This book is for my daughter, Hannah, with much love.

About the Author

Curt Simmons is a technology author and trainer, focusing on Windows operating systems, Internet technologies, and digital photography. He is the author of more than 50 computing books, including *Windows XP Headaches, Second Edition* and *How to Do Everything with Your BlackBerry, Second Edition,* both published by McGraw-Hill/Osborne. When he is not writing or training, Curt spends time with his wife and two daughters. Visit Curt on the Internet at http://www.curtsimmons.com, or send him an e-mail at curt_simmons@hotmail.com.

About the Technical Reviewer

Bill Bruns is the coordinator of technology and media at the College of Education and Human Services at Southern Illinois University. For eight years, he has also been a technical editor, working on more than 125 books relating to the Internet, web servers, HTML, operating systems, and office applications. Bill, his wife Debbie, his daughter Marlie, son Will, and his three bearded dragons live on the edge of the Shawnee National Forest in Carbondale, Illinois. You can reach him at billbruns3@yahoo.com.

How to Do *Everything* with Windows® XP

Third Edition

How to Do *Everything* with Windows® XP Third Edition

Curt Simmons

McGraw-Hill/Osborne

New York Chicago San Francisco Lisbon
London Madrid Mexico City Milan New Delhi
San Juan Seoul Singapore Sydney Toronto

The **McGraw-Hill** Companies

McGraw-Hill/Osborne
2100 Powell Street, 10th Floor
Emeryville, California 94608
U.S.A.

To arrange bulk purchase discounts for sales promotions, premiums, or fund-raisers, please contact **McGraw-Hill**/Osborne at the above address. For information on translations or book distributors outside the U.S.A., please see the International Contact Information page immediately following the index of this book.

How to Do Everything with Windows® XP, Third Edition

234567890 FGR FGR 0198765

ISBN 0-07-225953-1

Vice President & Group Publisher	Philip Ruppel
Vice President & Publisher	Jeffrey Krames
Acquisitions Editor	Megg Morin
Project Editor	LeeAnn Pickrell
Acquisitions Coordinator	Agatha Kim
Technical Editor	Bill Bruns
Copy Editor	Lisa Theobald
Proofreaders	Susie Elkind, Emily Rader
Indexer	Valerie Perry
Composition	ITC
Illustrator	ITC
Series Design	Mickey Galicia
Cover Design	Dodie Shoemaker
Cover Illustration	Jacey

This book was composed with Adobe® InDesign®.

Contents at a Glance

PART IV Optimize, Troubleshoot, and Fix Windows XP

Contents

Acknowledgments

I would like to thank everyone at McGraw-Hill/Osborne for giving me the opportunity to write the third edition of *How to Do Everything with Windows XP*. Thanks to Megg Morin, my acquisitions editor, for getting me started. Also, a big thanks to Agatha Kim, Bill Bruns, and Lisa Theobald for their editorial eagle eyes and for keeping things moving in the right direction. Finally, thanks to my agent, Margot Maley, and to my family for being so supportive of my work.

Introduction

Welcome to the third edition of *How to Do Everything with Windows XP*! In my opinion, Windows XP is the best operating system Microsoft has produced to date, no matter if you are using Windows XP Home or Professional Edition, Windows XP Media Center, or Windows XP Tablet PC. How would you like an operating system that is friendly, easy to use, makes the best use of the Internet and digital media, and rarely—if ever—locks up or acts weird? I thought so. Windows XP is all of these things and more. In fact, no matter what you need, Windows XP can probably do it!

In this book's third edition, you'll find out about the new developments with Windows XP, including Service Pack 2 and Media Player 10.

Seeing as the XP in Windows XP stands for *experience,* you might be wondering, "Then is Windows XP right for me if I'm new to computing?" The answer: absolutely! XP provides for a full range of experience with this new operating system. Not only is it the easiest operating system to learn that Microsoft has ever produced—you'll be a pro in no time—but it is also the most powerful. If you're just starting out, all you need is Windows XP and this book, you'll have the operating system mastered in no time.

Speaking of this book, *How to Do Everything with Windows XP* is designed to be your one-stop source for help in using Windows XP. This book helps you get started in Chapter 1 and takes you through everything you might want to know how to do. You'll learn what you need to know quickly and easily, often using a step-by-step format.

This book starts you out at the beginning:

In **Part I**, "Get to Know Windows XP," you learn all about the Windows XP interface (such as the Start menu). You also learn how to launch the computer and shut it down, manage your computer with the Control Panel, configure system settings and folders, install applications, use accessories, and manage hardware and printers—plus much more!

In **Part II**, "Get Connected," you learn all about getting connected to the Internet with your Windows XP computer. You'll find out how to use Internet Explorer 6, Outlook Express, plus you'll learn how to create a home network using Windows XP. This part also covers more advanced networking topics, such as Remote Desktop and Windows Firewall.

In **Part III**, "Cool Things You Can Do with Windows XP," we check out the fun stuff XP provides. You learn about playing games on Windows XP, how to use the XP Media Player, and how to use the Movie Maker tool for editing and saving your own home movies. You'll also see how to make the most of digital photos on Windows XP and how to extend Windows XP with Plus! packs and PowerToys.

In **Part IV**, "Optimize, Troubleshoot, and Fix Windows XP," you learn about the tools and utilities Windows XP provides to make your work much easier. You'll learn about disk management, System Information, Windows Help and Support, System Restore, and much more!

Within this book, you'll also find a special **Spotlight** section that gives you a look at how to create a custom CD, along with custom jewel case graphics. Be sure to check it out!

Finally, the book wraps up with the **Appendix**, which covers installing Windows XP. In fact, if there is something you can do with Windows XP, this book covers it!

I've written this book in an easy-to-read format. You can read it cover to cover, or you can skip around and find specific information you need—the choice is yours. To help you along the way, this book includes

- **How To sidebars** These boxes tell you how to do things, usually in a step-by-step format. Be sure to check them out—they are full of quick and helpful information.
- **Did You Know? sidebars** These boxes contain ancillary information you might find useful and even entertaining.
- **Voices from the Community** These sidebars contain helpful tips, tricks, and fixes from other Windows XP experts.
- **Notes** These provide you with helpful information. You should always read every Note.
- **Tips** These provide you with a friendly piece of advice or a little extra information that might make your work and play with Windows XP easier. Be sure to read them!
- **Cautions** These point out a potential problem or pitfall—so beware!

Are you ready to experience Windows XP? Then it's time to get started. Before you do, though, I would love to hear from you. Visit me on the Internet at http://www.curtsimmons.com, or send me e-mail at curt_simmons@hotmail.com.

Part I

Get to Know Windows XP

Chapter 1

Explore the XP Desktop

How to...

- Start your computer
- Explore your Desktop
- Examine icons
- Manage and configure the Recycle Bin
- Use the Taskbar and Start menu
- Log off, restart, and shut down your computer

You got what you asked for—at least what most of you asked for! For years, computer users had been saying, "We want a robust, stable operating system that plays nicely with hardware and makes it easy to do just about anything." Windows XP, your dream come true, combines power and stability and the security features of Service Pack 2. Windows XP is the operating system of choice for both home and business use.

If you are new to Windows, or perhaps to computing in general, this chapter was written especially for you. Windows XP is a powerful system that can do practically anything you need (except paint your house), and it is the easiest operating system to use that Microsoft has ever produced. In this chapter, you'll get to know Windows XP by learning about the basic system features that will enable you to use your computer effectively and efficiently.

Start Your Computer

If you have just purchased a new computer with Windows XP preinstalled, your first task is to unpack it, attach your peripherals (your keyboard, mouse, printer, speakers, and so forth), and then start the computer. Your computer comes with a booklet that explains how to attach peripherals and start the computer. Most computers have a power switch on the back of the case that you must switch on. Some models have an On switch on the back and also another button on the front of the case that gives you easy starting access. Check out your computer's documentation to find the On switch.

Once you flip the switch and your computer has power, you will most likely see a brand-name screen or maybe even a black screen with a bunch of information about your computer's hardware, and then you will see the Windows XP starting screen as your computer boots up. If your computer is new and has Windows XP preinstalled, the first time your computer boots up, Windows XP may ask you some questions to customize your computer and finish the installation. (See the appendix for more information about installation.) At some point, Windows XP will ask you to enter a username and a password. This is the username and password you will use each time you log on to Windows. Windows XP can be a secure operating system, so you can expect usernames and passwords to be very important. You can learn all about Windows XP user-management in Chapter 12.

Get to Know Your Windows XP Desktop

Windows XP uses a Desktop for the standard user interface, as have previous versions of Windows, such as Me and 2000. The Desktop is where you access your system components, applications you want to use, the Internet, and basically everything else. Think of the Desktop as, well, a *desktop*. The ideal desktop has everything you need within quick and easy reach. On your computer, the same idea holds true.

As you can see in Figure 1-1, the Desktop contains an open area, the Recycle Bin (usually on the right-hand side), and a Taskbar at the bottom that contains the Start button on the left and a Notification Area on the lower-right side.

The items you see on your Desktop may vary from those shown in Figure 1-1, especially if you have just bought a new computer with Windows XP preinstalled. The manufacturer of your computer (such as Compaq, HP, or Dell) may have set up a number of preconfigured options and even advertisements to appear on the Desktop. In short, if you have a new computer, you may have a lot of…well, *junk* on your Desktop, and Windows XP itself even includes several advertisements there. You may see an icon you can click to launch MSN Internet software (which you can do or not do—the choice is entirely yours), and several other ISP advertisements, and you may see all kinds of other stuff, depending on your computer manufacturer. You can safely ignore these icons or drag them to the Recycle Bin to get rid of them forever. You can learn more about using the Recycle Bin in the next section.

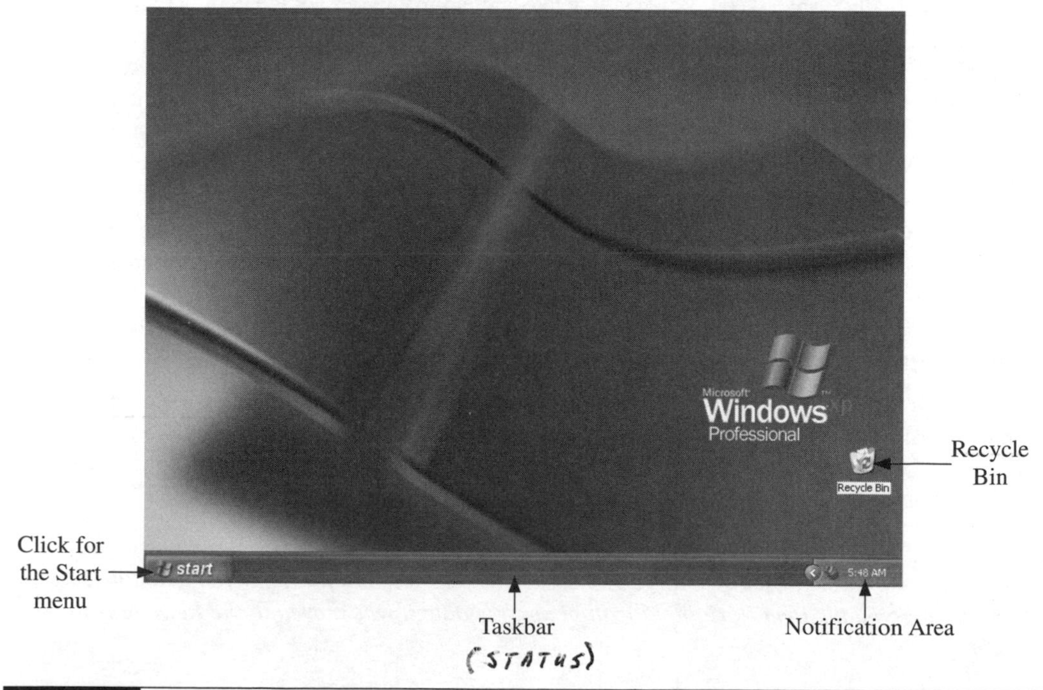

FIGURE 1-1 The Windows XP Desktop

You may also see a number of shortcuts. *Shortcuts* are simply icons on your Desktop that enable you to access some system component or application quickly and easily without having to wade into the operating system and retrieve it. A shortcut icon appears on your Desktop with a little arrow in the corner.

Shortcuts can be helpful, but if you have too many, they can clutter up your Desktop and make it confusing. The good news is that you do not have to keep any advertisements or shortcuts on your Desktop that you do not want. Simply delete them. When you delete a shortcut, you are not deleting the program, just the little icon on your Desktop that points to the program. This feature lets you decide what should be on your Desktop and what should not.

Check Out the Recycle Bin

By default, Windows XP provides you with only one permanent Desktop icon, which is the Recycle Bin. If you have used Windows in the past, you may be thinking, "Wait a minute—where is My Computer, My Network Places, and the usual stuff I see?" These icons are still around, so don't worry; in an effort to make the Desktop cleaner and more configurable for your needs, common icons, such as My Computer, now reside on the Start menu. So, what is the Recycle Bin? The Recycle Bin is a place where you put garbage. You can remove old files and items you no longer need and add them to the Recycle Bin.

Want to know a secret? When you delete a file from your system (anything at all, a document, picture, shortcut—whatever), it isn't really deleted. It is sent to the Recycle Bin, where it waits to be deleted. Why? The Recycle Bin is an excellent Windows feature that prevents you from losing data that you may actually want to keep. When you delete an item from your computer, it is removed from its current location and placed in the Recycle Bin. It stays in the Recycle Bin until you choose to empty the Recycle Bin or the Recycle Bin becomes too full. Only then is the item deleted forever.

Now, before you get too happy, keep in mind that this secret applies to files on local hard drives on your computer. It is not true for network drives or removable storage drives, such as floppy disks and CD-RWs (CD-rewritables). Once you delete something from one of these locations, it is immediately deleted instead of being stored in the Recycle Bin, so be careful!

I will give you an overview of the other Desktop elements, because we will use them extensively throughout the book. However, the Recycle Bin is covered only in this chapter, so I'll spend a little more time with it to make sure you know "how to do everything."

Use the Recycle Bin as a Way Station

As mentioned, any time you delete an item, it is sent to the Recycle Bin. You can open the Recycle Bin and see what is inside by double-clicking the Recycle Bin icon on your Desktop (you can also right-click the icon and click Explore). You can see the items in the Recycle Bin that are waiting to be deleted, as shown in Figure 1-2.

In the View menu, you can choose Thumbnails, Tiles, Icons, List, or Details. By using these choices, you can see large icons, small icons, a list of files, or even a detailed list telling you the item's original location and the date it was moved to the Recycle Bin.

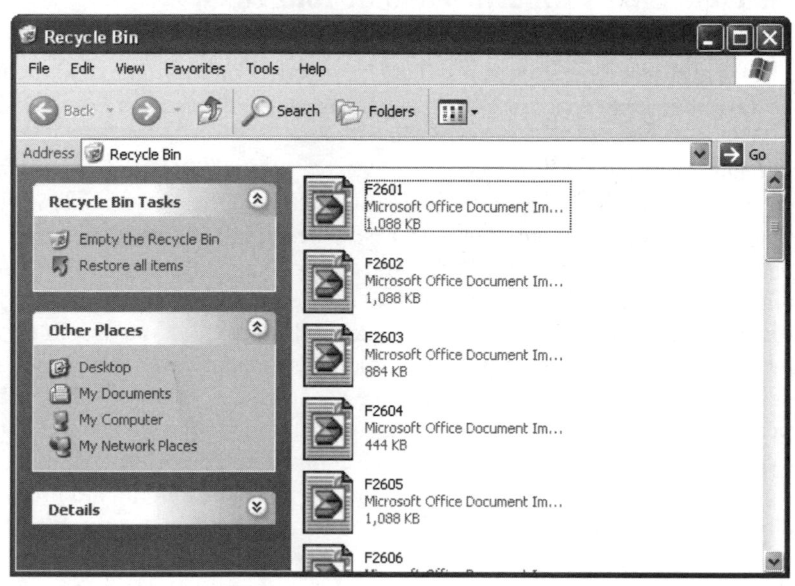

FIGURE 1-2 Items in the Recycle Bin

Two buttons are available in the Recycle Bin Tasks window on the left part of the Recycle Bin window. You can click the Empty the Recycle Bin button, which permanently deletes the items in the Recycle Bin. You *cannot* recover these items once they have been emptied from the Recycle Bin, unless you use a third-party program, such as Norton SystemWorks.

TIP *You can also empty the contents of your Recycle Bin by right-clicking the Recycle Bin icon on your Desktop and clicking Empty Recycle Bin on the menu that appears.*

You also have a Restore All Items button in the Recycle Bin Tasks window. Suppose you accidentally delete a file and it is moved to the Recycle Bin? No problem. Clicking the Restore All Items button moves all the files in the Recycle Bin back to their original locations on your computer. But what if you have deleted 30 files and you want to restore only one of them? No problem—select the file in the list by clicking it. The Restore All Items button changes to Restore This Item. Click the button and the selected file is put back in its original location.

NOTE *You can also move an item out of the Recycle Bin by dragging it to the Desktop. Put your mouse pointer over the file you want to take out of the Recycle Bin, and then press and hold down your left mouse button. Continue holding down your left mouse button, and drag the item to your Desktop; then let go of the mouse button. The item will now reside on your Desktop.*

Change the Recycle Bin's Properties to Suit Your Needs

You can also change the Recycle Bin's properties, which basically changes the way it behaves. Right-click the Recycle Bin on your Desktop and click Properties on the contextual menu that appears. You see a Recycle Bin Properties window that has a Global tab and a Local Disk tab, as shown in Figure 1-3.

The two radio buttons at the top of the Global tab enable you either to configure your drives independently or use the same setting for all drives. This feature applies to you only if you have more than one hard disk in your computer. In most cases, the default setting that configures all of your drives the same way is all you need. Next, you see a check box that tells your computer to delete items immediately instead of moving them to the Recycle Bin. As you can guess, this feature automatically deletes items when you click Delete. This provides you absolutely no protection in the event that you accidentally delete a file you want, however. Let's say you are writing your life's story and you accidentally delete the document. If you selected this check box, the document would immediately be removed from your computer—you would not be able to retrieve it. I strongly recommend that you do not select this check box to enable this option. No matter how good your computing skills, you will make a mistake from time to time and accidentally delete something. The Recycle Bin is your safety net so that you get that document back. By selecting this check box, you have no protection—so don't do it!

Next, you see a sliding bar that represents the maximum size of the Recycle Bin. Like everything else on your computer, the Recycle Bin stores items in a folder on your hard drive.

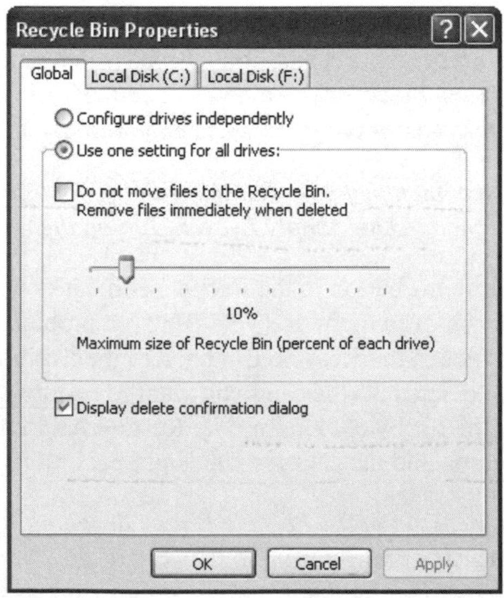

FIGURE 1-3 Recycle Bin Properties

The sliding bar enables you to set a limit for how big the Recycle Bin can grow before it forces you to empty the contents and permanently delete items from your system. By default, this setting is configured for 10 percent. This means that 10 percent of your hard drive's space can be used by files in the Recycle Bin before the Recycle Bin tells you to empty it. That is, for example, if you have a 10GB hard drive, you can store up to 1GB of deleted data in the Recycle Bin before it must be permanently removed and deleted from your computer. Under most circumstances, this 10 percent setting is all you need, but you can change it to a higher or lower percentage if you want. Just be sure to ask yourself why you are changing the setting and make sure you have a good reason for doing so.

NOTE *Keep in mind that you do not have to wait until your Recycle Bin is full to empty it—and, in fact, most people don't. Some people empty it every time they put documents in it, while others empty it on a weekly basis after they have reviewed its contents to make sure nothing was accidentally deleted. There is no right or wrong approach, of course; find what works best for you.*

Finally, you see a Display Delete Confirmation Dialog check box at the bottom of the Global tab. This tells Windows to give you that aggravating "Are You Sure?" message every time you delete something. This option is selected by default, and although the configuration message is sometimes a pain, it is a good safety check, so I recommend that you leave this setting enabled.

Aside from the Global tab, you have a Local Disk tab—you may see several of these tabs if your computer has more than one hard drive. You can't do anything on these tabs if you selected the Use One Setting for All Drives radio button on the Global tab. If you want each drive to have different settings and you selected the corresponding option on the Global tab, you can configure each drive independently. The tabs have the same options, such as the slider bar for the percentage of the hard drive you want to use for the Recycle Bin. The real question is, why would you configure drives differently? The answer is all about drive space.

Let's say your computer has two hard drives. One has 5GB while the other has only 1GB. You can spare 10 percent of the 5GB drive for the Recycle Bin, but what if your 1GB drive is already crowded? You might not want 10 percent of that drive used for the Recycle Bin, so you can give it a lower percentage, such as 5 percent. Again, under normal circumstances and with most computers, you don't need to worry about any of this, but it's good to know the options are there in case you have some specific hard drive space issues.

Manage Your Taskbar

The Taskbar is the small bar across the bottom of your Desktop (refer back to Figure 1-1). The Taskbar contains your Start menu, which is explored in the next section, and a Notification Area, which is the separate box on the right side. Any applications that you have open or any windows that you have minimized also show up on the Taskbar. If you want to view one of these programs or windows on your Desktop so that you can work with it, just click its corresponding icon.

The Notification Area (called the System Tray in previous versions of Windows) contains a clock, probably a volume control icon, and maybe several other icons, depending on what is installed on your computer. The Notification Area is an easy way to access some applications you may use frequently. If you right-click any of the items in the Notification Area, you can usually close or remove the item from the Notification Area, or you can click Properties so you can configure the item. For example, if you right-click the clock in the Notification Area, you can then choose Adjust Date/Time. This action opens a simple window where you can change the current date and current time. These settings are easy and self-explanatory.

You can customize the Taskbar in a number of different ways. See Chapter 3 for details and step-by-step instructions.

Explore the Start Menu to Get to All the Programs

If you have ever visited a theme park, you know that typically one main entrance leads you to all of the attractions the park has to offer. Windows XP's main entrance is the Start menu, which appears on your Taskbar in the lower-left portion of your screen.

The Start menu is your gateway to most Windows components and the applications that you install. If you have used Windows previously, the Start menu is certainly nothing new. However, in Windows XP, the Start menu has been completely redesigned so you can access your programs, documents, and common Windows components more easily. If you click the Start button, a pop-up menu appears, as shown in Figure 1-4.

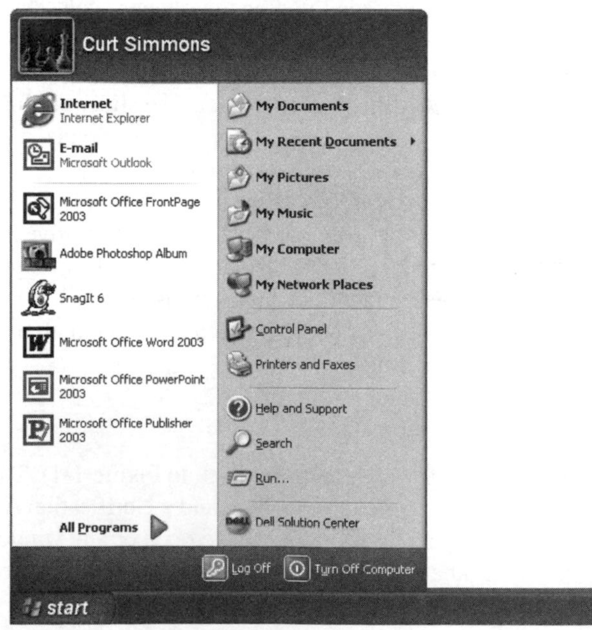

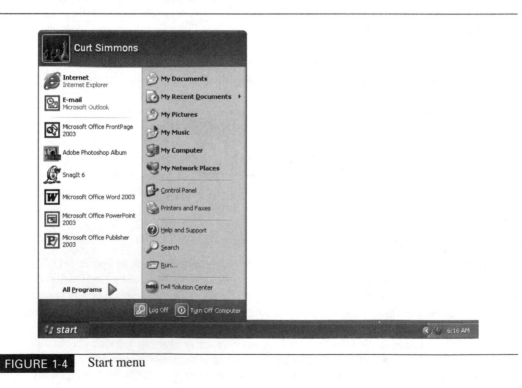

FIGURE 1-4 Start menu

Because the Start menu has been redesigned for Windows XP, I'll devote more time to it in Chapter 3, where you can learn all about the available options and how to configure the Start menu so that it is just right for you.

Log Off Your Computer

Windows XP is designed to be a "multi-user" computer. This means several different people can use the same computer but keep their settings, files, and folders separate. For example, at home you and some family members may share the computer; or if your computer is on a network, several different users may access it. In Windows XP, all of your settings and documents are tied to your user account. This way, several people can use the same computer and have different computer settings, documents, and even e-mail accounts. If someone else uses your computer, Windows XP keeps track of that person's settings as well as your own settings.

With all of this in mind, Windows XP enables you to log off the computer so that someone else can log on without having to restart the computer. To log off, click the Start menu and click Log Off. A dialog box appears asking if you want to Switch User, which allows someone else to log on to the computer, or you can choose to Log Off. If you choose to switch users, the current user's applications continue to run in the background while the new user logs on. If you choose to log off, all applications are closed. Either way, you are taken to the Windows XP logon screen where you can select your username and password to log on.

Restart or Turn Off Your Computer

When you have finished using Windows XP, you can choose to shut down the computer, or, in the case of problems or if something new is installed, you can restart it. To shut down or restart your computer, click the Start menu and then click Turn Off Computer. A dialog box appears that contains three button options:

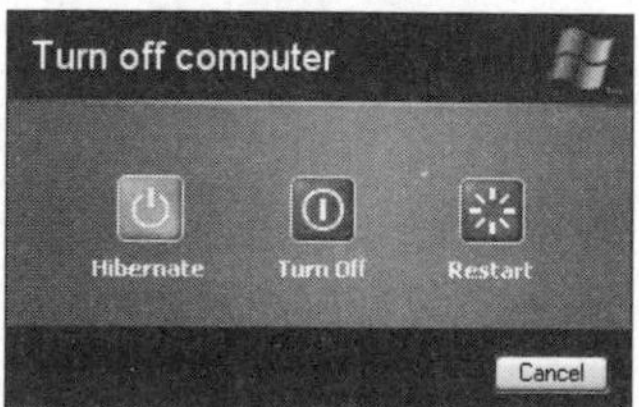

- **Stand By or Hibernate** Whether Stand By or Hibernate appears depends on how the manufacturer set up the Power Options for your computer (which are adjustable from the Control Panel).
    - Choosing Stand By puts your computer into a low-power state, but it remains available for use. Move the mouse or press a key on your keyboard, and the computer returns to its regular power state. To put your computer into hibernation, you can hold down the SHIFT key and click Stand By.

- Choosing Hibernate saves all of your current Desktop settings to your hard disk and then powers down the computer. When you power back up, you return to the same applications and files you were working on when you chose to hibernate.

- **Turn Off** This option shuts down Windows XP and powers down the computer safely.
- **Restart** This option shuts down Windows XP and immediately restarts it again. The computer is not fully powered down.

You should always shut down your computer or restart it using these options. Do not shut down or restart by turning the power off and back on. While this method does work, it may damage your operating system and possibly your computer motherboard, which contains all the main circuitry for your computer.

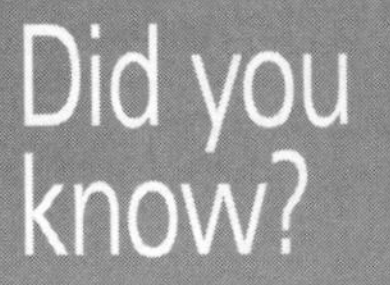

To Turn Off or Not to Turn Off, That Is the Question!

I teach several online courses, and as I'm teaching, students frequently want to know if they should leave their computer on when it is unattended, or should they always shut down? Does frequently shutting down damage the computer?

These are common, but very important questions. First things first: you can shut down or restart your computer without damaging your system or hardware—but you shouldn't shut down or restart a bunch of times during the day. For any given day, shut down and/or restart only once or twice. Many people get up in the morning, turn on the computer, and leave it on for the entire day. This is perfectly fine.

Computers today support a number of power-management features that enable the computer to go into a "standby" mode when it is not being used. I'll show you how to configure these options in Chapter 3. With power management features enabled, you really don't have to turn off your computer at all! I have five computers in my study, and they all remain on 24 hours a day, seven days a week. The only exception is if I'm traveling and going to be away for several days; only then do I turn off the computers.

Chapter 2

Manage Your Computer with the Control Panel

How to...

- Access the Windows XP Control Panel
- Discover XP categories
- Access Control Panel icons
- Use Control Panel icons to configure your computer

Quick—how many of you know how to set the clock on your VCR? I thought so. The proverbial joke about using a VCR and staring at the unsettable, blinking *12:00* certainly has a great element of truth. The reality of electronic devices and computers is simply this: you don't have to know everything about the device or computer to use it. You need to know some basic functions, but for the most part, you can ignore many features and use the product without problems. However, if you know how to set your VCR clock, you can record all kinds of television shows automatically and use a number of other management features of your VCR. True, you don't *need* to know how to set the clock, but you can use your VCR much more effectively if you do.

Windows XP, along with other computer operating systems, are much the same. You don't have to know a whole lot of technical stuff to use XP, but if you know how to configure its features and functions, it will do more work for you. While it is true that computer operating systems are becoming more complex with each new release, they are also becoming easier to use because they give users more management tools. One of those tools in Windows XP is the Control Panel. The Control Panel provides a number of tools that allow you to determine how various components of Windows XP look and act. If you know how to use these tools, you gain greater control over XP, and—just as with your VCR clock—your XP system will more effectively meet your needs.

In this chapter, you'll learn how to manage your Windows XP computer using the tools provided in the Control Panel. This chapter explores all of the Control Panel options; shows you what they do; and then shows you how, when, and why to configure them. Because of their specific nature, some Control Panel tools are best explored in other chapters, and I'll direct you to those chapters in such cases.

Access the Control Panel

You can access the Control Panel in three major ways. First, you can click the Start menu and click Control Panel. This is probably the most common and easiest way of accessing the Control Panel. Second, you can access the Control Panel from within any other XP window by simply typing **Control Panel** in the Address bar found on the window. This will cause the current window to change to the Control Panel. Finally, many folders give you a link to the Control Panel (as long as they use the XP view) in the Other Places box on the left side of the folder window. For example, if you happen to be in My Computer, just click the Control Panel link in the Other Places box to switch to the Control Panel. No matter how you get there, when the Control Panel opens, your initial view will appear as shown in Figure 2-1.

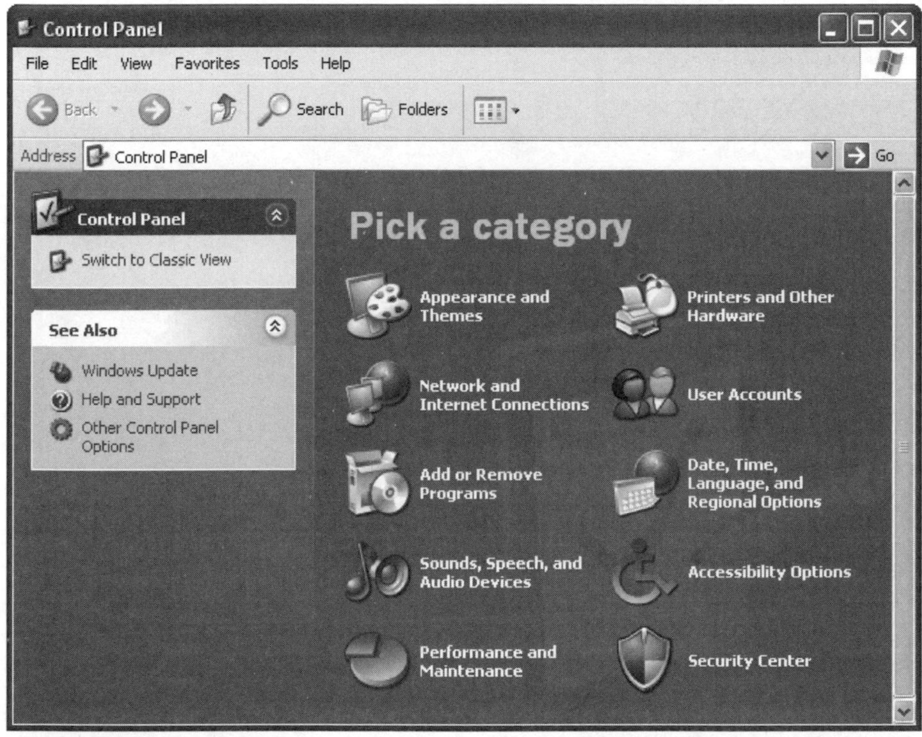

FIGURE 2-1 Control Panel

If you've used any version of Windows, you will first notice that the Control Panel in Windows XP looks a little different. The Windows XP Control Panel is divided into *categories.* If you click a category, the window that opens presents a list of tasks you may want to perform and related Control Panel icon(s) you may want to choose, as you can see in Figure 2-2.

Now, before you get too concerned about these differences, let me tell you that the task and icon options are essentially the same. For example, as you can see in Figure 2-2, I have the option to change the computer's theme, Desktop background, screen saver, and screen resolution. If I click one of these tasks, the Display Properties window opens so that I can make the change. Or I can simply click the Display icon option and open the same set of windows. There is no difference—it's just that the task option tries to help you locate the tasks you want to perform in case you don't know which Control Panel icon to select. Notice that when you use the task option, you'll also get some See Also suggestions and Troubleshooters options in the boxes on the left.

Now, all of this may sound great, and it can be helpful. However, you need to know two important things. The Category view does not provide you access to every Control Panel tool that is available—it provides you access only to the more commonly used tools. Even though

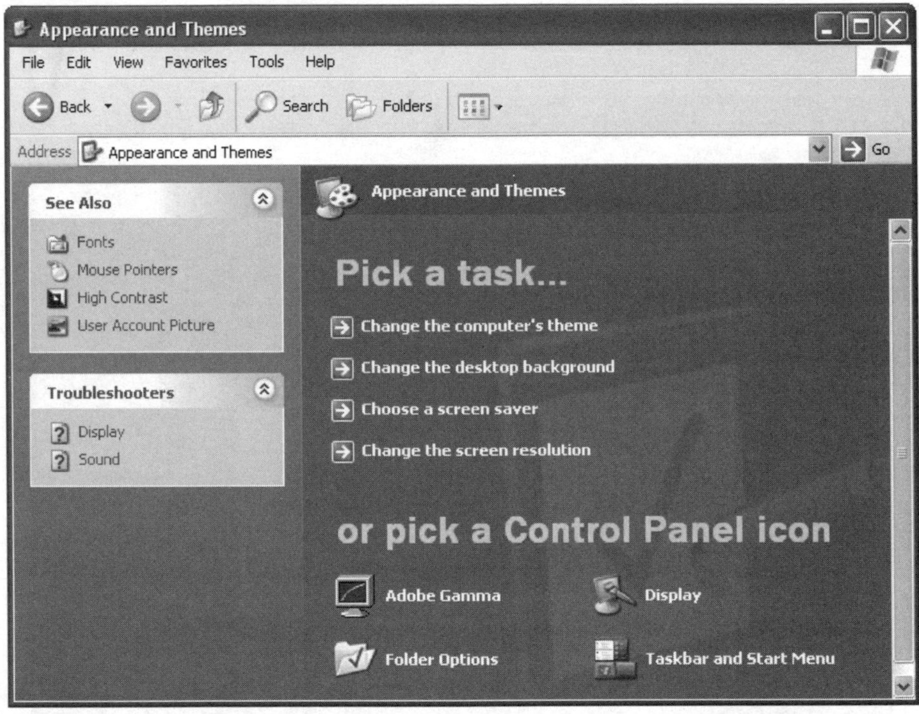

FIGURE 2-2 Appearance and Themes Control Panel category tasks and icons

Microsoft considers the tools found in Category view the most common, many Control Panel tools are not available from this view. So, to see all of your Control Panel options, click the Switch to Classic View link found on the left side of the Control Panel. This will give you the typical icon list found in previous versions of Windows, as you can see in Figure 2-3.

You can switch back and forth between Category view and Classic view by clicking the link in the Control Panel box on the left side of the window. You can access items in either view as needed—just use whichever view you like best.

Now that you have taken a look at XP's Control Panel views, turn your attention to the programs the Control Panel offers. In the following sections, we will explore all of the Control Panel icons, and you will learn what you can do with each. To see all of the Control Panel icons, you need to use the Classic view; so click the Classic View link in the Control Panel box to switch to that view, if you haven't done so already.

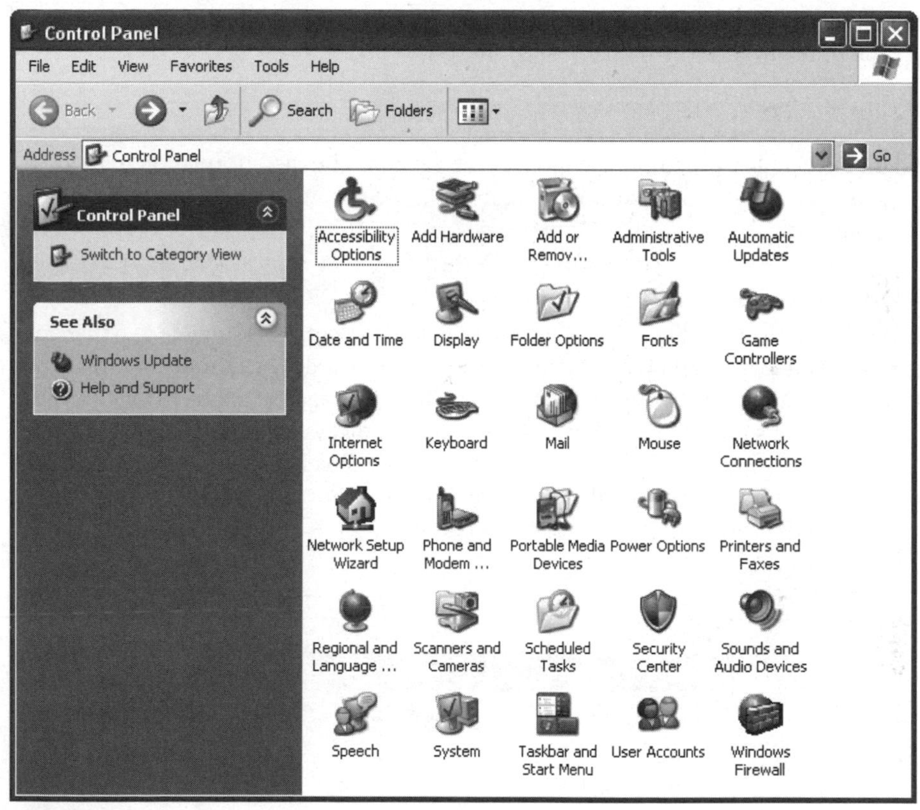

FIGURE 2-3 Control Panel Classic view

To avoid repeating information in this book, some Control Panel icons are briefly discussed in this chapter with a reference to another part of the book where the configuration is explored. Some configuration options are much more complicated than others and deserve their own chapters.

Accessibility Options

Accessibility Options enable you to configure the computer's input and output behavior for people with certain disabilities. These options make computing much easier for these individuals. Windows XP provides excellent support for accessibility configuration, and you use this icon in the Control Panel to configure most of them.

If you double-click Accessibility Options in the Control Panel, a Properties window appears with several different tabs that you can configure for special needs. The following sections tell you about each of them.

Keyboard

The Keyboard tab enables you to change the way the keyboard inputs information to the Windows XP operating system, as shown in Figure 2-4. The following sections explain the available options.

StickyKeys

First, you see that you can enable StickyKeys. The StickyKeys option is provided so that you do not have to hold down several keys at one time on the keyboard. For example, let's say that you want to press CTRL-ALT-DEL to open the Windows Task Manager window. Normally, these keys are pressed at the same time, but StickyKeys enables the keys to "stick," so that you can press CTRL, then press ALT, and then press DEL, one at a time. This is an excellent feature for people who can use only one hand on the keyboard. To enable StickyKeys, just select the Use StickyKeys check box, and then click the Settings button.

FIGURE 2-4 Keyboard tab

When you click Settings, a new window appears with a few check boxes. First, you can enable the StickyKeys shortcut, which enables you to turn on StickyKeys by pressing the SHIFT key five times in a row. You can also select or deselect these options:

- Choose Press Modifier Key Twice to Lock to specify that the CTRL, SHIFT, or ALT key remains active if you press it twice (press it a third time to unlock it).
- Turn StickyKeys off if two keys are pressed at the same time.
- Make a sound when a modifier key is pressed (CTRL, SHIFT, or ALT).
- Show StickyKeys status onscreen.

Once you enable or disable these options as desired, you can then use StickyKeys by pressing the SHIFT key five times in a row. A message appears on your screen telling you that the StickyKeys option is enabled, and a StickyKeys icon appears in your Notification Area. Once you play around with StickyKeys, you'll see how easy to use and how helpful this option is.

FilterKeys

FilterKeys are provided in Windows XP to help your operating system "filter" keystrokes. If a user has difficulty using the keyboard, FilterKeys can be used to ignore brief or repeated keystrokes. To use FilterKeys, select the check box on the Keyboard tab and then click the Settings button.

Once you click the Settings button, select the Use Shortcut check box so that you can turn on FilterKeys by pressing the right SHIFT key. You can use the remainder of this window to determine how FilterKeys behave by using (or not using) the following options:

- Ignore repeated keystrokes. For example, if I press the T key twice quickly, it will be filtered so that only one *t* appears on the screen. Click the Settings button to adjust the rate as desired.
- Ignore quick keystrokes and slow down the repeat rate.
- Beep when keys are pressed or accepted.
- Show FilterKeys status onscreen.

As with StickyKeys, the FilterKeys option is easy to use. Play around with the settings to meet your specific needs.

ToggleKeys

The ToggleKeys option is a simple feature that tells the operating system to play a tone when you press CAPS LOCK, NUM LOCK, or SCROLL LOCK on your keyboard. To turn on this feature, select the Use ToggleKeys check box. If you click the Settings button, a dialog box appears in which you can enable a shortcut to turn on ToggleKeys by pressing and holding down the NUM LOCK key for 5 seconds.

Beneath the ToggleKeys settings on the Keyboard tab is a check box that enables additional keyboard help when using programs. This feature turns on keyboard help pointers that may be supported in some applications that you use.

Sound

The Accessibility Options Sound tab gives you two options to enable Windows sounds to help you. This tab contains two check boxes for these options.

The first option is the SoundSentry. Depending on what happens with Windows XP (or what you do), certain warning or notice sounds are made. The SoundSentry option enables these warnings to appear on your screen instead of as a sound. This feature is helpful to Windows XP users with impaired hearing. To use the SoundSentry, select the Use SoundSentry check box. If you click the Settings button, you can decide what the screen should do to give you the warning (such as flash the active title bar).

Your second option on this tab is to use ShowSounds. The ShowSounds option tells your programs to display text for any sounds or verbal speech cues they might give you. You enable this option by selecting the Use ShowSounds check box.

Display

The Display tab enables you to use high-contrast colors on your display to make reading easier.

To enable this feature, select the Use High Contrast check box. If you click the Settings button, you can enable the keyboard shortcut, which is LEFT ALT-LEFT SHIFT-PRINT SCREEN, by selecting the check box for that purpose. You can also use this window to determine how high contrast should be used, such as white on black, black on white, or a custom combination. You can experiment with these settings to find which one works best for you.

Also notice on the Display tab that you can adjust the cursor settings. Use the slider bars to adjust the cursor blink rate and its width. These settings can make the cursor easier to see.

Let Windows XP Help You

A neat feature of Windows XP is its ability to provide aids to make your work easier. One of the features you can activate lets you single-click to open an item and underline icon titles only when you point to them. These are great features if a user finds it difficult to double-click with the mouse. To activate these features, open any Explorer window and choose Tools | Folder Options. In the General tab, choose the Single Click to Open an Item (Point to Select) radio button and then choose the Underline Icon Titles Only When I Point to Them radio button. Finally, click OK.

—Thomas H. Reichert, Staff Writer
ThemeXP.org
www.themexp.org/

2

Mouse

The Mouse tab provides a simple check box that enables you to control the mouse pointer on your screen with the numeric keypad on your keyboard, so that you do not have to use the mouse. Click the Settings button to enable the keyboard shortcut to this option, which is LEFT ALT-LEFT SHIFT-NUM LOCK. You also use the Settings page to control how fast the mouse pointer moves and related settings.

General

Finally, the General tab, shown in Figure 2-5, provides some basic control options for accessibility.

You have the following options:

- Turn off accessibility features if the computer is idle. This option enables you to specify that accessibility features should be turned off if the computer is idle for a certain period of time. Use the drop-down menu to select the desired idle time.
- Show a warning message when turning a feature on.
- Make a sound when turning a feature on or off.

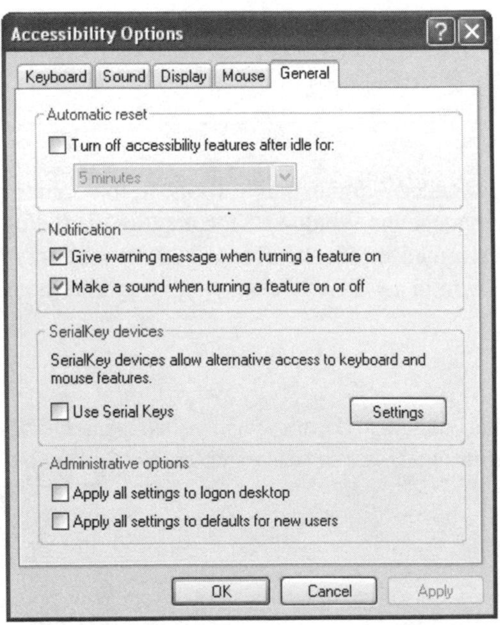

FIGURE 2-5 General tab

- Support SerialKey devices. SerialKey devices (also called augmentative communication devices) are additional input devices attached to your computer that are used by people who cannot use a standard keyboard and mouse. This setting tells Windows XP to support these devices.
- Use administrative options. If you are an administrator for the computer, you can choose to apply all accessibility options that you have configured to the logon desktop (the area where you select your user account and enter your password) for all new users. In this way, the accessibility options are available and configured for each person who uses the XP computer.

Add Hardware

The Add Hardware icon that appears in the Control Panel is actually a wizard you can use to help install hardware devices on your computer. This wizard is explained in detail in Chapter 6.

Add or Remove Programs

Add or Remove Programs enables you to install new programs, remove programs, add or remove components of installed programs, and install and remove Windows components. These features are explored in Chapter 4, so refer to that chapter for step-by-step information.

Administrative Tools

Windows XP includes a folder called Administrative Tools. In this folder, you will find several different tools that help you manage the Windows XP computer, including the Computer Management console and Performance Monitor. Because of the more complex nature of these tools, we'll explore and use them in a variety of chapters throughout the book.

Automatic Updates

Automatic Updates enable your computer to download and install updates to Windows XP automatically from Microsoft's Web site. The feature is safe and easy, and you can find out more about it in Chapter 19.

Date and Time

The Date and Time icon in the Control Panel enables you to set your operating system's clock, as you might guess. When you double-click the icon, you see a simple interface that contains a calendar noting the current date. You can change the date by using the drop-down menus. Likewise, you see a clock with a scroll menu where you can change the current time and the time zone. Notice that you also have a Time Zone tab where you can adjust your time zone. As you can see in Figure 2-6, this interface is very easy to configure.

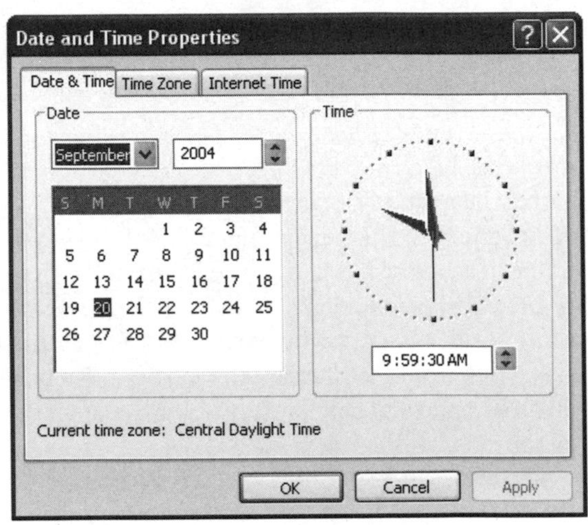

FIGURE 2-6 Date and Time Properties window

If you need to adjust your computer's date and time, you don't have to use the Control Panel icon. Just right-click the time in your Notification Area and choose Adjust Time/ Date. You can also double-click the time. Either action opens the same Date and Time Properties window.

The XP Date and Time tool Internet Time tab allows you to synchronize your computer with an Internet time server to make sure that your computer always has the exact time. This feature, if configured, occurs automatically and without interrupting you, but you must be connected to the Internet for synchronization to occur. Also, if you are using Windows XP in a corporate network that uses a proxy server or a firewall, the time synchronization feature may not be allowed and consequently will not work.

Display

The Display icon in the Control Panel enables you to configure your Desktop and other display settings so that your computer looks the way you want. You can configure a number of settings, and you can learn all about using the Display features in Chapter 3.

Folder Options

Windows XP enables you to configure the appearance of your folders. Several options are available, and you can learn all about them in Chapter 4.

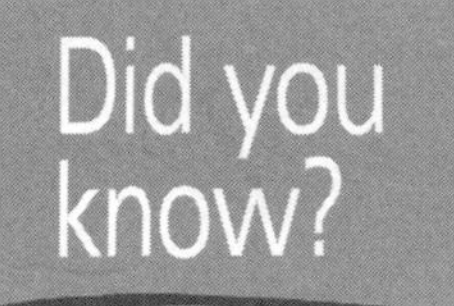

Proxy Servers and Firewalls Protect Computers

Many corporate environments use proxy servers or firewalls. To protect the internal network from the various risks posed by Internet traffic, proxy servers or firewalls examine all traffic flowing into the network from the Internet. The configuration of the proxy server or firewall may cause some Internet traffic to be filtered, or not allowed to pass. Proxy servers and firewalls access Internet content for internal network clients, so that no client is ever in direct contact with the Internet. This feature ensures that the internal network is safe and that unauthorized content does not enter the network from the Internet. In fact, your Windows XP computer contains a personal firewall you can use to help protect it against attacks from the Internet. See Chapter 13 to learn more.

Fonts

The Fonts folder in the Control Panel holds all of the fonts that your computer can use. When you open Fonts, you see a list of all of the fonts available. There isn't anything you can configure here, with the exception of removing or adding fonts to the folder. In general, this is not something that you need to do, because Windows XP and your applications handle the fonts that are needed and used. You can determine which fonts you want Windows XP and your applications to use by configuring the Display properties or configuring a specific application's properties. You can also double-click any font in the Fonts folder to learn more about the font and to see a sample of how the font looks.

Game Controllers

The Game Controllers icon in the Control Panel provides a location to manage any gaming devices attached to your computer, such as joysticks and other playing devices. You can learn all about this icon in Chapter 14.

Internet Options

The Internet Options in the Control Panel can be used to configure, as you might guess, Internet Explorer and possibly other Internet applications. You can access this same Properties window from within Internet Explorer itself, and these options are explored in Chapter 9.

Keyboard

The Keyboard icon in the Control Panel enables you to configure how your keyboard operates. When you double-click this icon, you see two tabs, which are explained in the following sections.

Speed

The Speed tab enables you to configure how fast your keyboard responds to keystrokes. The Speed tab gives you a few simple options for adjusting your keyboard's speed.

First, you see two slider bars for character repeat. The first, Repeat Delay, determines how much time passes before a character repeats when you hold down a key. If you are a fast typist, you will probably want this setting moved to Short.

The Repeat Rate slider bar determines how fast a character repeats when you hold it down. The Repeat Delay determines how fast the initial repeat begins, while the Repeat Rate determines how fast the characters are actually repeated. A medium setting (between Slow and Fast) is typically all you need.

At the bottom of the window, you see the Cursor Blink Rate. Use the slider bar to change the rate; you can see the cursor blinking on the tab for test purposes. The best setting is typically toward the Fast end of the slider bar.

Hardware

The Hardware tab lists the type of keyboard that is attached to your computer. Two buttons are available that allow you to troubleshoot the keyboard if you are having problems, or you can click the Properties button to access the device's properties sheets. You can learn more about configuring devices for your system in Chapter 6.

Mouse

The mouse is a universal input device that lets you point and click your way into Windows oblivion. The mouse itself is a simple device, but, surprisingly, you can access a number of configuration options for the mouse by double-clicking the Mouse icon in the Control Panel. You'll see a few tabs and several different options, and the following sections show you how to configure your mouse so that it operates and behaves in a way that is best for you.

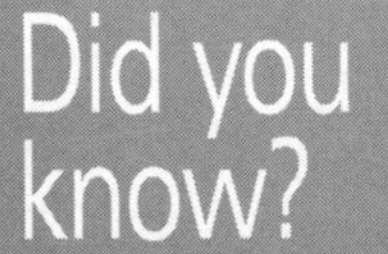

You Can Get Check Box Help

A lot of check boxes in Windows Control Panel pages turn on or off certain features. Sometimes the explanatory text isn't so easy to understand. Although this book explains all of these check boxes to you, you can also get additional help in Windows XP by right-clicking any check box text and clicking What's This? Another dialog box appears that explains more about the check box item. Sometimes the help text that appears is great, and sometimes it's not so great—but it is good to know this feature is available to you.

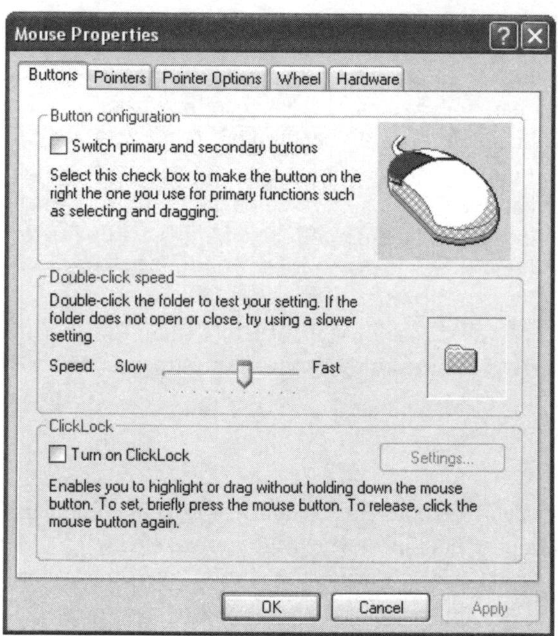

FIGURE 2-7 Buttons tab

Buttons

The Buttons tab, shown in Figure 2-7, provides a place where you can determine how your mouse buttons work.

First, you can check the box to Switch Primary and Secondary Buttons so that your mouse functions as a left-handed mouse. If you choose the right-handed option, the mouse buttons are as follows:

Left button	Select or drag
Right button	Context menu or special drag

If you choose the left-handed option, the mouse buttons are as follows:

Left button	Context menu or special drag
Right button	Select or drag

As you can see, choosing the left-handed option reverses which button performs which action.

Next, you can use the slider bar to speed up or slow down your mouse's double-click speed. Most people use a medium setting (where the slider bar is in the middle), but find the setting that works best for you.

Finally, you have an option at the bottom of the window called ClickLock. ClickLock enables you to drag items around your Desktop without having to hold down the mouse button continuously (left mouse button for right-handed users). Select the Turn on ClickLock check box to use it, and then click the Settings button that becomes accessible. The Settings window gives you a slider bar so you can determine how long you have to hold down the left mouse button before it locks into place, allowing you to drag items without holding it down.

You'll need to play around with the slider bar setting for ClickLock to find which setting works for you, but keep in mind that short ClickLock settings are usually more aggravating than helpful. This setting causes your left mouse button to lock very quickly every time you press it, so don't start out with a short setting when you are configuring ClickLock.

Pointers

The Pointers tab provides a place to configure the way your pointer appears on your Windows XP computer. What you are doing may cause your mouse pointer to change its appearance. For example, a typical pointer is simply an arrow; but if your system is busy, your mouse pointer changes to an hourglass. You can use the Pointers tab to customize the pointers as you wish.

At the top of the window, you see a Scheme drop-down menu that enables you to select preconfigured Windows schemes. Scroll down and select some of them. You'll see the various pointers change in the Customize window. Select a scheme that you want and click Apply to use that scheme.

Aside from using the standard Windows XP pointer schemes, you can also create your own schemes by modifying the desired pointers. If you click the Browse button, you can choose to use a different cursor file, such as one you have downloaded from the Internet or obtained from a CD-ROM. You can then select a desired pointer and create and save your own custom pointer scheme.

Although animated pointers are fun, they often put a burden on computer processors and may affect the performance of your computer. For this reason, you may want to avoid using them.

Pointer Options

The next mouse configuration tab provides Pointer Options, as shown in Figure 2-8. This simple tab gives you a series of check boxes or slider bars you can use to configure how your mouse pointer moves around the screen.

You can play around with these settings to determine which (if any) of them you would like to use:

- **Motion** Use the slider bar to determine how fast your pointer moves when you move your mouse. You can try different adjustments to find the speed you like. If you click the Accelerate button, you can also select how fast your pointer moves when you begin moving your mouse.

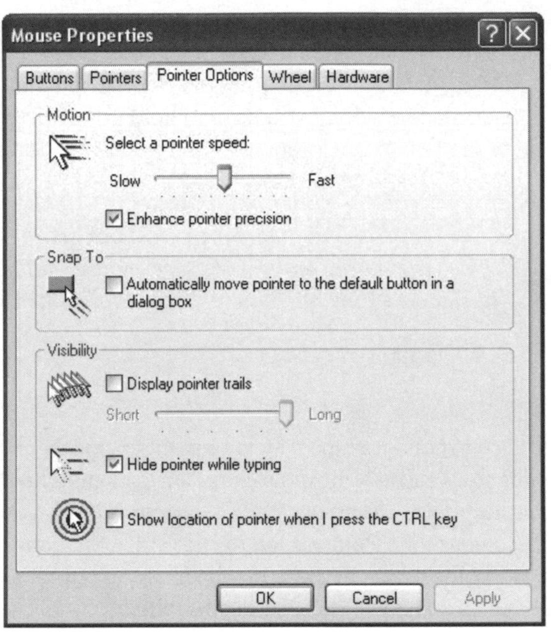

FIGURE 2-8 Pointer Options tab

- **SnapTo** This option automatically moves your mouse pointer to the default button in any given dialog box. You can try this option to see whether you like it, but many users (myself included) find SnapTo more aggravating than helpful.
- **Visibility** The visibility options control how your pointer looks when in motion—you have three check box options. First, you can choose to use a mouse trail, which leaves a disappearing trail when you move your mouse. Some people like this setting, some don't (it gives me a headache), but you can experiment with it. Next, you can choose to hide your mouse pointer when you type. This just makes your mouse pointer disappear when not in use. Finally, you can choose to use the CTRL key to make your mouse pointer appear when you press the key.

Wheel

For mice that use a control wheel in addition to right and left buttons, use the Wheel tab to determine how quickly the wheel moves the mouse. The configuration option here allows you to set how many lines are scrolled when you move the wheel, or you can choose to move through an entire page. Select the desired radio button and enter a scroll value to experiment with these settings.

Hardware

The Hardware tab lists the type of mouse that is attached to your computer. Two buttons are available that allow you to troubleshoot the mouse if you are having problems, or you can click the Properties button to access the device's properties sheets. You can learn more about configuring devices for your system in Chapter 6.

Network Connections

The Network Connections icon in the Control Panel enables you to configure networking components so that Windows XP can participate on a local or remote area network. You can learn all about networking with Windows XP in Chapter 11.

Network Setup Wizard

The Network Setup Wizard provides a quick and easy way for you to create a home network. You can find out more about creating a home network in Chapter 11.

Phone and Modem Options

The Phone and Modem icon in the Control Panel provides a place where you manage phones and modems attached to your computer. In the past, modems were painfully difficult to set up and troubleshoot, but Windows XP makes modem configuration much easier. As you might guess, modem setup and configuration is a lengthy topic, and you learn how to do it all in Chapter 8.

Power Options

Windows XP is equipped to save energy by using power schemes that you can configure. These options can automatically turn off your monitor or hard drive after a certain period of inactivity. Power options are also available within Display properties, and Chapter 3 explores these power options.

Printers and Faxes

The Printers and Faxes folder is devoted to any printers or fax machines attached to your computer and includes a helpful wizard you can use to set up these devices. As you can imagine, printing and faxing can be a complex topic, so check out Chapter 7 for all the details.

Regional and Language Options

Regional and Language Options in the Control Panel provides you a place to configure your computer to use different language symbols, currency, and other specific regional representations. For example, let's say that you are using Windows XP in France, and you want Windows XP to calculate money in European currency. You can enable this option by using Regional and Language Options. When you open Regional and Language Options, you see a standard Regional Options tab, a Languages tab, and an Advanced tab. Each tab contains drop-down menus so you can select the desired regional settings.

Scanners and Cameras

Reflecting the popularity of scanners and digital cameras, Windows XP includes a Control Panel icon to help you manage these hardware devices. You can learn about the installation and management of scanners and cameras in Chapter 7.

Scheduled Tasks

The Scheduled Tasks folder in the Control Panel contains several wizards you can use to set up a variety of PC maintenance utilities to run in the background. These options are all covered in Chapter 19.

Security Center

The Security Center, which is a new feature from Service Pack 2, helps you stay protected from Internet threats and makes certain everything is configured as it should be. You can find out more about the Security Center in Chapter 13.

Sounds and Audio Devices

The Sounds and Audio Devices icon in the Control Panel provides a place to make some basic configuration changes to the way your Windows XP computer handles default Windows sounds as well as any multimedia and sound devices attached to your computer. If you double-click the Sounds and Audio Devices icon in the Control Panel, the Properties window appears with five tabs, which are explored in the following sections.

Volume

The first tab, Volume, allows you to make basic settings for the volume level of your sound card or other device, as you can see in Figure 2-9.

The slider bar adjusts the overall volume for the device; but if you click the Advanced button, you'll see the standard volume control interface for Windows, where you can control CD volume, microphone volume, and other settings.

In the bottom part of the window are options for setting your computer's speaker volume; and if you click the Advanced button, you can select the type of speakers you are using, such as desktop speakers, a headset, and other types. All of these settings are simple and self-explanatory.

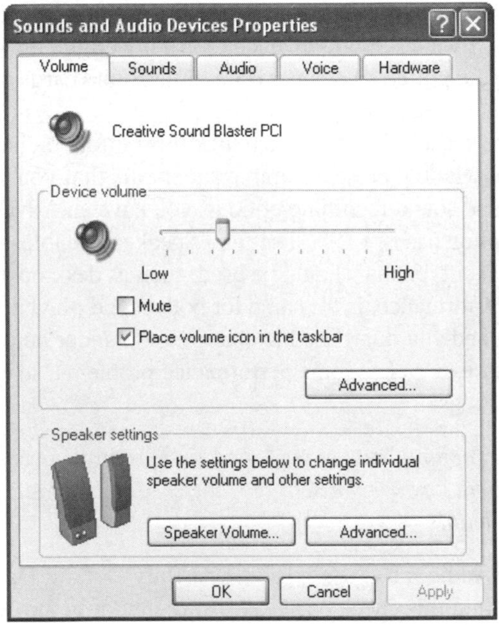

FIGURE 2-9 Volume tab

Sounds

On the Sounds tab, you can use different sound schemes to determine which sounds Windows XP plays for different events that occur. For example, when you receive an e-mail, Windows plays a sound. A number of these sound schemes are available, and the default sounds are applied when Windows XP is installed, so you do not have to configure anything here—but you can make changes to suit your personal taste.

You can use the drop-down menu to select a Windows scheme, such as Windows Default, and then you can select each sound in the Sound Events window, click the Browse button, and change the sound as desired by selecting a different one. You can then save this new scheme by clicking the Save As button.

At the bottom of the window, you see a slider bar to adjust the sound volume, and a check box that enables you to display the volume control in your Notification Area. I recommend that you keep this check box selected so that you can easily control the volume from your Taskbar.

Audio

The Audio tab presents you with three different types of audio input and output: sound playback, sound recording, and MIDI music playback.

For each type, you can use the drop-down menu and select the preferred device. This means that a particular device on your computer should be preferred over other devices for that type of input or output. For example, I want Sound Playback to use my computer's sound card to play sounds, so my sound card is the preferred device. If multiple sound cards or devices can be used, just use this drop-down menu to select the preferred device.

For each device, you also see a Volume button. Click this button to change the volume as desired. The Volume Control window presents simple slider bars that you can adjust as needed.

For the sound playback and sound recording options, you have an Advanced button. The sound playback Advanced option has two tabs. The first, Speakers, enables you to use a drop-down menu to select the speaker type that should be used, such as desktop speakers, headphones, and so on. The second tab, Performance, is the same for both sound playback and sound recording. The default settings are best, and you don't need to change them under normal circumstances. If you do change them, you may experience some performance problems, so keep that in mind when playing around with these settings.

The sound card, microphone, and other sound devices on your computer should come with instructions about any special settings that need to be made. Check your computer documentation for details.

One final note about the Audio tab—you'll see a Use Only Default Devices check box at the bottom of the window. Selecting this check box makes sure that only the default devices installed on your computer can be used. Should you enable this option? If your programs require a certain sound card or device and you have multiple sound cards or MIDI devices installed, then yes. If not, then don't worry about this check box.

Voice

The Voice tab works in the same way as the Audio tab, except you can configure voice playback and voice capture options.

Hardware

Finally, the Hardware tab lists all the sounds and multimedia device categories for Windows XP. By clicking a category, you can see the actual device or software installed to manage that category. You can't do much here, but you can access the device's troubleshooter and properties sheets. See Chapter 6 to learn more about hardware management.

Speech

The Speech icon in the Control Panel allows you to configure text-to-speech translation, as shown in Figure 2-10. This means that Windows XP can read aloud any text in Windows that you want read.

By default, the Microsoft Sam voice is selected for you, which is the only voice option available in the default XP installation. You can use the Preview Voice button and the Audio Output button to hear the voice and to select the device that you want to use for voice playback (which is typically

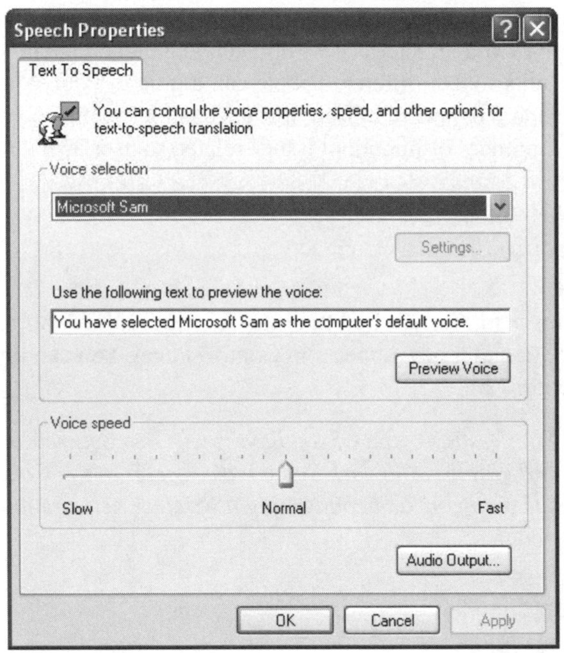

FIGURE 2-10 Speech Properties

your computer's sound card). You can also use the slider bar to slow down or speed up the rate at which the computer reads information to you.

System

The System icon in the Control Panel contains seven different tabs, such as Hardware, System Restore, Automatic Updates, Remote, and others. These tabs manage different components of your Windows XP system, and they are explored in various other chapters throughout this book.

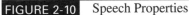

TIP *You can also quickly access this same Properties window by right-clicking My Computer from the Start Menu and choosing Properties.*

Taskbar and Start Menu

The Taskbar and Start Menu icon enables you to configure these items to suit your needs. You can learn about Taskbar and Start menu configuration in Chapter 3.

User Accounts

The User Accounts icon gives you an interface with which you can create new user accounts and manage existing user accounts so that different people can log on to your Windows XP computer. Without a valid username and a password, different users cannot log on, so you use this window to create these accounts. A number of important issues related to user account management are covered in Chapter 12.

Windows Firewall

Windows Firewall, which was formerly called Internet Connection Firewall, includes some updates from Service Pack 2, and it now appears in Control Panel. You can find out more about Windows Firewall in Chapter 13.

NOTE *You'll also see a Wireless Link icon (if you have a wireless network adapter installed on your computer) and Wireless Network Setup Wizard icon in the Control Panel. You can find out more about setting up and configuring a wireless network in Chapter 11.*

Chapter 3

Configure System Settings

How to...

- Customize your Start menu and Taskbar
- Customize the appearance and behavior of the Windows XP Desktop
- Customize your folders

One of the first reports about Windows XP, released several months before it was available to the public, concerned Windows XP's new Start menu and new interface. Windows XP does provide you with a significant interface makeover from earlier versions of Windows, and once you begin making your way around Windows XP's interface, you may decide that you want to change some things about the way Windows XP looks and behaves. That's fine, and Windows XP gives you a number of different options for configuring the interface, including folder view options, so that the operating system is easy to use and helpful to you. In this chapter, you'll explore how to customize your Start menu, Taskbar, XP Desktop, and folder view.

Customize Your Start Menu and Taskbar

When you first booted Windows XP, one of the first things you probably noticed is that Windows XP's Start menu looks different from that of previous versions of Windows. If you're new to Windows, this isn't such a shock; but for the rest of us, the new Start menu takes some getting used to. It's simple enough, however, and the next two sections show you how to use and customize the Start menu.

Use the Start Menu

The XP Start menu, shown in Figure 3-1, gives you an easy place to access the most common Windows configuration items as well as items that are popular specifically to you.

The Windows XP Start menu is divided into two portions, as you can see in Figure 3-1. The left side lists programs, and the right side provides access to common Windows folders, as well as Help and Support, Search, and Run options. I mentioned earlier that the Start menu lists items that are popular to you—this means that if you open a program, the Start menu will remember it and place an icon in the Start menu so you can more easily open the program next time.

Let's consider an example. I recently installed Microsoft Word on my XP system. To open Word, I have to choose Start | All Programs | Microsoft Word. Once I open Word a time or two, the Word icon is added to my Start menu. The next time I want to use Word, all I have to do is choose Start and click the Word icon.

In a nutshell, the Start menu is simply adding shortcuts to itself on your behalf. You can easily manage these icons by right-clicking them. This action gives you typical menu options for the shortcut, such as Open, Send To, Copy, Remove from This List, Rename, and Properties. If you want to remove the shortcut from the Start menu, just choose Remove from This List. This action removes the shortcut only from the Start menu—it does not remove the program from your computer, so don't worry.

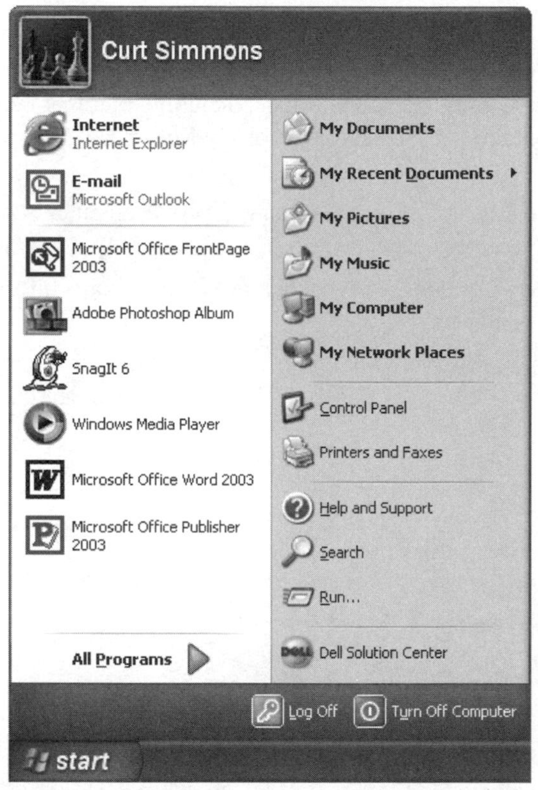

FIGURE 3-1 Start menu

When you right-click an item, you also see an option called Pin to Start Menu. This action simply moves the item to the top-left portion of the window, where it will always be visible. You'll notice that Internet Explorer and Outlook Express icons are available there by default, but you can remove them if you like by right-clicking the items and choosing Remove from This List.

Finally, you can also click All Programs to access typical Windows menus and installed applications.

NOTE *If you want to use Internet Explorer and Outlook Express from the Start menu, they have easy usage options if you right-click the icons. For example, you can choose to read e-mail, browse the Internet, or even access the Internet Properties window. See Chapter 9 for more information about configuring Internet properties.*

On the right side of the Start menu, you see common Windows items that you will need to access:

- **My Documents, My Pictures, and My Music** The My Documents folder is the default storage location for files of all kinds, including pictures, music, and movies. My Documents contains default subfolders of My Music, My Pictures, My Videos, and others.
- **My Recent Documents** My Recent Documents gives you quick access to the documents and files you have recently opened.
- **My Computer** My Computer is the default folder that stores information about drives connected to your computer.
- **My Network Places** My Network Places contains information about other computers and shared folders on your network and the Internet. You can learn more about My Network Places in Chapter 11.

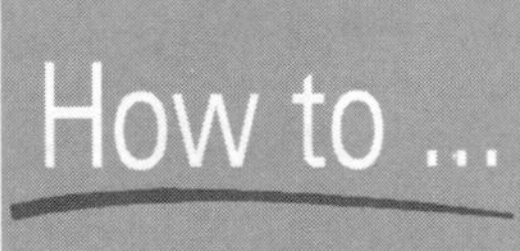

Reduce Clutter in My Recent Documents

As a writer, I use a lot of documents, as you might imagine. Although the My Recent Documents folder is very useful to me, it can get overcrowded, so that it becomes more confusing than helpful. So, what do I do if I need to remove some documents from My Recent Documents—or even all of them? First, let me clear up an important point. Like all items on the Start menu, My Recent Documents simply stores *shortcuts* to those documents, not the actual documents themselves. You can remove some items from My Recent Documents—or all of them—without deleting any of the actual documents from your computer. In fact, you can remove anything from the Start menu without damaging or deleting items on your computer, because all of the items on the Start menu are shortcuts.

So, if you want to remove items from My Recent Documents, you can do one of two things. First, you can choose Start | My Recent Documents and, on the pop-out menu that appears, right-click any item you don't want in the folder and click Delete—doing this deletes the shortcut, not the document itself. Second, if you want to empty every document completely from the folder, access the Advanced tab of the Customize Start Menu window and click the Clear List button. See the next section for more information about customizing the Start menu.

- **Control Panel** The Control Panel is the default location for managing all kinds of programs and services on your XP computer. Chapter 2 is devoted to the Control Panel.
- **Set Program Access and Defaults** You can use this option to make basic settings to the way Windows XP handles programs.
- **Connect To** If you have any network connections, such as a local area connection, dial-up connection, DSL connection, and so forth, you'll see a Connect To option on the Start menu. By clicking Connect To, you can immediately access your connections. If you don't have any network connections configured, you'll not see this option.
- **Printers and Faxes** Get direct access to your Printers and Faxes folder from the Start menu. See Chapter 7 to learn more about printers and faxes.
- **Help and Support** Windows XP includes a Help and Support feature that can answer your questions and even locate answers on the Internet. See Chapter 21.
- **Search** The Search feature enables you to find items on your computer or items on the Internet, including other people.
- **Run** The Run dialog box can be used to start programs or connect to network shares quickly.
- **Log Off/Turn Off Computer** These standard icons enable you to log off or shut down/ restart the computer. See Chapter 1 for details.

Customize the Start Menu

To customize the Start menu, you need to access the Start menu's properties. To access the Start menu's properties, open the Control Panel, double-click the Taskbar and Start Menu icon, and then click the Start Menu tab. If you don't see a Taskbar and Start Menu icon, switch the Control Panel to Classic view using the Control Panel link on the left side of the window.

TIP

You can also access the Start menu's properties in two other quick ways. First, you can right-click any empty area of the Taskbar and choose Properties, and then click the Start Menu tab. Even easier, just click Start, then right-click an empty area of the Start menu, and then choose Properties.

No matter how you've chosen to get there, you arrive at the Taskbar and Start Menu Properties window, shown in Figure 3-2.

You have the option on the Start Menu tab to use either the current XP Start menu or the Classic Start menu, which is simply the Start menu found in previous versions of Windows. Because the two are different, the following sections explore the configuration of each.

FIGURE 3-2 Taskbar and Start Menu Properties

XP Start Menu

To continue using the XP Start menu, click the Customize button. Doing this takes you to a Customize Start Menu window, which has a General tab and an Advanced tab. On the General tab, shown in Figure 3-3, are three different customization options:

- **Select an Icon Size for Programs** You can choose to use large or small icons on the Start menu. Small icons may be harder to see, but you can put more shortcut icons directly on the Start menu. Large icons are selected by default.
- **Programs** This selection menu changes the number of program shortcut icons that appear in viewing range when you click Start. Basically, it changes the size of the Start menu. By default, your Start menu displays 5 program shortcut icons; the maximum is 30.
- **Show on Start Menu** This option allows you to show Internet and e-mail applications on the Start menu and then provides a drop-down menu for selecting the application (Internet Explorer and Outlook Express, by default). If you have other browser or e-mail clients installed on your computer, you can use the drop-down menu and select a different browser and/or e-mail client, or just clear the check boxes if you don't want these items displayed at all.

FIGURE 3-3 Clear any check box items you do not want to use.

On the Advanced tab are some additional options that you may find very useful, shown in Figure 3-4.

First, you see a few check boxes collectively called Start Menu Settings. You have two options:

- **Open Submenus When I Pause on Them with My Mouse** This check box asks you whether you want a submenu to appear when you pause your mouse over an item on the Start menu; by default you must click the item to see the folder window. By default, folders such as My Documents and My Computer are stored as links on the Start menu, and you click them to open the folders in a different window. However, if you choose to have these folders appear as menus instead of links (see "Change Menu Item Behaviors" a bit later), an arrow appears next to the menu item. If this option is selected in the Advanced tab, when you hover your mouse over the item on the Start menu, a submenu automatically appears. For example, let's say I have chosen to display My Documents as a menu instead of a link, and I have a folder called My Stories stored in My Documents. Using the submenu option, if I pause the mouse over My Documents on the Start menu, a pop-out menu appears listing my other folders, including My Stories, and I can click My Stories to open it. If you want to use the menu option instead of a link, I'll show you how in "Change Menu Item Behaviors."

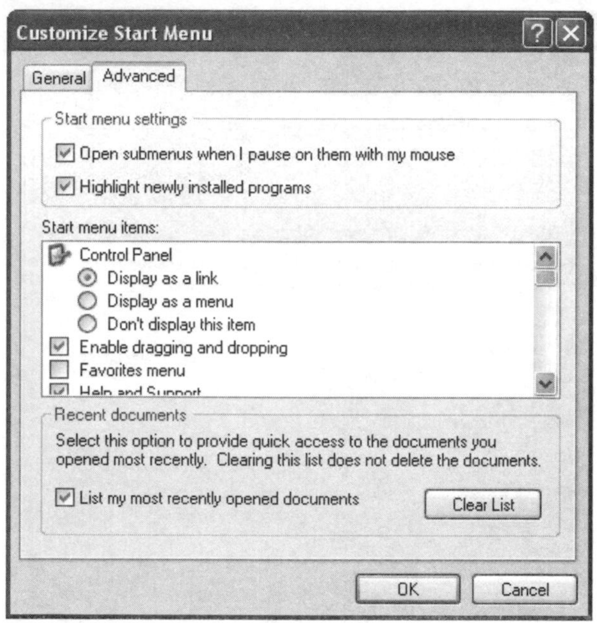

FIGURE 3-4 Advanced tab

At first glance, it may seem that the hover option is best; but if you have all folders on the Start menu configured to display menus, then every time you roll over one of the folders with your mouse, a menu will pop out. Some people find this very aggravating. You can play around with these settings and find the solution that is right for you.

- **Highlight Newly Installed Programs** When applications are first installed on your XP computer, they are highlighted until you use them for the first time. This serves as a simple reminder that you have new stuff you haven't used. If this gets on your nerves, just clear the check box.

Change Menu Item Behaviors The next part of the Advanced tab is a scroll window where you can select the folders and Windows items that appear on the Start menu and choose how those items are displayed. For example, the Control Panel, by default, is shown on the Start menu as a link. You can change this behavior so that it is shown as a menu or not at all. Simply scroll through the list and click the desired check boxes and radio buttons to determine what Windows items you want to include and how those items are presented (link or menu). You may want to experiment with these settings until you find the combination that is right for you—remember that you can make changes to these settings as many times as you like.

Show Recently Used Documents The last part of this configuration tab allows you to show recently used documents on the Start menu. For example, let's say that you're writing your life story. Once you open the document and then close it, the Start menu will put it in My Recent Documents, which is a folder that will now appear on the Start menu. Then, you can easily access the document from the Start menu the next time you need it.

Classic Start Menu

The Classic Start menu can be used instead of the new XP Start menu. In the Taskbar and Start Menu Properties window, click the Classic Start Menu option on the Start Menu tab. This option allows you to use the Start menu that appears in previous versions of Windows. If you want to use the Classic Start menu, select the radio button and click the Customize button, which gives you a single Customize Classic Start Menu interface, as shown in Figure 3-5.

You'll see the same basic Start menu options, just in a different format. If you want to add items to the Classic Start menu, click the Add button and a wizard will help you select items on your computer to add. Use the Remove button to remove items. The Advanced button opens Windows Explorer so you can manually add and remove items that you want. You can also re-sort the items and clear recent documents, programs, Web sites, and so on. The Advanced Start Menu Options window that you see enables you to, among other things, display a number of Windows items and use expandable (menu) folders. These items are self-explanatory—feel free to experiment and try new configurations.

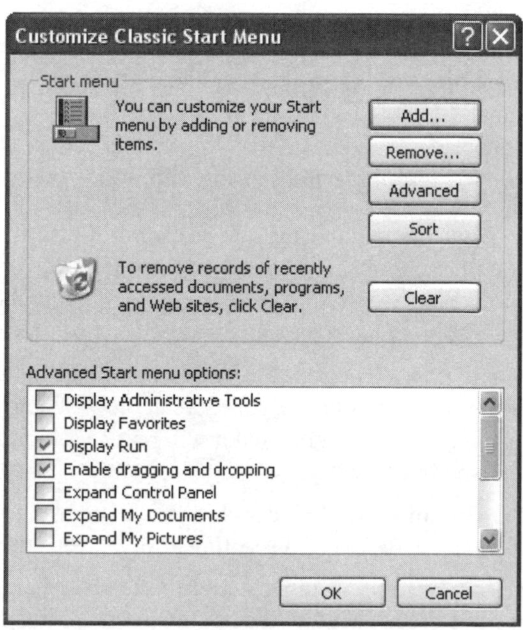

FIGURE 3-5 Customize Classic Start Menu

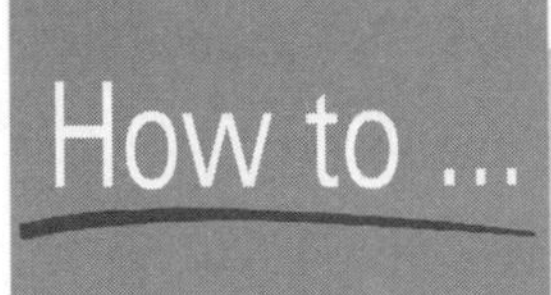

Add More Start Menu Shortcuts

Always keep in mind that the Start menu contains shortcuts to items that you want to access. Therefore, you can add just about anything to the Start menu. You can place an icon, folder, document, or essentially anything else on the Start menu. Here's how:

1. When you locate an icon, folder, document, or other Windows item that you want to add to the Start menu, right-click the item and click Create Shortcut.
2. Normally, a message will appear asking whether you want to put the shortcut on the Desktop. Click Yes.
3. On the Desktop, use your mouse to drag the new icon to the Start button on your Taskbar, and then release the mouse. The shortcut will be copied to the Start menu and will appear in your list of items.

Customize the Taskbar

Along with Start menu properties, you can customize your Taskbar properties as well. You can access the Taskbar and Start Menu Properties window by double-clicking the icon in the Control Panel. Or, just right-click any empty area of the Taskbar and click Properties, and then click the Taskbar tab, as shown in Figure 3-6.

You have two basic customization areas—Taskbar Appearance and Notification Area. In the Taskbar Appearance area, a few check box options enable certain features:

- **Lock the Taskbar** You can drag the Taskbar to different places on your Desktop. For example, if you want the Taskbar to appear on the top of the screen instead of the bottom, just drag it to the top. If you select the Lock the Taskbar check box, the Taskbar will be locked on the bottom of the screen and you will not be able to move it.
- **Auto-Hide the Taskbar** This feature keeps the Taskbar out of your way. When you are not using the Taskbar, it disappears below your screen view. When you need it, just point your mouse to the location of the Taskbar and it will reappear. Some people like this setting, so be sure to experiment with it.
- **Keep the Taskbar on Top of Other Windows** As you are using various windows, they may cover up portions of the Taskbar. This setting always keeps the Taskbar on top.
- **Group Similar Taskbar Buttons** This feature keeps similar items together. For example, if you open two Web pages and then minimize them both, they will appear next to each other on the Taskbar.

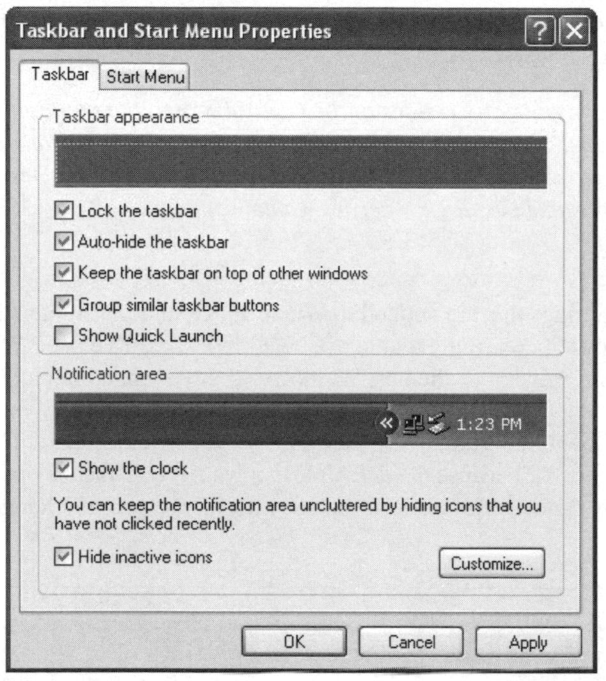

FIGURE 3-6 Taskbar tab

TIP *You can learn more about general Taskbar usage in Chapter 1.*

The Notification Area on the right side of your Taskbar has icons for a number of functions that are working on your computer, and it can notify you of certain application functions. Two simple check box options are located here. You can choose to show the clock in the Notification Area, and you can choose to hide inactive icons. The hide inactive icons feature simply "cleans up" the Notification Area so that only active icons are seen. You can try both of these settings to see whether you like them.

Configure Your Display

One of the primary places you configure the way your Windows XP system looks is through your Display properties. If you remember from Chapter 2, Display is an icon in the Control Panel that you can open to configure various settings that affect the appearance of your Windows XP display. Just click Start, and choose Control Panel, and then double-click the Display icon to open the properties sheets. Once you open Display Properties, you see several tabs, all of which are explored in the following sections.

The Display icon officially resides in the Control Panel, but you don't have to open the Control Panel to access the properties sheets. Just find an empty area on your Desktop (a place where there is no folder or icon), right-click the Desktop, and choose Properties. The same Display Properties window appears.

Themes

A *theme* is a group of settings that are applied to Windows XP under a single name. The settings usually relate to each other, creating a theme of some kind. If you've used Windows before, you are familiar with the concept of themes. Windows 95 gave you a bunch of options in the Windows Plus! pack, such as Mystery, The 70's, and Underwater. However, you are not used to seeing a Themes tab, shown in Figure 3-7, in the Display Properties window. The Themes option is placed here in Windows XP because the default Windows XP interface is one among a number of themes that you can choose. You can use the XP interface; you can change to a different

FIGURE 3-7 Themes tab

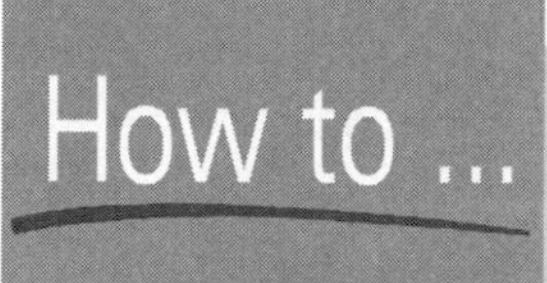

Remove a Theme

In the Windows courses that I teach, students are often frustrated by themes. If you have installed the Windows Plus! Pack for Windows XP, a bunch of additional themes are included on this tab. Let's say you choose the Underwater theme. If you later decide you no longer want the theme, how can you remove it? Because themes change all kinds of settings, including icons and fonts, manually removing a theme's settings can be difficult. The best way to remove a theme is to return to the Themes tab and select a different theme. Alternatively, you can choose the XP or Windows Classic theme to return to a default Windows interface. You can then make the customization changes you want on the other Display Properties tabs.

theme; or you can even use a Windows Classic theme, which basically gives you the plain-vanilla Windows interface you saw in Windows 9*x*, Me, and 2000. Simply use the drop-down menu to select a desired theme, and click Apply to see all of the settings the theme has to offer. You can also modify any theme (including the default XP interface theme) by making modifications to the other tabs available in the Display Properties window.

Desktop

The second tab you see in the Display Properties window is the Desktop tab (formerly called Background), shown in Figure 3-8. The Desktop tab lets you decide how your Windows XP Desktop area should look. In other words, the Desktop tab lets you decide what color, style, or even picture appears on your Desktop.

Using Backgrounds

Windows XP gives you several built-in options that you can choose for your background in the list on the Desktop tab. If you scroll through the list, you see that two kinds of files are present. Some files give your Desktop a pattern, while others give your Desktop a picture.

If you look in the list on the Desktop tab, you see that each file has a name and an icon next to it. Background patterns and pictures are simply JPEG, BMP, GIF, and related picture file formats (which you commonly see on the Internet), as well as HTML files (which are also used for Web pages).

On the Desktop tab, you can select one of the files and it will appear in the test monitor window. By default, pictures are set up to stretch across your screen so that they take up the entire Desktop area, and patterns are set to tile so that they repeat until the entire Desktop area is used. This process causes the pattern to fill the entire test screen, so you can see how it looks

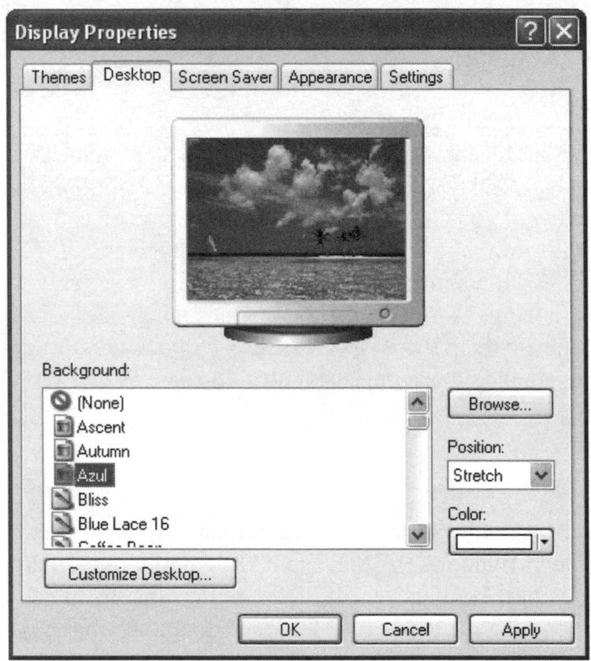

FIGURE 3-8 Desktop tab

before you decide to use it. You can also use the Center option in the Position drop-down menu to center the pattern in the middle of the test screen, which will give you a different look. If you like what you have selected, click the Apply button at the bottom of the window and the new pattern will be applied to your Desktop. If you don't like it, just pick something else on the Desktop tab. You can look at all of the patterns and even reapply different patterns until you find the one you want.

If you choose to center a picture or pattern, an area of your Desktop will still be showing. Windows XP enables you to alter the color of the remaining Desktop area. For example, let's say you choose a wallpaper from the Background list on the Desktop tab and you center the picture. You will have additional leftover background space. You can use the Color drop-down menu and select a color for the remaining portion of the Desktop area.

Do you have to use an additional background picture or pattern? It is important to remember that all of this stuff is optional. Windows XP gives you a basic background upon installation; if you are happy with that background, you don't have to change anything. However, all of the options explored in this chapter are provided so that you can configure your Windows XP computer to look the way you want. Keep in mind that Windows XP can display any common graphics file format (such as GIF, JPEG, or BMP files) as wallpaper for your Desktop, so be creative! If you want to use something different, such as picture files stored on your computer, you can simply click the Browse button to locate the file on your PC or even the Internet. Here's how:

1. On the Display Properties Desktop tab, click the Browse button.
2. In the Browse window that appears, navigate to the location on your computer where your picture files are kept (such as the My Documents or My Pictures folder).
3. Once you locate the desired picture, select it and then click the Open button in the Browse window.
4. The picture will appear in the test window on the Desktop tab. Click OK for your picture to be displayed on your computer's Desktop.

Once you have finished your background pattern and selected anything else from the Desktop tab that you want to use for the main pattern, just click Apply and then click OK.

Customize Your Desktop

Also on the Desktop tab (toward the bottom) is a Customize Desktop button. If you click this button, you are taken to the Desktop Items properties sheet, which contains a General tab and a Web tab.

On the General tab, shown in Figure 3-9, you can choose which Desktop icons you want to display, such as My Documents, My Computer, My Network Places, and Internet Explorer.

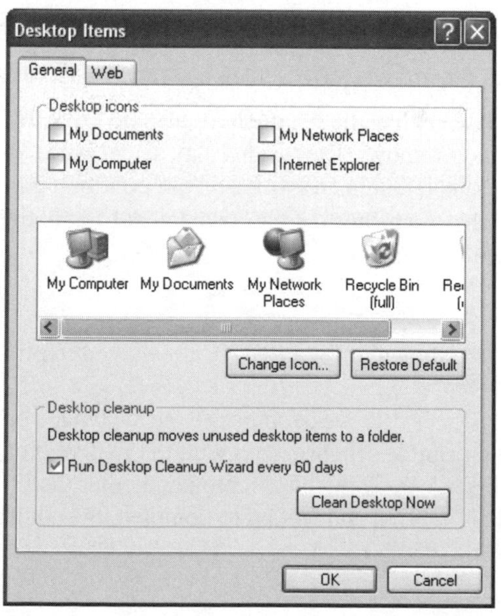

FIGURE 3-9 General tab

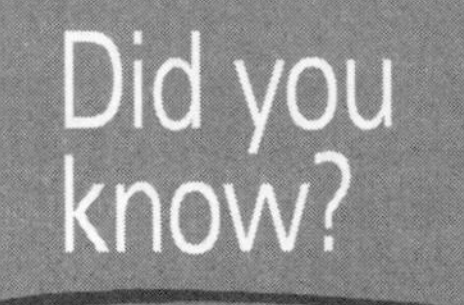

You Can Use Several File Types for Your Desktop

JPEG (as well as GIF) files are standard file types for pictures and graphics used on the Internet. When surfing the Internet and looking at pictures or graphics, you are usually looking at JPEG and GIF files. HTML files are Web pages. You can display an entire Web page as your background if you like, and you'll see how to do this later in this chapter. In a nutshell, virtually any picture on the Internet can be used on your Windows Desktop, as long as it is a BMP, JPEG, GIF, DIB, or HTML file or document.

All of these items are selected by default. You also see a window showing the default icons that are used for each Desktop item. If you want to use different icons, click the Change Icon button and select different icons from the provided list. If you manage to get them all fouled up, just click the Restore Default button to return to XP's default icon settings.

At the bottom of the General tab, you see the option to use the Desktop Cleanup Wizard. The Cleanup Wizard is configured to run every 60 days by default, but you can run it at any other time by clicking the Clean Desktop Now button. This wizard simply removes old shortcuts and puts them in a folder called Unused Shortcuts. If you create a lot of shortcuts and don't use them very often, this wizard can help keep your Desktop free of clutter. The wizard is easy to use—just follow these steps:

1. On the Desktop Items General tab, click the Clean Desktop Now button.
2. The Desktop Cleanup Wizard welcome screen appears. Click Next to continue.
3. In the Shortcuts window, review the list of shortcuts and click the check boxes next to the ones that you want to remove. The wizard may select some of them for you, so make certain you want any selected items removed before continuing (if you don't, clear the check boxes). Notice that each shortcut has a date next to it, noting the last time it was used. Click Next when you're done.
4. Click Finish.

The Desktop Items Web tab, shown in Figure 3-10, allows you to place a complete Web page on your Desktop.

You can place an HTML file on your Desktop or use the Web page option to place an actual Web page on your Desktop that can be synchronized with the real Web page on the Internet. To place a Web page on your Desktop, click the New button and enter the URL in the New Desktop Item dialog box. You'll need an Internet connection to complete the addition of the Web page.

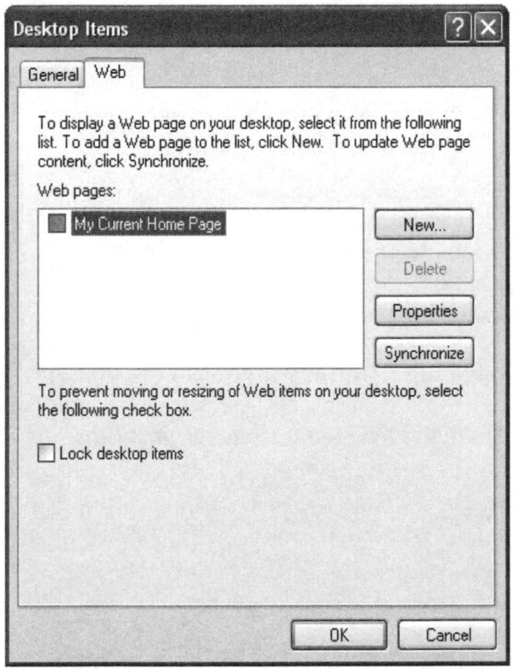

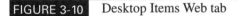

FIGURE 3-10 Desktop Items Web tab

NOTE *When you choose the Web page option, the entire Web site is downloaded and stored on your computer so that you can use the site as if you were actually using a browser.*

Once you click OK, a confirmation message appears. If the Web site requires you to enter a password, click the Customize button and enter it; otherwise, click OK.

TIP *Once the Web page is displayed on your Desktop (and perhaps gallery items as well), you can select the Lock Desktop Items check box on the Web tab so that no items can be moved or resized by accident. In other words, once your Desktop is just as you want it, use the lock feature so that you or someone else doesn't accidentally change the Desktop.*

Screen Saver

The Screen Saver tab provides two functions: it enables you to configure a screen saver for your computer and enables you to configure power management options. A screen saver is a simple program that runs once your computer has been idle for a certain period of time. In the past, the screen saver protected monitors from "burn in." When a monitor was left unattended for too long and one continuous picture or window was displayed, the image could burn itself onto the monitor and always be sort of floating in the background. Monitors today aren't really susceptible to this problem, so screen savers are used more for decoration. The following two sections explore both screen savers and Windows XP's power-management features.

Use a Screen Saver

The Screen Saver tab is easy to use, as you can see in Figure 3-11. Just use the drop-down menu to select a screen saver, and a sample of it will be displayed in the test window. Once you find one you like, click the Apply button.

Once you select a screen saver that you want to use, you have a few other options as well:

- **Settings** The Settings button, which opens a small window specific to the screen saver, allows you to configure the screen saver. These settings are easy and self-explanatory. You can play around with them to find the settings you want.

- **Preview** If you click Preview, your screen first goes blank, and then the screen saver begins, so you can see whether you like it. Just move your mouse to get control of your system again.

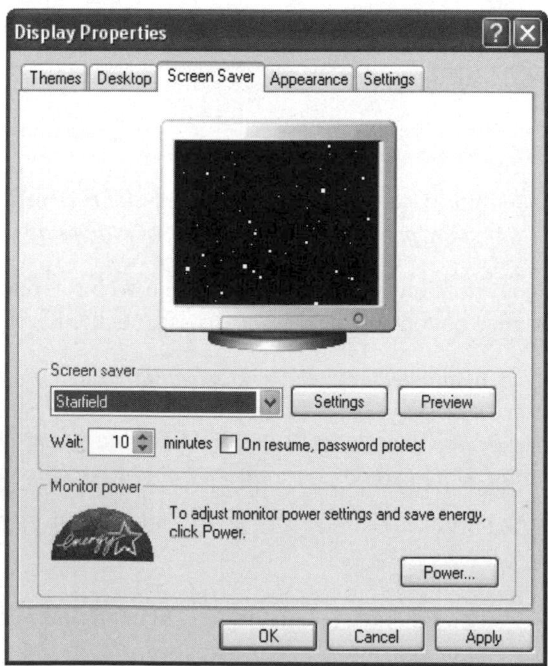

FIGURE 3-11 Screen Saver tab

Did you know?

You Can Use Your Own Pictures for a Screen Saver

Windows XP offers a My Pictures screen saver. This feature lets you use any pictures stored on your computer as a screen saver. The system rotates through the pictures after a specified period of time. You designate a folder the program accesses, such as My Pictures, where the pictures are stored. You can then set transition effects as desired. Select My Pictures Slideshow in the screen saver list, and then click the Settings button to set it up.

- **Wait** This scroll box enables you to set the amount of time that should pass before the screen saver comes on. The default time is 14 minutes. There is no right or wrong setting, but to protect your screen, keep the setting under 30 minutes; also, do not set the time setting so low that it comes on after 1 minute or so of inactivity—you'll find such a setting very aggravating.
- **On Resume, Password Protect** This check box option returns you to the Windows Welcome screen when you move your mouse to regain control of the system. In other words, you'll have to log back in each time the screen saver comes on. In previous versions of Windows, the Screen Saver tab offered a Password Protect option—this is the same thing, but it is enabled with your user account so that you have only one password to remember.

Use Power Options

The Screen Saver tab also provides a button to access energy-saving options: the Power button. After clicking the button, the Power Options Properties window appears (which has the same properties sheets you see if you click Power Options in the Control Panel), as shown in Figure 3-12.

On the Power Schemes tab, you have a few options for managing how your computer conserves energy when it is idle. First, you see a drop-down menu called Power Schemes that contains a few basic schemes:

- **Home/Office Desk** When using this scheme, your monitor is automatically turned off after 15 minutes of inactivity, your system goes on standby after 20 minutes of inactivity, and your hard disks are turned off after 30 minutes of inactivity.
- **Portable/Laptop** This scheme uses the same settings as Home/Office Desk.

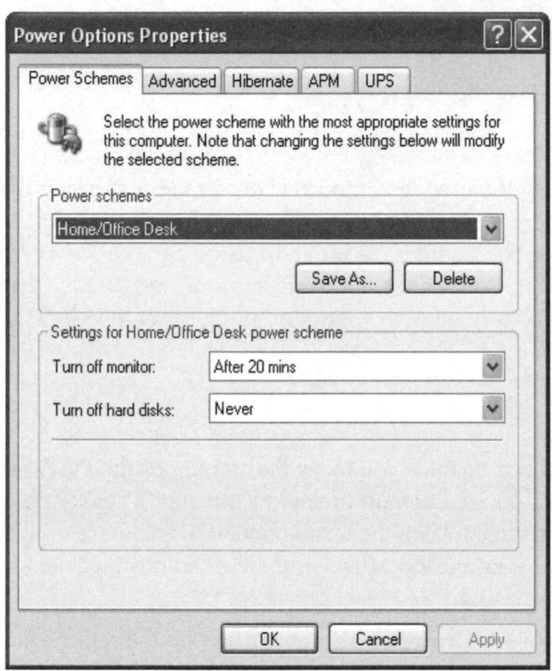

FIGURE 3-12 Power Options Properties window

- **Presentation** This setting is used for laptops or computers used for teaching or presentations. Essentially, the power options are turned off and the system never goes on standby.
- **Always On** When using this scheme, your monitor is automatically turned off after 30 minutes of inactivity, your hard drives after one hour of inactivity, and your system never goes on standby.
- **Minimal Power Management** This setting turns off your monitor after 15 minutes of inactivity but never turns off the hard drive.
- **Max Battery** This setting contains the same settings as Minimal Power Management.

Okay, here's the deal. You can use a particular scheme and change any of the settings you want by using the drop-down menus. For example, let's say I want to use the Home/Office Desk scheme, but I do not want my monitor to turn off until 30 minutes of inactivity. No problem; I just use the drop-down menu for the monitor and change it to 30 minutes. You can also change all of the settings and click Save As to create your own scheme. Just give the scheme a name, and it will appear in your scheme list.

The Power Options Properties window also has an Advanced tab (which really isn't that advanced). You have only two check box options that you can enable if you want:

- **Always Show Icon on the Taskbar** This option puts a power icon on your Taskbar.
- **Prompt for Password When Computer Goes Off Standby** This option requires you to reenter your password when your computer goes off standby before you can use the system again. This feature helps prevent anyone from gaining access to your system when you are away from it.

On the Hibernate tab, you can enable the hibernate feature by clicking the check box to turn it on. Hibernation allows Windows XP to store information that is in memory on your hard disk before it shuts down. When the computer is brought back online, XP can remember its previous state so that you do not lose any data.

The APM tab, which stands for Advanced Power Management, is used by computers that support the APM standard. Basically, APM allows your computer to use less power, and it gives you information about battery life if you are using a battery (such as with a laptop). There's nothing for you to configure, and if this tab tells you that your computer supports APM, you can enable it by selecting the single check box option.

The final tab is UPS, which stands for uninterruptible power supply. UPS devices are basically batteries that give your desktop computer enough power to remain online in the event of a power failure. This gives you enough time to do proper shutdown of the system. The UPS feature is typically employed on server systems and rarely on desktop systems, but if you have a UPS, you can enable it on this tab. Be sure to follow the UPS manufacturer's suggestions for configuration and settings.

Now that you see what options you have, what scheme should you use? While no exact answers are right for everybody, for the typical home user, I recommend the Home/Office Desk scheme with the default settings. This scheme ensures that your computer is using the least amount of energy once it becomes inactive for 15 to 30 minutes. This setting makes the best use of energy, but it will disconnect you from the network, if you are connected to one.

Appearance

The Appearance tab, shown in Figure 3-13, enables you to choose an appearance scheme for your Windows XP computer.

You have a few standard options here:

- **Windows and Buttons** You can use the drop-down menu to choose either XP style or Windows Classic style.
- **Color Scheme** A number of color schemes are available. Use this drop-down menu to select one you like. You can experiment with this setting and change it at any time.
- **Font Size** You can choose Normal, Large, and Extra Large from the drop-down menu.

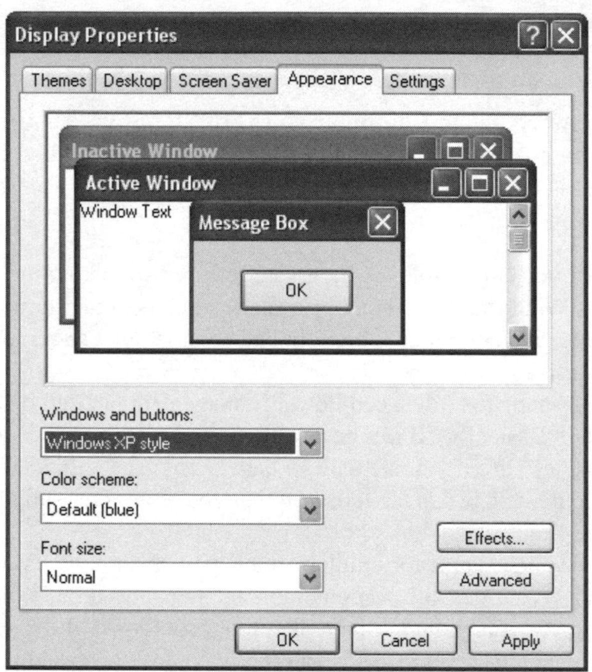

FIGURE 3-13 Appearance tab

- **Effects** Click the Effects button to open the Effects window, which gives you some basic check box options, such as fade and shadows under menus.
- **Advanced** If you click the Advanced button, you can make specific font and color changes to different Windows components, such as menus, buttons, active title bar, and a host of others. Under most circumstances, you will not want to edit all of the settings, but if you want to change something specific, just select it using the drop-down menu and configure the available options for it.

Settings

The final Display Properties tab is the Settings tab. You use this tab to manage the actual video-card hardware that resides within your computer. A few basic options are offered, as you can see in Figure 3-14.

First, you see a Screen Resolution slider bar. You can adjust the resolution to suit your needs, and, as you adjust it, you will see that your Desktop area gets either larger or smaller (including your icons) depending on the location of the slider bar.

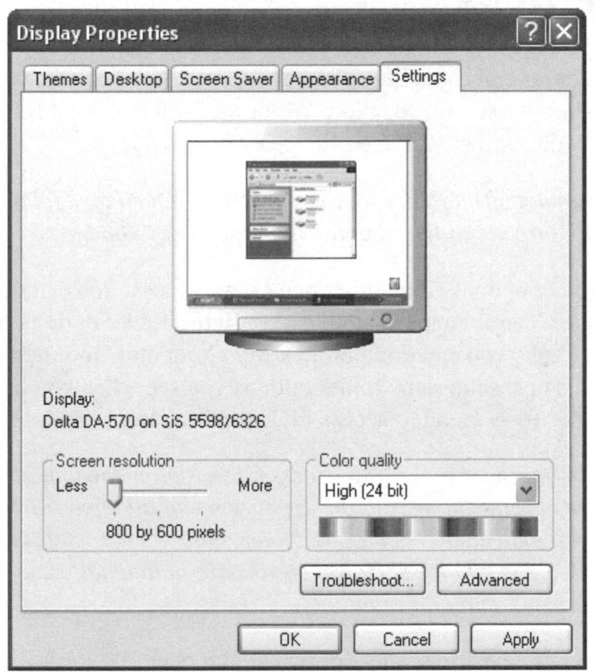

FIGURE 3-14 Settings tab

You also see a Color Quality drop-down menu that enables you to select the number of colors Windows XP can use to generate all of the graphics and pictures that appear on your monitor. True Color (32 bit) is the highest color scheme that you can use, and, depending on the quality of your video card, you may have only a few color options available. The higher resolution provides the best color performance.

You also have an Advanced button. This option opens the properties sheets for your video card. In general, the default settings found on these sheets are all you need, and you really should not change any of them unless your video card documentation tells you to do so. If you're having problems with your display, click the Troubleshoot button to get help from Windows XP.

TIP *Are you having problems with your screen flickering? No problem. On the Settings tab of Display Properties, click the Advanced button, then click the Monitor tab. Change the refresh rate to at least 90. This will usually stop the screen flicker aggravation. If you are using an LCD monitor, you will not see flicker and you can't change the refresh rate as noted here.*

Configure Folder Views

Aside from using an appearance scheme so that your folders appear with a certain color and font, Windows XP also includes several capabilities that enable you to customize your folders. Keep in mind that a folder is simply a storage location. Windows XP has several folders it creates and uses, and you can create your own as well (see Chapter 4).

TIP *Folder options do not affect folder toolbars, but you can change folder toolbars, which you will learn about later in this chapter, in the section "Toolbars."*

You can configure folder options from either one of two places. You can double-click the Folder Options icon in the Control Panel, or you can configure folder options from within any Windows folder. For example, you can double-click My Computer, and then choose Tools | Folder Options. Doing this opens the same folder options you see when you open the Control Panel icon. You can use the Tools menu to access folder options from any folder in Windows XP.

TIP *It is important to note here that if you access folder options within a window and make changes, you are making changes to the appearance of all of your folders. In other words, you cannot individually configure folder options for each folder—one setting applies to all folders in Windows. However, you can individually change View options (such as details, icons, and other options).*

Once you open Folder Options (regardless of where you open it), you see a simple interface with four tabs.

General

The major appearance changes you can make to your folders are performed on the General tab, which presents you with a list of radio buttons, as shown in Figure 3-15.

You can choose radio button options from three different categories:

- **Tasks** These options let you display Web content in your folders, including the blue links in the left side of your folders (which jump to another location when you click them). Web content also enables your folders to display HTML documents and graphics files. For example, let's say you have a picture file called My Dog. With the XP default view, a thumbnail icon appears showing you what the picture looks like. If you want to keep Web items in your folder, just keep Show Common Tasks in Folders selected. Otherwise, select Use Windows Classic Folders.

NOTE *My Computer and the Control Panel are always displayed with the Web page view, even if you do not select the Web page view option.*

- **Browse Folders** These options let you choose how your folders are displayed when you are browsing through a folder structure. For example, let's say you open My Computer and then you open the Control Panel. You can have My Computer open in a window, and then have the Control Panel open in a separate window. Or, you can

FIGURE 3-15 General tab

choose to use the same window so that with My Computer open, when you open the Control Panel, it replaces what you see in My Computer. There is no right or wrong option, but if you work with a number of windows at one time, you may find the Open Each Folder in the Same Window option less cluttering to your Desktop.

TIP *When using the Open Each Folder in the Same Window option, click the Back button on the folder's toolbar to return to a previous window. For example, if you open My Computer and then the Control Panel, just click the Back button to return to My Computer—just as you would when surfing the Internet.*

- **Click Items as Follows** You can have your mouse clicks act as though your Windows XP interface were the Internet. On the Internet, you simply click once with your mouse to open any item—all Internet movement is performed through hyperlinks that connect Web pages and Internet sites together. You can have your computer act this way as well, so that you only have to point to an item to select it, and then click it one time to open it (no more double-clicking). You can enable this option and try it out—it does take some getting used to, however. Just click the Single-Click radio button option to enable it.

View

The View tab contains a number of check boxes that enable you to make decisions about files and folders. The options found here concern the display of certain file types, folder views, and other lower-level settings. Windows XP does a good job of configuring the common settings, and changing them may cause problems—so my recommendation is that you do not make any changes to the options found on this tab unless you have a very specific reason to do so. Because you probably don't need to use these options, I will list here only some of the more common ones and indicate whether they are enabled by default:

- **Display All Control Panel Options and All Folder Contents** Do you remember how the Control Panel displays only the most common icons? If you don't like that feature, click this check box to turn it off (this option is not selected by default).
- **Do Not Show Hidden Files and Folders; Hide Protected Operating System Files** These two separate options, both of which are enabled by default, keep the hidden files and folders in Windows XP from being shown. Windows XP hides folders that hold operating system files, as well as many of the individual files that make Windows XP run. Obviously, you don't need to do anything with these files, and Windows XP hides them to help prevent tampering or accidental deletion. You should leave these settings as they are so that Windows XP continues to hide system files and folders.
- **Hide Extensions for Known File Types** This option provides for hiding file extensions. For example, let's say you create a Microsoft Word document called Cat. The document's full name is Cat.doc. The hide extensions option hides the .doc extension and all other extensions for files that Windows recognizes. This makes your folder files cleaner and easier to read. This option is enabled by default; however, you may want to turn on file extensions, which can help you get more familiar with the kinds of files you are working with.
- **Remember Each Folder's View Settings** You can use the View menu in a particular folder to determine how the folder appears and what you can view (you can learn about these options in the "Configure Folder Views and Toolbars" section later in this chapter). This setting tells Windows to remember each folder's view settings. This option is enabled by default and you should keep it enabled.

File Types

The File Types tab lists every type of file supported in Windows XP. Your operating system and applications do a great job of managing this list, so you do not need to perform any configuration here unless explicitly instructed to do so by some application's technical documentation.

TIP

Removing file types from this list can prevent certain application files from functioning in Windows XP. Do not remove any of these files! Let Windows XP and your applications manage this task.

Offline Files

Offline Files allows Windows XP to store network files locally on your computer and then synchronize your local copy with the network copy. For example, let's say that a document resides on a network server at work, but you need to take that document home on your laptop one evening and make some changes to it. With Offline Files, the document is stored on your local computer instead of the network server. You can work with the file and make changes to it when you are at home. Then, when you reconnect to the network at work, the local file can be synchronized with the network file. In other words, the changes you made at home are added to the network file so that the network file is up-to-date.

The Offline Files tab enables you to turn on offline file support and configure some basic functions for offline files. Typically, the default check boxes are all you need here.

Configure Folder Views and Toolbars

Once you have made some decisions about how you want your folders to appear using the Folder Options window, you can customize your folder views and toolbars. When you open a folder, you see a View menu, which is shown open in Figure 3-16.

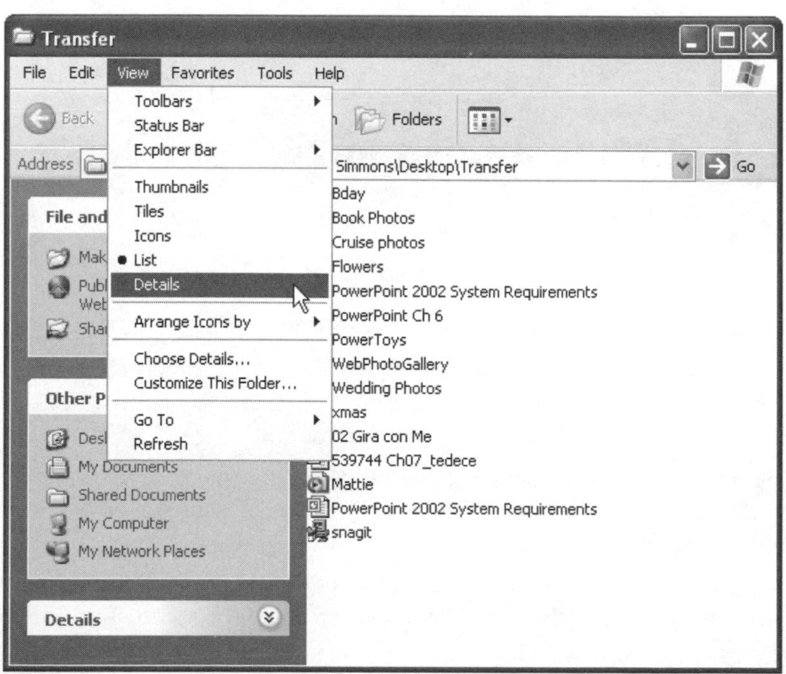

FIGURE 3-16 View menu

Most of the options you see on this menu are self-explanatory, and you can try the different setting options to determine what you like best. The following sections explore your major options.

Toolbars

First, you have the Toolbars item—when you hold your mouse over this item, a submenu pops out. This submenu allows you to choose the toolbar items you would like to use. Some of these are enabled by default, but you can enable or disable them by clicking them with your mouse. You have these options:

- **Standard Buttons** Enabled by default, this option provides you with the standard toolbar buttons, such as Back, Forward, Up One Level, Search, and so forth. You need these, so keep this option enabled.
- **Address Bar** Enabled by default, this option gives you the Address bar, so you can move to different areas of your computer or even the Internet. For example, you could access a folder by simply typing the path to the folder (such as **C:\My Documents**) or an Internet address.
- **Links** This option, which is enabled by default, gives you a Links button on your toolbar so you can access links or resource locations that you commonly use.

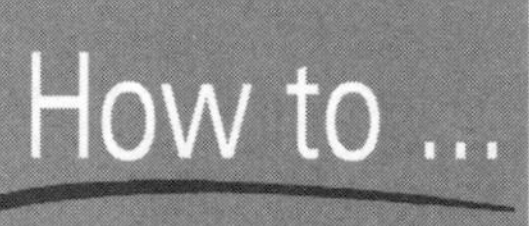

Create a Customized Toolbar

Follow these easy steps to create a customized toolbar:

1. In a desired folder, choose View | Toolbars | Customize.
2. In the Customize Toolbar window, select any item in the left portion of the window that you want to add to your toolbar, and then click the Add button. Continue this process until you have moved all options that you want.
3. In the right portion of the window, select any item that you do not want to use on your toolbar, and then click Remove. Continue this process until you have removed any options you do not want.
4. In the right portion of the window, select an option and use the Move Up or Move Down buttons to adjust the order that the items appear on the toolbar, as desired.
5. Click Close when you are done.

Aside from these standard options, you can also lock the toolbars and you can click Customize. This option opens a Customize Toolbar window, as shown in Figure 3-17, where you can add and remove various toolbar buttons and options. This feature allows you to configure your folder toolbars so they are exactly what you want.

Status Bar

The Status bar is the small bar that runs along the bottom of your folder window. It tells you what is going on when you are trying to use or connect to other resources. This bar works just like the Status bar in Internet Explorer, and you can choose to use it or not by choosing View | Status Bar to add or remove a check mark next to the item.

Explorer Bar

This option has an additional pop-out menu that lists various Explorer items you can select, such as Search, Favorites, History, and others. If you select one of these items, an additional pane appears in your window to provide the Explorer option. For example, if you select the Search option, the window provides a search section. You can experiment with these settings to find ones that are useful to you.

Icon Appearance

The remainder of the View menu contains a number of different icon and list options to determine how the contents of a folder are displayed. For example, you can use large icons, small icons, a list, and so forth. Click these options to experiment with them until you find the appearance that you like best.

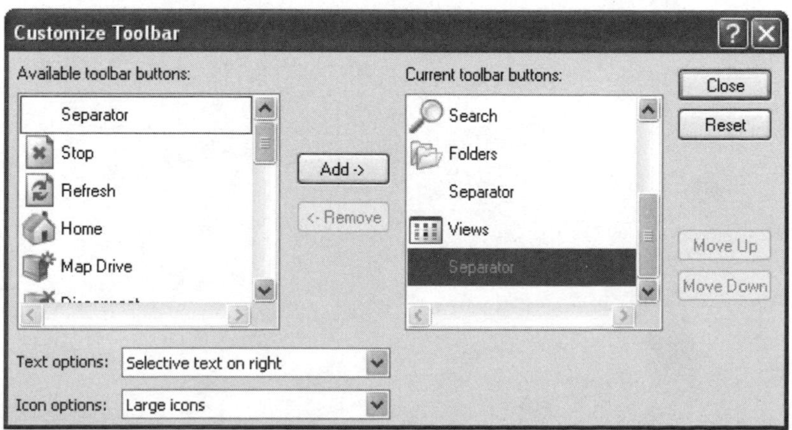

FIGURE 3-17 Customize Toolbar window

Did you know?

Your Folders Can Take You to the Internet

One of the design goals Microsoft has for Windows XP is to make the operating system more integrated with the Internet. Notice that the folder's Address bar looks a lot like the Internet Explorer browser's Address bar. This similarity is by design, and, as you might guess, you can jump from a local folder to the Internet without even changing to a different window. In the folder's Address bar, just select what is currently listed, press BACKSPACE or DEL, type the Internet URL you want, and press ENTER. Your computer will launch an Internet connection and take you to the Internet site—very cool!

NOTE

You can learn more about files and folders and how to use folder menus in Chapter 4. You'll also note that the View menu has a Customize This Folder option. This option essentially allows you to share the folder on a network, and you can learn all about sharing in Chapter 4.

Chapter 4

Manage Components, Programs, Folders, and Files

How to…

- Install and remove Windows XP components
- Install, manage, and remove programs
- Create and configure folders and files

The Windows XP operating system is a rich, robust system that is full of tools and features that help you make the most of your computing experience. Moreover, you can easily add new programs and even Windows XP components so that your computer will do exactly what you need it to do. From Microsoft Office to Adobe Photoshop Elements to games and tax programs, you can purchase and install multitudes of programs on Windows XP, as well as several additional XP tools that are not included by default. In this chapter, we'll look at how to manage programs and components on your XP system, how to add and remove them, and how to manage folders and files so you can keep up with the files you create.

Manage Programs with Windows XP

A *program* is software that you install on Windows XP to perform some task. Programs can come in many forms, such as applications, games, and utilities. The purpose of a program is to give your computer some functionality that is needed. For example, Windows XP does not ship with advanced photo-editing software. To perform photo editing on Windows XP, you need a program that provides this functionality, such as Adobe Photoshop Elements. The program is installed on Windows XP from a CD-ROM; after installation, you can use the application on your Windows XP computer.

If you purchased your computer with Windows XP preinstalled, a number of programs are probably already installed on your computer. Choose Start | All Programs to see all of the programs that are currently installed.

NOTE *In Windows XP, new programs that you have not opened are displayed in yellow when you look at them by choosing Start | All Programs. Once you open a program, this highlight is removed so you can keep track of which programs you have explored and which ones you have not. If you don't like the highlight feature, you can remove it by accessing the Start menu properties. See Chapter 3 for more information about Start menu customization.*

Before installing a program, you should make certain that it is compatible with Windows XP. Before you purchase a program, check out the information on the box—it should tell you on the box that the program will work with Windows XP. The odds are also very good that applications that functioned well under Windows 98/Me and/or Windows 2000 will work with Windows XP, although compatibility cannot be guaranteed. Once you are sure your program will work under Windows XP, you need to install the program. You can install a program in two ways, as explained in the following sections.

Did you know?

Compatibility Issues with Service Pack 2

You are probably running Windows XP Service Pack 2 (SP2) on your computer at this point (if not, see Chapter 19). However, the new SP2 Windows Firewall can cause some problems with certain applications and games. You can generally configure Windows Firewall to work with these applications and games, but you'll need to configure Windows Firewall to allow an *exception* for the application or game. You can learn more about Windows Firewall and how to configure an exception in Chapter 13.

NOTE *In addition to software considerations, the program you want to install may also require a certain amount of RAM (Random Access Memory), a minimum amount of available hard disk space, possibly a certain graphics card, and perhaps other requirements. Make sure your system can accommodate these needs before you buy—or be ready to update your system or buy other equipment to support the new program.*

Use a Program's Setup Feature

Programs that you purchase are placed on a CD-ROM for easy installation. In fact, most programs today include an auto-start file to help you get the program installed quickly and easily. For example, when you place the CD-ROM into the CD-ROM drive, the disk spins, and then a dialog box appears on your screen asking whether you want to install the application. This procedure varies from manufacturer to manufacturer, so you'll need to follow the documentation or onscreen instructions that came with the program you purchased.

If you put the CD-ROM into the CD-ROM drive and nothing happens, you can manually start the setup program by opening My Computer. Right-click the CD-ROM icon, and then choose either Install or AutoPlay. If nothing happens, right-click the CD-ROM icon and choose Explore. You'll probably see some folders and files in the CD-ROM folder. Find an icon called Setup.exe, as shown in Figure 4-1. (You may not see the .exe extension if the Hide Extensions for Known File Types option is enabled; see Chapter 3 for more details.) Double-click the Setup icon and the installation should start. Once you have started the installation process, follow the instructions that appear.

NOTE *You should always examine the setup instructions that come with any program. Every program is different, so be sure to follow the particular manufacturer's instructions for installing the program on your computer.*

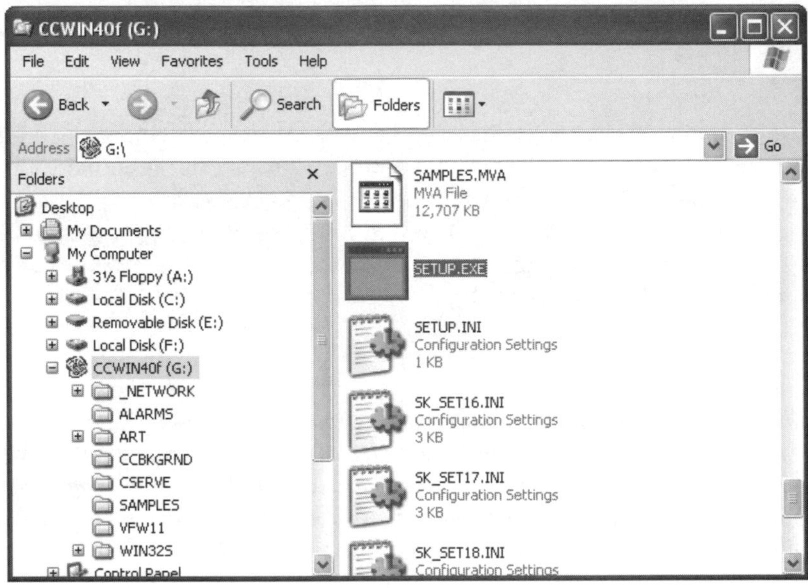

FIGURE 4-1 Setup.exe

Install Programs Using Add/Remove Programs

As you might guess, you can also use Add or Remove Programs in the Control Panel to install a program. You'll see an Add New Programs icon on the left side of the screen, as shown in Figure 4-2. Once you click the icon, you can click the CD or disk button to begin an installation from a CD-ROM or disk. If you want to see whether your XP operating system needs any updates from Microsoft, click the Windows Update button. Essentially, the Install option found here looks for the Setup.exe file on a disk or CD-ROM. Otherwise, the setup routine works in the same way that it would if you had used AutoStart or manually started Setup.exe.

Uninstall a Program

Just as you can install programs on Windows XP, you can also uninstall them. For example, let's say that you use a particular application and, at a future date, you purchase a different application to replace your older one. If the application you purchase is not an upgrade to the old one, you may want to remove the old application from Windows XP. After all, the application takes up disk space; and because you're not going to use it any longer, you don't need it cluttering up your system.

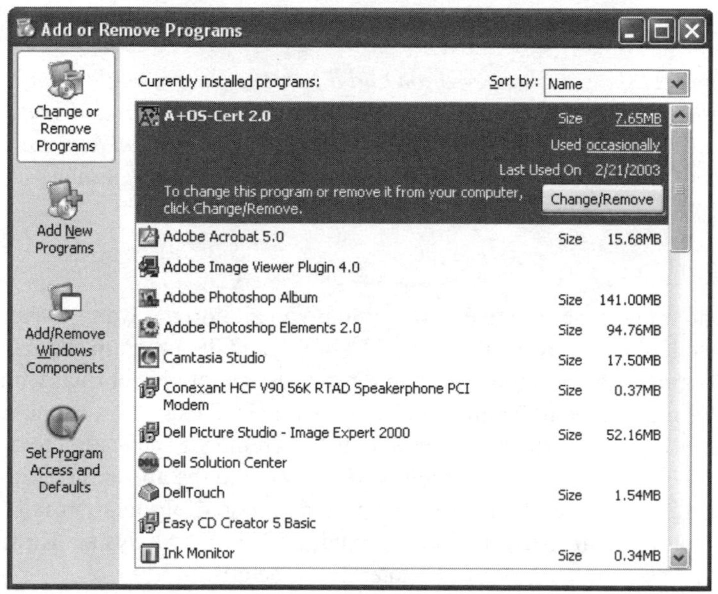

FIGURE 4-2 Add New Programs in Control Panel

NOTE

Once you remove an application from your system, you may not be able to use any of the files generated by that application. For example, if I remove Photoshop Elements from my computer, I may not be able to open any Photoshop Elements files (PSD) (unless I have another program that can read them). Make sure you no longer need an application before removing it from your computer.

Use a Program's Uninstall Option

Some programs come with their own uninstall option. You put the CD-ROM into the CD-ROM drive, and a window appears that allows you to install additional components or to remove existing ones—or the entire program. Microsoft Office, for example, offers this feature. Some programs also offer a built-in uninstall routine. You can choose Start | All Programs, point to the program's folder, and a menu pops out with an uninstall option. Not all programs have this feature, so don't worry if you do not see this option.

Use Add/Remove Programs

If you have a tricky program that doesn't help you with the uninstall, you can, once again, use Add/Remove Programs in the Control Panel. When you open Add or Remove Programs, you'll see a list of programs. The programs listed in this window are installed on your computer.

To remove one of them, simply select it and click the Change/Remove button. Follow any additional prompts that appear.

Some programs show a Change button and a Remove button, while some show only a Change/Remove button. If you have programs that can be upgraded or if additional parts of the program can be installed, you'll see both Change and Remove. This arrangement allows you to install additional portions of the program or remove the program or components from your computer.

If All Else Fails…

Sometimes, you end up with programs that really like you and do not want to leave your computer. No uninstall option is available on the CD-ROM, and the program is not listed in Add or Remove Programs as an option you can uninstall. Although this normally does not happen, you can still remove the program by deleting its folder. This is not a recommended action, though, because you may experience problems by forcing an application to delete itself. However, this option can be used when absolutely necessary. See the upcoming How To box for step-by-step instructions on forcefully removing a program. Also, if trying to install or uninstall a program has left you with a bunch of problems, Windows XP offers a System Restore feature that can help you get things sorted out. See Chapter 21 for details.

Under no circumstances should you delete a program's folder if you can use the CD-ROM or Add or Remove Programs option. Deleting the folder does not allow Windows XP to delete and clean up after the application properly, so this should be considered a last-resort option. Also, before using this option, check your program's documentation for specific information about uninstalling the program from Windows XP.

Download Programs from the Internet

The Internet contains a wealth of applications that you can download and use on your computer—many of them for free. For those that are not free, you can often download an evaluation version of a program to determine whether you like how it works on your computer before actually purchasing it. You can also download all kinds of Windows utilities and games.

When you choose to download an application from the Internet, you click a link on the Web site that starts the download to your computer. When this happens, a dialog box appears in which you can choose whether to open the application from its current location or save it to disk. If you choose to open the application, the setup files are downloaded to your computer and setup begins. If you do not, the files are all saved to a place that you specify in this dialog box (such as your Desktop or My Documents folder). You can then start setup yourself when you are ready. There is no right or wrong here, just a matter of preference.

How to ... Forcibly Remove a Program

If you cannot use Add or Remove Programs or the program's uninstall option, you can forcibly remove a program by following these steps:

1. Open My Computer, and double-click your C drive icon.
2. Locate a folder called Program Files and double-click it. You may need to click the View All Contents link as prompted.
3. Look through the folders and find the one that contains the program you want to uninstall. Typically, the name of the folder will state the program's name or the manufacturer's name.
4. Right-click the folder and click Delete to remove it from your computer. Make sure you are deleting the correct folder before completing the action.

TIP *If you are given the option to perform a custom install, do it! Sometimes, other programs, and even spyware, are installed with downloaded applications, and a custom installation will help you see and choose exactly what is being installed.*

If you choose to save a program to disk when you start the download, the program is downloaded in a *compressed* format. Compressing a file saves time when downloading. Usually, the application will appear as a simple icon. Double-click the icon to uncompress and start the installation. Windows XP includes compression software so you can open and use compressed folders (see the section "Use Folder Compression," later in this chapter). For specific installation steps, refer to the Web site where you downloaded the program.

Use Windows XP's Compatibility Mode

Windows XP includes a new feature called *compatibility mode* that allows it to act like a previous version of Windows—specifically, Windows 95, 98, Me, NT, or 2000. Compatibility mode allows you to use older applications that might not work with Windows XP. When in compatibility mode, Windows XP acts like the previous version of Windows (which you select), so that the application is "tricked" into thinking it is installed on the correct operating system.

It is important to note that compatibility mode is intended for standard applications and even games. However, compatibility mode is not designed for use with programs that run portions

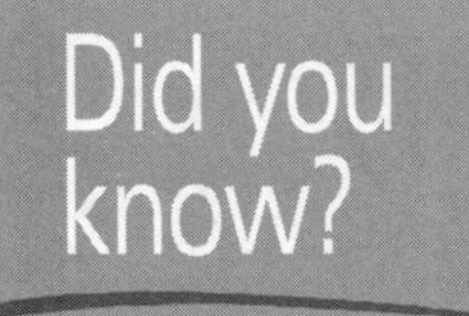

About Downloaded Programs and Viruses

Internet programs are a great way to get utilities, applications, and games for your computer—and computer viruses and spyware as well! Computer viruses are made up of malicious code that often hides within other code—such as in a setup program for an application. Spyware consists of programs that hide in your computer and gather personal information about you. To protect your computer from infection, I highly recommend that you purchase some antivirus software for your Windows XP computer. This software watches for viruses, identifies them, and kills any that have been loaded on your computer. Visit your local computer store or an Internet store to shop for antivirus software, and make sure you keep it updated regularly. See the software's instruction manual for details. Microsoft also has a new—and free!—tool, Microsoft Antispy, that can find and destroy spyware and adware. You can download it at www.microsoft.com (or you may find it magically appears on your computer via Automatic Updates).

Aside from using antivirus software, another great way to keep from getting a computer virus resides right in your own head—common sense! Be wary of downloading programs from Internet sites that do not appear to be on the up and up. Do not run programs that you receive via unsolicited e-mail, Internet pop-up boxes, or from unknown sources in other ways. Your best bet is to download software from respected Internet sites and companies only. When in doubt—don't download!

of your system configuration. For example, antivirus programs that are not compatible with Windows XP should not be used, because the program may damage your system in compatibility mode. The same is true for disk-management utilities and backup software. In other words, if the application is used to manage the operating system or some portion of the operating system, it should not be used with compatibility mode—you need to upgrade and get the compatible version of the software.

The Program Compatibility Wizard helps you use compatibility mode:

1. Open the Program Compatibility Wizard by choosing Start | All Programs | Accessories | Program Compatibility Wizard.
2. Click Next on the Welcome screen that appears.
3. In the next window, choose a radio button option. You can choose to view a list of programs, use the program currently in your CD-ROM drive, or locate the program manually. Then click Next.
4. In the selection window, choose the application that you want to run in compatibility mode, as shown here. Click Next.

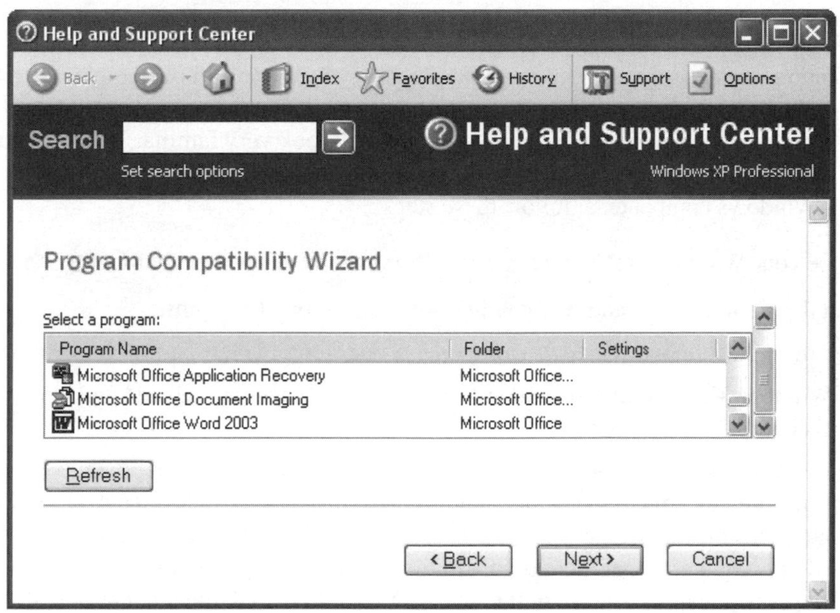

5. Choose the appropriate radio button so that your XP computer will act like Windows 95, NT 4.0, 98/Me, or Windows 2000. Click Next.
6. The Test window appears. Click Next to open the program and test its functionality.
7. A window appears asking you whether the program worked correctly. Choose the correct radio button, and then click Next and Finish.

Manage Windows XP Components

Windows XP provides a way for you to include additional Windows components that are not installed by default. This way, you don't end up with a bunch of operating system junk that you'll never use. However, unlike Windows 9*x* and Me, most of the components that you will use are already installed on your computer, so the odds are good that you will never need to add or remove Windows XP components. If you need to, however, this section will show you how to use the Add/Remove Windows Components feature of Windows XP.

NOTE

The components available to you depend on whether you are using the Home or Professional version of Windows XP. The Professional version has more options and more networking components than are needed by home users, so don't be surprised if your component list doesn't quite match the examples you see in the following sections.

Install Windows Components

Installing Windows components is very easy. Once again, you'll use Add or Remove Programs in the Control Panel (that's right, Add or Remove *Programs*). If you have used Windows 2000 before, the Add/Remove Windows Components feature will look very familiar. Even if you haven't, the tool is easy to use.

To install Windows components, follow these steps:

1. Locate your Windows XP installation CD-ROM and insert it into your CD-ROM drive.
2. Open the Control Panel and double-click Add or Remove Programs.
3. Click the Add/Remove Windows Components button on the left part of the window.
4. The Windows Components Wizard appears. Select the category desired and click the Details button.
5. In the Subcomponents menu that appears, shown here, select the component you want to install (the box next to the component is checked when you select it). Additional subcategories may appear as well. If you select the item and the Details button is not grayed out, you know that there is an additional subcategory to view. Also notice that the wizard gives you a description of the item you want to install, the amount of disk space required, and how much disk space you have available. Make your selections and click OK (and possibly OK again) until you have returned to the main window.

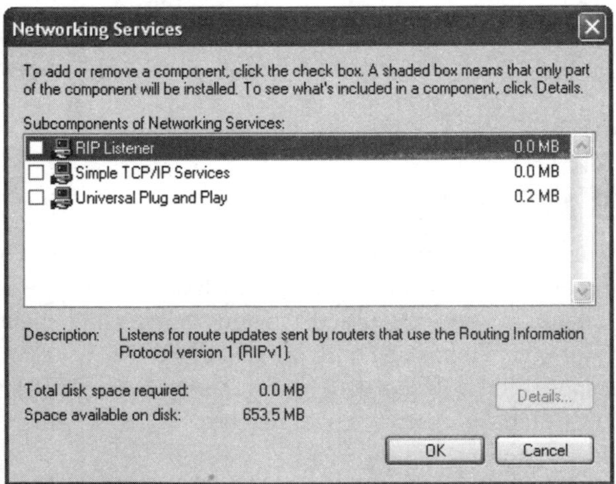

6. Click OK. Windows XP examines your system and installs the component you selected.
7. The completion window appears. Click Finish.

Remove Windows Components

Just as you can install any Windows components you want to use, you can also uninstall components that you do not want. This action frees up more disk space on your computer that can be used for other purposes. To remove a component, uncheck the selected check box so that Windows will remove it. You may need your installation CD-ROM for this action as well.

Manage Folders and Files

As you may have learned from the first few chapters of this book, Windows XP manages data by using various folders to store that data. Just as you would not dump a bunch of single papers into a filing cabinet and expect to find what you need, Windows XP doesn't store information in a haphazard way; it uses folders to keep operating system files, program files, and even your own files organized. In this section of the chapter, you will learn how to manage your files and folders.

Before we begin, I would like to offer a big warning. You can manage your own folders and files, but you should never make changes to any of the folders and files found in C:\Windows. These folders and files are used by the Windows XP operating system to function. Tinkering with them can—and probably will—cause Windows XP to stop working. So you should manage your own files and folders and let Windows XP manage its files and folders.

Create, Rename, and Delete Folders

You use folders in Windows XP to store data, such as documents, pictures, spreadsheets, you name it—any type of file or application can be stored in a folder. Depending on your needs, you may not require additional folders. After all, Windows XP automatically tries to place files in your My Documents folder or one of its subfolders, such as My Pictures. However, you may need to create your own folders to manage data. For example, each time I begin work on a new book, I create a folder on my computer where I store all of the files for the book. Within that folder, I then create additional folders for each chapter. This way, a specific folder exists for each chapter document and the graphics files for that chapter, so I can keep it all organized. You can create folders within folders, and folders within those folders, to as many levels as you want or need.

TIP

Although folders are great, don't get too wild with folder creation. Too many folders can be more confusing than helpful, so keep your folder structure in check to make sure that it actually meets your needs.

The good news is that you can easily create, rename, and delete folders as needed. To create a new folder, open the folder in which you want to create the new folder, such as My Documents, or simply open your C drive. Choose File | New | Folder. A new folder appears. Press the BACKSPACE key on your keyboard and type a desired name for the new folder.

Fixing a Common Folder or Drive Problem

I have been troubleshooting Windows XP from the beta stage(s). Since XP's release, I've worked with Microsoft newsgroups and have kept my Windows XP Web site (www.kellys-korner-xp.com) available to the public, where each new find, fix, or workaround is kept current and readily obtainable.

Even after the releases of Service Packs 1 and 2, a common issue continues to be a consistent problem. It has been problematic for many users; the newsgroup posts concerning this behavior are prolific.

The problem occurs when changes are made to the desktop and folder settings, which you might do inadvertently. Suddenly your folders start looking like My Pictures or My Music. You may find that the Play All option doesn't work, or that Common Tasks appear on the Desktop. Don't worry. These problems can be fixed easily by restoring the original settings. Click Start | Run. In the Open dialog box, type **regsvr32 /i shell32** and then click OK. This command resets registry entries to their original settings.

—Kelly
Troubleshooting Windows XP
www.kellys-korner-xp.com

TIP *If you want to create a new folder directly on your Desktop, right-click an empty area of your Desktop, and choose New | Folder.*

At any given time, you can rename a folder by right-clicking the folder and choosing Rename. Then type a new name and press the ENTER key. This feature makes it easy to keep your folders organized.

Finally, you can delete any folder by right-clicking the folder and choosing Delete. This moves the folder, and everything in the folder, to the Recycle Bin. Do keep in mind that everything in the folder is deleted as well, including files, applications, and other folders—anything at all.

Use Folder Menus

Windows XP folders contain a standard set of menus at the top of the folder window: File, Edit, View, Favorites, Tools, and Help. You can use these different menus to perform various actions with respect to folders and the files within a folder. Many of the options are self-explanatory. This section describes the most commonly used menu features.

File Menu

The File menu enables you to manage files and folders. Aside from using the File menu to create a new folder, you can also select a file or folder, choose File, and then choose any of the following options (which may or may not appear, depending on the file, folder, or application you've selected):

- **Open** This feature either opens the file or folder window, or it opens a window that allows you to select an application with which to open the file. You can use this option if you are having problems opening a file.
- **Print** For files, this option prints the file.
- **Edit** For image files, this option opens a program that can edit the image file. For example, if you select a picture file and then click Edit, Paint will open by default.
- **Preview** For image files, the Preview option opens Image Preview so you can quickly take a look at the file.
- **Send To** This pop-out menu enables you to send a folder or file to a particular location, such as a floppy disk or an e-mail message. You can also right-click any folder or file and get this same option.
- **New** This pop-out menu enables you to create another folder or a specific type of file. You also see a list of file types available, which vary depending on the applications installed on your system. This feature enables you to start a new file of your choice directly from this location.

In the lower part of the menu, you can perform other basic tasks, such as creating a shortcut for the item, deleting it, renaming it, and even closing the item.

Edit Menu

The Edit menu provides several easy features you can use to manage the folders or files within the folder. The following list describes these features:

- **Undo Delete** Accidentally delete something? No problem; choose this option to restore what you deleted (this works only if you have performed no other operations since you deleted the item).
- **Cut, Copy, and Paste** You can cut, copy, and paste items from one folder to another using these commands. Let's say you want to remove a document from one folder and place it in a different folder. Just select the document, choose Edit | Cut, open the folder where you want to place the document, and choose Edit | Paste.
- **Copy or Move to Folder** You can copy or move items to another folder by using these options. When you choose one of them, a window appears that enables you to copy or move the file or folder.

TIP *Do you need to copy or move several items to the same target folder? You can do them all at the same time! Just click the first item, and then, holding down the* CTRL *key on your keyboard, click the remaining items you want to copy or move—all of the items you click will be selected. Then choose Edit and choose the option you want. You can perform this operation when cutting, deleting, moving, or copying items manually.*

- **Select All and Invert Selection** Use Select All to select all items in the folder. This feature is helpful if you want to copy or cut all items in a particular folder. You can also use Invert Selection to give you the exact opposite of what is currently selected. For example, let's say you have five files in a folder. Two of the files are selected. If you use Invert Selection, the two previously selected files will not be selected and the three previously unselected files will be selected—this feature is helpful if you tend to do things completely backward from time to time.

View Menu

The View menu enables you to configure the appearance of your folder, and you can learn about this option in Chapter 3.

Favorites Menu

The Favorites menu works just like Favorites in Internet Explorer (and it is, in fact, exactly the same). See Chapter 9 for details.

Tools Menu

The Tools menu contains just a few folder items you should know about:

- **Map Network Drive** For computers connected to a network, you can use this item to map a network drive. This feature enables you to access a network folder, with an icon placed on your computer that makes the folder looks like it is local to your machine. To map a network drive, choose this option and a dialog box appears, where you can select a drive letter that is not in use and then enter the network UNC (for Universal Naming Convention, or path name) path to the shared folder to which you want to map.
- **Disconnect Network Drive** If you no longer want to use a particular network drive, use this option to disconnect it from your computer permanently.
- **Synchronize** This option enables you to synchronize data changes between information in a folder on a network server and the same folder on your computer. As you work with the contents of the folder, you can use this option to synchronize the two folders so that they contain the same data. To use the synchronization feature, choose the option and then click the Setup button to set up the folders you want to synchronize. You can learn more about the synchronization feature in Chapter 5.

Did you know?

How to Use a UNC Path

A Universal Naming Convention is a method used to connect to network folders or files on Windows networks. You can use the UNC path in the Run dialog box or in the Address bar of any Explorer window in Windows XP. The UNC path is represented by two backslashes (\\), then the name of the computer you want to connect to, then the share name, and then the file name. Each portion of the path is connected by a single backslash. So, if I want to connect to a particular file called *bass* in a shared folder called *fishing* on a computer named *Curt123,* the UNC path is \\curt123\fishing\bass.

Help Menu

The Help menu gives you a quick and easy way to open Windows XP Help files.

TIP *Folder toolbars contain a number of icons that essentially repeat what is available in the menus. The difference is that you can click an icon for easy access instead of wading through menu options. For example, by clicking buttons on the toolbar, you can cut items, undo a delete, copy to a folder, and perform other tasks. You can also create customized toolbars, which are described in Chapter 3.*

Share a Folder

Windows XP contains networking capabilities so your computer can share folders and printers on a network. It is important to note here that you cannot share individual files—you can share only folders, which provide access to files. For example, let's say I have a Word document called *My Dog*. I can't share My Dog by itself, but I can put My Dog in a shared folder so that others on the network can access the document.

You can share any folder in Windows XP by right-clicking the folder, choosing Properties, and then opening the Sharing tab. If the folder you want to share resides within another folder, you can right-click the folder you want to share and choose Sharing.

NOTE *It is important to note here that Windows XP must have its networking components configured before any folders can be shared. If you don't see the Sharing option, you do not have networking components installed. See Chapter 11 to learn how to set up Windows XP for networking.*

The Sharing tab, shown in Figure 4-3, is easy to configure. Just select the Share This Folder on the Network check box and enter a share name for the folder. If you want other people on

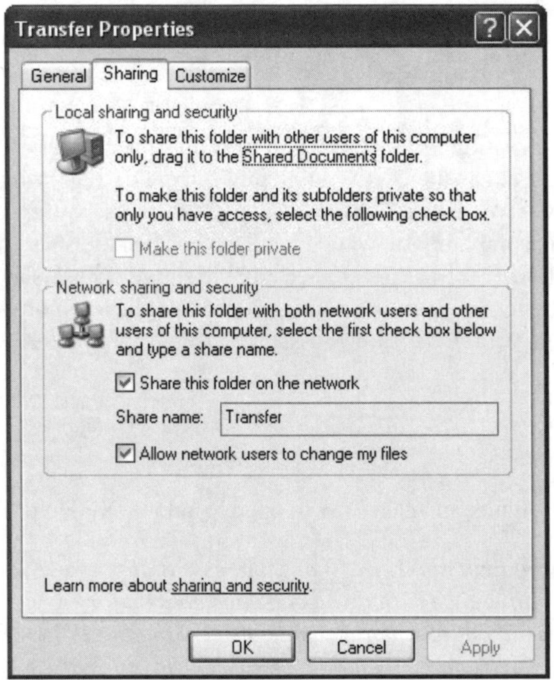

FIGURE 4-3 Sharing tab

your network to be able to make changes to the contents of the folder, select the Allow Network Users to Change My Files check box. Remember, the name you give a folder is how the folder will appear to other users, so make the name easy to understand—something like *Public Docs,* not *Pubdcs,* which no one can decipher. Also, if you are using Windows Firewall incorrectly, it may prevent others from accessing your shared files. See Chapter 13 for more information about Windows Firewall.

In Windows XP, some folders that are tied to your user profile are automatically shared with the other people who use your computer (called *local users*), if there are any. The My Documents (and all subfolders, such as My Music and My Pictures), Desktop, Start Menu, and Favorites folders are automatically shared among local users. However, if you want to keep one or more of these folders private so that only you can view it, select the Make This Folder Private check box. Note that this option works only on My Documents, Desktop, Start Menu, and Favorites folders, and any subfolders of these folders; it is grayed out for any other folders you create, because these folders are automatically private. If you create your own folder that you want to make available to local users, you don't have to share it on the network—you can just drag it to the Shared Documents folder on your computer, and all local users will be able to access it.

Use Folder Compression

Windows XP includes a built-in feature to help you conserve disk space: *folder compression.* Compression shrinks the normal size of a folder and its contents to free up more disk space that you can use for other purposes. Compression in Windows XP is quick and easy to use.

Create a Compressed Folder

You can create a compressed folder just as you create any other folder. In the folder where you want to create the new compressed folder, choose File | New | Compressed Folder. If you want to create a compressed folder on your Desktop, right-click an empty area of the Desktop, and choose New | Compressed Folder. Either way, a new compressed folder appears. Compressed folder icons have a zipper on them so you can identify them, like the icon shown here.

Add Items to and Remove Them from a Compressed Folder

You can add files and folders to a compressed folder and then remove them just as you would in any other folder in Windows XP. Once you drag a file or folder into a compressed folder, the item is compressed. Once you drag the item out of the folder, it is automatically decompressed—there's no configuration to worry about. Additionally, you can perform all other actions with the file, such as opening, renaming, deleting, and so forth—just as you would if the file were in a regular folder.

Use Extraction

Windows XP uses the WinZip technology to compress folders. A part of that technology is the *extraction* option. This feature enables you to pull all items from a compressed folder and place them in a folder that is not compressed. This action extracts—or decompresses—the items so they are no longer compressed. If you right-click a shared folder, you will see the extraction options. You can extract the folder to a different folder or other location, or even choose to e-mail the compressed folder. No matter what option you choose, the WinZip utility opens and helps you with the procedure. If you choose the Extract All option, a little wizard begins so you can choose where you want the extracted folder to go.

Remove Compression from a Folder

So what do you do if you have a compressed folder that you do not want to be compressed any longer? You simply right-click the folder and click Extract All, which essentially re-creates the folder and all data—just without the encryption.

Although anything residing in a folder can be compressed, you should not compress folders that contain programs. Compression may prevent the program from operating correctly.

About Files

As you have already learned, files are placed in various folders on your computer for safekeeping and organization purposes. Files are created by various programs you have installed on your system and have different file extensions. For example, a Microsoft Word document has the .doc extension, while a document you create with Paint might have the .bmp extension (bitmap). In short, some kind of program is necessary to create a file of any kind. The good news about files is that you do not have to manage them individually. You can right-click any file and see the same options you get with a folder, such as Send To, Copy, Cut, and so on. You can also drag and move files around to different locations on your computer without damaging them.

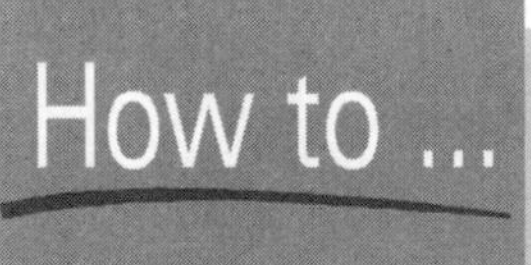

Solve File Extension Mysteries

For a number of reasons, a file may not get an extension or may not have one. For example, have you ever received a file attachment in e-mail and not been able to open it? This problem could occur for two reasons: either your computer does not have an application installed that can read the file or the file extension is missing. Such conditions cause your computer to say, "I don't know what this file is or which application to open it with." In these instances, you normally see a window asking you to pick an application to attempt to open the file. If you receive a file that does not have an extension and you know which application is supposed to open it, you can easily fix the problem by right-clicking the file, choosing Rename, and giving the file a name that includes the extension, such MyDog.doc. This helps your computer know what application to use so the file can be opened.

Chapter 5

Use the Accessories that Come with Windows

How to . . .

- Access Windows accessories
- Use Windows accessories
- Configure Windows accessories

Windows XP continues the Windows tradition of providing a group of programs on your computer collectively called *accessories*. Accessories are just that—programs that help you do some kind of job or specific function. They are not large applications, like Microsoft Word or Microsoft Excel, but rather are small programs that are designed to help you in some way. If you've used accessories in earlier versions of Windows, such as Windows 2000 or Windows Me, you won't find many surprises here. However, if you are new to Windows in general, this chapter will show you a new world of stuff available on your XP operating system.

As you might guess, a few of the accessories or accessory categories deserve their own chapters or by their nature belong in a different chapter. For example, Windows Movie Maker naturally needs its own chapter, and you can learn all about it in Chapter 16. You can locate the accessories on your Windows XP computer by choosing Start | All Programs | Accessories. You see a pop-out menu listing the accessory programs.

Accessibility

In Chapter 2, you learned about the Accessibility Options found in the Control Panel. A few other accessibility options are available in your Accessories menu as well. *Accessibility* refers to a number of Windows XP tools that make Windows XP easier to use for people with certain disabilities. If you point to Accessibility, a pop-out menu appears, which provides five additional options.

Accessibility Wizard

The Accessibility Wizard is a Windows XP feature that helps you set up and make decisions about the appearance and functionality of your computer so that it meets your needs. The wizard is easy to use and understand—just follow these steps:

1. Choose Start | All Programs | Accessories | Accessibility | Accessibility Wizard.
2. Click Next on the Welcome screen.
3. In the Text Size window, select the size of text you want Windows XP to use. Click Next.
4. In the Display Settings window, you see some check box options that enable you to select how your display appears. You can choose to change the font size, use Microsoft Magnifier, or disable personalized menus, as shown in Figure 5-1. You may also be able to switch to a lower screen resolution, which increases the size of items on screen, depending on your video card. Make your selection and click Next.

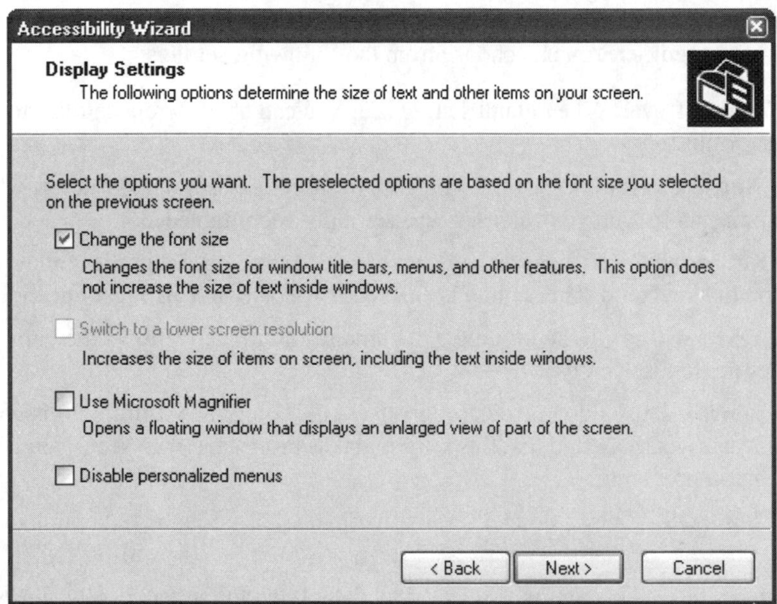

FIGURE 5-1 Display Settings

NOTE *You can also configure your own Display settings to meet your personal needs. See Chapter 3 for details.*

5. The Set Wizard Options window appears, which gives you a series of check boxes where you can select the type of disability you have, so the wizard can help you select some options. For example, if you select the I Am Blind or Have Difficulty Seeing Things on My Screen check box, the wizard continues and enables you to select various scroll bars, icons, display settings, and so forth. The other options available provide different features, depending on your needs. Select the check box that best describes your needs and click Next.
6. Depending on your selection in Step 5, your wizard options will vary. Continue to follow the wizard steps until you reach a summary screen. Review your settings, and then click the Finish button to complete the wizard. The options you selected will then be configured on your computer.

Magnifier

Magnifier gives you a window at the top of your Desktop that magnifies whatever you point at with your mouse, and the objects can become quite large.

If you choose to use the Magnifier option, a Magnifier Settings window appears after you first click Magnifier in the Accessibility window. This simple window gives you a few options for the operation of Magnifier. You can choose from the following settings:

- **Magnification Level** The default setting is 2. You can try different settings to find the one that is right for you.
- **Follow Mouse Cursor** Selected by default, this option has Magnifier show whatever you are pointing to with your mouse—this setting is recommended.
- **Follow Keyboard Focus** If you begin using your keyboard, Magnifier follows what you do on the keyboard. This setting is enabled by default and also recommended.
- **Follow Text Editing** When typing a document, Magnifier follows the cursor and magnifies the text as you type or edit.
- **Invert Colors** This option inverts (or reverses) the colors in Magnifier. It is not selected by default, but you may find that this setting makes things easier to see if you have certain vision problems.
- **Start Minimized** This option tells Magnifier to start as a minimized option on your computer.
- **Show Magnifier** This option is selected by default, and it automatically shows Magnifier at the top of your screen.

Narrator

Microsoft Narrator is designed to help people with low-vision problems. Narrator can read aloud items on the screen, so that your work with Windows XP is easier. It is important to note that Narrator works only in English, and it may not work with every program installed on your computer. The following are the Narrator options:

TIP *For Narrator to work, your computer must have a sound card installed and speakers of some kind.*

- **Announce Events on Screen** This option has Narrator announce new windows that appear or system messages.
- **Read Typed Characters** This option has Narrator read typed characters out loud.
- **Move Mouse Pointer to the Active Item** This option automatically moves your mouse pointer to the active window item for you.
- **Start Narrator Minimized** This option starts Narrator as a minimized item.

NOTE *If you need to make changes to the voice used for Narrator, you can click the Voice button on the Narrator configuration window, or you can just access Speech in Control Panel for the same options.*

Onscreen Keyboard

The onscreen keyboard gives you, well—an onscreen keyboard! The keyboard appears on your screen, and you can use your mouse to click the keys, just as you would tap keys on a regular keyboard. The onscreen keyboard is a limited version, but you can learn about other options available to you at www.microsoft.com/enable.

Utility Manager

Utility Manager is a little tool that enables you to manage all of the Accessibility tools easily. You can start Utility Manager at any time by pressing the Windows key and the U key at the same time. Utility Manager gives you a simple window that tells you which Accessibility tools are currently running; this may help you in troubleshooting problems. You can also use the check box options to have the desired utilities start when you log on, when you lock your Desktop, or when Utility Manager starts.

Communications

The Communications option in Accessories provides you with a pop-out menu where a variety of communications tools are present. Use this menu to access the Network Setup Wizard, Internet Connection Wizard, NetMeeting, Remote Desktop Connection, and other tools. As you might guess, these options are explored in the Internet and networking chapters of this book, which are found in Part II.

Entertainment

Want to have some fun with Windows XP? You access some of the options in the Entertainment menu, such as your Volume Control, Sound Recorder, and Windows Media Player. Volume Control and Sound Recorder provide you with simple interfaces that let you adjust your computer's sound output and record your own voice, provided that you have a microphone attached to your computer. You can learn all about Windows Media Player in Chapter 15.

System Tools

The System Tools menu gives you several tools that can help your Windows XP computer run better and solve problems. As with the other major menu sections, these tools deserve their own chapters, and you can learn about them in Part IV of this book.

Address Book

The Address Book found in Accessories is actually the same Address Book built into Microsoft Outlook Express, which is a part of your Windows XP operating system. The Address Book feature is very easy to use and a great way to maintain phone numbers, e-mail addresses, and other information. You can learn more about it in Chapter 10.

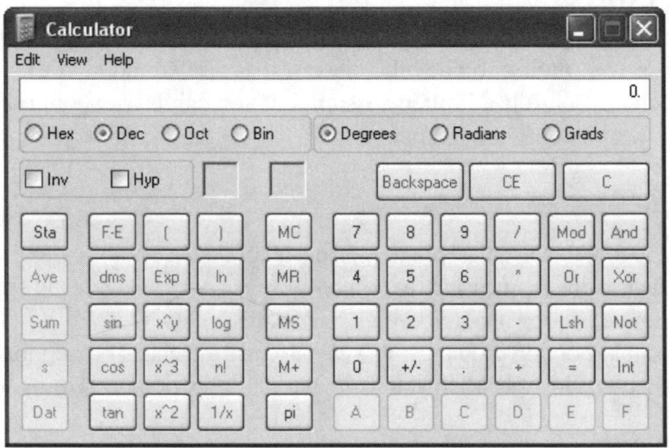

FIGURE 5-2 Scientific and standard calculator

Calculator

Windows XP provides you with a quick, onscreen calculator that you can access at any time using Accessories. Your onscreen Calculator works just like any other calculator—use it to count your money, pay your bills, or figure out how much you owe the IRS.

A quick note about the Calculator: you can use the View menu to see a standard calculator or a scientific calculator—or both, as shown in Figure 5-2. Then use the Calculator just as you would a desktop version, but with your mouse or keyboard keypad.

Command Prompt

The Command Prompt in Windows XP is the same as the one found in Windows 2000. From the Command Prompt, you can run programs and utilities, try to fix problems, and make use of a number of other command-line functions and features. In most cases, you'll find command-line syntax and options from the Help files of various Windows XP programs and utilities. If you are interested in using the Command Prompt, check the Help files of the desired application to find out how the Command Prompt might be useful for the task you are currently performing.

*You can also access the Command Prompt by choosing Start | Run, typing **cmd** in the Run dialog box, and clicking OK.*

Notepad

Accessories also includes a simple text editor program—Notepad. You can open text-only documents in Notepad and make changes to them. Advanced computer users often use Notepad to make text-based changes to their Windows configuration (which is not something you should

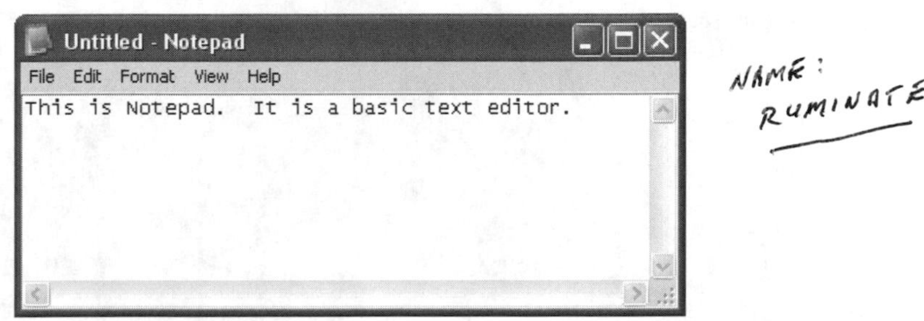

FIGURE 5-3 Notepad is a basic text editor.

try on your own!). You can use Notepad for simple tasks such as typing a message of some kind, sending it via e-mail, or printing it on your printer.

Notepad, shown in Figure 5-3, enables you to open, create, and save text files. You can use the Edit menu to perform cut and paste operations and to choose the font you would like to use.

However, Notepad is simply a basic text editor. You cannot format paragraphs or text (making text italic or bold, for example), and you cannot create any tables or use other word processing features. Notepad simply does text—nothing else.

Paint

Windows Paint is a low-level graphics-creation program that enables you to generate or open various graphics files and save a created graphics file as a bitmap (BMP), JPEG, TIFF, GIF, or other standard file format type. You are limited in what you can do with Paint, but you may find its moderate functionality useful in a variety of ways.

The best way to learn to use Paint is to open it and play around with the toolbar and menu options. You can spend about half an hour playing with Paint and you'll discover most all there is to know. I'll use this section to get you on your way.

First, you can use Paint to open any standard graphics file, such as a BMP, TIF, JPEG, GIF, PNG, or ICO. An example of a JPEG file is shown in Figure 5-4. Once you have the graphics file open, you can click on any of the toolbar buttons to make changes to the graphic. Your toolbar options include a paintbrush, a pencil, a spray can, text, and various line shapes.

Synchronize

The Synchronize tool found in Windows XP (which is the same one found in Windows 2000 and Windows Me) enables you to synchronize data on your computer with data on a network. For example, let's say that you have a collection of Word documents. You regularly edit those documents, but they are centrally located on a server on your network. You want to keep a copy

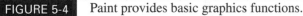

FIGURE 5-4 Paint provides basic graphics functions.

of those documents on your laptop computer so you can work on them during your bus ride home. If you work on those documents offline, they will have to be synchronized with the network server so that they will be up-to-date. Sure, you can manually copy those documents to the server, but for files you use regularly, why not have XP do the synchronization automatically for you? The following sections will show you how.

Making Files Available Offline

Using the synchronization feature is easy. Begin by choosing Synchronize from the Accessories menu. Doing this opens the Items to Synchronize window. To use the synchronization feature, you must have files made available to you offline. For example, let's say you want to use a network folder called *Company Docs*. You want to make this folder available locally on your laptop so you can access it whenever and wherever you want. This is called making the folder available *offline*. A copy is stored on your computer so that you don't have to be connected to the network to access the folder's contents. Making folders available offline is easy in Windows XP:

1. Access the network folder that you want to make available offline.
2. Right-click the network folder and choose Make Available Offline.

3. Windows XP will automatically begin the synchronization process, copying the folder with all its documents to your computer's hard drive. If you want to make subfolders in the folder available offline, you are prompted about making those available offline as well. The synchronization window shows the progress as the copy action is performed. Once synchronization is complete, the network folder appears on your computer in My Network Places.

Setting Up Synchronization

Once you have made offline folders available, you can then set up synchronization so that it will occur with your offline folder and the online folder as you specify. Access the Synchronize tool in Accessories and then click the Setup button. You see a Synchronization Settings window with three tabs.

The first tab is Logon/Logoff, shown in Figure 5-5. As you can see, you are able to select which folders you want to synchronize whenever you log on or log off your computer (either one or both actions). Select the desired offline folders and select the automatic synchronization method check box options that you want. You can also have Windows prompt you before synchronization occurs by selecting that available check box option.

The Scheduled tab allows you to create a schedule that defines when offline folder synchronization should occur. For example, let's say you have an hour-long lunch break each

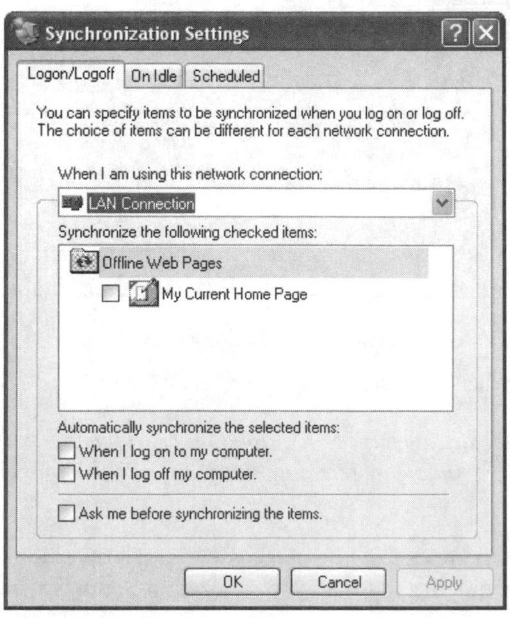

FIGURE 5-5 Logon/Logoff tab

day at work, and you want your XP computer to synchronize offline folders with the network during your lunch break. To create this configuration, you need to create a schedule that specifies the time and days of the week that synchronization should occur. To do so, simply complete the following steps:

1. On the Scheduled tab, click the Add button. Doing this opens the Scheduled Synchronization Wizard. Click Next.
2. In the Connections window, select a connection; then select the desired offline folder(s) that you want to synchronize by selecting their check boxes.

You can create different schedules for different offline folders as needed.

3. In the Start Time and Start Date window, use the drop-down menus and radio buttons to select the start time, the start date, and how often the synchronization should occur (such as every day, weekdays, and so on). Make your selections and click Next.

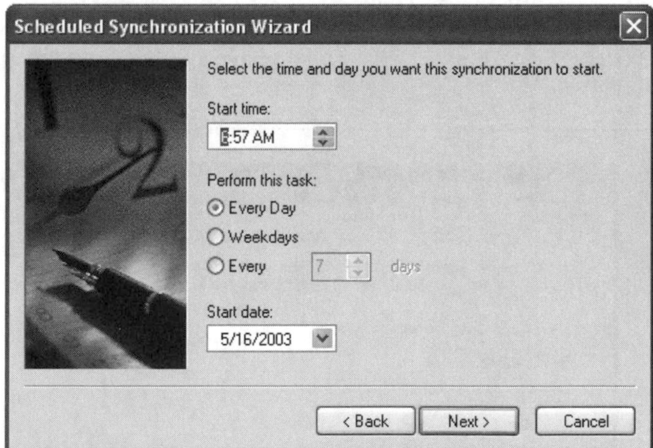

4. Enter a friendly name for the schedule and click Next.
5. Click Finish to save the schedule.

If you need to see the documents in an offline folder, you can easily do so from the Items to Synchronize window by selecting the desired folder and clicking the Properties button.

After you have created schedules that you need, you can always edit or delete them using the available buttons on the Scheduled tab of the Synchronization Settings window.

Synchronization can use any kind of connection on your computer to connect to the network—whether a typical LAN connection or a dial-up/broadband connection. Just use the Setup button to select the desired connection for the synchronization that you want to perform.

Windows Explorer

Another accessory you find in the Accessories menu is Windows Explorer. In previous versions of Windows, Explorer was considered the main tool that you use to browse and manage files and folders. In Windows XP, as well as Windows 2000 and Windows Me, Explorer is considered an accessory because the Web view features of these operating systems make Explorer not so indispensable. However, Explorer is still available if you like working with it.

Windows Explorer provides a single interface to view all of the folders on your computer and to make additions to or deletions from them. As you can see in Figure 5-6, Windows Explorer presents your entire folder in a hierarchy. You click the plus-sign box next to what you want to expand and continue to click the plus-sign boxes until you reach the folder you want. Once you reach that folder, just select it to see all of its contents in the right pane.

TIP

If you don't like the Tile/Icon view, just open the View menu and choose the List, Thumbnails, or Details option.

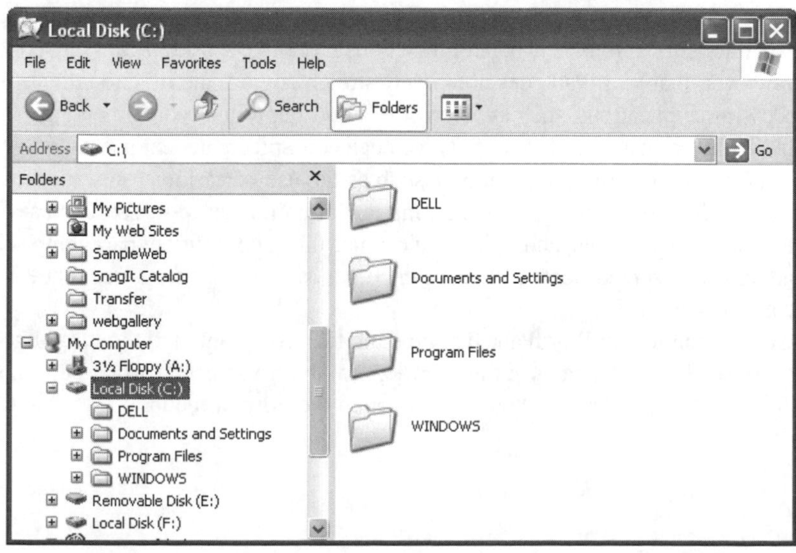

FIGURE 5-6 Windows Explorer

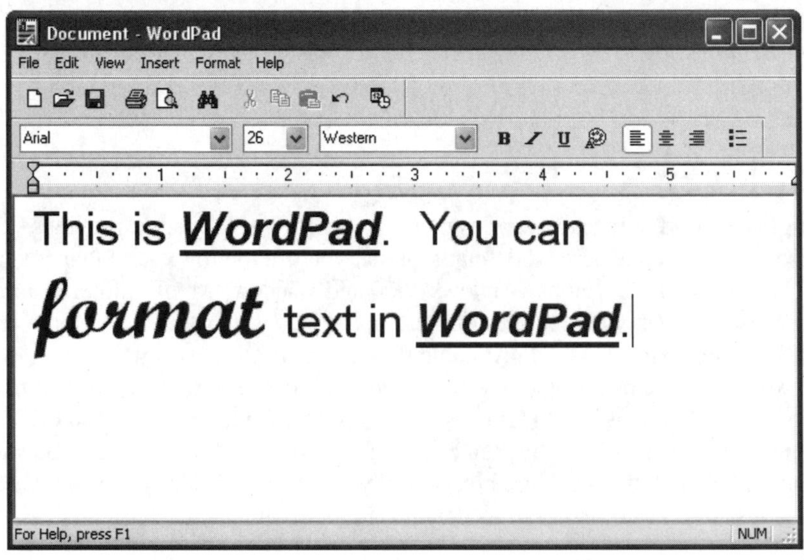

FIGURE 5-7 WordPad

WordPad

WordPad is a text editor similar to Notepad, but it functions more like a word processing application. Keep in mind, however, that WordPad does not by any stretch contain the functionality of most major word processing applications, such as Microsoft Word, but it does contain enough functions to be very useful. With WordPad (see Figure 5-7), you can edit and create text just as with Notepad, but WordPad supports major formatting features, such as the use of various fonts and text styles. When you save a WordPad document, the formatting is maintained as well. You can use WordPad to create all kinds of text documents, and while you can use tabs and different paragraph schemes, you cannot create tables or spreadsheets within the documents. However, for a free text editor, this one is certainly not bad at all.

You can easily format text in WordPad. Just type the text you want, and then highlight the text using your mouse. Then, you can use the WordPad toolbar to select a format button, such as bold, italic, font changes, and so on. You can also open the Format menu to see a list of other options.

Chapter 6

Manage Hardware

How to...

- Install new hardware
- Manage hardware with Device Manager
- Install new hardware drivers
- Use multiple hardware profiles
- Troubleshoot hardware problems

The term *hardware* refers to physical devices that your operating system uses to accomplish some task. Your keyboard, mouse, CD-ROM drive, floppy drive, modem, and sound card, plus the multitude of other devices attached to your computer, are all collectively called hardware. In the past, installing new hardware devices was difficult; but since the days of Windows 95, installing and configuring hardware has become much easier. Windows XP continues this advancement—in fact, Windows XP can often automatically install and configure new hardware without any help from you.

Nevertheless, you may experience hardware problems if you have upgraded from previous consumer versions of Windows, such as Windows 98 and Windows Me. Simply put, Windows XP is a powerful system, and it must have powerful and compatible hardware on which to run. If you purchased a new computer with Windows XP preinstalled, you have nothing to worry about unless you want to add hardware. Still, hardware does not have to be a computing monster, and this chapter shows you how to install, configure, and troubleshoot hardware problems in Windows XP.

Understand Hardware

If you are like me, it's usually helpful to understand a potential problem before you try to solve it, so this section tells you a bit about hardware—why it has been a problem in the past and what Windows XP does to reduce hardware problems. In the past, computer operating systems were "dumb," in the sense that you had to tell them what hardware devices were installed or connected to the computer. You had to specify what sound card, video card, printer, modem, and other hardware devices were installed on your computer. You then had to provide a driver for hose hardware devices. A *driver* is a piece of software an operating system uses to communicate with a particular device. For example, for your operating system to communicate with your modem, a driver must be present so the operating system can manage and use the modem. Each hardware device has its own driver—usually provided by the hardware device manufacturer. To make the hardware work, you had to install it, provide a driver, and then (usually) configure the operating system to work with the device, and vice versa (as well as keep the device from interfering with other devices). As you can imagine, this process sometimes became very maddening for even the experienced user.

All of this began to change with Windows 95, which introduced a technology called Plug and Play (which was often referred to as "Plug and Pray"). The idea was to create an operating system that was "aware" of its environment. The operating system could automatically detect when new hardware was added and attempt to install it. You might have to provide a driver for the hardware via a disk or CD-ROM, but Windows 95 also had its own database of generic drivers that could be used for typical pieces of hardware. All of this sounded wonderful—but if you have used Windows 95, you know that Plug and Play was not perfect. It didn't work well with some hardware, and some hardware didn't work well with Plug and Play.

Windows 98, Windows 2000, Windows Me, and Windows XP all use a more grown-up version of Plug and Play. Windows XP has a very extensive driver database, so it can automatically detect and install most devices. This is a great feature, because most of us would rather do something else than tinker with hardware installation. Windows XP can take care of the entire process—most of the time without any intervention from you.

Plug and Play in Windows XP is designed to install and remove devices from your computer. How does it work? Here's the chain of events that occurs when you install or connect a new device to Windows XP:

1. Windows XP detects that a new hardware device has been added to the system. You will usually see a bubble message appear in your Notification Area telling you so.
2. Windows XP installs the new device and finds a generic driver for the device in its database.
3. Windows XP allocates resources to the device so the device can work with your computer.

That's it—in most cases, you don't even have to reboot the computer. When you remove a device from your computer, Windows XP

1. Detects that a hardware device has been removed.
2. Removes the device from the system and uninstalls the device's driver.

The Golden Rules of Windows XP Hardware

In the introduction to this chapter, I mentioned that Windows XP will demand hardware that can handle the power of Windows XP. To avoid hardware problems, you should follow some simple XP hardware rules.

First of all, if you have purchased a new computer with Windows XP preinstalled, the hardware that was also installed on the computer will work fine with Windows XP. The computer manufacturer works with Microsoft to ensure that your computer's hardware is compatible, so you have no worries if you fall into this category.

However, what happens if you later want to upgrade to a different device or upgrade an older computer to Windows XP? What if you want one of those new, awesome video cards or a new modem? No problem. You can purchase a new device and add it to your computer, and you can often upgrade an older computer to Windows XP. If you follow some basic rules, you are likely to have few or no problems with hardware. Here they are—the golden rules of Windows XP hardware:

- If you want to upgrade a computer to Windows XP from a previous version of Windows, you must check out the computer's hardware carefully and compare it to the hardware requirements of Windows XP (see the appendix). XP may not run on older hardware, and the older computer may not have enough RAM to power the XP operating system. Do your homework first!
- Buy only Plug and Play–compliant hardware. How do you know? Because the new hardware device will say "Plug and Play" right on the box. There is little hardware out there these days that is not plug-and-play, but if a device doesn't say "Plug and Play" on the box, keep moving—don't buy it!
- Look for a Microsoft seal of approval or a "compatible with Windows XP" statement on the box as well. A lack of these doesn't mean the device will not work, but it should be a warning sign to you. Approved, well-tested hardware will tell you on the box that it is compatible with Windows XP.
- Check out the Windows XP Web site at www.microsoft.com/windowsxp for up-to-date information about hardware compatibility.
- Stick to recognizable brand names. Remember, as with most things in life, you get what you pay for. If you choose to purchase FlyByNight's Jiffy Modem on the Internet for $9.95 (with a set of steak knives), don't be surprised if it doesn't work well.

Install a Plug-and-Play Device

Now that you know about the rules for purchasing a new hardware device, installing it is rather anticlimactic. First, always check the device manufacturer's documentation that came with the hardware device for instructions. Most hardware manufacturers include specific step-by-step instructions that tell you exactly what to do to install or attach the device to your computer. If the device is plug-and-play and supported by Windows XP, installing the device should be very easy. Just follow these steps:

1. Attach the new device to the correct port or slot on the back of your computer. If the device is an internal device, shut down and unplug your computer from the power outlet and follow the manufacturer's instructions for removing the computer's case and installing the device in the correct slot.

You absolutely must unplug your computer from the power outlet before removing the case. Just because your computer is turned off does not mean that power is not flowing to some of its components. Play it safe and unplug the computer!

2. If the device is an internal device, replace the computer cover and plug the computer back in. If the device is external, make sure it is attached to your computer correctly and then turn on the device.

NOTE *In some cases, you should not turn on the external device before booting Windows XP. Check the device documentation to make sure.*

3. Turn on your computer and boot Windows XP. Windows XP will automatically detect the device and install it on your computer. With some types of devices, some instructions may appear. Just follow them as directed. In most cases, installation is handled automatically, and you will receive a bubble message from the Notification Area telling you that the device has been installed.

TIP *If you are installing a USB device, parallel printer, or PC card, you probably will not need to reboot the computer. These devices can be automatically detected and installed, so make sure you read the device's installation instructions.*

Remove a Plug-and-Play Device from Your Computer

If you want to remove a plug-and-play device from your computer, Windows XP will automatically detect the change and remove the internal software and driver. Just shut down Windows XP and remove the device. If you are removing an internal device, remember to unplug the computer from the power source. Once you are done, reboot Windows XP. Windows XP will detect that the device is missing and uninstall the driver for the device.

NOTE *You can also manually remove a device from Windows XP without physically removing it from your computer. See "Use Device Manager," later in this chapter. Also, for USB devices, parallel printers, and PC cards, you can simply remove the device without having to shut down your computer.*

Install a Non-Plug-and-Play Device

As I mentioned, virtually all hardware devices sold today are Plug and Play–compliant. However, it is possible for a hardware device to work under Windows but not support Plug and Play. Also, you may have an older device that you want to use that does not support Plug and Play. To accommodate these needs, Windows XP includes an Add Hardware Wizard in the Control Panel. This wizard (which has been around since Windows 98) is designed to help you install non-plug-and-play devices, as well as troublesome plug-and-play devices.

Before I show you how to use the wizard, I do want to note here that you should use plug-and-play hardware if at all possible. You'll see the best performance and experience the fewest problems if you use plug-and-play hardware that is compatible with Windows XP. In most circumstances, you should never have to use the Add Hardware Wizard. With that said, however, you can try to use devices that are not plug-and-play with the Add Hardware Wizard.

To use the Add Hardware Wizard, follow these steps:

1. Choose Start | Control Panel.
2. Double-click the Add Hardware icon.
3. Click Next on the Welcome screen. The wizard tells you that Windows XP will now search for any plug-and-play devices on your computer. A report appears containing all currently installed devices. If the device *is* in the list but is not working, select it and click Next to have Windows try to troubleshoot it for you. If the device *is not* in the list, follow the remaining steps. Select the Add a New Hardware Device option, shown in the following illustration, and click Next. The next window asks whether you want Windows to search for the device again or whether you want to select it manually from a list.

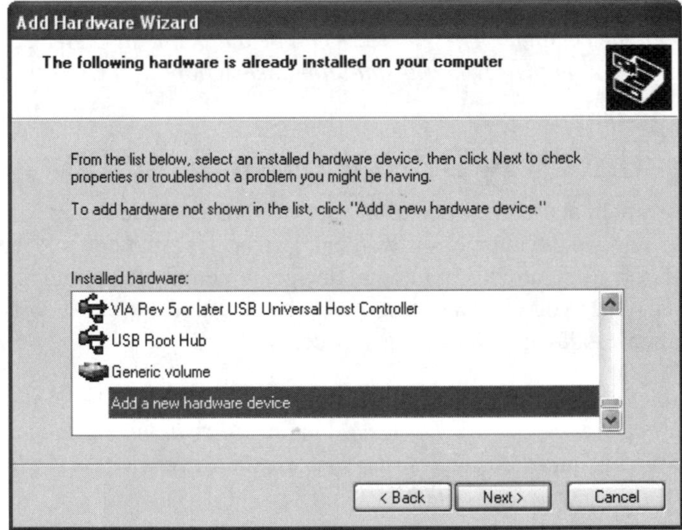
Add Hardware Wizard
The following hardware is already installed on your computer
From the list below, select an installed hardware device, then click Next to check properties or troubleshoot a problem you might be having.
To add hardware not shown in the list, click "Add a new hardware device."
Installed hardware:
VIA Rev 5 or later USB Universal Host Controller
USB Root Hub
Generic volume
Add a new hardware device
< Back
Next >
Cancel

4. Make your selection and click Next.
5. If Windows does not find the device or you want to select from a list, the Hardware Types window appears. Select the type of hardware you want to install and click Next.
6. Depending on the type of device you select, a new wizard may appear (such as in the case of a modem). You can also click the Have Disk button if you have installation files on a floppy disk or CD-ROM. Make your selection and click Next.
7. Follow any additional screens that may appear and click Finish.

Use Device Manager

Once you install devices on your computer, you can manage them in a few different places. First, for certain devices—such as printers, scanners, cameras, and modems—an icon appears in the Control Panel. These devices require more management than others do, so Windows XP helps you by giving them a specific Control Panel option (these are also explored in later chapters). Next, all devices installed or attached to your computer can be managed from a tool called Device Manager.

You can access Device Manager in one of two ways. First, right-click My Computer and choose Properties. Click the Hardware tab. Notice that you can access the Add Hardware Wizard and Device Manager from this tab. Just click the Device Manager button to open it. You can also access Device Manager using the Computer Management tool found in Control Panel | Administrative Tools. Either way, the Device Manager interface is the same, as shown in Figure 6-1.

As you can see, Device Manager provides an interface similar to Windows Explorer. You see different categories of hardware devices, each with a plus sign next to it. Click the plus sign to expand the category to see the actual devices. Notice that at the top of the window, you can open the View menu to choose to view devices either by type or by connection. These options show you how different hardware devices are connected and how they are using resources on your computer. This view option can be helpful when troubleshooting.

Examine a Device's Properties

As I noted, you can use Device Manager to examine specific properties for a device. Just select the device in Device Manager, right-click the device icon, and click Properties. Once you access

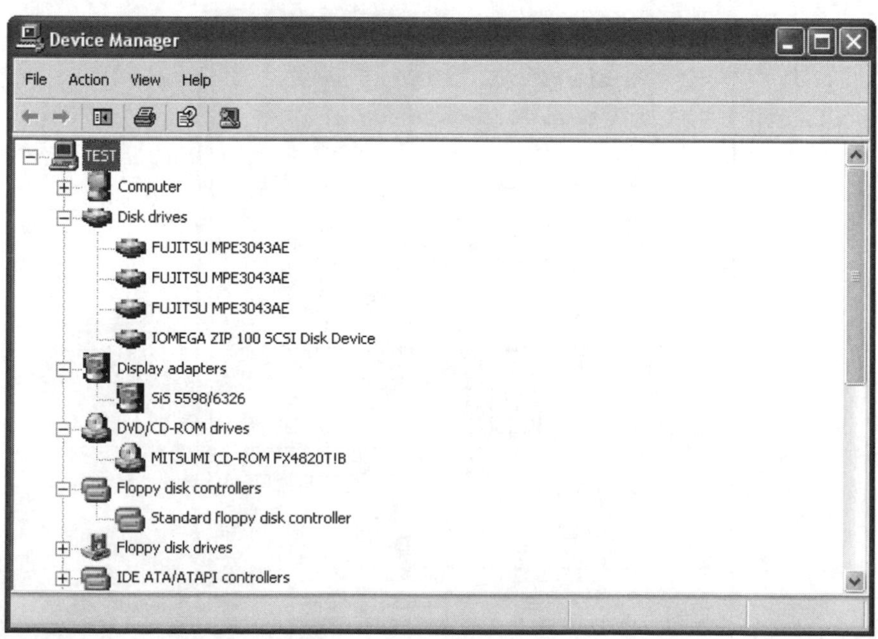

FIGURE 6-1 Device Manager

the Properties window, you see several tabs for the device. What you see may vary according to the device, but you typically see three basic tabs—General, Driver, and Resources. The following sections explore each of these.

General

The General tab gives you information about the device, but one piece of information can be particularly helpful. Along with information on the type of device, manufacturer, version number, and so on, is a message about the status of the device, as shown in Figure 6-2.

As you can see in Figure 6-2, the device is working properly. If it were not working properly, you would see a message here telling you what might be wrong (such as a bad driver).

At the bottom of the window, you see a button that will open the Windows Troubleshooter to help you solve any existing problems with the device. You also see a drop-down menu that enables you to disable the device. This feature allows your system to stop using a device even though it is still installed, which can be helpful when troubleshooting problems.

Driver

As you might expect, the Driver tab, shown in Figure 6-3, gives you information about the device's driver. You can use this tab to see the publisher of the driver and its date, and whether or not the

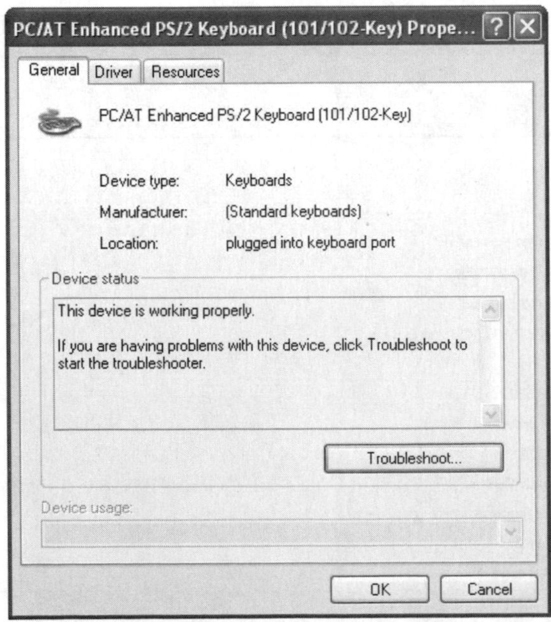

FIGURE 6-2 General tab

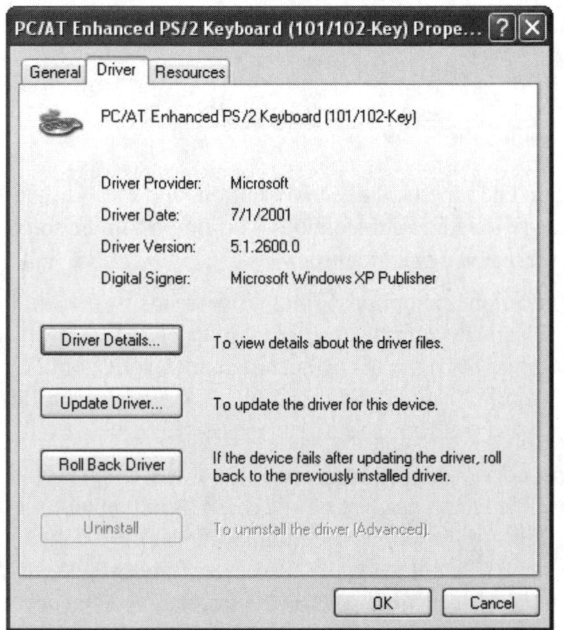

FIGURE 6-3 Driver tab

driver is digitally signed. A *digitally signed* driver means that the publisher has included a digital signature to ensure that the driver is authentic. Microsoft recommends that you use only signed drivers to ensure compatibility with Windows XP. You'll also see four buttons that allow you to manage the driver—Driver Details, Update Driver, Roll Back Driver, and Uninstall.

If you click the Driver Details button, a window appears that gives you more information about the driver. Typically, this is not information that you will need, but it may be useful to support personnel should you ever need to get telephone or Web support from Microsoft.

If you click the Update Driver button, you can install a new driver for your device. From time to time, hardware manufacturers publish new device drivers. You can download these new drivers from the manufacturer's Web site and install them on your computer. These new drivers often resolve conflicts or problems and ensure compatibility with your operating system. When you want to install a new driver, simply access the Driver tab for the device, and then click the Update Driver button. This action opens a Hardware Update Wizard; the upcoming How To box shows you how to use it.

The next button on the Driver tab is the Roll Back Driver option. Let's say you download a new driver for a hardware device. You use the Update Driver option to install the new driver, but now your device is not working. You want to return to using the old device driver, but how? In the past, that process could be difficult, but Windows XP includes this very helpful roll-back

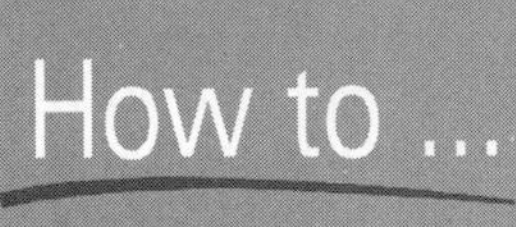

Install a New Driver

To install a new driver, follow these steps:

1. On the Driver tab, click the Update Driver button, and the Hardware Update Wizard appears. You'll see two radio button options: you can install the software automatically or select the driver that you want to install.
2. If you choose the automatic option, Windows searches its driver database for the best driver and installs it (after this choice, skip to Step 5). However, if you have obtained a new driver from the device manufacturer, you should choose the Install from a List or Specific Location radio button, click Next, and follow the next steps.
3. In the selection window that appears, choose the location that Windows should search for the new driver, or you can choose the Don't Search option so that you can manually choose the location of the new driver. For example, if you have the driver on floppy disk, you can make that selection, or if you have downloaded the driver, you may just want to select it manually. However, Windows does not guarantee that you are making a good selection, so just be sure you have the correct and most current driver for your device before using this option.
4. In the Update window, select the driver file that you want to install, or click the Have Disk button to select the driver from a disk (such as a floppy disk). Make your selection, click Next, and Windows installs the new driver.
5. Click Finish to complete the wizard.

feature. When you install a new driver, a backup file is created, and the old driver is saved on your computer's hard disk. In the event that you want to roll back to the old driver, simply click the Roll Back Driver button, and the new driver will be removed and the old one reinstalled. If you like to install new hardware and are constantly on the prowl for better drivers, this feature can be a real lifesaver.

The final option is the Uninstall button. The Uninstall button simply removes the driver from your computer, which essentially uninstalls the device from the operating system. If you click this option, a warning message appears asking whether you are sure you want to continue.

NOTE

Remember, if you simply remove a device from your computer, Windows XP will detect the removal and automatically uninstall the driver. Under most circumstances, you don't need to use the Uninstall option on the Driver tab, but the option is made available to you if you want to uninstall the driver without physically removing the device from your computer. However, the next time you reboot, Windows will redetect and reinstall the device unless you physically remove it from the computer.

Resources

The Resources tab, shown in Figure 6-4, tells what computer resources the device is using. For some devices, you can use this tab to manually change the resource allocation that Windows XP has established for the device. As you can imagine, you have to know what you're doing before tinkering with these settings, and I do not advise you to make changes here without qualified assistance.

TIP *Making incorrect changes on the Resources tab can cause the device to stop functioning and may cause other devices to stop functioning as well.*

The best thing about this tab is that it tells you if any conflicts have occurred with other devices. As you can see in Figure 6-4, no conflicts exist; however, if there were conflicts, this tab would indicate the kind of conflict and the other device that was conflicting with it. Again, this information is very helpful when troubleshooting a device that is not working properly. It is important to note that not all devices give you a Resources tab, so don't worry if you don't see one for the particular device you are inspecting.

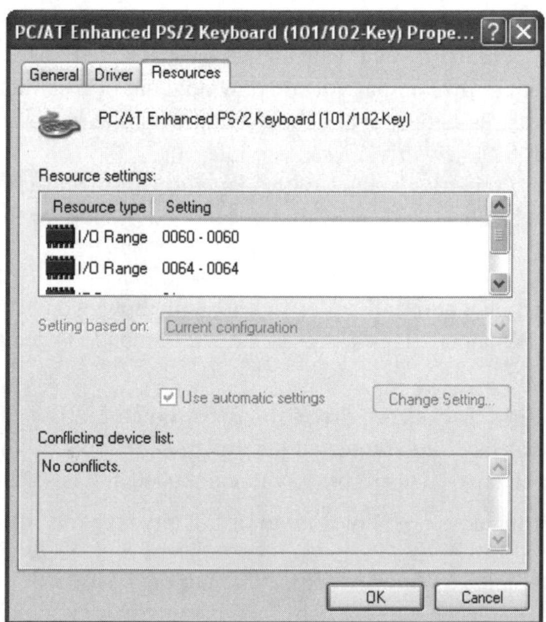

FIGURE 6-4 Resources tab

Did you know?

What Is an IRQ?

Devices installed on your computer use interrupt request lines (IRQs) to gain access to the processor. Your computer's processor is the brain of the computer; it performs all computations and calculations. Most system components use the processor to accomplish tasks. The IRQ enables the device to get to the processor. Because processors in Windows XP can handle only one processor task, or thread, at a time, the IRQ enables the device to get access to the processor in an organized way. The IRQ prevents two different devices from trying to access the processor at the same time (although certain devices can share an IRQ). IRQ conflicts were very common device problems in the past, but Windows XP automatically handles these settings for you. With Windows XP using newer hardware, IRQ conflicts are now quite rare.

Driver Signing

Windows XP also includes a device driver signing feature that checks device drivers for digital signatures. A *digital signature* is essentially a stamp on a piece of software that says "I am who I say I am" and "I haven't been tampered with since I was packaged." This certification is intended to assure you that the driver that you are downloading or installing is actually from the desired source. In short, driver signing is a security feature that helps you use new drivers and that allows XP to inspect each new driver to ensure integrity.

If you access System Properties in the Control Panel (or just right-click My Computer and choose Properties), you can click the Hardware tab and then the Driver Signing option. You see a single window that gives you three options:

- **Ignore** This setting ignores all driver signing and allows you to install drivers without any checks from Windows. This setting is not recommended because it essentially turns off driver signing.
- **Warn** This setting checks each driver file for a signature. If one is not found, a warning message is presented before you install the driver. At that point, you can choose whether or not to install the driver. This setting is recommended and is selected for you by default.
- **Block** This setting does not allow you to install any unsigned drivers.

You also notice an Administrator check box at the bottom of the window. This feature allows any user with an administrator account to apply the desired driver signing setting to all users. For example, let's say that your XP computer is used by several people at work; however, you are the only local administrator. You can choose the driver signing setting you want and then use the Administrator check box option to apply the setting to all other users. By doing this, you can configure the desired level of security, and no other user can change it. If you want to learn more about users and groups in Windows XP, see Chapter 12.

Use Hardware Profiles

Hardware profiles enable your computer to provide different hardware configurations. For example, let's say that you want a laptop computer to load all devices in one profile, but only a few necessary ones when you are traveling. You can create two different hardware profiles for each need. When you start your computer, you will be prompted for the hardware profile you want to load.

Under most circumstances, you probably will not need different hardware profiles. The best example is when using a laptop computer, although some people choose to use different hardware profiles for different users. For example, let's say you are teaching your five-year-old child how to use your computer. You can create a hardware profile that disables the CD-ROM drive, printer, and modem, for example, so that the child can't do anything to damage these devices (and believe me, I know a thing or two about teaching a five-year-old child to use a computer).

Create a New Hardware Profile

Windows XP has a default hardware profile that uses every device on your system. If you access the System icon in the Control Panel (or right-click My Computer and choose Properties) and then click the Hardware tab, you see the Hardware Profiles button. Click this button and you can see the Hardware Profiles window, which lists your original configuration (Current), as shown in Figure 6-5.

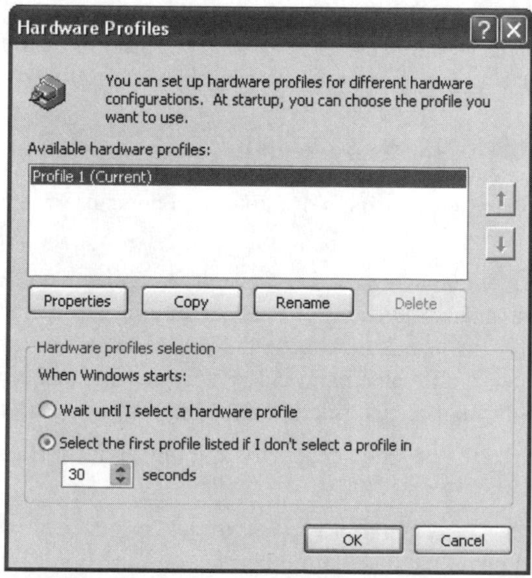

FIGURE 6-5 Hardware Profiles

If you want to create a new hardware profile, click the Copy button. This feature enables you to copy the default hardware profile that uses all devices, and then make changes to it as you want. When you click the Copy button, a dialog box appears prompting you to give the new profile a name. Enter a name and click OK. The new hardware profile now appears in the list.

Configure the Hardware Profile

Once you have created the new hardware profile, you'll want to decide on its configuration. First, reboot your computer. You'll see a menu appear in which you can select either the original profile or the new one you just created. Select the new one in the list and click OK. Once Windows XP boots, you can then use Device Manager to disable any devices you do not want used under this new profile. From that point on, those devices will not be available in the profile, but your original, separate profile configuration will not be changed.

Delete a Hardware Profile

If you decide that you no longer want to use a hardware profile you created, you can easily delete it from your computer by accessing the Hardware Profiles window, selecting the profile you no longer want, and then clicking the Delete button.

Hardware Troubleshooting Tips

I wish I could tell you that you will never have hardware problems with Windows XP. Although many of you will escape hardware difficulties, I'm afraid some of you will have problems (I have had problems as well). Fortunately, hardware problems do not have to be too difficult to solve if you take appropriate actions. Here's a list of my best troubleshooting tips regarding Windows XP hardware:

- Relax. If a problem occurs or you can't get a device installed, work through the problem calmly and slowly. A hardware problem or failure will not cause your computer to disintegrate.
- If plug-and-play doesn't seem to be working well on your system, use Add/Remove Windows Components (located under Add/Remove Programs in the Control Panel) to ensure that Universal Plug and Play is installed. Choose the Networking Services category and then click the Details button. In the selection window that appears, make sure Universal Plug and Play is selected. If it is not, just select it and click OK to install it.
- If you are trying to install a new device, verify that the device is plug-and-play and that it is supported by Windows XP.
- Check the device to make certain it is attached to the correct port or installed in your computer correctly. Reread the installation instructions and don't forget to power down and unplug your computer!

- Check your Windows XP installation CD-ROM. When the auto-screen appears, click Documentation. You will find a bunch of Readme files. These are text files that contain information about known problems or hardware incompatibilities. Check out these files to see whether your device is listed and a solution is provided.
- Use Windows Help to access the Hardware Troubleshooter. This feature can often help you solve problems with a particular device.
- If a device is installed but not working or not working properly, check the General and Resources tabs of the device's properties sheets in Device Manager. These tabs may tell you what is wrong with the device.
- If a hardware device is installed and not working well, the odds are very good that a driver problem exists. Check the manufacturer's Web site for an updated driver.
- If you cannot get the device to work properly, call the manufacturer for technical support. Often users are hesitant to seek telephone help, but these services are provided to help you solve problems. Take advantage of them!

If you are still having problems, call Microsoft Technical Support. You should find a telephone support number and related information with the documentation that came with Windows XP. Again, don't hesitate to get help from Microsoft if you need it.

Chapter 7

Use Printers, Fax Machines, Scanners, and Digital Cameras

How to...

- Install a printer
- Manage printers
- Use the print queue
- Manage faxes
- Install and configure scanners and digital cameras

Windows XP makes external hardware easy to use. In Chapter 6 you learned about installing and managing hardware in Windows XP. In this chapter, we'll explore some specialized hardware devices, specifically printers, scanners, and digital cameras. For years, both desktop and home-based computing have supported printers, and later, scanners and digital cameras. Windows XP makes using these devices easier than ever, and in this chapter you'll learn how to install and manage them.

Check Out the Printers and Faxes Folder

Like its predecessors, Windows XP contains a folder (now called Printers and Faxes) that stores information about any printers or fax machines connected to your computer and enables you to set up new printers and virtual fax machines. The Windows XP Printers and Faxes folder is found in the Control Panel. If you open the folder, you see a simple interface (shown in Figure 7-1) that gives you an icon for any existing printers that are set up on your computer. You also see options to open wizards to help you set up new printers and a setup icon for virtual fax machines.

Install a New Printer

You can use the Add Printer Wizard in the Printers and Faxes folder to help you install a new printer on your computer. Before tackling the wizard, however, you do have a little work to do away from your keyboard. First, make certain that your printer is compatible with Windows XP. If you are thinking of buying a new printer, read the label carefully. The printer should explicitly say that it is compatible with Windows XP.

The odds are very good that if a printer is compatible with Windows 2000 or Windows Me, it will work just fine under Windows XP. The only potential problem could be an incompatible driver. Check out Chapter 6 for more information about device drivers.

Before starting the wizard, you also need to unpack, set up, and attach your printer's cable to the correct port on your computer. You will probably be using a USB port on the back of your computer, and your computer may even have a picture of a printer next to the port where you

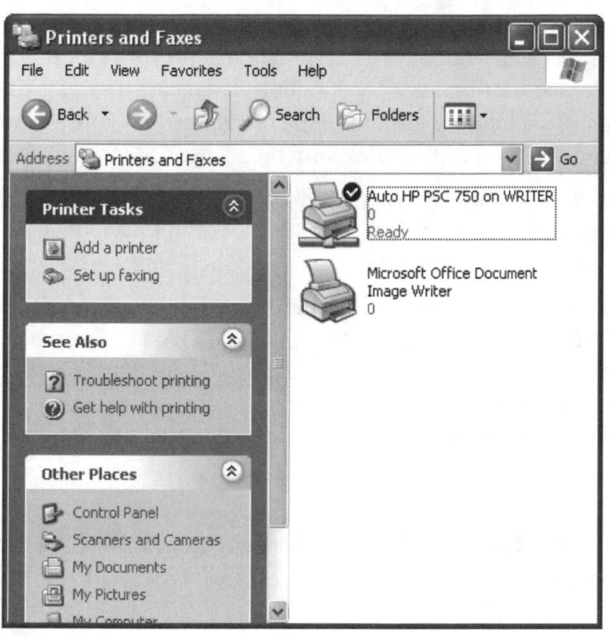

FIGURE 7-1 Printers and Faxes

should connect it. You may also be using a USB printer, in which case you need to connect the printer USB cable to the USB port or hub. The important thing here is to break out the printer manufacturer's instruction booklet and take a few minutes to read through it. The instruction booklet will tell you exactly how to attach your printer to the computer and how you should proceed with the setup. In fact, some printers are shipped with their own setup program found on a CD-ROM. The key to success is to read and make sure you know what you are supposed to do to get the printer correctly installed on your computer.

Once the printer is attached to your computer and you have read the printer documentation, you may need to use the Add Printer Wizard to get the printer installed (check the instructions that came with your printer). If you need to use the Add Printer Wizard, it is very easy. Make sure your printer is attached to your computer correctly and that it is turned on. Then, just follow these easy steps:

1. In the Printers and Faxes folder, double-click the Add a Printer option in Printer Tasks.
2. Click Next on the Welcome screen.

3. The next window gives you two radio buttons for selecting either a local printer or a printer connection (network printer). A local printer means the printer is attached directly to your computer, or you are using a remote TCP/IP printer that is using a local port to your computer (see Chapter 11 for more information about setting up remote printers). If you are on a network and you want to use a printer attached to another computer, click the Network option. Make your selection and click Next. (If you are installing a network printer, skip to Step 10.)
4. The Add Printer Wizard searches your computer for a printer. If the wizard finds one, the printer is automatically installed. If the printer is not found, a message appears asking whether you want to install the printer manually. Click Next.
5. Select the port to which your printer is attached, as shown here. Under most circumstances, your printer will be attached to the printer port, LPT1. You can use the drop-down menu to select a different port, or you can use the Create a New Port radio button. Typically, however, you will need to use LPT1. You may also need to create a new TCP/IP port if you are using that connection type. Consult your printer's documentation for more details.

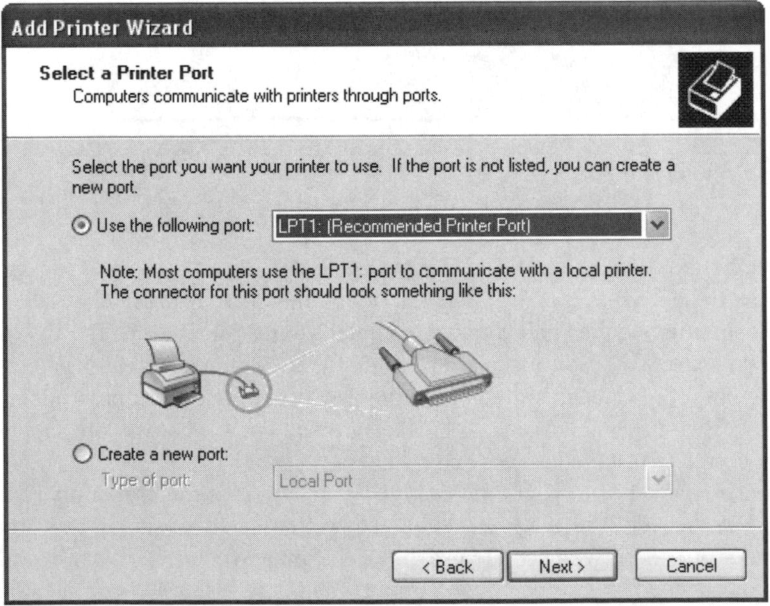

6. In the Install Printer Software window, shown next, select the manufacturer of your printer in the left list and select the printer model in the right list, and then click Next. If you have an installation disk, click the Have Disk button to install the printer software from a floppy disk or CD-ROM. However, keep in mind that the drivers on the CD-ROM may have been updated, so you should check the manufacturer's Web site for updated drivers.

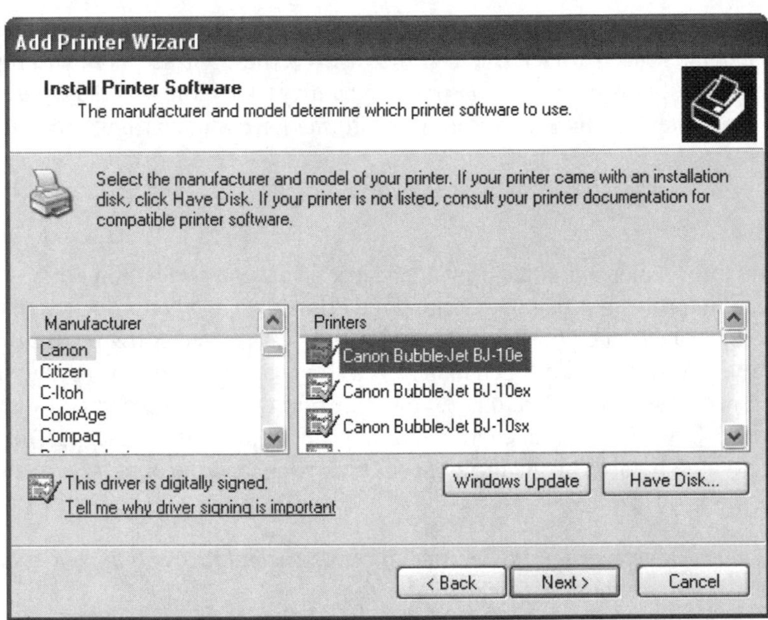
Add Printer Wizard
Install Printer Software
The manufacturer and model determine which printer software to use.
Select the manufacturer and model of your printer. If your printer came with an installation disk, click Have Disk. If your printer is not listed, consult your printer documentation for compatible printer software.
Manufacturer
Canon
Citizen
C-Itoh
ColorAge
Compaq
Printers
Canon Bubble-Jet BJ-10e
Canon Bubble-Jet BJ-10ex
Canon Bubble-Jet BJ-10sx
This driver is digitally signed.
Tell me why driver signing is important
Windows Update
Have Disk...
< Back
Next >
Cancel

7. In the Name Your Printer window, type a friendly name and click either Yes or No to use the printer as the computer's default printer. Click Next.
8. The next window asks you whether you want to share the printer so that others on your network can use the printer (if you have file and printer sharing enabled). Choose the desired radio button (see Chapter 11 to learn more about sharing devices and information on a network).
9. The next window asks you whether you want to print a test page. Simply choose either Yes or No, and click Next. Click Finish to complete installation.
10. If you chose to install a network printer in Step 3, a window appears so you can enter the network path (UNC) to the printer or queue name or you can connect using a URL. If you are not sure, just click the Browse button to locate the network printer you want to use. In an office network, consult your network administrator for the correct printer connection information. Make your selections and click Next.
11. Set up locations for the network printer. Enter a friendly name for the printer and click the Yes radio button if you want your Windows programs to use this printer as the default printer. Click Finish.

Configure Your Printer

Once you install a printer, a printer icon appears in the Printers and Faxes folder. You can use this printer icon to access the printer's properties sheets so that you can configure a number of different options for your printer. Several options are available, and some of them are a bit confusing. However, the following sections explain each of the options to you. To access the printer's properties sheets, right-click its icon in the Printers folder, and then choose Properties. You see a printer Properties window with several tabs. Depending on your printer, you may have more tabs than those listed here—consult your printer documentation for more information about configuration options for your printer.

General

This tab gives you information about the printer, and also gives you two button options. First, you have the option to print a test page by clicking the Print Test Page button. After you click the button, a window appears asking you whether the test page was printed correctly. If it was not, click No, and the Windows Help files open to help you solve the problem. The second option is Printing Preferences. When you click this button, the Printing Preferences window appears, as shown in Figure 7-2, where you can choose to print pages in portrait, landscape, front to back, and so on. You see both a Layout and a Paper/Quality tab, and the options here are self-explanatory.

TIP *Be sure to check your printer's documentation for special instructions about quality settings and features that may be available to you.*

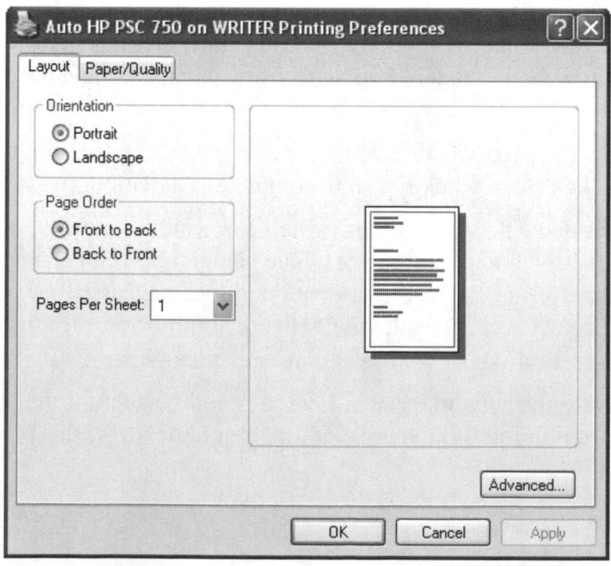

FIGURE 7-2 Printing Preferences

Sharing

The Sharing tab allows you to share the printer. If you want to share the printer, simply click the Share Name radio button and enter a desired name. Network users will see this name when they want to connect to the shared printer. Windows XP also has a feature that allows you to provide different drivers to network users. Remember from Chapter 6 that a driver is a piece of software that your computer uses to communicate with some device. Different operating systems use different drivers. If you want to allow Windows operating systems other than XP to connect to and use the shared printer, you can configure drivers for those systems. When network users connect to your computer, your XP computer automatically downloads the printer driver to their computers. However, if a Windows 95 computer wants to connect, the drivers used for XP probably will not be compatible. By clicking the Additional Drivers button on the Sharing tab, you can choose to provide the appropriate drivers for that operating system. Place a check mark in the check box next to the operating system that you want to select and click OK, as shown in Figure 7-3. You may need to provide your printer's floppy disk or CD-ROM so that XP can get the needed driver files.

If you download additional drivers from the manufacturer's Web site, keep in mind that they may be in a compressed folder. You need to decompress the folder first before trying to use the drivers. Right-click the downloaded compressed folder and click Extract All.

FIGURE 7-3 Additional Drivers

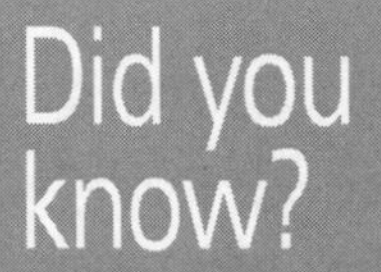

About Configuring Network Permissions and Access

It is important that your Windows XP computer be configured to use a network and share resources on a network. Also, the person who owns a network printer can allow you to use the printer or not—depending on what permissions he or she assigns. Just because you see a printer on your network does not mean that you have permission to use it. When in doubt, ask a network administrator. If you are trying to connect to a printer in a home network, make sure the shared network printer is set up, functioning, and available. You can learn how to set up your computer for network service in Chapter 11.

Ports

The Ports tab enables you to make changes to the physical or logical port that is used for printing. For example, the typical printer port is labeled LPT1. However, configuration issues with your computer may make it necessary to connect the printer to a different port. If you are using a network printer, you may need to change the port that is printed to as well. The Ports tab enables you to make these changes by changing the current port, as well as adding, removing, and deleting ports. All of these actions tend to be more advanced, and under most circumstances, you should never have to make any configuration changes here. However, if you need to adjust or change ports that are in use, Windows XP provides the Add, Remove, and Configure options to make port configuration easy.

It is important to remember that you do not need to change printer ports unless you have physically moved your printer to a different port on your computer or the network path to a particular network printer has changed.

Advanced

The Advanced tab, shown in Figure 7-4, isn't really all that advanced—it just provides you with a bunch of configuration options for printing that are not necessarily related to each other. The following options are available on this tab:

- **Availability** Use the radio buttons to configure the time that the printer is available. By default, the printer is always available, but you can place restrictions on when the printer can be used, if necessary. This setting is typically used in network environments in which you want to make certain that users can print only during work hours.
- **Priority** This setting can range from 1 to 99, with 1 being the default. This setting simply tells you that higher priority documents will print before lower priority documents (with 99 being the highest). You typically do not need to make any changes to this setting.

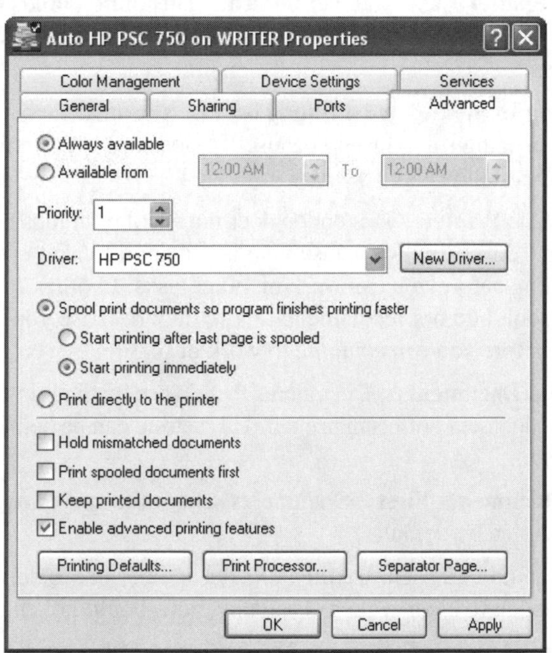

FIGURE 7-4 Advanced tab

- **Driver** From time to time, your printer manufacturer may produce a new driver for your printer. The new driver may increase performance or solve compatibility problems with a new version of Windows. If you need to update the printer driver, you can do so by clicking the New Driver button on this tab. This action opens a portion of the Hardware Update Wizard that can help you install the new printer driver. See Chapter 6 for more information about device drivers.
- **Spooling** This simply means that print jobs are stored on your hard disk while the computer waits for the printer to be ready. For example, let's say you print ten Word documents. It may take several minutes to print the documents, so while one document is printing, the others wait in the spool until it is their turn. Why? The answer is simple: spooling moves the documents to the hard disk so you get control over your application without waiting for them to print. Without the spool, your application would be tied up until the print job finishes. With the spool, you can return to work or play and not have to wait for the file to print. You have the following spool options:
  - **Spool Print Documents so Program Finishes Printing Faster** This option is enabled by default and tells your printer to spool print jobs to your hard disk. You should leave this setting enabled.

- **Start Printing after Last Page Is Spooled** This option holds the print job until the application spools all of the pages. This frees up your application faster but delays printing longer.
- **Start Printing Immediately** Printing begins as soon as the first page is spooled. In other words, printing starts faster because XP does not wait until the entire document is spooled. This is the default setting.
- **Print Directly to Printer** This option does not spool print jobs but sends them directly to the printer. This setting will cause your application to wait until the document finishes printing before you can work on other tasks. In other words, this setting does not use the spool. I do not recommend this setting, because you'll end up waiting for jobs to print before you can continue to work or play.

- **Hold Mismatched Documents** Documents that do not match printer setup configuration are held in the queue instead of being printed. This setting can be helpful in troubleshooting mismatch problems.
- **Print Spooled Documents First** Documents sent to the spool are always printed first. This setting is enabled by default.
- **Keep Printed Documents** This setting tells the spooler not to delete documents out of the spool once they have been printed. Typically, you should not enable this setting.
- **Enable Advanced Printing Features** This option, enabled by default, gives you advanced printing options, which will vary with the type of printer. You may be able to manage page order, pages per sheet, and other printing options. Consult your printer's documentation for more information.

The final portion of the Advanced tab allows you to access printer defaults (Printing Preferences window) and print processor options; you can also set up a separator page here. You should not make changes to the print processor configuration unless your printer documentation tells you to do so. The other setting options are self-explanatory.

Security and Device Settings

The Security tab allows you to configure the users and/or groups that can access your printer if it is shared on a network. If you are using Windows XP Home Edition, you will not see a Security tab because your system is configured for Simple File Sharing. If you are a Windows XP Professional user, you'll see the Security tab only if Simple File Sharing is turned off. See Chapter 4 to learn more about file sharing.

The Device Settings tab may contain additional configuration options, such as paper feed options, depending on your printer. See your printer's documentation for more details.

TIP *Depending on your printer, you may see additional tabs, such as Color Management and Services. These tabs apply specifically to your printer, and most of the time they do not need to be edited. See your printer documentation for additional details.*

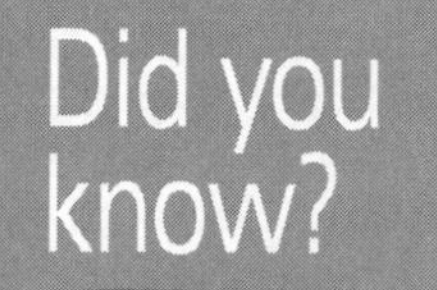

About Printer Pooling

In some network environments, printer pools are used. A *pool* is a collection of identical printers that are seen as one logical printer. For example, let's say you print to a printer named Company. To you and the computer, Company appears as one printer; but with pooling, Company can actually be five printers, for example, that are connected together. This feature allows all users to print to the same printer instead of five individual printers appearing on the network. If you need to enable printer pooling on your XP computer and have several printers connected to different ports, you can select the check box option available on the Ports tab. Also refer to your printer's documentation for more information about pooling options.

Manage Print Jobs

Once your printer is set up and configured the way you want, you can print all kinds of documents and files—almost anything you like. As you are printing documents, a small printer icon will appear in the Notification Area. This icon represents the *print queue,* which is the line of documents in your print spool that are waiting to be printed. You can manage the print queue by right-clicking this icon and then choosing the printer's name. Doing this opens a small print queue window:

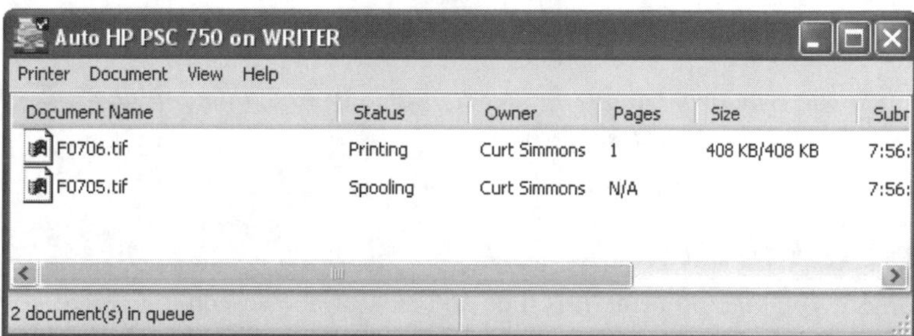

As you can see, one file is printing while another is spooling and waiting to be printed. You can take several actions by using the menus to manage documents in the print queue. From the Printer menu, you can

- **Pause Printing** This action stops all printing.
- **Cancel Print Documents** If you send a bunch of documents to the printer and change your mind, you don't have to waste your paper and ink. Just use the Cancel option to dump everything out of the print queue.

From the Document menu, you can

- **Pause** Select a print job in the list and click Pause to stop printing.
- **Cancel** Select a print job in the list and click Cancel to cancel it.

You can perform the same management action using the Printers and Faxes folder. Using the default XP folder interface, the Tasks list in the Printers and Faxes folder gives you a quick link so you can see what is in the queue, pause printing, and even adjust printer preferences and delete printers.

If you use the Document menu, you can pause printing, resume printing, restart printing, and even cancel documents that are currently in the print queue. For example, let's say that you want to print 10 documents. You send all of them to the print queue, but you suddenly realize that you do not want to print the ninth document. You don't have to waste your paper—just open this print queue window, select the ninth print job, and choose Document | Cancel.

You can also remove any document from the print queue by right-clicking the document in the queue and clicking Cancel.

Troubleshoot Common Printer Problems

Windows XP includes better printer support than previous versions of Windows, so troubleshooting does not have to be a major chore. Keep in mind that you should consult your printer documentation when you experience a problem, because some issues you need to resolve may be specific to your printer. The following sections tell you about some of the most common printer problems and their solutions.

You can use the Windows Troubleshooter tool to help you solve problems. See Chapter 21 for more information about troubleshooting.

Printed Text Is Garbled

You have a document you want to print, it is nice and neat on the screen, but when you print the document, the text comes out garbled. This is a common problem that is typically caused by one of two things. First, the document that you are trying to print may be damaged or corrupted. You can test this by printing a different document. If the text still appears garbled, the most likely cause of the problem is your printer driver. Your printer driver may not be compatible, the wrong driver may be installed, or the driver may have become corrupted. Use the Details tab of the printer's properties sheets to reinstall the driver or install the correct driver.

The Printer Does Not Work

If your printer does not seem to work, make sure it is turned on and that it is attached to the correct port on the back of your computer. If this doesn't solve the problem, you may need to reinstall the driver and reboot Windows XP. Sometimes internal issues can prevent a printer from working, and a reboot may take care of the problem. If these actions do not solve the problem, consult your printer documentation. You may have a printer hardware issue.

Printing Is Very Slow

If printing to a local printer is very slow, you may be running low on hard disk space. Remember that your printer uses part of your hard disk space to spool documents for background printing. You should have at least 10MB of free hard disk space available.

If you have enough free disk space, check your spool settings on the printer Properties window's Advanced tab to make sure spooling is enabled. Also, try defragmenting your hard disk to see if that helps. For more information about defragmentation, see Chapter 19.

A Certain Document Will Not Print

If a certain document will not print, try to print a different document from within the same application. If you can print another document within the same application, the problematic document is most likely corrupted. If printing is sporadic with the application or several applications, turn off the printer, wait 10 seconds, and turn it on. This may resolve the problems (you may try rebooting your computer as well).

Print Quality Is Poor

If your files will print, but the print quality is poor, you may need to make changes to printer-specific tabs within the printer's Properties window. Consult your printer documentation for help.

Use Fax Support in Windows XP

Fax modems have been around for some time now, and support for fax modem capabilities continues in Windows XP. Using a fax modem, you can fax documents to other fax machines, just as you would with a physical fax machine. Faxing tends to be application specific, but I will mention a couple of things about faxing with Windows XP. First, if your modem is installed, you can double-click the Set Up Faxing option in Printer Tasks in the Printer and Faxes folder and access the Fax Console. The Fax Console allows you to manage incoming and outgoing faxes as well as send faxes from this simple console (which looks a lot like Outlook Express).

If you want to send a new fax, Windows XP even includes a wizard to help you set up the fax job—which you learn more about in the following How To box.

Use Scanners and Digital Cameras with Windows XP

During the past few years, the popularity of scanners and digital cameras has exploded. After all, we all like to use electronic pictures that we can print, e-mail to friends and family, or just store on the computer's hard drive instead of in an album under the couch. Because of these devices'

Use the Fax Wizard

To use the Fax Wizard, follow these steps:

1. In the Fax Console, choose File | Send a New Fax or just click the New Fax icon on the toolbar.
2. The Send Fax Wizard appears. Click Next on the Welcome screen.
3. In the Recipient Information window that appears, enter a recipient's name in the To field, and enter a fax number. If you want to send the fax to more than one recipient, click the Add button to enter additional recipients. Click Next when you're done.
4. In the Preparing a Cover Page window, use the Template drop-down menu to select a desired cover page template, and then enter text for the subject line and a note if desired. Click Next when you're done.
5. In the Scheduling Transmission window, select when you would like to send the fax and at what fax priority you would like to send it. Click Next.
6. In the Delivery Notification window, select whether you would like to receive a delivery notification message when delivery is complete. You can even choose to send yourself an e-mail confirmation. Make your selections by clicking the desired radio buttons and then click Next.
7. Click Finish.

popularity, Windows XP includes a Scanners and Cameras folder in the Control Panel that looks much like the Printers and Faxes folder. You can use the Add Device Wizard to add scanners and cameras to your system, and then manage them from this folder.

Install Scanners and Cameras

Installing a scanner or digital camera is a lot like installing a printer. First, always consult the documentation and instructions that came with the scanner or digital camera for setup and management information. Some models include their own installation disk or CD-ROM, so be sure to check out the documentation carefully. Also, make sure any scanner or camera you purchase is compatible with Windows XP.

You can use the Add Device Wizard in the Scanners and Cameras folder in the Control Panel to install a new scanner or camera. You may not need to use the wizard, however. In many cases, Windows can automatically detect your scanner or camera via Plug and Play; but if it does not, you can use this wizard to assist you.

Like the Add Printer Wizard, the Add Device Wizard is easy to use. Just connect the scanner or camera to your computer, turn it on, and then follow these easy steps:

1. Click the Add an Imaging Device icon in the Scanners and Cameras folder in the Control Panel.
2. Click Next on the Welcome screen.
3. Select the make and model of your camera or scanner, or click the Have Disk button to install it from a floppy disk or CD-ROM. Make your selection and click Next.
4. Select a port for the device (refer to your scanner or camera documentation), and click Next.
5. Give the device a friendly name, and click Next.

Once you have your scanner and/or camera installed on Windows XP, icons for them will appear in the Scanners and Cameras folder, shown in Figure 7-5.

It is important to note that in many cases, you will not have to use this wizard to install a camera or scanner. Because of Plug and Play, you can often directly plug a scanner or camera into your computer's USB port, and Windows XP will automatically detect the camera or

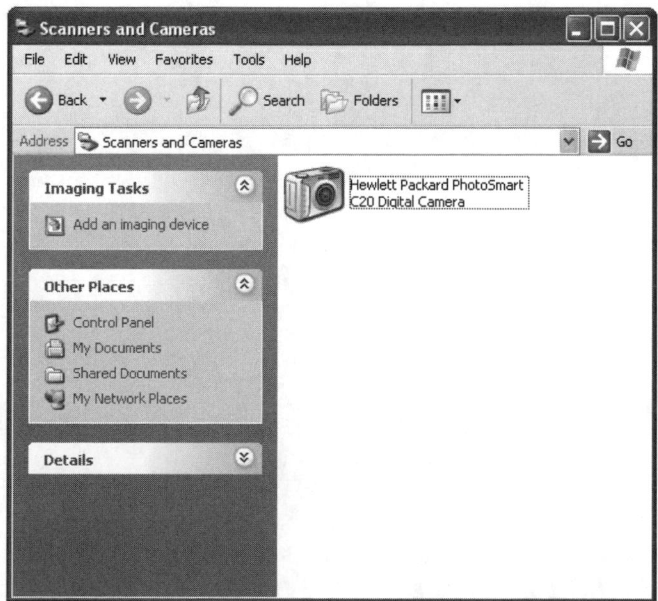

FIGURE 7-5 Scanners and Cameras folder

scanner and show it to you as an external hard drive (which you can then open and access). Of course, you should read the camera or scanner manufacturer's installation instructions for Windows XP and follow them—this will help reduce the likelihood of any problems.

Manage Scanner and Camera Properties

You can right-click a scanner or camera icon in the Scanners and Cameras folder in the Control Panel and click Properties to access the device's properties sheets. As you might guess, the contents of the properties sheets depend on the type of device and the make and model, much like with printers. Various options are available to you. For example, you can have a camera or scanner always save files to a certain folder, and for some devices you can manage color settings here. Check your scanner or digital camera documentation for information about configuring these properties sheets.

Be sure to check your scanner or camera manufacturer's Web site periodically. Often, you'll find information about updates and how-to steps for troubleshooting common problems.

Part II Get Connected

Chapter 8

Create Connections to the Internet

How to...

- Configure your modem
- Set up dialing rules and options
- Create Internet and dial-up connections
- Create broadband connections
- Edit dial-up connections

Simply put, Internet connections give you access to the Internet—a way to connect your computer to an Internet Service Provider (ISP) so that you can use the Internet and send and receive e-mail. In the past, connectivity to the Internet was one of those "extra" computing services—something only advanced computer users wanted. Not so today; virtually every computer is sold with the hardware and software necessary to connect to the Internet, and more and more computer users every day are joining the World Wide Web.

Like previous versions of Windows, Windows XP provides the software you need to connect your computer to the Internet. Internet connectivity in Windows XP is easier than ever, and some helpful wizards will guide you every step of the way. In this chapter, you'll see how to set up your computer with an Internet connection so that you can be surfing the Internet in no time!

Internet Connections 101

Before we jump into the business of creating and managing Internet connections, let's first make sure you're up to speed about those connections. An Internet connection allows your computer to access the Internet: you can send e-mail, look at Web pages, and download information with your Internet connection. An Internet connection is achieved through an ISP. The Internet itself is free, but generally you must pay an ISP a fee (usually monthly, but annual and semiannual plans are also available) to access the Internet.

Think of the Internet as a busy freeway. To get on the freeway (the Internet), you must drive onto an access ramp (access the ISP) so your car (your computer) can enter the traffic. All information you send and receive over the Internet comes through server computers at your ISP before reaching your computer, so your ISP can also be thought of as the middleman that stands between your computer and the Internet. The *connection* to the Internet, then, is a physical connection that exists between your computer and your ISP. A few different types of connections exist, but they fall into two distinct categories—dial-up and broadband. The following sections explore both of these types.

Connecting with a Dial-Up Connection

The most common type of Internet access is a dial-up account. With this type, your computer uses a modem connected to your telephone line to dial an access number—just as you would make a telephone call. Once the ISP answers the call, your computer sends username and password information so it can be authenticated (validated) by the ISP. After the ISP authenticates your information, you can use the Internet through the ISP. Dial-up access is the most common type of access, with 56 Kbps (or 56K) modems being the most common modem speed. Virtually all new computers sold today are equipped with an internal modem—it is considered a standard piece of hardware. All computer operating systems, including Windows XP, give you software wizards and helpful information so you can easily set up an Internet connection with your modem—you'll explore modem configuration later in this chapter.

Connecting with a Broadband Connection

Today's Internet contains rich multimedia and surfing experiences. You can view all kinds of graphics, listen to music, and even watch movies and concerts over the Internet. Although a great addition, multimedia and the cool Web pages of today are much larger in size than they once were—and 56K modems are quite slow. Therefore, many people are turning to broadband "always on" Internet access. Broadband Internet access gives you much faster speeds than dial-up connections, and you do not dial any kind of access number to connect—because your computer is always connected to the ISP, it is always connected to the Internet. If you want to use the Internet or e-mail, you simply open your Internet browser or e-mail client and begin—there's nothing for you to connect to or anything else to do.

Three main types of broadband connections are available:

- **Cable** Cable Internet access uses existing cable TV connections to provide Internet access over the cable line, just as television programs are accessed over the cable line. To use cable access, the cable modem is connected to your computer's Ethernet port. You can then connect to a cable outlet and use the Internet at any time. Cable Internet access can provide speeds beginning around 400 Kbps and may be quite higher, depending on the cable company and the amount of activity of other users who are accessing the same cable network. Your ISP will provide you with a cable modem for your PC (which it likely rents to you), or you can acquire one yourself.
- **DSL** DSL (Digital Subscriber Line) typically provides a dedicated, secure line that connects directly to your ISP. This copper line connects directly to a switchboard of sorts at the phone company, which connects to your ISP. DSL is the most popular type of broadband connectivity available today, and it can give you super-fast speeds—often up to 800 Kbps and higher. However, DSL must be supported by your phone company and ISP, so it is typically limited to more populous areas at this time. To use DSL, a special DSL modem is connected to your computer that uses the existing phone line in your home for the DSL connection.
- **Satellite** Satellite connections use a small satellite dish that mounts on your roof or to a pole in your yard. Information is sent and received over the disk to a satellite in orbit, which then beams data back to the ISP. Satellite connections are not that popular—yet—but they are especially helpful to people who cannot get cable or DSL. Satellite connections can give you speeds of around 400 Kbps and are currently offered by major ISPs, such as Starband (www.starband.com) and DIRECWAY (www.direcway.com). To use satellite access, you must have a satellite dish, a modem for your PC, and special software to run the connection. Your ISP provides all of this when you purchase the satellite access.

Connectivity Costs

As I mentioned, the Internet itself is free, but you must pay an ISP to provide you with a connection—and you'll pay more for a faster connection. A typical dial-up connection will cost around $20 a month for unlimited access and an e-mail account. If you live in a city where several ISPs are competing, you may get unlimited access for as little as $10 a month.

Broadband solutions cost more than dial-up connections. Cable and DSL unlimited access with one e-mail account will typically cost you around $40 a month. Watch for special deals where the cable or DSL hardware and setup are free. Shop around for the best deal. Finally, if you want satellite access, you can expect to pay around $60 a month for unlimited access and one e-mail account. However, the hardware and setup are often hefty—$400 or more, depending on your purchase plan.

Configure Your Modem

As I mentioned in the previous section, the most common type of Internet access is a dial-up account, which uses a modem in your computer. Unless you have paid for DSL, satellite, or some other broadband service (and have the hardware to connect to your computer), you will access the Internet via your internal modem.

Configuring modems has been a painful experience for Internet users in the past. I remember staying up late at night and literally pulling my hair out trying to get a modem to work correctly. Although modems can still be complicated, we're a long way from those days, and setting up your modem in Windows XP should be no problem.

Before getting into the details, I do want to mention that dial-up connections tend to be problematic for computer users, because you have to work with two different components. You have to configure the actual connection (which we will do in the section "Create Connections to the Internet"), and you have to configure your modem, which the connection uses. Just remember as you work with connections that successful Internet access requires the configuration of a connection and your modem. The following sections show you how to configure your computer's modem.

Install a Modem

Your computer probably has an internal modem currently installed—after all, modems are a standard piece of hardware these days. You may have purchased a different modem, a particular one you want to use—that's fine, too. Windows XP should automatically detect and install a plug-and-play modem, so modem installation works just like that of any other piece of hardware. Check out Chapter 6 for more information about installing devices.

Did you know?

Your Modem's Actual Speed

So, you're using a 56K modem—you should get 56 Kbps speeds, right? Wrong! First of all, as a result of regulations, the highest speed you are likely to get with a 56K modem is about 48 Kbps. Even then, the speed must be matched with your ISP's modem, and telephone line conditions can lower the speed. If you have used the Internet, you may wonder why you get different connection speeds at different times. Local, ISP, and Internet traffic all affect modem speed, so you are often at the mercy of your ISP and phone line traffic in general. This is one reason that connections are often faster early in the morning or late at night.

Configure Modem Properties

To make modem configuration easier, a Phone and Modem Options icon is included in the Control Panel. If you double-click the icon, you see a Phone and Modem Options window that contains Dialing Rules, Modems, and Advanced tabs. The following sections show you what you can configure on each of these (and why you would want to).

Modems Tab

Today's modems do a good job of setting themselves up. You don't have to worry about inputting a lot of information to make the modem work, but you may want to adjust some of the settings to meet your needs. The Modems tab, shown in Figure 8-1, provides a simple interface that lists the modem(s) installed on your computer and provides you with a few buttons.

You'll see Add and Remove buttons at the bottom of the screen. If you click the Add button, the New Modem Wizard appears and searches for additional modems attached to your computer. If the wizard finds one, it automatically installs it. If it doesn't find one, you can select it from a list. This is the same type of installation wizard you see when installing various other hardware devices (see Chapter 6). If you select a modem in the list and click Remove, the modem's software is uninstalled from your computer. Under most circumstances, you don't need to use either of these buttons—unless you just love modems and want to use two or three of them on your computer.

You'll also see a Properties button. Select the desired modem in the list (if more than one appear), and then click the Properties button to see properties specific to that modem. Several properties tabs appear. The General tab, shown in Figure 8-2, tells you the status of the device (whether or not it is working). You can click the Troubleshooter button to start the Windows XP Troubleshooter if you're having problems with the modem, and you can also use the drop-down menu at the bottom of the screen to disable the device if necessary.

Modem Tab On the Modem tab, you have three basic options. First, you can adjust the slider bar for the modem's speaker volume. A lower setting is typically best here, unless you love to hear

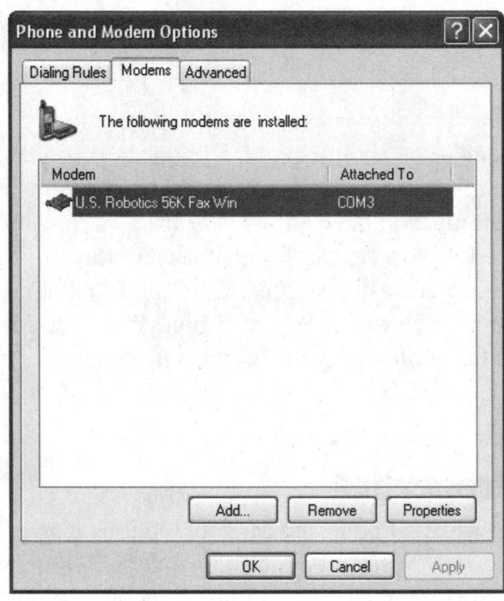

FIGURE 8-1 Modems tab

that familiar modem connection noise. Next, you see a Maximum Port Speed drop-down menu. You can use this drop-down menu to set a maximum speed at which you want the modem to connect. Typically, you'll leave this setting at the default so that you'll get the highest connection speed possible. Finally, a Dial Control section with a Wait for Dial Tone Before Dialing check

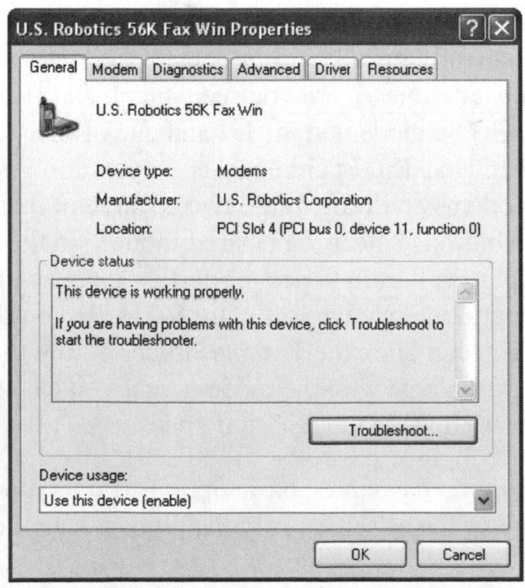

FIGURE 8-2 General tab

box is probably enabled and, typically, should remain enabled so that your modem checks for a dial tone before dialing the number.

Diagnostics Tab On the Diagnostics tab, you can run a query, which is simply a test your computer runs with the modem to make sure it is working properly. You can also view a log file. The information you see here is basically a lot of commands, and few will have any meaning to you, but this information can be helpful if you have to call technical support concerning problems with your modem.

Advanced Tab The Advanced tab gives you a single Extra Settings field, where you can enter additional modem string commands. You don't need to do anything here unless your modem documentation or the technical support explicitly instructs you to make a change. The extra initialization commands entered here are most often used to solve problems with modem connectivity.

Driver Tab Finally, the Driver tab is like all such tabs for hardware in Windows XP. Use this tab to update or change drivers for the device. See Chapter 6 to learn more about drivers and the configuration options presented on this tab.

Dialing Rules Tab

In the Phone and Modem Options window, the Dialing Rules tab, shown in Figure 8-3, provides a place to configure locations. In Windows XP, a *location* is a place from which you dial up to the Internet. For each location, you can configure different dialing rules. For example, let's say you use a laptop computer for your work. Some days you dial from the Dallas office, and some days you dial from the Seattle office. Depending on your location, the dialing rules and

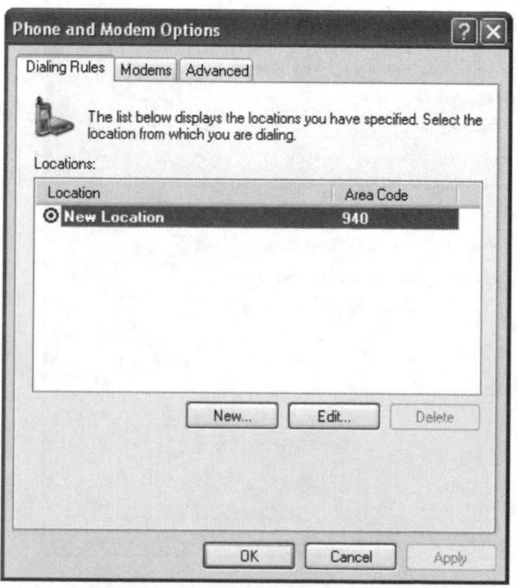

FIGURE 8-3 Dialing Rules tab

preferences you need will be different. Rather than having to reconfigure your dialing rules manually each time you travel, you can simply create different locations and use those locations as needed. By clicking the desired location, you can use the rules configured for that location immediately and easily.

To create a new location, click the New button. The New Location window appears with three tabs. Also, if you want to make changes to a location, select the location and click the Edit button, which gives you the same tabs that appear in the New Location window. Either way, you can create new locations or edit existing locations using these tabs, which are explored in the following sections.

If you're using Windows XP from a home or office on a desktop system that stays in one place, then all you need is the default "My Location," which you can edit as necessary.

General Tab The General tab, shown in Figure 8-4, enables you to make some basic dialing rules configurations. First, you can name the location by entering a recognizable name in the provided text box. If you travel, you may consider naming the location after cities or areas, such as Dallas, Canada, Northwest, and so on.

Next, use the Country/Region drop-down menu to select the country or region for the location and then enter the area code. You then see a collection of options called *dialing rules.* These are simply fields where you enter information, if necessary, that tells Windows XP how to dial the connection. For example, if you need to dial 9 to access an outside line, a field is provided for entering this information. You also see configuration options to disable call waiting and to use either tone or pulse dialing.

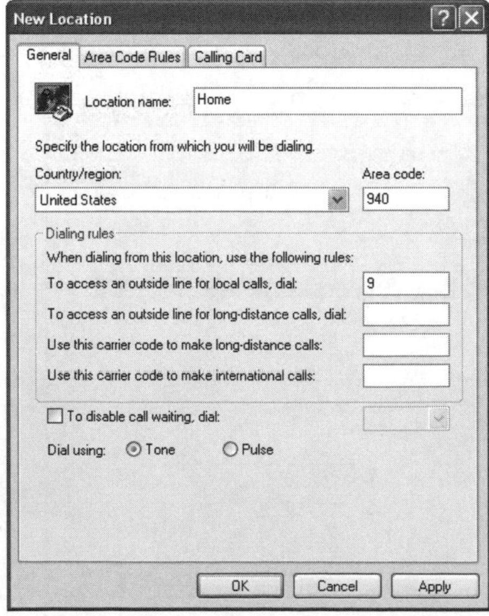

FIGURE 8-4 General tab

Area Code Rules Tab In the past, dialing an area code typically meant you were making a long-distance call. However, in many cities, several area codes are now considered local. Windows XP has to know how to handle different area codes, and that's the reason for area code rules. If you click the Area Code Rules tab, shown here, you can generate a list of area code rules specific to a particular location. Obviously, area code rules from one location to the next may vary, so Windows XP gives you the option to configure area code rules on a location-by-location basis.

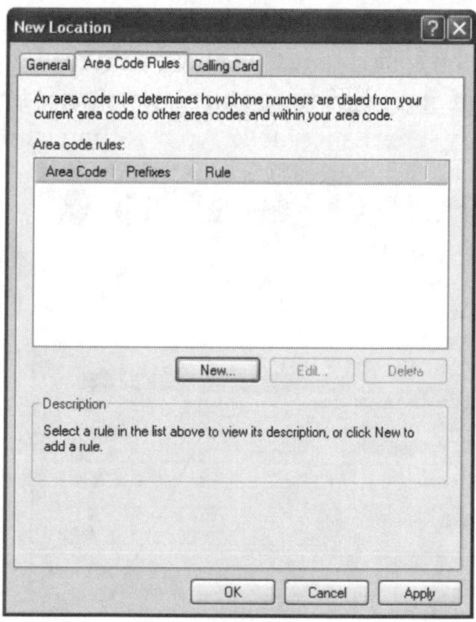

To create a new area code rule, click the New button, which opens the New Area Code Rule window, shown next. Enter the area code for this rule in the Area Code field. In the Prefixes section of the window, you can specify how prefixes are handled for the area code, such as to use all prefixes or to limit them to a specific set. Under the Rules section of the window, you can tell Windows XP to dial 1 in front of the area code or include the area code for all numbers.

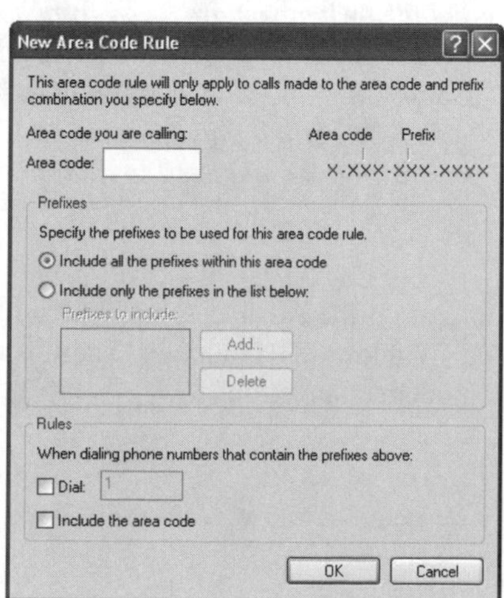

8

As you generate your list of area code rules, you can edit them or delete them at any time using the Edit and Delete buttons on the Area Code Rules tab.

Create only area code rules that you actually need. Too many area code rules become more confusing than helpful.

Calling Card Tab The final New Location window tab is Calling Card. In this tab, you can use the provided list to select the type of calling card you want to use, and then you can enter the account number and PIN. If you don't need to use a calling card for long-distance calls, you don't need to configure anything here, of course. If your calling card is not listed on the menu, click the New button and enter the necessary information about your calling card.

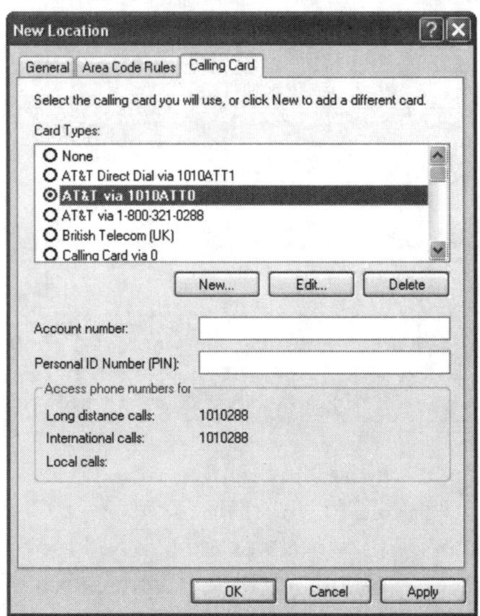

NOTE

Using calling cards is a great idea when you are away from home, but the feature doesn't always work well. Your computer has to negotiate the call and the calling card number with the phone system, and depending on your location, that negotiation process simply doesn't work well all of the time. It's still a good feature, though, and one you should consider working with if you travel a lot and need to dial in with a calling card.

Advanced Tab

The final Phone and Modem Options tab is the Advanced tab, which lists information about telephony software installed on your Windows XP computer. There is nothing that you need to configure in this window for your modem connection.

Create Connections to the Internet

Once you are sure your modem is installed and you have configured any connection and dialing rules you need, you can turn to creating your Internet connection. Remember, your Internet connection uses your modem to dial a connection, and your modem uses the modem settings to manage the call. Think of these two items as a duet—two pieces that work together to accomplish one goal.

Fortunately, creating connections to the Internet is made rather easy by the Internet Connection Wizard included in Windows XP. If you have used a previous version of Windows, you are probably familiar with the Internet Connection Wizard. However, in Windows XP, the Internet Connection Wizard is hidden from view because Microsoft wants you to use the Create a New Connection Wizard—explained in the next section. Still, if you would rather use the Internet Connection Wizard, it can be found in C:\Windows\Internet Explorer. Once you start the wizard, it walks you through a series of steps, collecting information from you to create a connection.

Create Connections Using the Network Connections Folder

In the Control Panel, you'll find a Network Connections folder. This folder looks similar to the Printers and Faxes folder. A wizard here can help you create different kinds of connections; you will see an icon for any connections that currently exist, as shown in Figure 8-5.

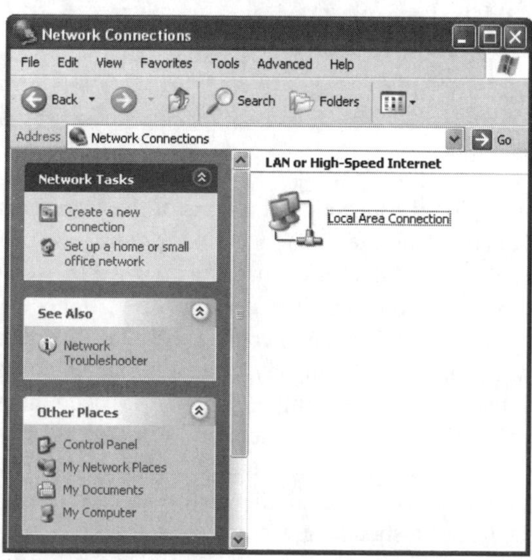

FIGURE 8-5 Network Connections

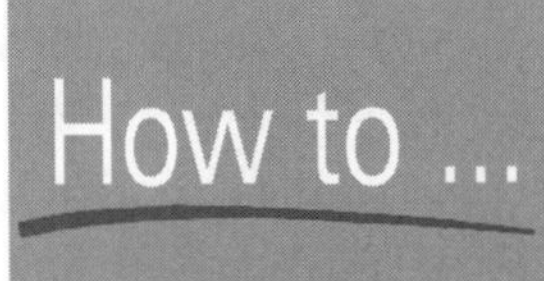

How to ... Create a Broadband Connection

The New Connection Wizard gives you the option of creating broadband connections for your computer. It is important to note here that you may not need to create a broadband connection if you are purchasing broadband connectivity. Typically, cable, DSL, and satellite all come with their own software (and frequently their technicians will hook up your connection for you), so make sure the broadband connection is something that will actually be useful to you before creating it. If you do need to create one, follow these steps:

1. In Network Connections, click the Create a New Connection icon.
2. Click Next on the Welcome screen.
3. In the Network Connection Type window, select Connect to the Internet and click Next.
4. In the next window, choose to set up the connection manually, and then click Next.
5. In the Internet Connection window, select the Broadband Connection radio button and click Next.
6. In the Service Name window, enter a friendly name for the service (such as the name of your ISP). Click Next.
7. In the Internet Account Information window, you can choose to make this connection the default connection, and you can enter your username and password for the connection. Make your selections and click Next.
8. Click Finish to complete the connection. The new connection now appears in your Network Connections folder.

Up to this point, we have explored connections in terms of the Internet. You can use the Internet Connection Wizard to create an Internet connection for an ISP—but why does Microsoft include yet another wizard here? The Internet Connection Wizard is used only for Internet connections. While it is true that you can use the Create a New Connection Wizard for an Internet connection, you can also use this wizard to create other dial-up or broadband connections. For example, let's say you work for a small company. Instead of using expensive networking technology for remote users, the company may implement dial-up accounts where you can dial up to a private server and get information from the network. Regardless of what it's used for, the Create a New Connection Wizard is very simple and straightforward. If you need to create an additional dial-up connection, just double-click the wizard to start it. Answer the questions it poses to you, and, once you have finished, a new connection icon will appear in the Dial-Up Networking folder.

Edit a Dial-Up Connection

All connections you create within Windows XP are stored in your Network Connections folder in the Control Panel. You can open this folder, right-click a connection of your choice, choose Properties, and make changes to the connection as needed. This is a great feature that prevents your having to re-create connections when something changes. Different types of connections will have different tabs, but typically, most modem and broadband connection properties have General, Options, Security, Networking, and Advanced tabs. The Networking tab lists components that cannot be changed for a dial-up connection, and we'll explore the Advanced tab in Chapter 13. The following sections, however, show you what you can configure on the General, Options, and Security tabs.

General Tab

The General tab, shown in Figure 8-6, enables you to change the phone number the connection uses to dial your ISP. Phone numbers can frequently change, so access this tab to make adjustments as necessary. You can use this tab to tell the connection to use the dialing rules you have configured for your modem. You can also make configuration changes directly to your modem from this tab by clicking the Configure button. This action opens the modem Properties window that we explored in the first half of this chapter.

Options Tab

The Options tab gives you options for telling Windows XP how to handle dial and redial for your ISP. This tab, shown in Figure 8-7, simply gives you a number of check box options.

FIGURE 8-6 General tab

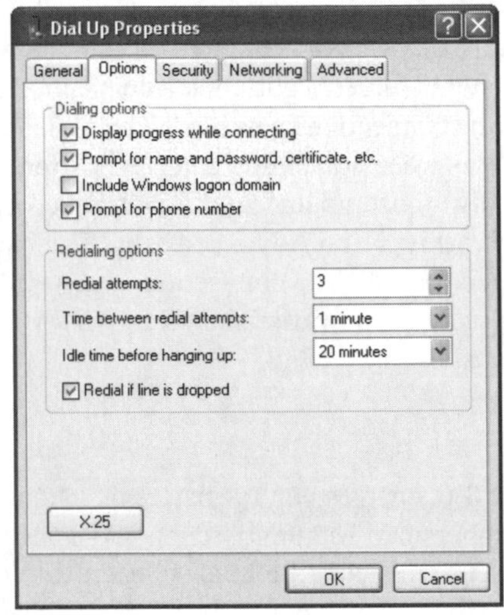

FIGURE 8-7 Options tab

You can choose to display progress while connecting, prompt for username and password, prompt for phone number, and so on. You can also determine how many redial attempts should be made before Windows gives up on the connection and how much time should be idle between each connection.

TIP

Does your Internet connection hang up by itself? For example, let's say you're surfing the Web and you take a break to eat a quick snack. When you return to your computer, the connection has been severed. How can you stop this behavior? Simple—use the Options tab and change the Idle Time Before Hanging Up drop-down menu to Never (or at least set it to a longer period of time).

Security Tab

The Security tab contains your username, password, and other security information your connection uses to authenticate with the ISP or dial-up server. You should refer to your ISP documentation or dial-up server authentication information before making any changes on this tab.

You may be familiar with Windows XP's ability to share an Internet connection with other PCs in your home or office. You can learn all about this configuration option in Chapter 13.

Chapter 9

Surf the Internet

How to...

- Use and configure Internet Explorer
- Get going with Windows Messenger
- Check out MSN Explorer
- Use the Web Publishing Wizard

Windows XP continues the Windows tradition of being an operating system that is easy to use on the Internet. As you learned in Chapter 8, creating connections to the Internet is quick and easy, and Windows XP includes all the software you need to use the Internet and to send and receive e-mail. In this chapter, we'll consider the tools that allow you to surf the Internet, hold virtual meetings on the Internet, and publish information to the Internet. You can learn all about e-mail in Chapter 10. If you're new to the Internet and this is your first attempt to surf, don't worry, this chapter tells you everything you need to know!

Understand Internet Terms and Technology

Windows XP includes two software tools that allow you to surf the Internet—Internet Explorer 6 and MSN Explorer. Both of these tools are Web browsers. A *browser* is simply a program your computer uses to access and view Web pages and content. At its core, the Web is made up of Hypertext Markup Language (HTML) documents. HTML is a kind of programming language your browser reads to draw and create the nifty Web pages you see. HTML documents are transferred from place to place using the Hypertext Transfer Protocol (HTTP). HTTP is a communications protocol that is a part of the Transmission Control Protocol/Internet Protocol (TCP/IP) suite of protocols. These common protocols and programming languages are universally used on the Internet. Now, do you really need to know anything about HTML, HTTP, or TCP/IP to use the Internet? Not at all—which is good news! However, it may help to know that just as you need Microsoft Word to read a Word document, you need a Web browser to access and read Web pages.

Internet Explorer and MSN Explorer are built right into the Windows XP operating system. You can find the Internet Explorer icon (a blue *e*) on the Start menu or on your Taskbar if Quick Launch is enabled (see Taskbar properties to turn it on), and the MSN Explorer icon appears as a multicolored butterfly. You can use either of these tools to surf the Internet, and this chapter will show you how to use both of them.

Understand the Internet Explorer Interface

You can start Internet Explorer by clicking the Internet Explorer icon on your Taskbar. It is probably available on your Start menu as well. This action opens the Web browser and, if you have a dial-up connection to the Internet, probably launches the connection automatically. If you have not configured a connection for your computer, the Internet Connection Wizard appears instead of Internet Explorer. (See Chapter 8 to learn how to configure an Internet connection.)

One thing you'll notice right away about Internet Explorer is that it looks a lot like any other folder on your computer. This is by design. Microsoft has made Windows XP integrate closely

Did you know?

You Don’t Have to Sign Up for MSN to Use Windows XP

You’ll see MSN pop up from time to time and in various places in Windows XP—including the Windows XP Help files and MSN Explorer. This might make you think that MSN should be your Internet Service Provider—however, this is not the case. You don’t have to use MSN to use any of the MSN Windows XP features, so don’t think you have to use Microsoft’s ISP to make the best use of Windows XP on the Internet. However, as you use Windows XP, you’ll definitely get the feeling that Microsoft would like you to be an MSN customer. That’s fine, but just remember: the choice is completely up to you.

with the Internet so that your computer can look and feel more like a Web page. The Internet Explorer browser, like your XP folders, contains several menus across the top, toolbars, and a primary interface area, as shown in Figure 9-1.

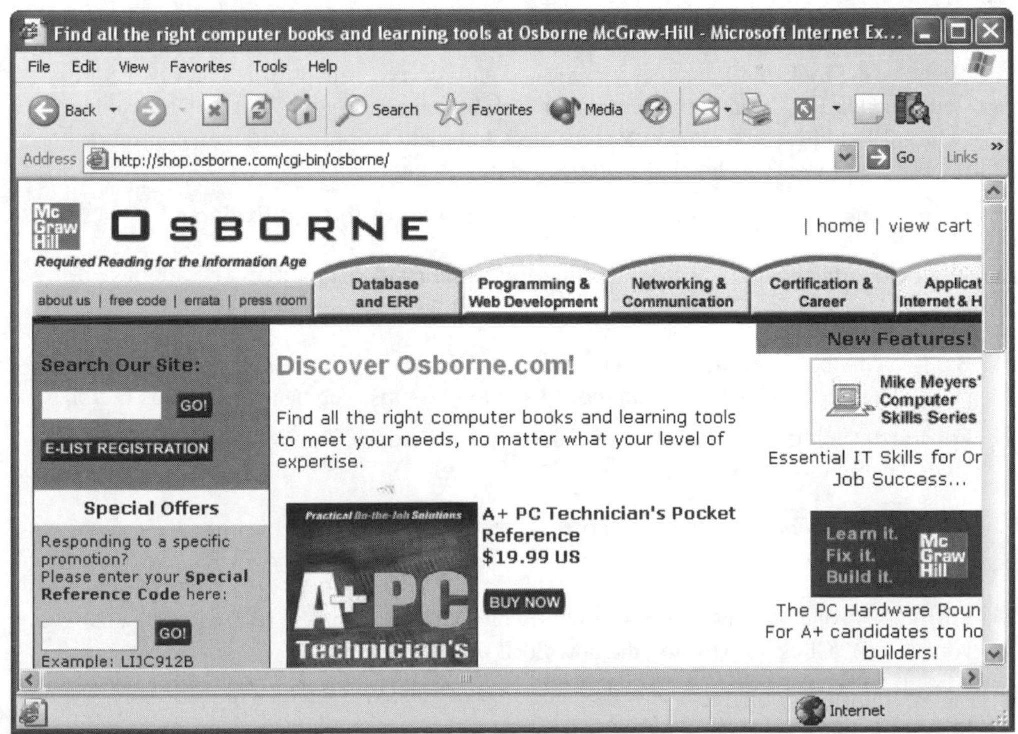

FIGURE 9-1 Internet Explorer

At the top of the Internet Explorer window, you see several common menu options: File, Edit, View, Favorites, Tools, and Help. These menus are virtually the same as folder menus that you learned about in Chapter 4; however, a few differences are specific to Internet Explorer. The following list highlights these menu functions and points out major features:

- **File** This menu contains typical options: Open, Save, Save As, Print, and related File menu options. You also have a Send feature that enables you to send a Web page to a friend via e-mail, send the link via e-mail, or create a Desktop shortcut to the page.
- **Edit** The Edit menu contains your typical Cut, Paste, and Copy functions.
- **View** The View menu enables you to control how your page is viewed by selecting different font sizes. You can also use this menu to change Internet Explorer's toolbars.

- **Favorites** The Favorites menu contains a few folders of generic favorites that Microsoft configures for you. You'll use this menu to add favorites that you want to keep. For example, let's say you find a Web page you really like. You don't have to remember where the Web page is located on the Internet—Favorites can do it for you. Just click Add to Favorites to save the Web page to your Favorites list. The next time you want to visit the page, just click the Favorites menu and click the page title you want to visit.

NOTE *If you have a lot of favorite items, you can click Organize Favorites to group them into different favorites folders. Doing this helps keep your favorites organized and easy to locate.*

- **Tools** The Tools menu enables you to send and receive e-mail using Outlook Express (see Chapter 10); synchronize with other Web folders; configure Windows Messenger (which I'll address in a moment); and access Internet Options, where you configure Internet Explorer (which I'll also address in this chapter).
- **Help** This option opens the Windows XP Help files for Internet Explorer.

Directly below the menus, you see the primary Internet Explorer toolbar. The options are fairly intuitive:

- **Back** This button returns you to the previous Web page you visited. Think of each Web page as a page in a book. You can move back to previous Web pages using this button.
- **Forward** In the same manner, you can move forward to other Web pages you have visited using this button.

TIP *The Back and Forward buttons apply to your current surfing session only. If the Forward button is grayed out, you haven't moved back any, so you are not able to move forward.*

- **Stop** Is a page not downloading correctly or taking too long (or have you just changed your mind)? Click Stop to stop the download process.
- **Refresh** Some Web page content changes frequently. Use Refresh to make sure you are looking at the latest version.

- **Home** This button returns you to your desired home page (see the next section on Internet Options for details).
- **Search** This action opens a search window hosted by the Microsoft Network (MSN) by default (but you can change it). You can then perform a Web search for a topic of your choice.
- **Favorites** This button opens your Favorites list in a different window.
- **Media** This button opens the Media Places pane so you can view multimedia on the Internet.
- **History** Want to know what Web pages the kids have been visiting? Just click History to view a list of previously visited Web pages. But beware, you can edit the History by right-clicking a listing and clicking Delete—which your Internet-savvy children probably already know how to do.

NOTE *The History list is a good way to find a Web page that you have visited when you have forgotten its address.*

- **Send Mail** This option opens an Outlook Express mail message. See Chapter 10 to learn more about Outlook Express.
- **Print** This option prints the current Web page.
- **Edit** You can play around with editing a Web page and changing its content by clicking this button. Internet Explorer selects a default editor for you, such as Microsoft Word if Word is installed on your computer; but you can change this default setting using Internet Options, which I'll explore in the upcoming sections.
- **Discuss** If you want to use discussion and newsgroups, you can click this button to set up a preferred discussion server.
- **Windows Messenger** This option enables you to send and receive instant messages to and from other users.
- **Contacts** Access Outlook Express's Address Book by clicking the button. You can learn more about the Address Book in Chapter 10.
- **Address** The Address bar is the place where you enter the Web address of a site you want to visit. For example, to visit Microsoft, just type **Microsoft.com** here and press ENTER. Although all Web addresses require the http://www portion of the address, Internet Explorer automatically puts in this part of the address, or Uniform Resource Locator (URL), for you if you don't type it. If you want to see a recent list of addresses you have visited, just click the down arrow at the end to access a drop-down menu.
- **Go** You can click this button after you enter a Web address in the Address bar. You can also press ENTER to go to the Web page, which is probably a lot easier.
- **Links** This list (or drop-down menu, depending on your configuration) gives you a list of predefined links—basically advertisements. However, you can right-click any of the default items and click Delete to get rid of them. Then you can drag any URLs from the Address line to the Links bar, and they will copy over to the Links bar for easy access.

Configure Internet Explorer Through Internet Options

You can make changes to the way Internet Explorer behaves so that the browser looks and acts the way you want. You have a variety of useful options, and I'll guide you through them so you can decide which ones are the best for you. You can configure Internet Explorer through Internet Options, which is found in your Tools menu. When you open Internet Options, you find seven different configuration tabs, and the following sections show you what you can do on each tab.

General Tab

The General tab, shown in Figure 9-2, contains three major categories—Home Page, Temporary Internet Files, and History.

The home page is simply the Internet site to which you want Internet Explorer to connect as a default site. Whenever you open Internet Explorer, it will always connect to this site first. If you want to change the site, type a new URL in the Address field. If you don't want to use a home page, click the Use Blank button. Also, if you are currently visiting the Web page you want to make your home page, click the Use Current button on the General tab (which keeps you from having to type the URL).

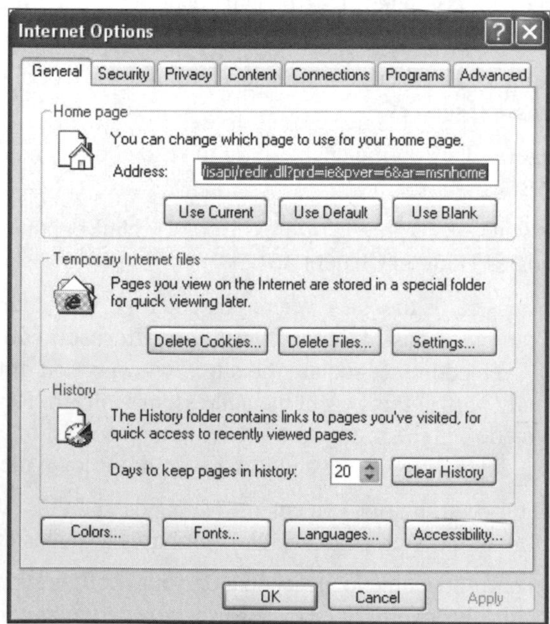

FIGURE 9-2 General tab

The Temporary Internet Files section enables you to determine how temporary Internet pages are stored. When you surf the Web, your computer stores pages that you visit in a Temporary Internet Files folder (including all of the graphics and photos from that page). This speeds up your access to those pages when you revisit them. You can change the default options by clicking the Settings button. Doing this opens a Settings window, shown here, where you can adjust how Internet Explorer uses the temporary pages.

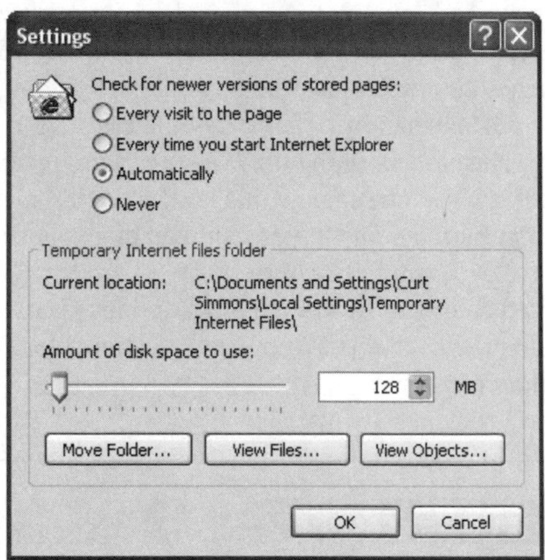

By default, Internet Explorer automatically checks for new material. This setting ensures that you are looking at the most current version of the Web page, and I recommend you leave this default setting. You also see that you can adjust the amount of disk space that is used for temporary Internet files (128MB). You can increase this setting if you like, but 128MB is quite a bit of storage just for temporary Internet files, and this is probably all the space you need. You can also use the buttons at the bottom of the Settings window to view your temporary Internet files and objects, and you can move the Temporary Internet Files folder to a different location on your computer (which doesn't help anything, so it's best just to leave it alone).

TIP *If you believe you are looking at an "old" page from your temporary file, click the Refresh button and the page will be re-downloaded from the Web server.*

Finally, you also see a History section on the General tab. Remember that History lists the sites that have been visited by Internet Explorer. By default, Internet Explorer keeps a history listing for 20 days—in other words, every site that has been visited in the last 20 days will appear. You can change or lower the period of time a history is kept, depending on your individual needs, and you can also click the Clear History button to clean out current History items.

9

At the bottom of the General tab, you see several buttons: Colors, Fonts, Languages, and Accessibility. These options enable you to change the way Internet Explorer looks and displays Web pages. These options are self-explanatory, so check them out if you want to make appearance changes.

Security Tab

The Security tab enables you to configure how Internet Explorer handles security issues on Internet or intranet sites, as shown in Figure 9-3. A typical home user does not need to make any configuration changes on this tab; and if you are using Internet Explorer on a business network, you should not make any changes here unless instructed to do so by your network administrator. Click the Internet icon, and you'll see that, by default, the Internet option (shown in Figure 9-3) is set to Medium. This setting gives you all of the browser functionality, but prompts you before downloading questionable content. You can change this level by using the slider bar to access different settings. For each slider bar movement, you can read an explanation of how the browser behaves. Typically, however, the Medium setting is best.

You can also use the Trusted Sites and Restricted Sites options. These options enable you to list sites that you know are safe or sites that you know are questionable. This, in turn, affects how your browser acts when handling these sites.

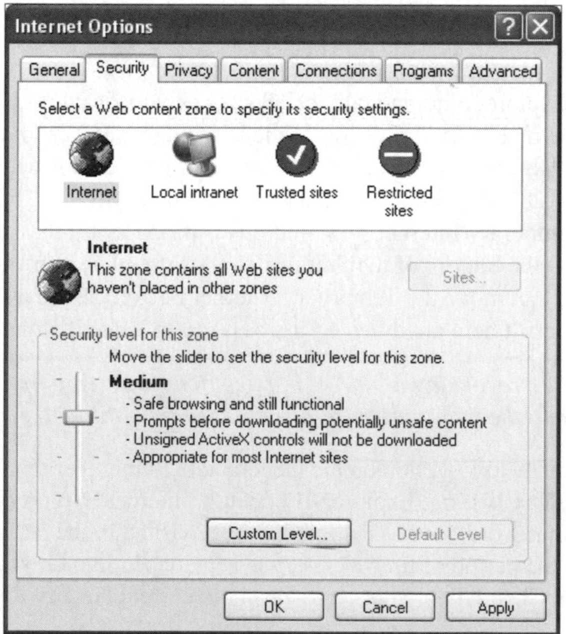

FIGURE 9-3 Security tab

Privacy Tab

The Privacy tab, shown in Figure 9-4, gives you a slider bar option so you can set a privacy configuration for your computer (first click the Default button on the tab). Web sites have become more interactive in the past year or so, and many of them want to collect information from you and your computer. This setting allows you to determine whether or not Web sites can set cookies with your browser and use personal information. By default, the Medium setting is used, which is typically all you will need. You can click the Advanced button to alter the cookie settings as desired.

If you have Service Pack 2 installed, you also see a Pop-Up Blocker, which can help IE prevent those annoying pop-ups. If you want to block pop-ups, select the check box option, and you can click the Settings button to create exceptions if necessary.

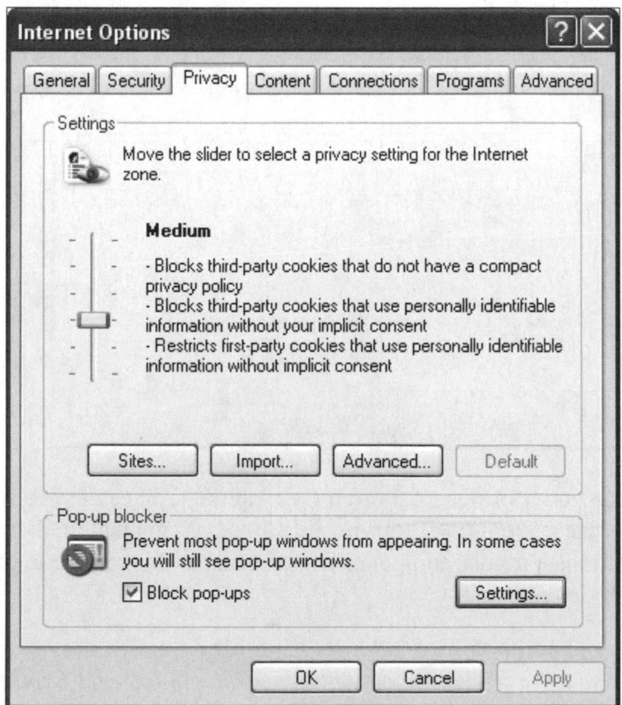

FIGURE 9-4 Privacy tab

Content Tab

The Content tab enables you to configure how Internet Explorer manages different kinds of content from the Internet, as well as information about you. This tab has three sections—Content Advisor, Certificates, and Personal Information, as shown in Figure 9-5.

The Content Advisor enables you to manage how (and if) Internet Explorer handles different kinds of potentially offensive Web content. If you click the Enable button, you see a Content Advisor window, shown here:

You see different categories of potential offensive material. You can use the slider bar to adjust the level of offensive content that users are able to view. This feature is great if you have children who use the Internet on your computer. You can enable this feature to prevent accidental access to offensive Web content.

NOTE *These settings are not foolproof. Internet Explorer examines the requested Web site for keywords that provide clues about offensive content. Internet Explorer can also use a site's rating system to determine whether it is safe. As you can see, a lot of this is up to the individual site, so don't think that your kids are safe when you enable these settings. You still need to monitor them, and you might consider investing in some third-party software that can also help manage access to offensive Web sites.*

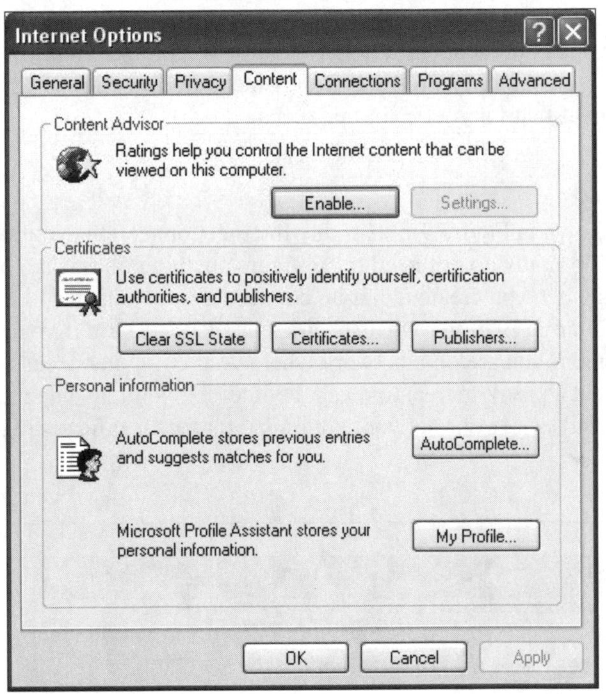

FIGURE 9-5 Content tab

Once you make some settings decisions, click Apply, and Windows XP will prompt you to enter a password. This prevents other users of your computer from changing the content settings. Also note that you can access the Approved Sites tab to create a list of approved sites, and you can also make some basic changes on the General and Advanced tabs. Normally, however, you don't need to use these tabs; if you do, you'll find them self-explanatory.

The second part of the Content tab is Certificates. In some organizations, Internet Explorer is configured to use various digital certificates to verify certain Web site authenticity. Home users do not use certificate options, so you don't need to configure anything here. In some circumstances you might want to use a digital certificate to communicate with a highly secure Web site. If this is the case, you will need to follow that Web site's instructions about obtaining and using a digital certificate. If you are using XP in a business environment, your network administrators will manage these settings for you.

Finally, you can use the Personal Information section of the Content tab to change or turn off AutoComplete. Internet Explorer tries to learn what Web sites and information you enter into

Web pages. If Internet Explorer recognizes what you are typing, it will try to complete it for you. You may find this helpful or aggravating. At any rate, you can click the AutoComplete button to change the behavior. This button opens another window with some simple check box options you can consider. Also, you see a My Profile button, which you can click to change personal information about yourself that Internet Explorer keeps.

Connections Tab

The Connections tab, shown in Figure 9-6, lists any Internet connections you have configured on your computer. You normally do not need to configure anything on this tab because you configure these options when you create a dial-up connection (see Chapter 8). However, you can use this tab to tell Internet Explorer what specific connection to use if your computer has multiple connections. If you are on a network where your computer accesses another network computer (called a proxy server) to reach the Internet, you may need to perform some configuration here. Consult with your network administrator for specific setting information.

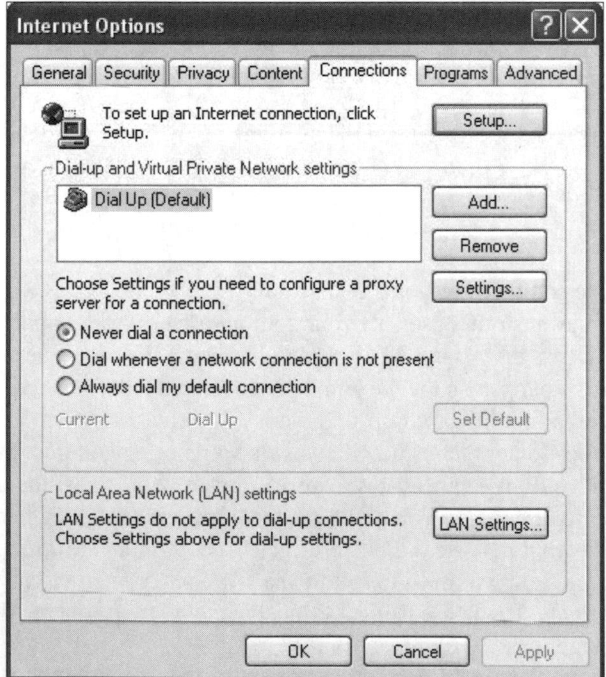

FIGURE 9-6 Connections tab

Programs Tab

The Programs tab, shown in Figure 9-7, enables you to choose which programs on Windows XP perform what options. For example, by default, Internet Explorer uses Outlook Express for Internet mail (in other words, if you are visiting a Web page and click a "send e-mail" link, Internet Explorer opens an Outlook Express mail message). However, you may want to use a different mail client you have installed on your computer. You can use this page to change the applications that Internet Explorer uses for HTML editing, e-mail, newsgroups, Internet calling, your calendar, and your contact list. If you plan to use both Internet Explorer and Outlook Express, you won't need to change any of these settings.

Advanced Tab

The Advanced tab contains a bunch of check box options for a variety of processes. For example, you can change some browsing behavior, multimedia settings, and printing settings (among others) just by checking or unchecking different options.

The real question, of course, is what do you need to change? In reality, nothing—under most circumstances. Do not start making changes on this tab unless you have a specific goal in mind. For example, Internet Explorer does not print background colors and images on Web pages,

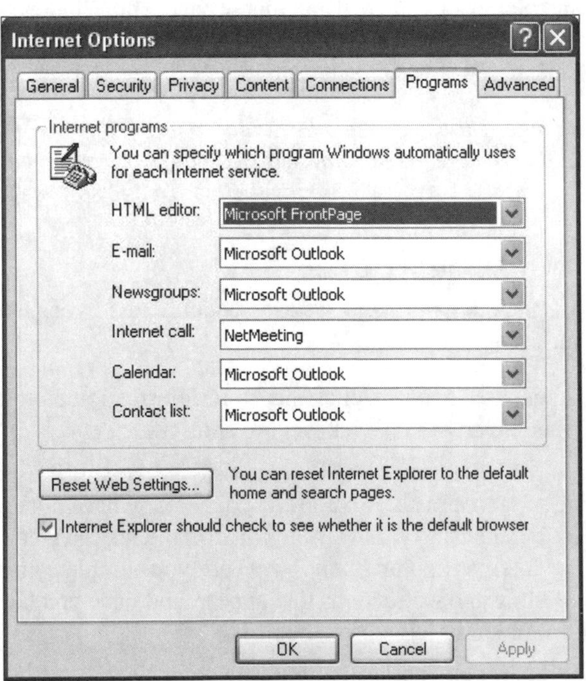

FIGURE 9-7 Programs tab

as a way of sparing your color ink cartridge from printing unnecessary graphics. However, if I want Internet Explorer to print them anyway, I can select the Print Background Colors and Images check box under Printing. The key is to identify a goal you want to accomplish and then determine whether you can enable or disable that option on the Advanced tab. The most common settings are already configured for you.

If you choose to ignore my advice and change a bunch of these settings, you can click the Restore Defaults button to put everything back to the original settings.

Windows Messenger

I have mentioned that Windows Messenger, formerly MSN Messenger, is available in the Internet Explorer browser. First off, MSN—the Microsoft Network—is both an Internet search engine and an ISP. You can visit www.msn.com and read news, get information, and search the Web. You can also sign up with MSN, and for a monthly fee, MSN will be your ISP—your onramp to the Internet.

Windows Messenger is included in Windows XP, and you do not have to be an MSN ISP customer to use the service. The service, in a nutshell, enables you to communicate directly with other Windows Messenger service participants. It is a quick and easy way to bypass your typical static e-mail. You can talk back and forth instantly and even use voice over the Internet instead of text. You can send files and pictures to others using this service, and Windows Messenger users can even use the service via Web-enabled telephones and personal digital assistants (PDAs). Overall, it's a cool service that you'll want to check out.

This type of messenger service is offered by other major ISPs and Internet sites, such as Yahoo! and AOL. However, these different messenger programs cannot interact with each other.

Set Up Windows Messenger

To set up Windows Messenger, click the Windows Messenger icon on your Internet Explorer toolbar and then follow these easy steps:

1. In the Welcome screen that appears, click the More Information button to read more about Windows Messenger, or just click Next to continue.
2. You need either an MSN/Hotmail e-mail account or a Microsoft Passport to use this service. The Passport is free (as is Hotmail). If you already have a free Hotmail account, just use your account name and password. If you don't, click the Get a Passport button. This opens another Internet Explorer window where you complete an application page to get a Passport. Follow the instructions that appear, and once you have a Passport, you can continue with Windows Messenger setup.
3. Enter your Passport name and password, and then click Next.
4. Click Finish.

Windows Messenger sets up and its opening window appears on your computer, as shown in Figure 9-8. You may be prompted to download the latest version, and you should choose to do so to take advantage of the latest features.

Use Windows Messenger

As you can see in Figure 9-8, Windows Messenger is an easy, scaled-down window option with a few buttons. You can use the window to set up your service for new contacts and other people with an MSN or Hotmail account, as well as for Microsoft Passport to send and receive messages. The window tells you which of your contacts are currently online and which are not. Messages are automatically displayed in the window as you receive them. This feature enables you to talk back and forth instantly. You can also place a phone call or call a pager number from the Windows Messenger window. As you can see, using Windows Messenger is very easy—just play around with it, get some of your friends signed up and online, and see how you like it!

NOTE *If you are using your computer with Windows Messenger turned on and you need to step away for a moment, you can let your friends know you are away from your computer. Choose File | My Status, and a list of options appear, such as "out to lunch," "be right back," "on the phone," and so on. Your messenger friends will see your status and know you are unavailable for the moment.*

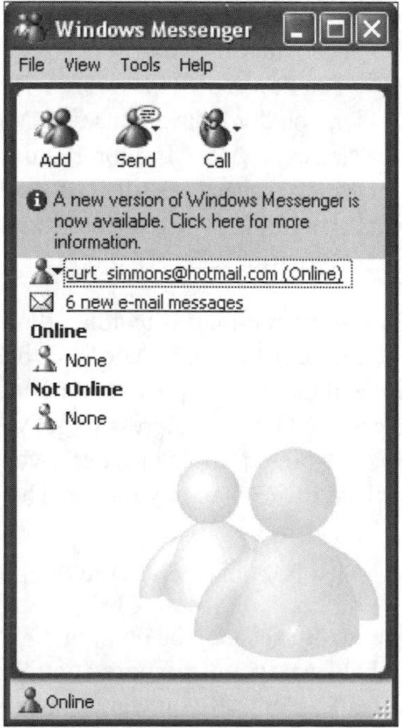

FIGURE 9-8 Windows Messenger

Change Your Windows Messenger Profile

Let's say some things change in your life and you need to update your Windows Messenger profile, or you just want to change what other Windows Messenger users can view about you. It's easy to change your profile, and here's how:

1. In Windows Messenger, choose Tools | Options.
2. On the Personal tab, click the Edit Profile button.
3. This action opens an Internet Explorer window that takes you to your account on the Microsoft Passport site.
4. Examine the information in your account and change it directly on the Web page as desired.

Use MSN Explorer

MSN Explorer can be used by anyone with a Hotmail or MSN account. MSN Explorer is also a Web browser, like Internet Explorer, but MSN Explorer can be used only by people who have an MSN ISP account, Hotmail e-mail account, or a Microsoft Passport. In short, if you are not a subscriber to one of these services, you can't use MSN Explorer. The reverse, however, is also true—if you are an MSN ISP subscriber, you don't have to use MSN Explorer—you can use a Web browser such as Internet Explorer or Netscape. MSN Explorer is used to browse the Internet, just like any other browser, and it also provides easy access to all of the MSN subscriber features, as well as e-mail. In other words, it puts everything in one central location. You do, however, need to consider a couple of setup issues before using MSN Explorer:

- Once you set up MSN Explorer, your e-mail is handled through Explorer—not another e-mail client such as Outlook Express. In other words, Explorer forces you to use e-mail from the Explorer interface, and Outlook Express will no longer work for POP3 (ISP-based) mail. However, you can use Outlook Express to get your Web-based mail, such as Hotmail. You can use Outlook Express for this purpose—you just won't be able to connect to your regular ISP to download POP3 mail any longer. The problem is in POP3 mail and Outlook Express.
- To read or write e-mail, you must be connected to the Internet.

Depending on your needs, these two issues may be enough of a deal killer for many—myself included. I am an MSN subscriber, but frankly, I want more control over my e-mail and settings, so I prefer to use Outlook and Internet Explorer. If you want to use MSN Explorer, however, it does have some nice features and a cool interface that is very easy to use. The How To box shows you how to set up MSN Explorer.

After you have set up MSN Explorer, you see that it looks a lot like Internet Explorer, but all things MSN are integrated into one location so that they are easy to use. If you need to make any changes, click the Help & Settings link at the top of the window. Besides this, MSN Explorer is very intuitive, and if you spend some time working with it, you'll be a pro in no time.

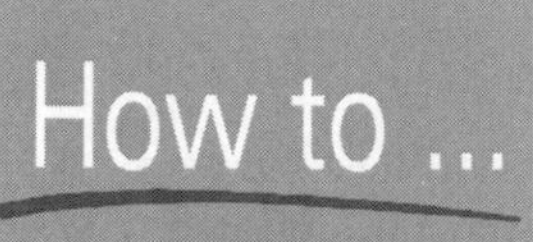

Set Up MSN Explorer

To set up MSN Explorer, just follow these steps:

1. Click the MSN Explorer icon on your Taskbar (it looks like a butterfly).
2. This opens an Explorer Getting Started page. Click the Type of Internet connection you use (dial-up, broadband, or local area network, for example), and click the Continue button.
3. MSN places a toll-free call to the Internet (if you are using a dial-up connection) and connects you with MSN. This sometimes takes a few minutes.
4. A message appears asking whether you want to sign up for MSN Internet access. Click either Yes or No, and click Continue.
5. A message appears telling you about upgrade issues, which are explained in the previous section. Click the Continue button.
6. Enter your MSN account information (username and password). Click Continue.
7. Enter your name on the next screen and click Continue.
8. Use the drop-down menu and select your occupation (or something close to it). Click Continue.
9. Enter your date of birth and click Continue.
10. Enter the ISP phone number that you dial to connect. Click Continue.
11. Additional screens may appear as necessary. Finally, you will be reconnected, and you will need to sign in with your username and password.
12. Once you've finished, you finally reach the Welcome screen. Notice that you can take a tour to orient yourself with MSN.

Use the Web Publishing Wizard

Along with Internet Explorer, Windows XP includes a related tool called the Web Publishing Wizard, which is available in any Windows XP folder that contains content. In the Tasks dialog box on the left side of the window, you see a Publish This Folder to the Web link. This feature opens the Web Publishing Wizard, which can help you publish items to an Internet site.

Often, ISPs give their customers a certain amount of server Web space. This means that you have a block of space on their server's hard drive where you can put Web pages and pictures. Friends and family can then access the Web address and view your files on the Internet. This feature could also be used by an intranet Web server. Let's say you have a small company that uses an intranet and you want to send files and folders to an address on that server. You can use the Web Publishing Wizard to accomplish this task.

Basically, all the Web Publishing Wizard does is gather information about what files you want to publish and to which Web server you want to publish them. The Web Publishing Wizard then takes this information, connects to the Web server, authenticates with it, and then transfers the files to the Web server. The wizard makes this an easy process for you.

To use the Web Publishing Wizard, you'll need information from your ISP or intranet server on how to access the Web server so you can transfer your files. Once you have this information, just start the Web Publishing Wizard, enter the information as requested, and then let Windows XP handle the rest for you.

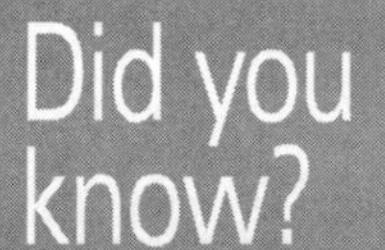

MSN also offers a Web storage solution so you can store files on the Internet as a simple backup method. Once again, you'll need an MSN, Hotmail, or Passport account to do this. This is a very cool feature—it's fun, free, and a big help; just choose the Publish option from the desired folder and choose the option to publish to MSN when the wizard appears. Follow the easy steps to complete it.

Did you know?

What Happened to NetMeeting?

If you have been cruising around Windows XP looking for NetMeeting (a more detailed conferencing application you can use to video conference with people over the Internet), never fear, it is still there. In truth, Windows Messenger does much of the same thing, and Microsoft would rather that typical users like you and I use Windows Messenger instead of NetMeeting because, frankly, it is easier to use.

However, NetMeeting does have a lot of cool features, so if you want to use it, click Start | Run. Type **conf** in the Run dialog box and click OK. The NetMeeting wizard will begin, and once you enter your information, you'll be able to start using it. The wizard will even let you put a shortcut to NetMeeting on your Desktop or Start menu for easy access.

Chapter 10

Run Outlook Express

How to...

- Set up Outlook Express
- Send and receive e-mail
- Configure interface views
- Use identities
- Create and manage message rules
- Customize Outlook Express
- Use the Address Book

If you are like many of us, you didn't have e-mail a few years ago, and the concept of e-mail didn't seem very important. Today, e-mail is a daily part of your life, and you don't know how you ever survived without it! That statement certainly describes me—I use e-mail every day for my work and to keep up with friends and family. Checking and managing the e-mail I receive consumes a significant amount of my time each day, and I don't know what I would do without it.

Like previous versions of Windows, Windows XP provides Outlook Express, which is a free e-mail client. An *e-mail client* is a software program that allows you to send and receive e-mail and manage the e-mail that you receive. Outlook Express 6 is included with Windows XP; and if you have used previous versions of Outlook Express, you won't find many differences in version 6. If you're new to Outlook Express, however, this chapter is just what you need to get your feet on solid ground. In this chapter, you will learn how to set up Outlook Express, manage e-mail accounts, and make the most of the additional features offered by Outlook Express.

How E-Mail Works

E-mail is primarily sent over the Internet to reach a certain person. Businesses and organizations also use e-mail, which is sent over their local network instead of the Internet; but most of us use e-mail that is sent over our Internet connection to the Internet. Like everything else on the Internet, e-mail uses a protocol to send mail between different computers.

Typically, e-mail uses Simple Mail Transfer Protocol (SMTP) to move mail from one place to another. An e-mail address is made up of a username and a domain name, such as *myname@mydomain.com*. When you send an e-mail to someone, e-mail servers first examine the *mydomain.com* portion of the address to find a *mydomain.com* server. Once this server is located, the mail is sent to the server. This server recognizes *mydomain.com* as its own domain, so it examines the username to see whether a user by that name exists. If *myname* is, in fact, a user, the mail is held on the server until it is downloaded. If the name does not match, the mail is sometimes sent back to the sender with a "user unknown" message. In many respects, e-mail is just like regular mail, where the address is inspected first, and then the name is inspected by the local post office. Of course, e-mail is a lot faster. You can send a message to any e-mail address anywhere in the world, and it normally arrives in a few minutes or less. Also, you can send any kind of electronic file as an attachment—pictures, documents, video, applications…you name it. Because it is so fast and can handle almost any kind of attachment, e-mail has become very popular in our fast-paced world.

Set Up Outlook Express

When you install Windows XP, Outlook Express is installed by default. You can see the Outlook Express icon on your Quick Launch toolbar (if you have it enabled), which looks like a letter with blue arrows around it. To use Outlook Express, you will need to set up your mail account so Outlook Express will know how to connect to a mail server to send and receive e-mail. This information is available from your ISP. You most likely received printed instructions about setting up your computer for a connection to the Internet (see Chapter 8). Once you have made this connection, you then use your documentation to set up Outlook Express.

NOTE *You do not have to use Outlook Express to send and receive e-mail with Windows XP. You can use Netscape, Eudora, or some other mail client instead. However, this chapter focuses only on Outlook Express because it is included with your XP operating system.*

To start, click the Outlook Express icon on your Taskbar, or choose Start | All Programs | Outlook Express if you don't see it on your Taskbar. Outlook Express opens, and you see the basic Outlook Express interface. Choose Tools | Accounts. Then click the Mail tab on the Internet Accounts window. Click the Add button on the right side of the window, and then click Mail. The Internet Connection Wizard appears, which will lead you through a series of steps in which you will enter your username, password, and so on. Have this information ready, and then follow these easy steps to complete the wizard:

1. Enter your display name. This is the name that you want other e-mail users to see when you send mail. Typically, you want to use your real name here and not something that can't be recognized, such as "Biker Dad" or "Sweet Cakes." However, if you want to be known by a nickname, that's okay, too. Click Next when you're done.
2. In the next window, enter your e-mail address and click Next. If you already have an existing account, you can use that, or you can set up a free Web-based e-mail account on the Internet with Hotmail, which is a part of MSN.

NOTE *Hotmail is not the only free Web-based e-mail account that is available. Yahoo.com, Netscape.com, Go.com, and many others also offer free e-mail accounts.*

3. In the next window, you'll need to enter your e-mail server information. Almost all e-mail servers use POP3 (Post Office Protocol 3) to manage e-mail messages, with the exception of free e-mail servers. Outlook Express needs to know whether your server is a POP3 server or a different kind of server, such as IMAP or HTTP. Check your ISP

documentation. Then, enter the incoming mail server name and the outgoing mail server name. Typically, both of these names will be in the form of *mail.mydomain.com.* You'll need to check your ISP documentation to know for sure. Enter the correct information, and then click Next.

4. In the next window, enter your logon name and your password. Check your ISP documentation to make certain you are entering the correct information—and do remember that passwords are case-sensitive. Also, you should not select the Secure Password Authentication check box at the bottom of the window unless your ISP documentation explicitly tells you to do so.
5. Click Finish to complete the wizard.

Filter HTML E-Mail for Added Security and Privacy

One of the important changes for Windows XP Service Pack 2 (SP2) is the ability to filter HTML e-mail in Outlook Express. HTML (in very simple terms) is a programming language that allows authors to format documents for the web (in this case, e-mail).

Why would you want to do this? While HTML can add nice graphical features to e-mail messages, it can also open the door to security risks. The use of HTML in e-mail can allow someone to run unauthorized programs, such as a virus or Trojan horse, on your computer. In the case of spammers, the use of HTML e-mail can confirm the existence of your e-mail address by calling back to the spam author's web server. This can lead to your getting even more spam.

With Windows XP SP2, Microsoft automatically turned off the option to view external images and content in Outlook Express. To view this setting, open Outlook Express. Choose Tools | Options, and click the Security tab. In the Download Images section, check the box next to Block Images and Other External Content in HTML Email. This is an excellent and necessary security option, but you can take your security one step further by blocking HTML in e-mail altogether.

To turn off HTML e-mail in Outlook Express, choose Tools | Options, and click the Read tab. Select the check box that says Read All Messages in Plain Text and click Apply at the bottom of that window to save your changes.

You can also send all your e-mail in plain text. This makes it more likely that those who read their e-mail in plain text see the e-mail in the same format that you sent it. Choose Tools | Options. Click the Send tab, and in the Mail Sending Format section, click the Plain Text radio button. Then click Apply at the bottom of that window to save your changes.

—Eric Vaughan
www.tweakhound.com

Outlook Express has the capability to support multiple accounts for the same user. For example, let's say you have a primary ISP with an e-mail address of *myaddress@myisp.com.* However, you also have an e-mail account at *youraddress@youraddress.com.* Can you use Outlook Express to access information on both of those accounts? Sure! All you need to do is configure both mail accounts using the previous steps. When you check your mail, Outlook Express will check both accounts.

Check Out the Outlook Express Interface

Outlook Express provides an easy-to-read and easy-to-use interface where you can quickly view e-mail messages. By default, Outlook Express uses four major *panes,* or views, to separate different mail components. These four panes make mail usage easy, and you can customize this interface as well (I'll show you how later in this chapter). Figure 10-1 gives you a look at the default Outlook Express interface.

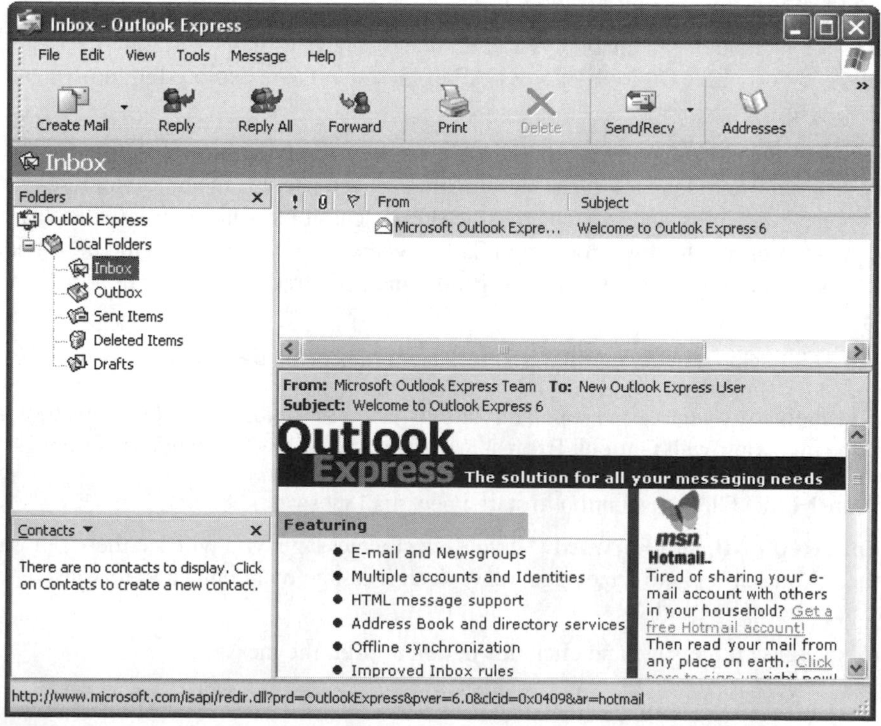

FIGURE 10-1 Outlook Express interface

Let's first take a look at your menu options. At the top of the Outlook Express window, you see common menus: File, Edit, View, Tools, Message, and Help. You have the standard options on these menus, such as Open, Save, Cut, and Paste; but you also have quite a few options that are specific to Outlook Express. The following list highlights the most important features:

- **File** Using this menu, you can perform standard open and save functions, and you can create additional mail folders in which you can store mail. You can also import and export mail settings, messages, and address books to and from other e-mail programs. You can also use the File menu to establish different identities. This way, two different people can send and receive mail using a single Outlook Express program. All of these options are easy and self-explanatory, but I'll explore the Identities feature later in the section "Use Identities."
- **Edit** The Edit menu contains typical editing functions. Use the Edit menu to delete e-mail, move e-mail between folders, mark e-mail messages in various ways, and perform other standard editing tasks.
- **View** You use this menu to change how current messages are viewed, as well as how the entire Outlook Express interface appears. See the "Change Outlook Express Views" section later in this chapter for more information.
- **Tools** The Tools menu enables you to send and receive e-mail, configure message rules, and customize Outlook Express. All of these items are explored in more detail later in this chapter.
- **Message** The Message menu contains typical message functions, most of which you can perform by clicking a toolbar button. You can also use this menu to block senders, create message rules, and "watch" messages or discussions. You can use Outlook Express to connect to newsgroups and flag messages so you can watch the message and all the replies. This is a great way to organize and keep track of information that is useful to you.
- **Help** Get help from the Outlook Express Help files or on the Microsoft Web site.

Below the menu bar, you see the standard Outlook Express toolbar. You'll use this toolbar quite a bit when working with Outlook Express. You have the following standard buttons:

- **Create Mail** Click this button to start a new mail message.
- **Reply, Reply All, and Forward** If you select a message, you will see these options appear. You can reply to a message, reply to all message recipients, and forward a message to someone else.
- **Print** Select a message and click this button to print the message.
- **Delete** Select a message and click this button to delete a message.
- **Send/Recv** Click this button to see a drop-down list of choices. You can Send and Receive, Receive All, and Send All.

- **Addresses** Click this button to open the Address Book.
- **Find** Click this button to find specific messages. You can search by sender, message subject, or keywords.

The final part of the Outlook Express interface is composed of the four primary panes:

- **Folders** The top-left pane shows your Outlook Express folder structure. You can easily move between your Inbox, Outbox, Sent Items, and Deleted Items, as well as additional folders that you can create using the File menu.
- **Contacts** The bottom-left pane shows your contacts. Contacts are people to whom you have sent e-mail. Outlook Express keeps up with your contacts and their e-mail addresses by maintaining this list for you.
- **New Message** The top-right pane contains a message list. These are messages that you have received but not deleted or moved into another folder.
- **Preview** The bottom-right pane contains the text of the selected message. This is an easy preview that allows you to skim through your messages without actually opening them.

Send and Receive E-Mail

Once you have set up an account, you can send and receive e-mail. Sending and receiving e-mail is very easy, and the following sections show you how.

Send an E-Mail

To send a new e-mail message, click the Create Mail button on your toolbar. A new mail message appears, as shown in Figure 10-2. To send a new mail message, type the recipient's e-mail address

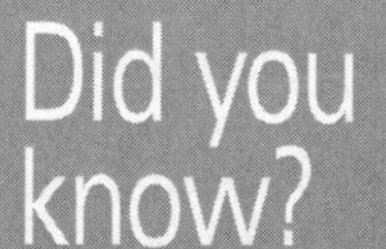

Advanced Message-Editing Features

Outlook Express supports advanced message-editing features. As you are typing your new message, notice that you have bold, italic, bulleted lists, and other button features on the message toolbar. You can also cut, copy, and paste message text as well. You can use the Format menu to use different color styles in your message and even use a background picture or graphic with the Message menu. You can also check your message for spelling errors by choosing Tools | Spelling, or just click the Spelling button.

All of these features are really nice, but do be aware that not all mail clients can receive these formatting features. Even though you style your text and add a background, some of your recipients may see only plain text.

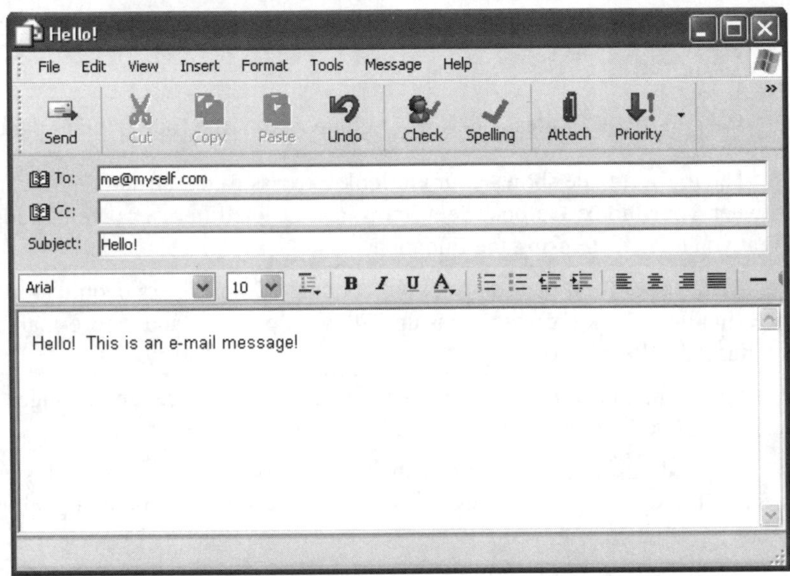

FIGURE 10-2 New mail message

in the To line and any additional e-mail addresses in the Cc line (if you want other individuals copied), enter a subject, and then type your message in the provided message box—it's that easy!

NOTE *When you enter a subject, be as descriptive as possible. E-mail users will often receive many e-mails on any given day. Descriptive subjects help identify important messages. Also, if your message is very important, you can attach a "high priority" notice with it. Choose Message | Set Priority | High, or click the Priority button and select a priority.*

When you've finished with your message, click the Send button. If you are currently connected to the Internet, the message is immediately sent. If you are not currently connected to the Internet, click the Send/Recv button on your Outlook Express toolbar. Doing this launches an Internet dial-up connection so the message can be sent.

Attach a File to an E-Mail

If you want to send an e-mail with an attachment, which is just a file of some kind, you can easily do so. Click the Create Mail button on your Outlook Express toolbar and follow these steps:

1. Enter the recipient's e-mail address, cc addresses if desired, and a subject, and then type any text in the message area.

2. To attach a file, choose Insert, and choose either File Attachment or Picture. (You can also choose to include the text from a file, which enables you to browse for the file and copy and paste the text from it.) You can also click the Attach button.
3. A browse window appears. Browse to the location of the file, and then select it.
4. Click the Attach button. The file now appears in your New Message window as an attachment, as shown in Figure 10-3.

NOTE *Want to know an easier way to attach a file to a message? Shrink your message window so you can see your Desktop, and then locate the file you want to include. Drag the file into the message portion of the window. Its name will appear in the Attach line and the file will be attached to the e-mail.*

Before sending attachments, you should consider putting the attachments in a new folder and compressing the folder. Doing this makes your transmission time shorter. To learn more about folder compression, see Chapter 4.

Receive Messages

When you are ready to check for messages, open Outlook Express and click the Send/Recv button on your toolbar. Doing this launches an Internet connection, so mail can be downloaded to your

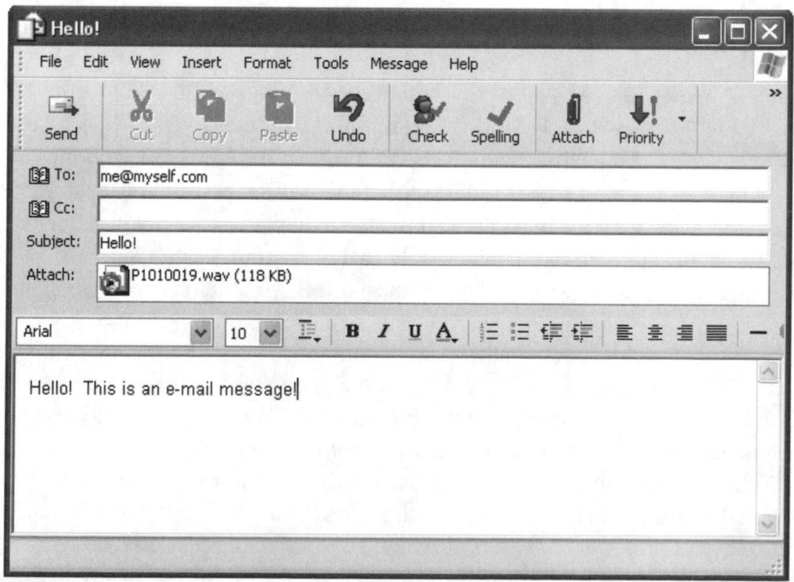

FIGURE 10-3 New Message window with attachment

computer. New e-mail messages appear in the New Message pane. If you click each message, you can read its text in the Preview pane, but do not assume that you see all of the message text in the Preview pane; scroll down with the slider bar to view the entire message. To open a message, double-click it. Doing this enables you to read the message in its own message window. Once you have received and read your messages, you can delete them, leave them in the Inbox, or drag them to a desired folder for safekeeping.

TIP

A great feature of Outlook Express is that deleted messages aren't really deleted—they are moved to the Deleted Items folder. You can click this folder and find a message that has been previously deleted and reread it. You can also right-click the Deleted Items folder and choose Empty Deleted Items to delete the items permanently if you need to free up disk space; however, I don't recommend you choose this global delete option. Invariably, you will need to refer to a mail item you thought you no longer needed.

Receive Attachments

Any attachments that are sent to you are automatically downloaded with the mail message. Messages with attachments have a small paper clip beside them in the New Message pane.

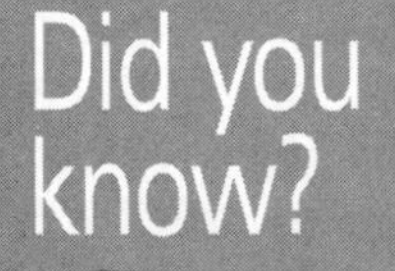

About E-Mail and Computer Viruses

There's a lot of talk and confusion about computer viruses and e-mail—and rightfully so. Generally speaking, computers do get viruses from e-mail. However, it is important to note that you cannot get a computer virus from the text of an e-mail. For example, let's say you download your mail, select a message, and the contents of the message appear in the Preview pane. Let's say you even open the message and read it. You cannot get a computer virus this way. There is, however, an exception to this rule: HTML e-mail messages. Because HTML is a computer language, it is possible to get a Trojan horse or other malicious code from an HTML message—this is why is important to keep your antivirus software up-to-date.

Computer viruses typically come in the form of some kind of attachment. Opening an attachment can give your computer a virus. Virus attachments normally contain some kind of executable code that launches on your computer and does all kinds of annoying and nasty things. In short—don't open attachments from someone you don't know, and be wary of attachments even from people you do know, who may have unintentionally sent you an infected file. Also, watch for the .exe and .vbs extensions on attachments (such as *attachmentname*.exe or *attachmentname*.vbs). These are executable files and are more likely to contain viruses than other attachments, such as a picture file. In addition, "macro" viruses can hide within word processing documents, such as a Microsoft Word document. All major brands of antivirus software include an "e-mail scan" feature that can check your e-mail attachments for viruses before you open them. This software is very inexpensive and a great investment.

In the Preview pane, you see a larger paper clip on the right side of the window. If you click the paper clip, a pop-out menu appears where you can choose either to open the attachment or save it to your computer (such as in the My Documents folder or your Desktop).

Change Outlook Express Views

As I have discussed, Outlook Express has a four-pane option that *I* think is great. However, *you* may not think it's so great and you may want to change it. That's fine, and it's easy to do as well. To change the appearance of the Outlook Express interface, choose View | Layout. A window appears with a single Layout tab, as shown in Figure 10-4.

As you can see, two sections appear—Basic and Preview Pane. You can select or clear the various check boxes to display the panes that you want. You can try different settings to find the ones that you like best. Also, if you click Customize Toolbar, you can add other toolbar icon features, which are discussed in more detail in Chapter 3.

In addition to using the Layout feature, you can also customize the current view, which enables you to determine which messages are displayed and which are hidden. You can use different views by choosing View | Current View. You can then select a desired option from the pop-out menu. As with an appearance configuration, you may need to play around with the settings to find the ones that are right for you.

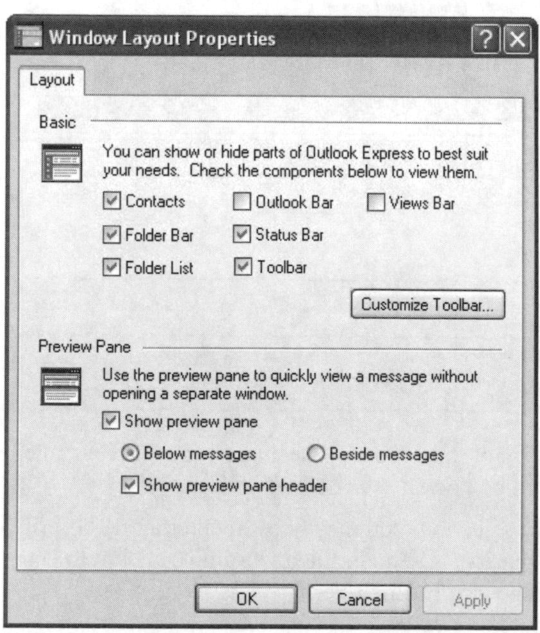

FIGURE 10-4 Layout tab

Create Message Rules

Message rules enable you to control how various messages are handled by Outlook Express. Message rules are most helpful to people who receive a lot of e-mail or who receive a lot of spam, or junk e-mail. You can set up rules to help you manage messages so that Outlook Express can automatically delete certain messages or move certain messages to other folders.

Rules are easy to create, but be careful of "overdoing it." Too many rules usually become more confusing than helpful, so plan carefully before you create a bunch of e-mail rules. Make sure you have a specific reason to create a rule or a specific problem you want the rule to solve.

Create a New Rule

To create a new rule, follow these easy steps:

1. In Outlook Express, choose Tools | Message Rules | Mail.
2. The New Mail Rule window appears. In the top portion of the window, select a condition for your rule. Scroll through the list and select the check box next to the desired condition.

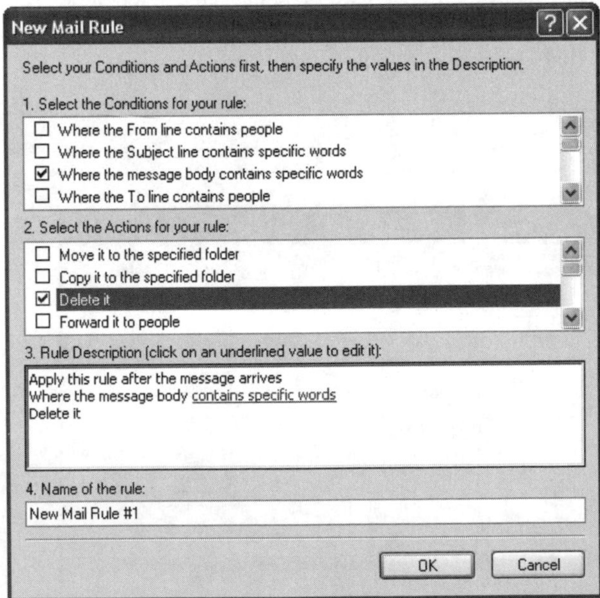

3. In the second portion of the window, select an action for your rule. Scroll through the list and select the check box next to the desired action.
4. Depending on your selection, you may need to enter a rule description or perform some editing. If a link appears (blue underlined wording), click it to enter some additional information that is needed for the rule.
5. In the bottom of the window, give the rule a friendly name and then click OK.

Manage Message Rules

Once you create message rules, you can manage them from the same Message Rules interface. Choose Tools | Message Rules | Mail. A window appears, listing your current rules. You can use the provided buttons to create new rules, delete existing rules, edit existing rules, and perform related management features. This interface is very easy to use and self-explanatory.

Block Senders

Let's say you meet Chatty Kathy in a chat room and you make the mistake of giving her your personal e-mail address. Now Chatty Kathy writes to you every day and sends you piles of junk mail. You decide you really don't like Chatty Kathy and you don't want any more mail from her. What to do? No problem. You can block Chatty Kathy so that your computer automatically moves her mail to the Deleted Items folder without informing you of the mail's arrival.

To use the Blocked Senders option, choose Tools | Message Rules | Blocked Senders List. A simple window appears. Click the Add button, enter the e-mail address of the sender you want to block, and click OK. The sender appears in the Blocked Senders list, shown in Figure 10-5. You can modify this list at any time.

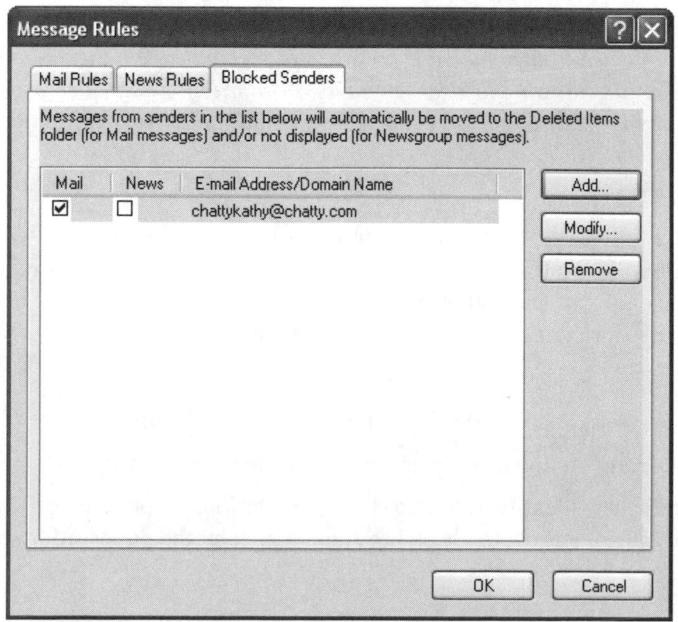

FIGURE 10-5 Blocked Senders List

You can also use the Message menu to add a new person to your Blocked Senders list immediately (and easily). When you get a message from someone and you know you don't want any more messages from that sender, just select the message in Outlook and then choose Message | Block Sender. That's all you have to do; any mail sent in the future from this sender will be removed automatically. Additionally, you can use the Message menu to create a rule from the message. Select the message, choose Message | Create Rule from Message, and you'll see the New Mail Rule window appear. These options give you quick and easy access to the Message Rules and Blocked Senders features of Outlook Express.

Use Identities

Let's face the facts—everyone wants to use a computer, and no matter whether your Windows XP computer is a home or office computer, multiple users may be accessing your machine. Microsoft recognizes this fact and has given you a number of new tools in Windows XP that enable you to manage multiple users easily on the same computer. Outlook Express also supports multiple people using Outlook Express with its Identities feature. With Identities, several people can use Outlook Express and Outlook Express's Address Book. You see only your e-mail and your contacts, so it's as though you are the only one using the mail client.

NOTE *Outlook Express provides only a moderate amount of security. You can require that different people log on to Outlook Express with a password, but your private folders are not really protected from someone who wants to snoop through them. Outlook Express provides identities for a multi-user computer, primarily for home users where family members are not likely to spy on each other's e-mail activity.*

Create an Identity

By default, Outlook Express creates the first identity for you, called Main Identity. If you are the only person using Outlook Express, you are the Main Identity and you don't need to configure anything else. However, if you want additional people to be able to use Outlook Express, you need to create identities for them. Creating and managing identities is very easy. To create a new identity, follow these steps:

1. In Outlook Express, choose File | Identities | Add New Identity.
2. In the New Identity dialog box, enter the name of the new identity.
3. If you want the new identity to have to log on to Outlook Express using a password, select the Require a Password check box, and then enter the password in the dialog box that appears.
4. Click OK when you've finished.

Manage Identities

Once you have created the identities for Outlook Express, you can switch among them at any time. For example, let's say that my wife wants to use Outlook Express to check her e-mail. She can simply open Outlook Express and then choose File | Switch Identity. The Switch Identities dialog box appears, and she selects her name from the list, enters a password if one is required, and clicks OK. The Outlook folders will change to her folders, and she is all set to check her mail, send mail, create message rules, or do whatever else she needs to do.

In addition to adding identities and switching identities, you can easily manage them by choosing File | Identities | Manage Identities. This option opens the window shown in Figure 10-6, where you can add or delete identities and change passwords as needed. On this window, you can also choose a default identity, which Outlook Express opens to each time it is started. By default, the Main Identity is used each time Outlook Express is started, but you can change this setting by using the drop-down menu.

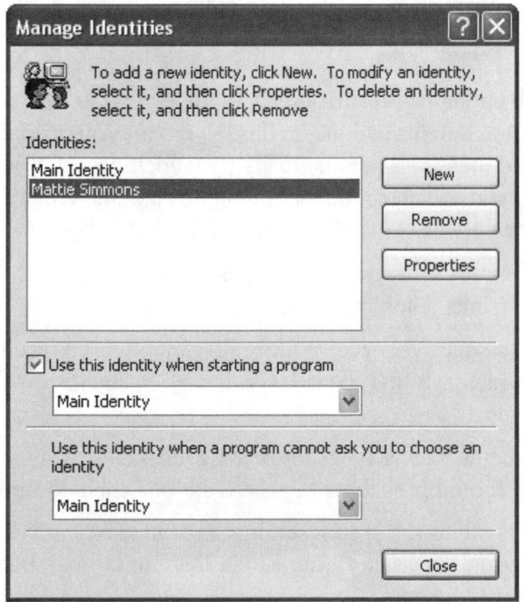

FIGURE 10-6 Manage Identities

Manage Your Accounts

When you first begin using Outlook Express, you set up an account so that your computer can send and receive e-mail to and from your ISP. Over time, that account information may change, or you may need to add other accounts. You can make changes to your accounts by choosing Tools | Accounts. This action opens a window where you can view your current mail account, news account, or even directory service account. Use the provided buttons to create a new account, edit an existing one, and perform other related account-management tasks. Before making changes to an account or creating a new one, remember that you will need information from your ISP for the correct username, password, and e-mail server information.

Customize Outlook Express

Outlook Express contains quite a few customization options that you can access by choosing Tools | Options. You'll see several tabs, but the good news is that each tab is rather easy to use. Most present a list of check box options you can choose from. The following list gives you an overview of what you can do on each tab. Remember that you can try different settings and change them later if you don't like them, and one of the best ways to find the settings that work for you is to experiment.

- **General** This tab contains information about the way your computer receives messages. Most of the default options on this tab are all you need. If you want Outlook Express to check for messages automatically by launching a dial-up connection at specified intervals, you can select the option on this tab and enter the amount of time you want to pass between checks (such as 30 minutes or so).
- **Read** This tab contains settings for messages you have received. You can choose to view messages in various colors and fonts.
- **Receipts** Some messages you receive (or send) can request a receipt—a return e-mail notification that the message was opened. Use the tab to enable this feature and determine how it should be used.
- **Send** This tab contains basic settings for sending messages. Almost all options are enabled by default, and you should probably keep these options enabled for the best functionality.
- **Compose** Use this tab to select font settings and business card settings and to attach stationery to your e-mail messages. Remember that not all mail clients can read these style features.
- **Signatures** You can automatically add a signature—such as your name and phone number—to all new messages you type. Use this tab to enter the text you want for the signature.
- **Spelling** Use this tab to enable automatic spelling and spell settings.

- **Security** If you want to use encrypted mail with digital certificates (which you probably won't), use this tab to enable the option.
- **Connection** This tab contains information about your dial-up connection. One item of interest here is that you can tell Outlook Express to hang up the dial-up connection automatically once mail has been sent and received. If you use the General tab to dial a connection automatically to get mail, you should use this option on the Connection tab so those dial-out sessions will be terminated automatically (unless you want your computer tying up the phone line all day).
- **Maintenance** This tab contains options for Outlook Express to handle deleted items. The default settings are all you need here.

Use the Address Book

A great feature of Outlook Express is the Address Book. You can use the Address Book to store e-mail addresses as well as postal addresses, phone numbers, and all kinds of other information. The Address Book is fully searchable and easy to use.

You can access the Address Book by clicking the Addresses icon on the Outlook Express toolbar. The Address Book provides you with a simple interface list of your contacts or groups, as shown in Figure 10-7.

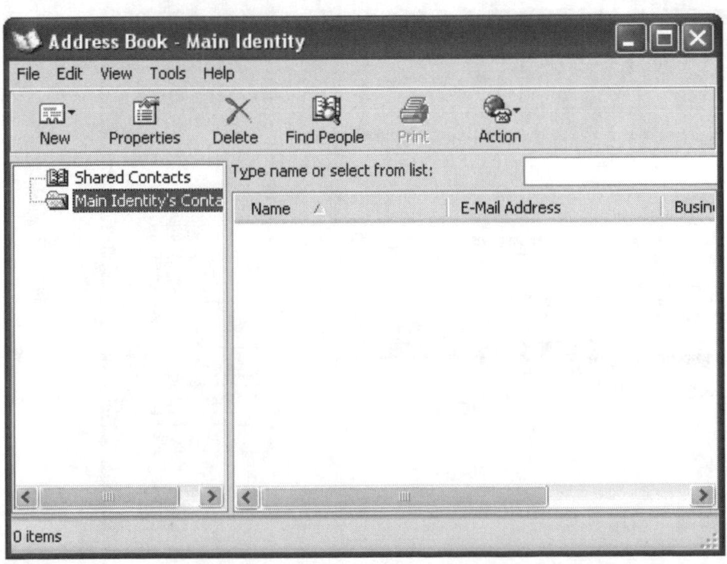

FIGURE 10-7 Address Book

Add a Contact

You can easily add a contact to the Address Book by clicking the New button on the Address Book toolbar and clicking New Contact. A window appears, shown in Figure 10-8, where you can enter the contact's information. Notice that several tabs appear, where you can enter all kinds of information. You need to complete only the tabs you want—you can enter very little or a lot of information about each contact. When you have entered all of the desired information, click OK. The new contact will be added to your Address Book.

You can use the same New button to create a group. You can use the group feature to group your contacts as needed. Many users create a Distribution List of people to which they can send particular types of e-mail. When you want to send the group a message, enter the group name on the To line of your new message, and everyone in the group will receive the e-mail. If you e-mail the same messages to a lot of people, this feature can make your life much easier.

Manage Addresses

As you can see, you can easily manage your Address Book by using the buttons on the toolbar. You can add new contacts or groups at any time, delete contacts or groups, launch a mail message from the Address Book, find contacts, and print the list. If you need to change a contact's information, select the contact in the list and click Properties. You can then make changes as needed. All of these features are quick and easy.

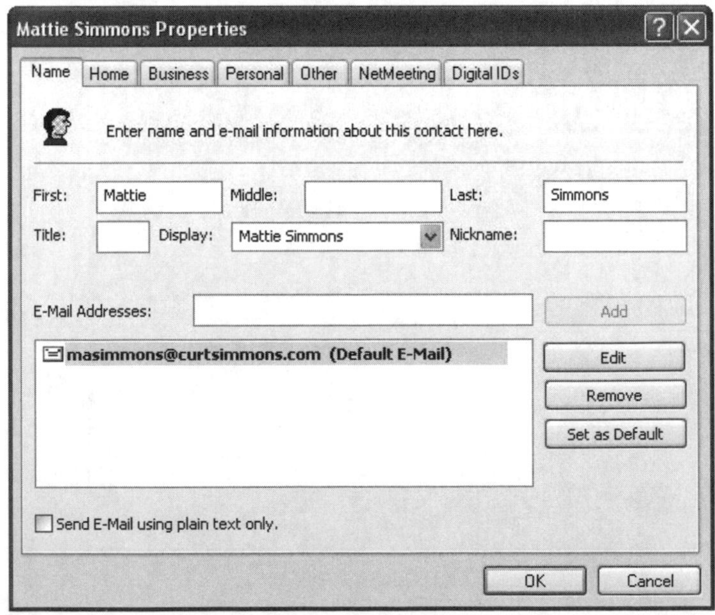

FIGURE 10-8 Create a new contact

Manage Address Book Identities

As I noted in the "Use Identities" section, the Address Book is tied to your particular e-mail identity. When you log on to Outlook Express with a particular identity, your Address Book is set up for you. In actuality, the Address Book gives you a folder where all of your contacts and groups are stored and not mixed up with other users' contacts and identities. This feature is useful and does not require any additional configuration from you—Outlook Express handles it automatically.

However, what if you want to switch identities while using the Address Book? Although you can't directly switch identities from within the Address Book while working in Outlook Express, you can do so if you access the Address Book from the Accessories menu on the Start menu. Choose Start | All Programs | Accessories | Address Book. The same Address Book opens, but if you open the File menu, you'll see the option for switching identities (which does not appear if you access the Address Book within Outlook Express).

Now you might wonder: why go to all of this trouble? The answer is simple. If you are using Windows XP and you need to reference an e-mail address, the Address Book is provided in Accessories so that you do not have to open Outlook Express to access it. The identity-switching option is provided in Address Book so that if you are logged on to Outlook Express with one identity, but need to access the Address Book using another, you don't have to wade through Outlook Express to switch identities first. In short, this option is provided to speed up your work and to make your life easier.

Chapter 11

Create a Home Network

How to...

- Plan a home network
- Create your home network
- Use Internet Connection Sharing
- Use My Network Places
- Use a direct cable connection
- Create a wireless network
- Use Windows XP Professional on a large network

Windows XP gives you plenty of home networking options. In fact, home networking in Windows XP has never been easier. If you are interested in networking two or more home computers (or computers in a small office), this chapter is just for you. Let's get our feet wet by talking about home networks and small office networks, and then you'll see what Windows XP offers to make networking easy.

Windows Networking Basics

Before you jump into the home-networking arena, you need to know a few basics about what it takes to create a wired home network. Networks, on a simple level, require both hardware and software to allow one computer to communicate with another computer. First, computers have to be equipped with a network adapter card, and they come in several forms. Most are internal cards that fit into an expansion slot on your computer, similar to sound and video cards. Network adapter cards can also be built into the motherboard, or they can function as separate USB devices. The network adapter card enables information to flow to and from your computer. A special connection, usually an RJ-45 connection (which looks like a large telephone cable), connects to the network adapter card. The cables from all of the computers connect through a device called a *hub*—a small piece of hardware with several places to plug in RJ-45 connectors. The hub routes information to and from computers so that the information travels to the appropriate computer.

Now if all that sounds a little overwhelming, don't worry, because other alternatives are available. With the growth of home networking, a number of solutions are available where cabling and a hub are not needed. For example, you can purchase network adapter cards that plug into your phone jacks. The computers use the existing phone wiring in your house to communicate with each other at no expense and interruption to you. Some versions also use power outlets, and you can easily create a wireless network (which we'll talk about later in this chapter) so your PCs and peripherals can communicate with each other. The key is to shop around and find a solution (and dollar amount) that works best for you. And you can always use standard networking cabling and hubs (as I do), which are not terribly expensive.

Many computers come equipped with a standard network adapter when you purchase them. Most new laptops even ship with a wireless network adapter. Check your computer documentation to find out what's included.

In addition to the hardware needs, your Windows XP software must also be configured for networking. This includes turning on Microsoft File and Printer Sharing and configuring the TCP/IP protocol so that computers can understand each other. Fortunately, in Windows XP, you get setup help from the new Network Setup Wizard, which we'll explore later in this chapter.

Plan Your Home Network

Before you try to configure your Windows XP computer for networking, you need to complete a few tasks to make sure your home-networking experience will be a positive one. I've arranged these tasks into a quick and easy, step-by-step format, so make sure you perform these before moving on to the next section in this chapter.

1. If you have only one Windows XP computer, it needs to be the primary computer. For example, if your computer is using Windows XP and another computer uses Windows 95/98 or Me, Windows XP will be the primary computer on your network. Shared peripherals, such as a printer or scanner, should be connected to the Windows XP computer. If you want to share one Internet connection, it should be on the Windows XP computer (especially if you are using a broadband solution, such as DSL)—although this is not a mandatory requirement, it does make the entire process a lot easier. Of course, if you have multiple peripherals, other computers can share those; just remember that Windows XP will be your primary, or server, machine for your home network.
2. Make a list of all the hardware you will need. Inspect your computers to determine whether you have available expansion slots or whether some computers already have a network adapter card. You'll need to determine what kind of network you want (whether to use typical wiring or phone wire, for instance). You can learn more about the different kinds of networks on the Web or from your local computer store. Keep in mind that some solutions provide faster network transfer speeds. If your budget allows it, always go for the fastest solution you can obtain. Also, many home-networking hardware components are sold as a single kit with a single instruction list. These kits are great solutions, as they make certain you have everything you need. Check out your favorite computer store for details.

NOTE

Your computer has different kinds of expansion slots. The most common type used for a network adapter card are PCI and PC Cards for laptops (although you can use USB in some cases). More than likely, you will have available PCI slots, so you'll want to buy a PCI network adapter. Consult your computer documentation for more information.

3. Once you determine which type of network you will use, buy the required hardware devices and install them. Follow the manufacturer's guidelines during the installation process.

CAUTION

Your computer must be powered down and unplugged from its outlet before you install a network adapter. See Chapter 6 for more information about managing hardware.

4. Check to make sure your computers and peripherals are connected together correctly, and check your Internet connection as well. Access the Windows XP Help files and search under "home networking" for more information.

Understand Internet Connection Sharing

Internet Connection Sharing (ICS), first introduced with Windows 98, enables you to have one computer connected to the Internet and all other computers on the network share the Internet connection. This feature is specifically designed for home networks or small office networks with 10 or fewer computers. Why is ICS so helpful? With ICS, you need only one Internet connection and one piece of hardware—each computer does not need its own modem or broadband hardware (such as a cable modem or DSL connection). Through sharing, you save money and aggravation because you don't have to configure each computer for Internet use.

While you are designing your home network, you need to decide whether you want to use ICS. On a practical note, ICS is designed for use with broadband Internet access (such as DSL, cable, or satellite). Although you can use ICS with a 56K modem, your modem will operate very slowly if several people are trying to use the Internet connection at the same time. (This effect results from the 56K modem's lack of sufficient bandwidth to perform at a desirable speed.) However, if users on your network do not access the Internet at the same time, the 56K modem's shared connection will probably be fine.

When you use ICS, your Windows XP computer should be the ICS *host*. Note that you don't have to use the Windows XP computer as the host—you can use a different computer, such as a Windows Me computer, but you will have fewer operational problems if the XP computer is the ICS host. All other computers on your network, called ICS *clients,* access the host to gain access to the Internet. Therefore, all Internet communications flow from your home network to the host computer and then to the Internet, and vice versa. Using this setup, your host computer has a connection to the Internet and a connection to your home network. All the client computers need only a network adapter so they can connect to the host (however, versions of Windows earlier than 95 need not apply). As far as the Internet is concerned, it appears as though only one computer is accessing the Internet.

NOTE

ICS does not work with some versions of American Online (AOL). Check with AOL to see whether your version is supported. It is also possible, although unlikely, that your ISP will charge you for multiple computer connections to the Internet. Check with your ISP to make certain you will not receive additional charges (and if you do, I would suggest you shop elsewhere).

Use the Network Setup Wizard

Once you have connected all of your hardware and your computers are connected to each other, you can run the Network Setup Wizard to set up home networking on your computers. (The Network Setup Wizard is supported only on computers using Windows 98, Windows Me, or Windows XP.) The following steps walk you through the Network Setup Wizard.

NOTE *You may have a custom setup CD-ROM, especially if you purchased a home networking kit. Refer to the kit's documentation about setup, but if you have a custom CD-ROM for the kit you purchased, you need to use the kit's setup program instead of the Home Networking Wizard.*

1. Turn on all computers on your home network so they are booted and operational.
2. On your Windows XP computer, choose Start | All Programs | Accessories | Communications | Network Setup Wizard.
3. Read the information on the Welcome screen and click Next.
4. The next window gives you more information about home networking. Make sure you have completed the preparation tasks listed, and then click Next.
5. The Select a Connection Method window appears, as shown in Figure 11-1. Essentially, the radio button options here ask you to describe how the XP computer connects to the Internet. (I assume that the XP computers connect to the Internet, and the other computers on your network will connect to the XP computer.) Select the desired radio button, and then click Next.

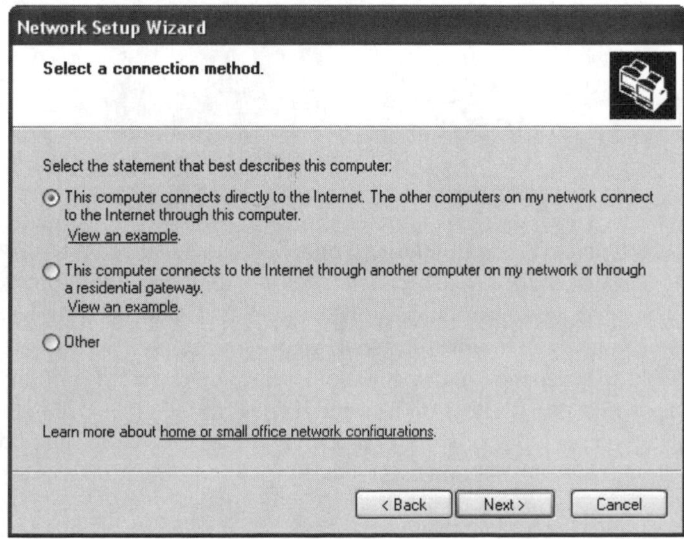

FIGURE 11-1 Select a Connection Method window

6. The Internet Connection window appears. In the box listing all entries in your Network Connections folder, select your connection to the Internet; then click Next.
7. If you're using a dial-up connection, the wizard will prompt you to dial a connection to the Internet.
8. In the provided window, enter a description for your computer and a computer name. Take note that if you are using a cable broadband connection to the Internet, you should probably not change the name of your computer, because the Internet Service Provider (ISP) may require that you use a certain name.
9. Review the changes that will be made to your computer and click Next. Windows XP automatically configures all of your computer's software and hardware components for networking, according to the selections you made so far.
10. Click Finish. You will need to restart the computer for the new changes to take effect.

Once you have run the Home Networking Wizard on the XP computer, you need to run the wizard on each computer that you want to include in the home network. You can use your Windows XP CD-ROM to run the Home Networking Wizard on those computers. You can find and start the wizard on the opening screen of the Windows CD-ROM.

So what do you do if you have problems connecting the computers together? Or what if you are really curious and want to know what the Home Networking Wizard did to your computer? For either situation, check out the properties of your local area connection, which are found in the Network Connections folder on the Control Panel. Right-click the Local Area connection, and you will see a General tab in the Local Area Connection Properties window (see Figure 11-2). Make sure that Client for Microsoft Networks, File and Printer Sharing for Microsoft Networks, and Internet Protocol (TCP/IP) are all selected—do *not* unselect them!

Did you know?

What TCP/IP Is

TCP/IP (Transmission Control Protocol/Internet Protocol) is an advanced topic and one that gives even network administrators severe headaches from time to time. Fortunately, Windows operating systems have evolved to help humans deal with TCP/IP. In a TCP/IP network, each computer must have a unique IP (Internet Protocol) address, which is a series of numbers, such as 131.107.2.200. In order for computers to communicate, you must configure each computer with an appropriate IP address in the same IP class as the other computers. Actually, it's all more complicated than this, but you can probably realize that having Windows XP set this up for you is a great help. Windows XP, like Windows 98/Me/2000, can give itself a private IP address in an appropriate range reserved for small networks. Windows XP does all the work, so you don't have to do anything—which is really nice!

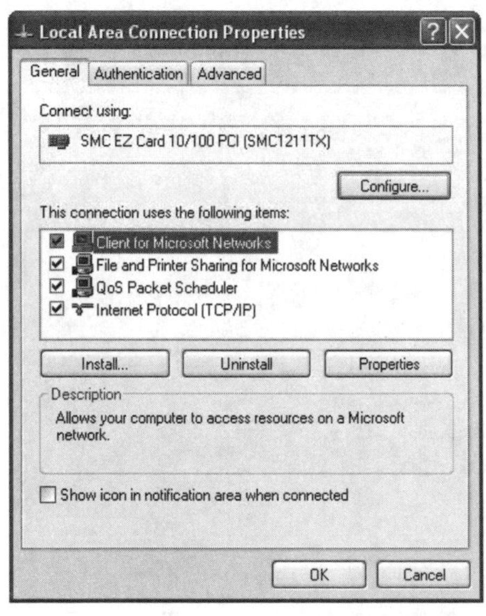

FIGURE 11-2 Local Area Connection Properties

Essentially, the communications protocol (TCP/IP) is configured so that your computer can talk with other computers, and the File and Printer Sharing software is configured so that your computer can function on a Microsoft network with other Windows operating systems. The computers on the network can share folders, printers, drives, and just about anything else. Just right-click the item you want to share and choose Sharing to configure it. See Chapter 4 for more information about sharing folders.

If you select Internet Protocol (TCP/IP) and click Properties, you will see that the Home Networking Wizard has assigned your computer an IP address and a subnet mask value, as shown in Figure 11-3. I won't go into the intricacies of TCP/IP here, but I would bet your IP address is something like 192.168.0.1. If you are having problems connecting another computer on your network to the XP computer, try adjusting the problematic computer's IP address. For example, you might want to give the other computer an IP address of 192.168.0.2 (or .3, or .4, or whatever). Just give the computer the same IP address as the XP computer with the exception of the last number (all IP addresses have to be unique—you can't give two computers exactly the same IP address). Use the same subnet mask on each computer (computers cannot see each other if different subnet masks are used). Click OK; make sure Client for Microsoft Networks and File and Printer Sharing for Microsoft Networks are enabled, and then click OK to exit the properties pages. After rebooting, the computer should now be able to share information. Again, if everything works according to plan, you will not have to make changes to any of these settings yourself—the Home Networking Wizard should take care of it for you.

Once you have run the Home Networking Wizard on your computers or have fooled around with the local area connection settings manually, you can open My Network Places and see the other computers that are available on your network.

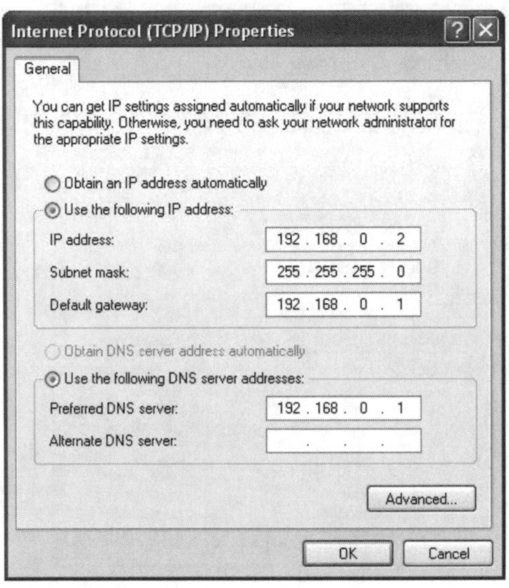

FIGURE 11-3 IP address and subnet mask values

If you want a quick and easy way to see the status of your connection and find out about your IP address, you can go back to the Network Connections folder and double-click your connection. You'll see a General tab, shown in Figure 11-4, that shows you whether you are connected and, if so, the duration and the speed of the connection. Click the Support tab to find your IP address and other addressing information.

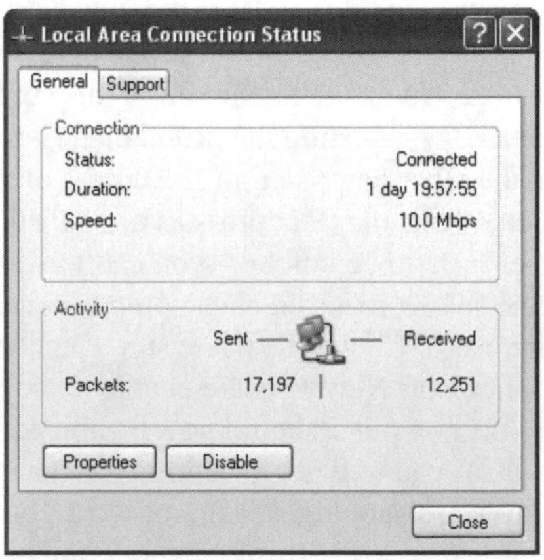

FIGURE 11-4 General tab

Set Up Your ICS Clients

If you decided to use ICS, you now have an ICS host and ICS client(s). In order for your client computers to access the ICS host, you need to tell Internet Explorer, Outlook Express, and any other applications that use the Internet how to access the Internet through the ICS host. Without this configuration, your applications will think your computer has a direct connection to the Internet. This configuration is easy, and this section shows you how to make the change with Internet Explorer and Outlook Express. If you are using other browsers, e-mail clients, or applications, consult their documentation for specific steps—it will be very similar to what you learn here.

Internet Explorer

To configure Internet Explorer to access the Internet through the ICS host, follow these easy steps:

1. Open Internet Explorer. If you get an error message about connecting to the Internet, click OK.
2. Choose Tools | Internet Options. Click the Connections tab.
3. On the Connections tab, select any existing dial-up connections in the window and click Remove.
4. Because you have configured your computer for ICS with a host computer during the Home Networking Wizard, your computer should use the default LAN setting to find the shared connection.

Outlook Express

To configure Outlook Express to access the Internet through the ICS host, you do not need to perform any configuration if you configured Internet Explorer. Outlook Express uses the connection settings Internet Explorer uses, so you don't need to do anything with Outlook Express.

Use My Network Places

My Network Places is an icon on your Desktop that you can click to browse your network. With this feature, you can see all the computers on your network, and you can see what resources each computer shares. You can also right-click My Network Places on your Start menu and click Properties to see the specific network configuration, which is the same thing as opening the Network Connections folder.

When you open My Network Places, you will see a number of items (exactly what you see will depend on your network). You can open Entire Network to see all of the computers on your network. You can double-click a computer icon to view the resources available. Any resources you access will show up in this folder for easy future access, and the Home Networking Wizard is also available from this location.

One item here you may find very useful is the Add Network Place Wizard, which appears as a Create a Network Shortcut action link in the Network Tasks section of the folder. The Add Network Place Wizard lets you easily add a folder to My Network Places for a network resource. This way, you can easily access the resource in the future just by opening My Network Places. To add a network place, follow these easy steps:

1. Click the Create a Network Shortcut icon in the Network Tasks box.
2. Click Next on the Welcome screen of the Add Network Place Wizard.
3. Select another network location or MSN to store Web data, and click Next.
4. If you want to connect to a network folder, a browse window appears where you can locate it. Locate the folder that you want and select it; then click OK.
5. Enter a desired name for the network place (make it a friendly name so you can easily locate it).
6. Click Finish to save the network place.

Create a Direct Cable Connection

Consider this scenario: Let's say you have a PC at home and a laptop computer at work. From time to time, you want to transfer files from the laptop to the PC, but you do not want the trouble and expense of setting up a home network just for these file transfers. You could e-mail the files to yourself and download them from home, but the files are multimedia files and you have only a 56K modem—downloading would make you old before your time. Now what?

The solution to this problem is quite easy—you can use a direct cable connection between the two computers to move the files. Windows XP makes this option very easy, too, because its own direct cable connection is available. To create a direct cable connection, you need a serial or parallel cable that you can use to connect the two computers together (a printer cable usually works, but it may not work well). Once you have your cable ready, follow these steps:

1. Open the Network Connections folder and click the Make New Connection icon.
2. Click Next on the Welcome screen.
3. In the Network Connection Type window, select Set Up an Advanced Connection and click Next.
4. In the Select the Type of Connection You Want window, you can choose either to accept incoming connections, which allows the other direct cable connection computer to connect to you, or to connect to another computer. Since you are setting up this computer to be the host, click Accept Incoming Connections, and then click Next.
5. In the Devices for Incoming Connections window, select the cable method that you want, such as your printer cable or LPT1, and then click Next.

6. You see a window asking whether you want to allow VPN connections. Click the Do Not Allow Virtual Private Connections radio button; then click Next. You can learn more about VPN connections in the "Virtual Private Networking" section later in this chapter.
7. In the User Permissions window, select the check boxes next to the users who are allowed to connect to your computer, and then click Next. See Chapter 12 to learn more about user accounts.
8. The Networking Software window appears. Accept the default selections and click Next.
9. Click Finish to create the connection.

NOTE *You must use the same port on both the host and guest. In other words, you can't use a parallel port on one and a serial port on the other.*

The host computer is now set up. Next, go to the guest computer and repeat these same steps—just select the Connect Directly to Another Computer option on the first page. After you set up the guest computer, you can move files between the computers through the connection.

TIP *You can actually configure both the host and guest as direct cable connection computers by selecting the Connect Directly to Another Computer radio button. The next screen asks you to select either host or guest. You may find using this route quicker and easier.*

Set Up a Wireless Network

Wireless networking has become very popular over the past few years for the home and small office user, and rightly so. After all, it lets you create a network without needing to connect a bunch of cables. If you have a laptop computer, you can freely move around your home or office and stay connected to the network without being tied down (literally!).

If you visit your local computer store, you'll find all kinds of home-networking cards, access points, routers, and other hardware provided by a variety of vendors. You'll even find wireless home-networking kits that are designed to get you started. As you are thinking about creating a wireless network, here are a few pointers to keep in mind:

- Wireless networks require use of a device that is similar to a hub, called an *access point*. Most access points are set up so you can connect a cable or DSL Internet connection directly to them for Internet sharing. While you can directly connect wireless computers using a method known as Ad Hoc, you'll probably be happier purchasing the access point.
- If you buy an access point and wireless network cards for your computers, it is best to use the same brand for both. Although all wireless networking components work on a standard (so that they *should* work well together), you are less likely to have problems if you stick with the same manufacturer.
- It is best to follow the manufacturer's setup instructions exactly. Wireless networks require that all wireless cards use the same channel and security key, so if you follow the manufacturer's installation and setup instructions, you are less likely to have problems.

Once you install a wireless network card on your Windows XP computer, you'll see a Wireless Network Setup Wizard in Control Panel. However, once again, it is best to use the manufacturer's setup software and instructions. Once the wireless network is configured, you can view the properties of the connection and adjust them as necessary using the wireless network connection in the Network Connections folder.

You should be able to get help from the wireless networking manufacturer's Web site and, most likely, a toll-free help line. Do not call Microsoft for support since you are using hardware and software created by another company. If you're having problems, though, don't hesitate to call the manufacturer for assistance.

Use Windows XP Professional on a Large Network

It's no secret that Windows XP is designed for high efficiency and operability in a Microsoft Windows XP or 2000 network. Windows XP Professional is designed to take full advantage of all that Windows networking has to offer. You don't have to be a networking guru to understand this fact, and if you do work with Windows XP Professional in a Microsoft network, you might hear some of these buzz words from time to time:

- **Web integration** Windows XP is designed to use the Internet or an intranet without any difficulty. In fact, using the Windows XP default view, your computer acts more like a Web page anyway. When you jump to the Internet or an intranet, the information you see integrates with your folder views, so that your XP computer appears to be one with the Internet. With easy Web integration, networks can disseminate information to their employees more easily, and you can get what you need from the network more easily.
- **Active Directory** Active Directory is a powerful Microsoft networking feature that enables administrators to organize and manage a highly effective and very large network. The benefit of Active Directory from your point of view is *simplicity.* Using My Network Places, you can easily search your network and find what you need, and then you can create a network place so that it appears right on your computer. Active Directory allows querying for all kinds of resources. For example, you can search for printers and find all of the printers in your network, or even just those in your department. Windows XP makes full use of Active Directory.
- **Group Policy** Group Policy is a feature that network administrators use to manage user Desktops. Simply put, Group Policy lets administrators control the way your computer looks and what you can do with your computer. First introduced in Windows 2000, Group Policy is a powerful tool that allows administrators to configure your computer without any help from you and even to install software without your intervention. On the down side, Group Policy allows network administrators to place restrictions on what you can and cannot do as well. The good news is that Group Policy is highly effective and makes computer environments easier to manage. Windows XP takes full advantage of Group Policy in Windows 2000 networks.

Did you know?

About Group Policy

In Microsoft networks using Windows 2000 or Windows XP Professional, Group Policy is a total network solution that allows network administrators to create standards, manage users, and manage software effectively and easily. Different Group Policy configurations can be used for different areas of a company and even for different departments, depending on Active Directory organization. Without your help or even your knowledge, your XP computer can be configured and updated, software can be installed and removed, and even Internet settings can be configured. All of this occurs over the network based on the Group Policy configuration set by network administrators. It is a total package and provides hands-off computing for you. You get to focus on your job, and your Desktop and network administrators get to handle everything else!

- **Security** In network environments, security is always a major concern. After all, you do not want intruders to gain access to computer data and steal company secrets. Windows XP Professional provides the highest industry standards for security, and in a network environment, Windows XP Professional can easily be configured to use the security standards that are in place for that network.

Virtual Private Networking

Virtual Private Networking (VPN) has been around for a few years, but it has recently become very popular. As a home user, you are probably not going to use a virtual private network, but it *is* possible, and if you are a part of a small office, you may find VPN quite helpful. If you are in a larger network, you may use a Windows XP laptop computer to connect to your corporate network using a VPN connection.

VPN enables Windows XP to create a private networking session using a public network. For example, let's say you work for a company based in Seattle. You travel to Atlanta for a conference. While you are in Atlanta, you want to access your company's network over the Internet. To ensure privacy, you can use a VPN connection. Or, what if your company has an intranet and you need to send very private files to another employee? You can create a virtual private network over the intranet for the file transfer.

NOTE *Your private network must support VPN in order for it to work. Also, if your network uses an ISP to access the Internet, it must support VPN as well.*

Configure Your Windows XP Computer for a VPN Connection

When you're ready to create the VPN connection on your computer, refer to the following steps:

1. Choose Start | Control Panel | Network Connections.
2. Double-click the Make New Connection Wizard, and then click Next on the Welcome screen.
3. In the Network Connection Type window, click the Connect to the Network at My Workplace radio button, and then click Next.
4. In the Network Connection window, click the Virtual Private Network Connection radio button. Then click Next.
5. In the Public Network window, select whether you want to dial the connection automatically, and specify the connection you want to use. Click Next.
6. In the VPN Server Selection window, enter the hostname of the computer you are dialing into or the IP address.
7. In the Default Connection window, you can choose to make this connection your default connection, and you can enter a username and password if they are required by the computer into which you are dialing. Click Next.
8. Click Finish.

Allow Other Computers to Connect to Your Computer

If you want to allow other computers to connect to your Windows XP computer, once again you can use the Make New Connection Wizard to configure your computer for incoming connections. To configure your computer for incoming connections, follow these steps:

1. Choose Start | Network Connections.
2. In the Network Connections window, double-click the Make New Connection icon and click Next on the Welcome screen.
3. In the Network Connection Type window, click the Set Up an Advanced Connection radio button, and then click Next.
4. In the Options window, click the Accept Incoming Connections radio button, and then click Next.
5. In the Devices for Incoming Connections window, select the check box next to the device that you want to use to receive incoming connections (such as your modem). Click Next.
6. In the VPN window, you can choose whether to allow VPN connections to this computer. Click either the Allow or Do Not Allow radio button, and then click Next.
7. The User Permissions window appears. Select the users who are allowed to dial in via this connection, and then click Next.

Did you know?

How VPN Works

VPN uses a protocol called Point-to-Point Tunneling Protocol (PPTP). To send private communications over the Internet to and from a corporate network, PPTP hides the data you are sending inside a *PPTP packet*. A PPTP packet looks and acts like all of the traffic on the Internet, but it actually hides the real network data inside. Think of a PPTP packet as a Christmas present; the wrappings and paper hide what is inside the box. The PPTP packet allows the data to traverse the Internet unharmed. When it reaches the private network, the PPTP wrapping is stripped away, revealing the real data hidden inside. To use PPTP, both your private network and your ISP must support VPN. Windows XP also supports a new, more secure version of PPTP called Layer 2 Tunneling Protocol (L2TP). (This information may not be that useful to you, but you will sound cool throwing around these terms at the company water cooler.)

8. In the Networking Software window, you can choose the networking software that will be used. Typically, TCP/IP, File and Printer Sharing for Microsoft Networks, and Client for Microsoft Networks are selected. Click Next.
9. Click Finish.

Chapter 12

Manage Users and Groups

How to...

- Understand XP permissions
- Manage and configure user accounts
- Manage and configure group accounts

Windows XP is designed to be a highly stable, highly secure desktop operating system for the home or office user. With Windows XP, you can easily allow other people to use your computer while preserving your personal settings and files. As far as users are concerned, each user can log in and log out of Windows XP and use the computer as if it were his or her own PC. For both the home and the office user, this feature has far-reaching advantages. Managing permissions, users, and groups is not a difficult task, but you must keep in mind a number of concepts when working with these features of Windows XP. In this chapter, you will explore setting permissions and managing and configuring user and group accounts.

Understand User Accounts

When Windows XP is first installed, two default accounts are created: administrator and guest. The *administrator account* has control of the entire Windows XP computer—the administrator can perform tasks on the computer to make any changes he or she desires. The administrator account cannot be deleted or disabled, so you (as the administrator) could never lock yourself out of your own computer, unless of course you forgot your password.

The second default account, the *guest account,* is provided for users who do not actually have a user account on the computer. The guest account does not require a password, but it also has no permissions to make changes on the computer. The guest account is disabled by default, but it can be enabled if you need to use it.

Windows XP provides these two built-in accounts, but from there, the issue of accounts and account configuration is up to you. As you are reading this section, you may be wondering how accounts really affect you. If you are a home user and the Windows XP computer is your primary home computer, you may be logging in with the default administrator account all the time. This account gives you complete control over the system, and when I use Windows XP at home, that is what I do. In addition to the default accounts, user accounts can be created to meet the needs of an administrator. For example, at an office, you may have your own user account so that you can use your computer as needed, but you can't change anything on it. With your home computer, you can, for example, use the administrator account yourself and configure other, more restrictive accounts for your kids or others who borrow your PC. The choice is completely yours, and Windows XP makes user management easy.

Windows XP offers two types of user accounts. The first is the administrator account created by default. The administrator can make changes or perform a variety of tasks on the computer. The second type is the *limited account.* This account type is good for most other users. With the limited account, the user can change desktop images and related personal data, and create, change, or remove his or her own password. The limited account user can also view any files he or she created and view files in the Shared Documents folder. This account type is great for kids, because it prevents them from adding or removing programs or hardware from the computer (which may end up with you being on the phone with technical support).

NOTE *Rarely, games do not work well (or at all) under the limited user account. If you find that this is the case, you'll need to use an upgraded account to run the games.*

Manage User Accounts

You can easily manage user accounts from two different places within Windows XP—from the User Accounts icon in the Control Panel and from the Computer Management console. We will start with the User Accounts icon in the Control Panel. If you click the icon, the User Accounts window opens, which gives you an easy-to-use graphical interface, as you can see in Figure 12-1.

In the User Accounts window, you'll see some tasks that you can perform and the current accounts that exist on your computer. You can easily create new accounts or change existing accounts; the following sections show you how to perform these actions.

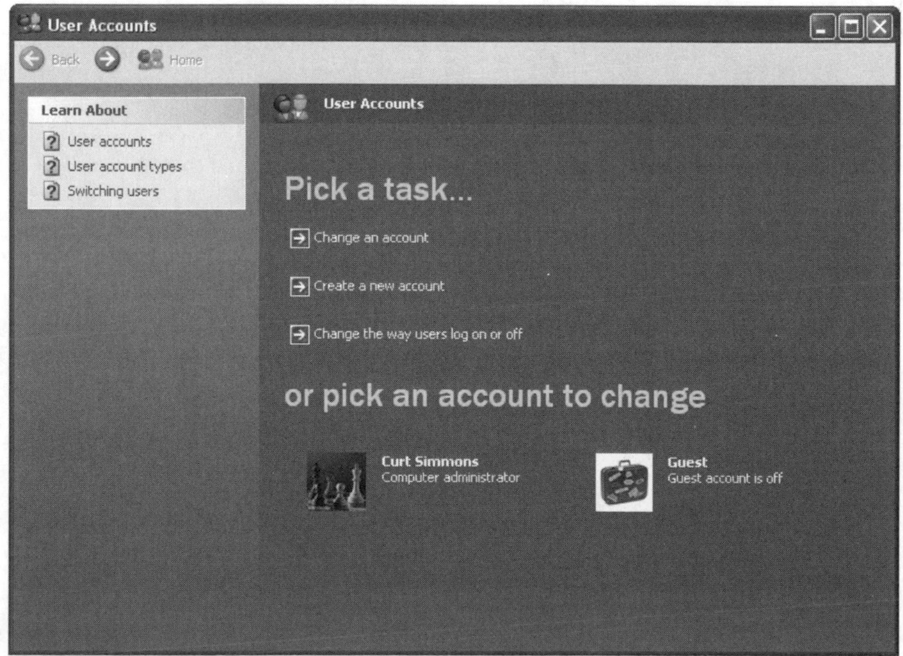

FIGURE 12-1 User Accounts window

12

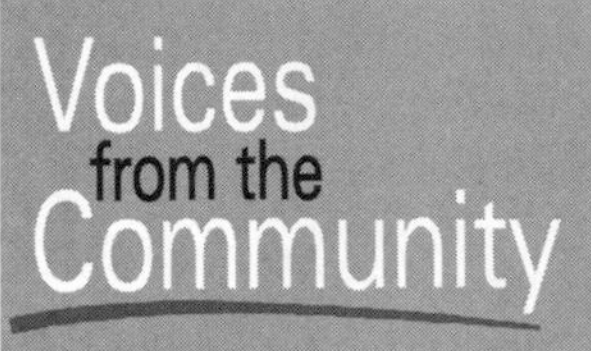

Create a Password Recovery Disk

Unlike Windows 9*x,* Windows XP is geared for use in a multi-user environment in an office or in a home setting. To keep individual user's information private, user accounts should be set up with each account given a unique password.

If you want some added safety in case you forget your password, you should create a password recovery disk. To do this, open the Control Panel and click User Accounts. Select the account for which you want to create a password recovery disk. From the Related Tasks list at the left, choose Prevent a Forgotten Password and follow the wizard's instructions to create the disk.

If you forget your password, click the green arrow on the Windows XP login screen, and you will see a link to use your password recovery disk. This will verify your access rights and prompt you to create a new password, which you can use to access your account. The new password is written to your recovery disk at the same time you create it.

If you upgraded to Windows XP from Windows NT or 2000, you will need to create new recovery disks. The old disks you created on the previous version will no longer work.

—Arie Slob
Vice President, Information Systems
helpwithwindows.com

Create a New Account

You can create new user accounts at any time, giving others access to your computer. To create a new user account, follow these steps:

1. If you want to create a new account, click the Create a New Account link in the User Accounts window.
2. A New Account Name window appears. Enter the desired name for this new account and click Next.
3. The next window asks you to pick an account type, as shown in Figure 12-2. Choose either Computer Administrator or Limited by selecting the appropriate radio button. If you're not sure, select each one and read the bulleted list of actions that can be performed by the account type.
4. When you've finished, click the Create Account button. The new account now appears in the User Accounts window.

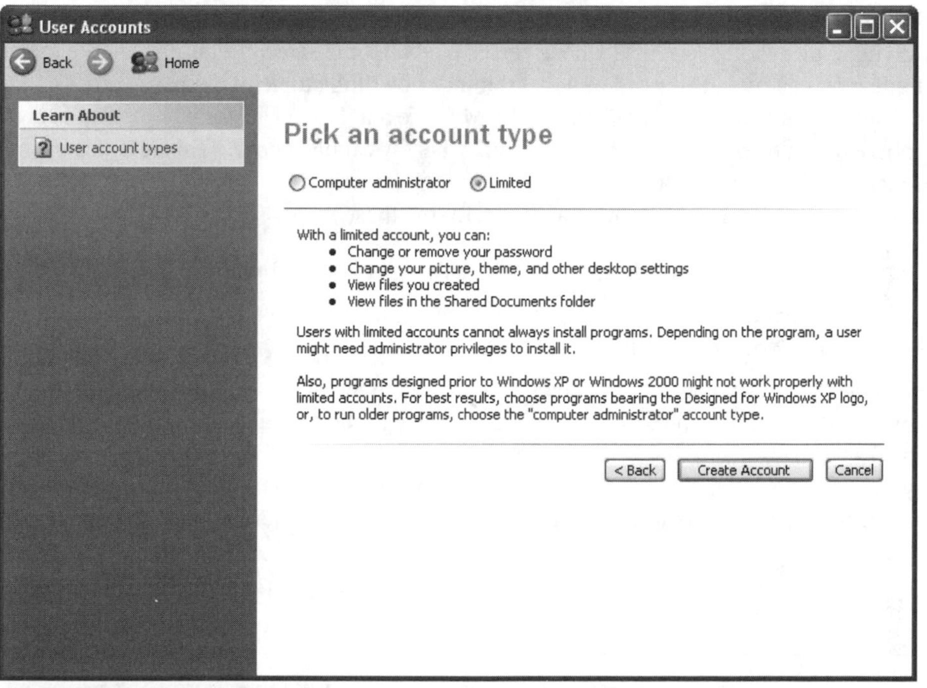

FIGURE 12-2 Pick an account type.

Change an Account

Any account that has been created can be easily edited or changed from the User Accounts window. You can edit the password or create a password for an account that must be entered before a user logs on to the computer. Passwords provide security and prevent unauthorized individuals from logging on to a computer using someone else's account. Depending on your needs, you may not want passwords attached to user accounts (such as for home use), but you should always keep the administrator account password-protected so that little Johnny doesn't decide to log on as you and remove all of your programs or delete your files!

In corporate environments, passwords are extremely important, and many highly secure environments go to great lengths to make sure passwords are so complex that they cannot be easily broken. You may not need to worry about such matters, but if you are going to use passwords to protect your computer, you should use a combination of letters and numbers for the password and it should be at least seven characters long. Also, passwords are case-sensitive—so, for example, Windows XP does not recognize *CURT345* as the same password as *Curt345*. For security purposes, it is always best to use a combination of letters (both uppercase and lowercase) and numbers. The more random a password looks, the more difficult it will be to break. Avoid using family names, pet names, phone numbers, birthdays, and other distinguishing words or numbers.

If you create passwords, Windows XP gives you the option of displaying a "password hint" that will appear on the Welcome screen. The purpose of the hint is to help you remember the password without giving it away to anyone else who accesses the Welcome screen (all users can see the hint). For example, you can use a password hint that reminds you of the topic of the password. On one of my XP computers, my password is *OldHOuse49*. My wife and I own a historic home that is always in some phase of remodeling, so for my hint, I put "where my money goes." This reminds me of my old house, and hence my password.

To make changes to an existing user account, follow these steps:

1. In the User Accounts window, click the Change an Account link.
2. A window appears, asking you to pick an account that you want to change. Click the account that you want to change.
3. Another window appears that allows you to change the name on the account, change the picture that appears on the Welcome screen, change the account type, create a password, or delete the account. Just select the option that you want and follow the instructions. As you can see, each user account is represented by an icon. If you click Change Picture, a window appears, as shown in Figure 12-3, where you can select a new picture or browse for a different one.

FIGURE 12-3 Change the picture.

Creating a Custom CD

Last year, I decided to give my eight-year-old daughter, Hannah, a unique Christmas present. Sure, I could have bought her any number of toys, but Hannah loves to dance, and she has a collection of songs she really loves to dance to on different CDs I previously purchased. The problem, of course, was each song was on a different CD, which made life really aggravating. So for Christmas, I decided to make a custom CD for Hannah. I used Windows Media Player to rip all of the songs she likes from her existing CDs, and then I created a playlist, burned the CD, and made a custom label for it. It was her favorite Christmas present that year and she still listens to the CD a year later.

In fact, custom CDs are great for a variety of purposes. They make great gifts for just about anyone. You can create a CD of favorite tunes for your parents' wedding anniversary, or you can create a CD of love songs for that special someone. You can make custom CDs of kids music, wedding music, party music, and the list goes on and on. My wife and I throw a big Christmas party each year, and we make custom CDs for that party so the music sets just the right mood.

In this special color section, I will show you how to create a custom CD. I'll walk you through the steps, giving you the necessary details, and when you're done, you'll have your own custom CD!

What You'll Need

To create your custom CD, you'll need a few items:

- A collection of songs that you want to rip
- Windows XP with Windows Media Player 10
- CD-R discs
- Microsoft Plus! Digital Media Edition or Microsoft Plus! SuperPack for Windows XP for creating CD and jewel case labels

NOTE

For information and to purchase Microsoft Plus! Digital Media Edition, go to http://www.microsoft.com/windows/plus/dme/dmehome.asp; for information and to purchase Microsoft Plus! SuperPack for Windows XP go to http://www.microsoft.com/windows/plus/PlusHome.asp. In addition to the label-making software, these packages include a bunch of other cool items.

- CD labels and, optionally, jewel case labels (with self-adhesive backs that stick to your media easily)

NOTE

You can find CD label packs at most computer and department stores (look in the section where CD-R discs are sold). The label-making software works with most major brands, such as A-1, APLI, Avery, Fellowes, Memorex, and more.

Get Ready to Rip Songs

Windows Media Player gives you everything you need to copy songs from various CDs, organize those songs, and then create your own CD using the songs you want. Before you get started, let's make sure you're up to speed with the current cool lingo: the process of copying a song from a CD to Windows Media Player is called *ripping,* while the process of creating your own CD is called *burning.* With Windows Media Player, you rip the songs you want to Media Player, organize them, and then burn them to your own CD, and viola—you now have a custom CD.

Before you begin, sit down with a piece of paper and list in order the songs you want to use on your personal CD. This way you'll have a working list to go by. Depending on the CD you are creating, think carefully about song order. If your CD includes both fast and slow songs, you may want to mix them up so not all slow songs are grouped together and not all fast songs are grouped together. Or, you may want to think in terms of a theme. Here are some examples:

- If you're making a CD of love songs for that special someone, consider putting songs in chronological order. For example, start with a few songs you both loved when you first met, followed by some songs important later in your relationship. If you have been with that special someone for years, you'll have a lot of material to choose from.
- If you are making a CD for a family member, such as a parent, brother, or sister, choose songs that represent different times of your life. For your brother or sister, you might want to include tunes you both loved as kids, and then some songs you listened to as adolescents, and finally some favorites from high school. This trip down memory lane is sure to be a hit!

- When your son or daughter graduates from high school, create a CD called "Songs of Your Life" and include toddler tunes, pre-adolescent tunes, and favorite teenager hits. Include music that has special family meaning or brings to mind certain family memories—this way they won't forget who you are when they go to college!

As you can see, you have lots to think about, which is why you always start with a piece of paper and construct your CD list before you begin. Once you're happy with your list, round up all of the CDs you'll need, and then you're ready to begin ripping those songs.

Rip Songs from a CD

First things first, you don't have to rip the songs in the order you want to burn them on your custom CD. You'll organize your songs later, so all you have to do right now is make sure you rip the songs you want. The following steps show you how to rip songs from a CD:

1. Connect to the Internet (you'll see why in a just a moment).
2. Open Windows Media Player.
3. Insert the CD from which you want to rip song(s) in your CD-ROM drive.
4. In Windows Media Player, click the Rip button on the Windows Media Player interface, as shown in Figure 1.
5. Notice the check box that appears next to each song. A check mark means Windows Media Player will copy the song. So, look at the CD song list and remove the check marks next to the songs you do not want to copy. As you can see here, I want to copy only three songs from this CD.

NOTE

If you're connected to the Internet, Media Player can find the names of the songs on the CD. If you don't see the song names here, just make sure you are connected to the Internet, and then click the Find Album Info button so Windows Media Player can gather the information.

6. Click the Rip Music button. Media Player begins ripping your selected songs. The songs copied to your computer will show up in your Media Library.

Repeat this process for each CD containing a song(s) you want to copy. Once you have copied all of your songs, go to Media Library. In Windows Media Player, click the Library button on the Media Player interface, and then expand All Music | Album, as shown in Figure 2. Click the CD title to see the copied songs. Now you're ready to organize them! The next section shows you how.

Windows Media Player

File View Play Tools Help

Now Playing | Library | Rip | Burn | Sync | Guide | Music | Radio | Movies & TV

Margaret Becker - Falling Forward | Rip Music | Find Album Info | View Album Info

	Title	Length	Rip Status	Artist	Composer	Genre	Style	Data Provider
1	I Don't Know How	5:20		Margaret Becker	Margaret Becker; Robbie Nevil	Religious		AMG
2	Cave It In	4:20		Margaret Becker	Byron Hagen; Margaret Becker; Quilan	Religious		AMG
3	Clay and Water	5:03		Margaret Becker	Margaret Becker; Tonya Leah	Religious		AMG
4	Horses	4:05		Margaret Becker	Brent Milligan; Dave Lichens; Margaret Becker; ...	Religious		AMG
5	Deliver Me	5:09		Margaret Becker	Margaret Becker; Robbie Nevil	Religious		AMG
6	Any Kind of Light	4:24		Margaret Becker	Margaret Becker; Robbie Nevil	Religious		AMG
7	Irish Sea	4:08		Margaret Becker	Margaret Becker; Tedd T.	Religious		AMG
8	Coins and Promises	5:11		Margaret Becker	Charles Garett; Margaret Becker; Quinlan	Religious		AMG
9	Crawl	3:05		Margaret Becker	Margaret Becker; Tedd T.	Religious		AMG
10	Take Me In	4:05		Margaret Becker	Margaret Becker	Religious		AMG
11	I Testify	3:41		Margaret Becker	Margaret Becker; Robbie Nevil	Religious		AMG

Figure 1. Click the Rip button to start the ripping process.

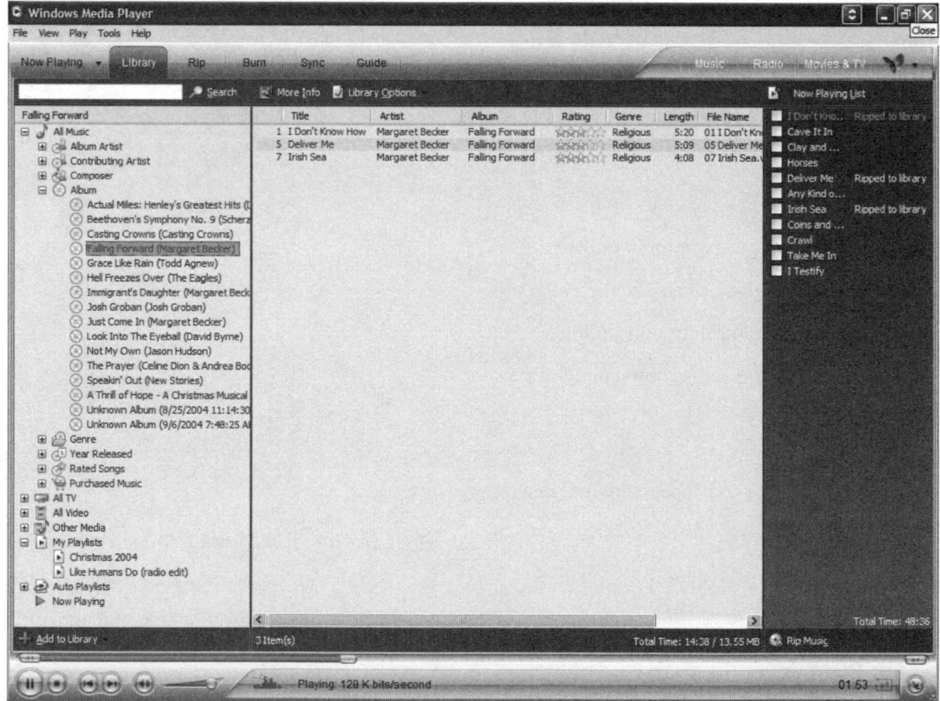

Figure 2. Your ripped music now appears in the Library.

Organize Your Songs into a Playlist

By creating a playlist, you can organize any collection of songs in Windows Media Player. A *playlist* is nothing more than a simple list of some songs you have selected in the Media Library. You can put any song in your Media Library on a playlist, organized in the order you want, and Media Player will store your custom playlist in the Media Library, just as it would albums, videos, or anything else you put there.

When you create a playlist, you decide which songs should go on the playlist and their order. You can then listen to that playlist anytime you like or you can burn the song list to a CD, creating your own custom CD. The good news is creating a playlist in Media Player is quite easy, so grab your song list for your custom CD and let's get started. The following steps show you how to create a playlist:

1. In Media Player, click the Library button to open the library.
2. In the Media Library, click the Lists button, then click New List | Playlist, as shown here.

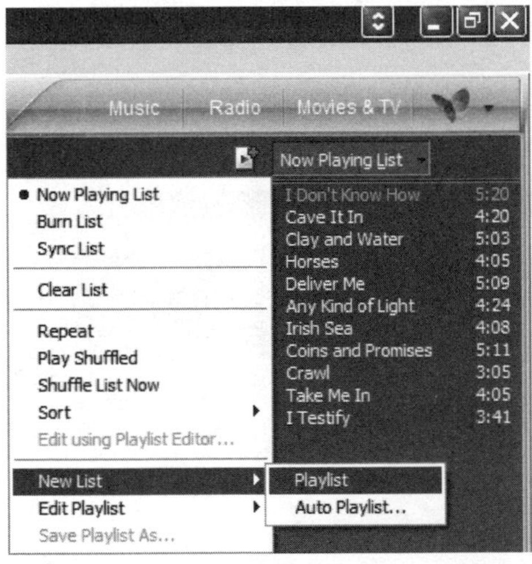

3. In the New Playlist window that appears, shown in Figure 3, click the album titles in the left pane to reveal the songs you have ripped. Drag a song to add it to the new playlist. Don't worry about order at this time, just click through your albums and select the songs you want to include.

4. Once all of your songs are on the playlist, click the Lists button and select Save Playlist As. In the Save As dialog box, enter a descriptive name, and click OK. The new playlist now appears in My Playlists in the Library.

5. Now you can adjust the order of your songs. Select a song and drag it to a new location on the playlist as desired, as shown here. Repeat this process for the other songs until they are in the order that you like.

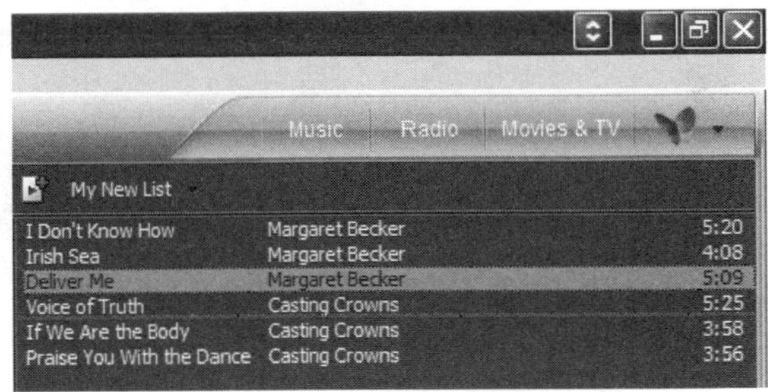

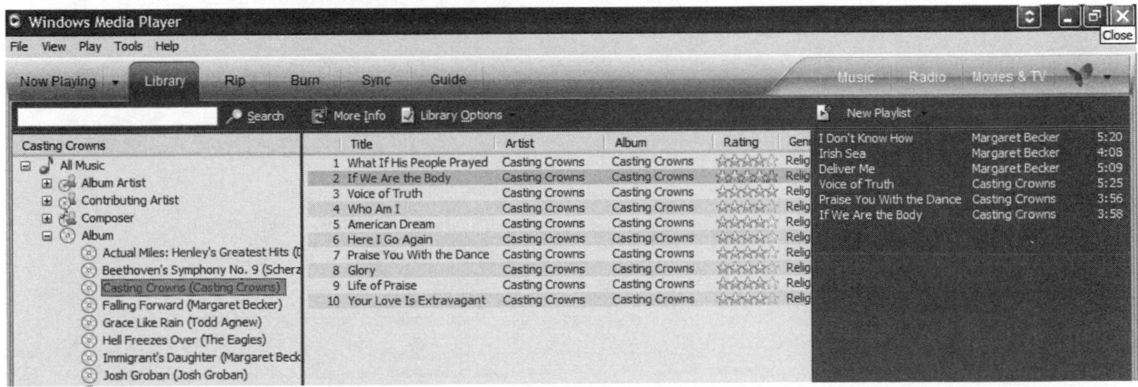

Figure 3. Drag a song to add it to the playlist.

Burn Your CD

You've ripped your songs and ordered the playlist; now all you need to do is burn your CD! Place a new CD-R disc in your CD drive and follow these steps:

1. Open Windows Media Player.
2. Click the Burn button on the interface.
3. In the copy portion of the Window, click the drop-down menu, as shown in Figure 4, and choose the playlist you created.
4. On the right side of the interface, click the drop-down menu toward the top and choose Audio CD. This option may already be selected for you, but make sure.
5. Now you're ready to burn your CD. Click the Start Burn button, found on the upper left side of the window. Windows Media Player will convert your songs to the standard CD format so the disc can be played on any CD player. Once the conversion takes place, the copy, or burn process, begins. This may take some time, so take a break while you wait.

Once the copy process is complete, you can eject your CD and you're done with your project! For safe measure, take the CD to any CD player and listen to it, just to make sure there are no problems. Now you're ready to create a personal label!

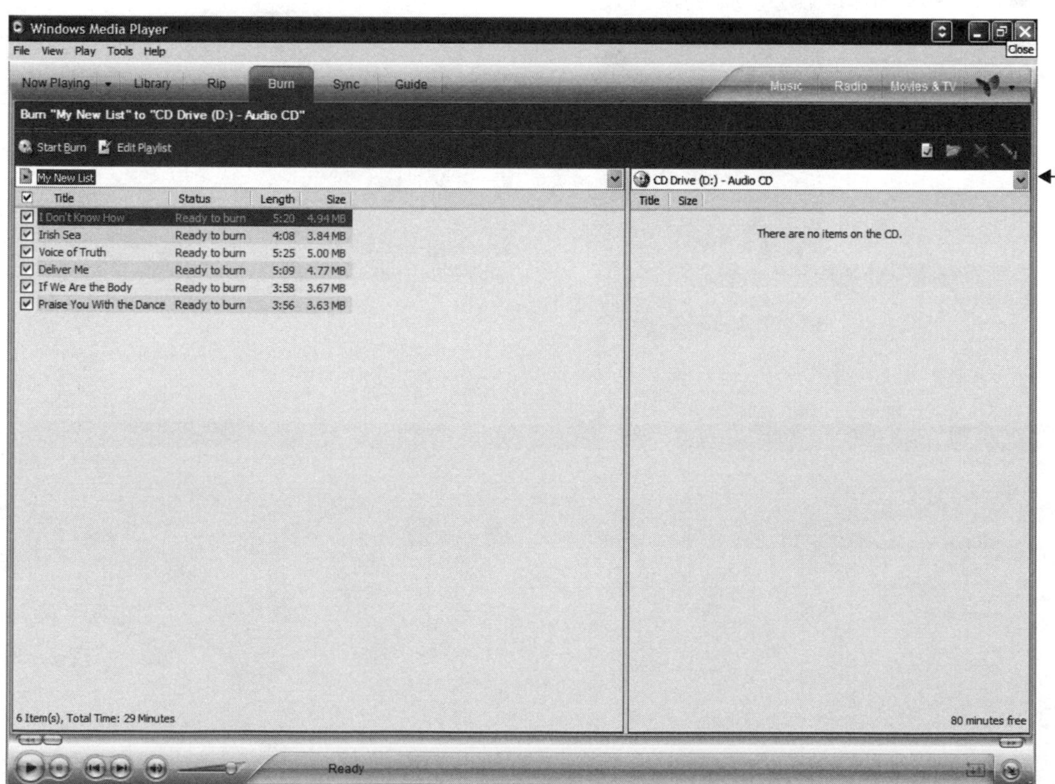

Figure 4. Choose the playlist you want to burn to CD.

Plan Your Label

Like most projects in life, your CD label project begins with a pencil and a piece of paper. Sit down for a few moments to think about what you want the label to convey. Do you want a custom label for the actual CD itself? What about creating a jewel case insert, complete with song information? The choice is completely yours, and the Plus! CD Label Maker can help you make what you want.

First, draw a basic sketch of your label. Think about song titles and the text you want to include on the CD. For custom backgrounds, you can use a digital photo or other graphics file. If you are into editing photos and creating graphics, use a program such as Photoshop Elements to create your own custom background. When planning your background, keep these tips in mind:

- Most graphic file formats, such as JPEG, TIFF, GIF, and BMP, will work with the CD label software. When in doubt, JPEG is a good choice.
- Create a background that matches the style of music and mood of the CD. In other words, think of the label as an extension of the CD's content: it is the first thing people will see, so make the graphic count.
- The background has to conform to a round CD with a hole in the middle. Make sure you aren't cutting a hole in someone's face. Experiment a bit to get the background graphic to look the way you want. You'll see exactly what I'm talking about later in this chapter.

Once you have a good idea and a sketch of what you want, you're ready to create your CD label. The rest of this chapter shows you how. First, we'll take a look at creating CD labels, and then we'll see how to make CD jewel case inserts.

Create Your CD Label with Plus! CD Label Maker

The Plus! CD Label Maker is a wizard that walks you through a series of steps, from selecting a template to printing the label. There are several different issues and items you need to consider, however, so let's look at each step in the following section. You may want to read these sections before you fire up the wizard, or you can start the wizard and simply follow along—the choice is completely up to you.

Start the Label Maker and Choose CD or Playlist

Launch the Plus! CD Label Maker by selecting Start | All Programs | Microsoft Plus! Digital Media Edition | Plus! CD Label Maker. The wizard jumps to life. Click the Next button on the Welcome screen to begin.

As shown in Figure 5, the wizard prompts you to choose a CD or playlist for the CD label. The wizard checks your computer's CD drive(s) for any music CDs, and it also pulls up any playlists from Windows Media Player. In the left column, select the CD or playlist you are creating a label for, and the contents of the CD or playlist will appear in the right pane. You may wonder why you need to take this step if you are only creating a label for the CD itself? In reality, you probably don't need to do this, but Label Maker wants to gather this information in case you later decide to make a label for your jewel case insert. You can include the song list on the jewel case insert, which is rather cool. Now, don't worry if the song list isn't exactly right and you want to

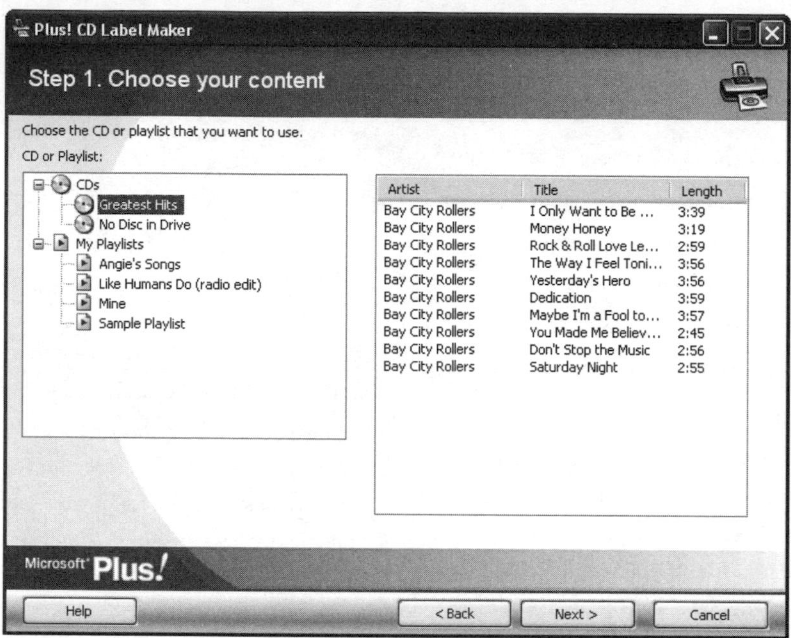

Figure 5. Choose a CD or playlist for the label.

do some editing. You can easily change it later when you are actually creating a jewel case insert. You'll see how coming up. Once you're happy with your selection, click Next to continue.

Choose a Template

The Plus! CD Label Maker uses templates to print your CD labels correctly. As shown in Figure 6, the most popular and common label manufacturers and their product names and numbers are listed in the left pane of the wizard. As you can see, I am using the Fellowes Neato CD Label. You'll probably notice that there several versions of the same product. No problem, just look on the outside package of your CD labels to find the product number (it's generally located in one of the corners on the packaging). Then find the product number in the templates list. My product number is 99943, so I have selected that option. You can also see a sample of my CD template on the right side of the screen in Figure 6.

What do you do if your product is not in the templates list? What if you find the product name, but can't find the actual product number? Don't worry; the odds are very good that an existing template will work just fine. Pull out one of your printable CD label pages and click through the templates to find one that is similar. Remember if you select a template on the left side of the wizard, a sample of it appears on the right side. Try to get as close a match as possible, and you should have fine results.

There are two more quick items I should mention here. First, depending on the template you're using, the Paper Section drop-down box may be enabled. If enabled, you'll see options for upper or lower, as you can see in Figure 6. These options appear if there are multiple print areas on your label paper. For example,

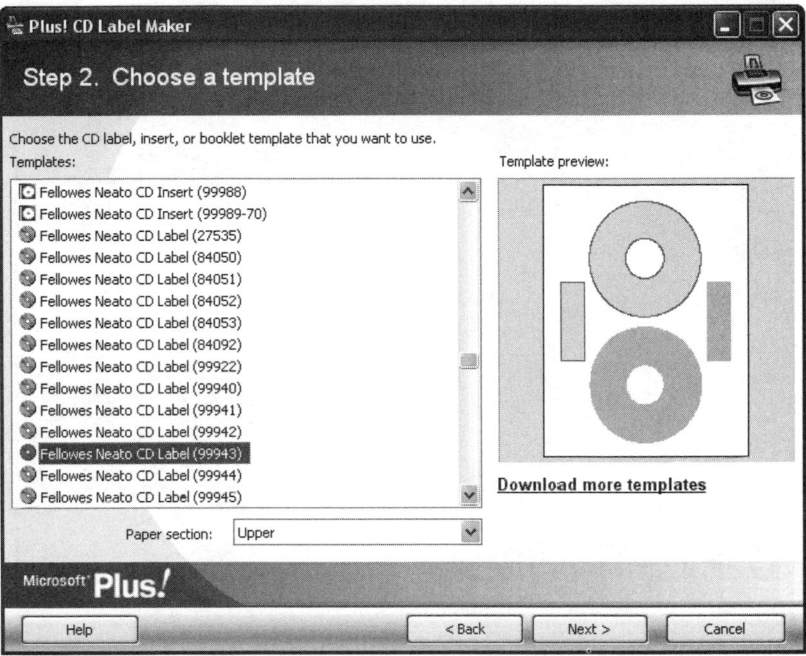

Figure 6. Choose a CD label template.

my label page has two labels, so I use the upper or lower selection option to tell the wizard which label I want to print to. Later, I can create a second label using the lower label.

NOTE

Unfortunately, you can't make a label duplicate on the same page. In other words, if you have a label page that provides two labels, you can't print the same label content on both at the same time. You'll have to run the page back through your printer and use the Paper Selection menu to change the print selection location. This is, of course, a bummer, if you're trying to make multiple copies of the same label since you'll have to run each page through twice.

Second, if you're connected to the Internet, you can also click the Download More Templates link to connect to Microsoft.com where you can see if any additional label templates are available. Click Next when you are ready to continue.

Design Your CD Label

Now comes the fun part—designing your CD label! First of all, orient yourself to the interface, as shown in Figure 7. You'll see a sample label, along with a tab for that label. Depending on the template you chose, you may have more than one label and more than one design tab for each one. For example, as you can see in Figure 7, my template can print both the label for the CD and a label for the spine of the jewel case. Choose which label you want to design first by clicking either the sample itself or the appropriate tab.

For CD labels, you can create a title, a footer, and choose a different background (or no background at all). The wizard gives you a default template, which is green with some music notes on it. You are free to use that one if you don't want to use your own background.

First things first, type the title text and footer text into the provided fields on the tab. Keep in mind that

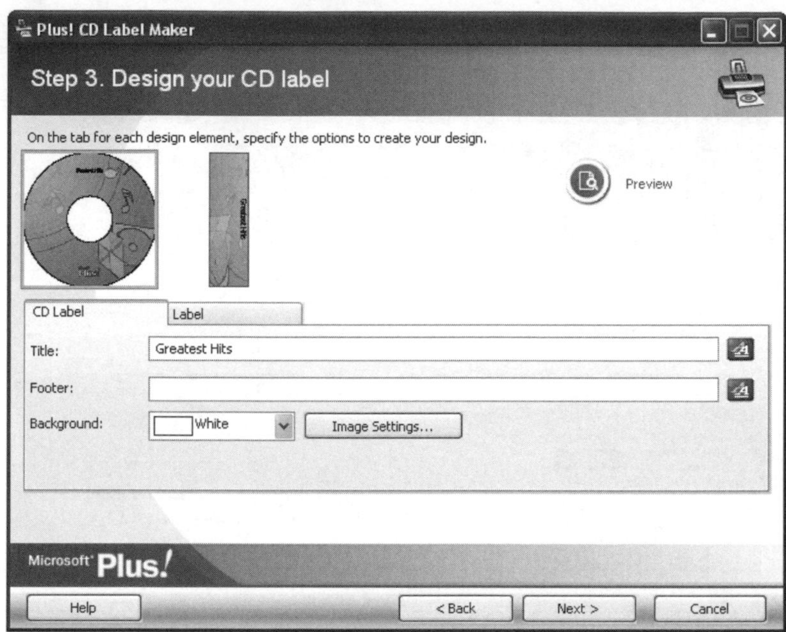

Figure 7. Each label has its own design tab.

the title and footer titles have to actually fit on the CD label, so try to keep the info short and sweet. Once you've entered the text, click the formatting button at the end of the text field (it looks like a double *A*). You'll then see a Font dialog box, shown in Figure 8, where you can select the font, style, and color for your text. Once you've made your selections here, click OK.

TIP

When choosing a font, style, and color, refer to the sketch you made earlier. Make sure the colors and fonts look good with the background you want to use and the background doesn't overpower and wash out your text.

Once you're done, click OK to return to the wizard where you can preview the label to see how your text will look when it is printed. Click the Preview button, located on the upper right, and then adjust the size of the preview so you can see it easily. Of course, you may not like what you see. Maybe the font is too big or the colors look bad. No problem; return to the Font dialog box to make any changes you like. You may need to go through several cycles of text formatting and previewing before the label looks how you want it to look. Repeat this same process for the footer, and if you don't want a footer, just leave the text field blank.

TIP

The background you choose greatly affects the text style and color. What I usually do is create my text, then move on to the background. Once I have the background just right, I go back to my text and make final adjustments.

Now you're ready to work on the background. As I mentioned previously, you can use any digital photo or graphics file as a background, as long as it is saved

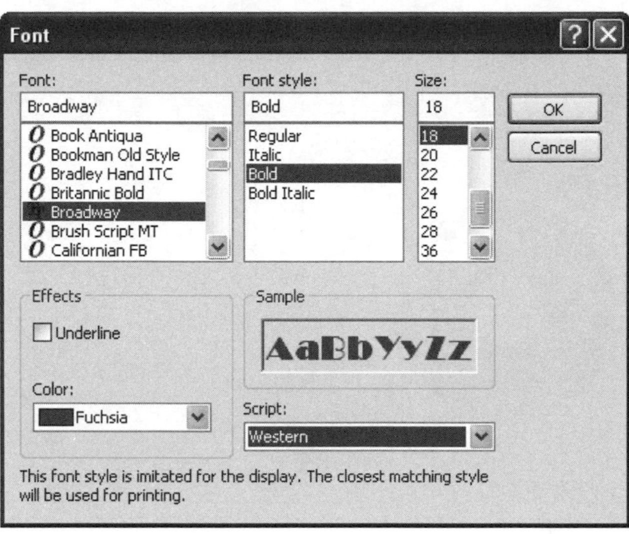

Figure 8. Use the Font dialog box to customize your text.

in a standard graphics file format such as JPEG. You can also use the default green background, or you can choose a solid background color. Here's how you do it:

1. On the wizard page, click the Image Settings button.
2. This opens a Background Image Settings dialog box, as shown in Figure 9. If you do not want to use a background image, select the Do Not Use Image radio button option and click OK.
3. This takes you back to the main wizard page. Now, choose a background color, or none at all, from the color drop-down menu. The none at all option gives you a plain colored label without an image.
4. If you want to use a background image, in the Background Image Settings dialog box, select Use Image, and then click the Browse button to locate the image. This action takes you to a standard Open window, with My Pictures being the default folder. As you can see in Figure 10, I have accessed a folder of vacation photos and selected the photo I want. Once you have selected the image you want, click Open.

TIP

As you open folders, do you see icons only and not a picture preview thumbnail, as shown in Figure 10? No problem, just click the View Menu button in the upper-right corner of the window and select the Thumbnails option from the menu that appears.

5. In the Background Image Settings dialog box, you can see a preview of your image on the label, as shown in Figure 11. The image will be grainy and slightly distorted, as it looks here, but don't worry, it won't come out that way when you print it. Select the Center, Stretch, or Tile option if your image is not large enough to cover the whole label, such as in the case of a graphics file or wallpaper file you might want to use. If you are using a digital photo, there is nothing you need to do here.

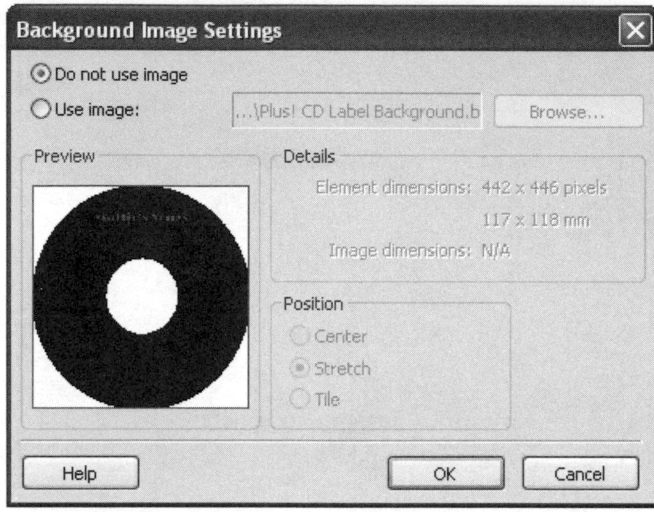

Figure 9. Select the background image–or not–for your CD.

6. Click OK when you're done to return to the wizard. To see your background and text (see Figure 12), click the Preview button. Note that the background will still look grainy and somewhat distorted. At this time, you may want to return to the Font dialog box and adjust your text so it looks better with your selected background.

Once you're happy with your background selection and text, you are ready to continue. Click the Next button.

Print Your Label

Now you are ready to print your label! The final wizard screen, shown in Figure 13, allows you to choose the printer you want to print to and the number of copies you want to make.

Figure 10. You can use a photo as a background.

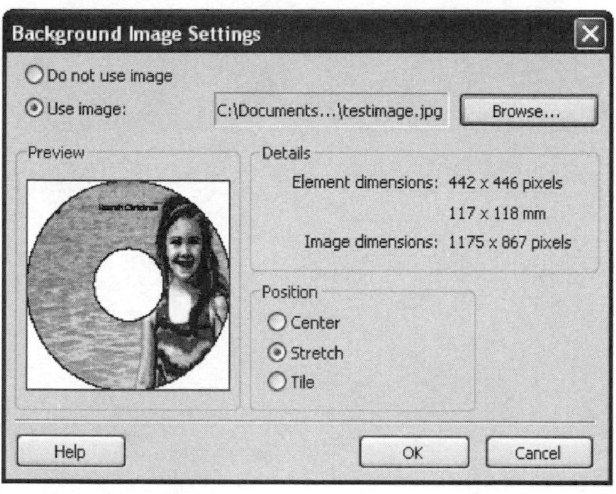

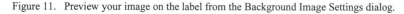

Figure 11. Preview your image on the label from the Background Image Settings dialog.

But wait! Before clicking the Print button, you may need to click the Properties button to tell the printer you're printing a graphic on a photo quality paper (which is what your CD label is made out of). Once you click the Properties button, you'll see a dialog box where you can select the paper and the printing quality. This dialog box, shown in Figure 14, may vary a bit, depending on your printer. From the Media drop-down list, you may find an option for CD Labels—if you do, select it; if not find something similar, or choose the Specialty Paper option.

Now you're ready to print your label for the first time. Insert the label paper into your printer and click Print! A final window will then appear, asking what you want to do next (such as print another copy, exit, print a jewel case insert, and so on).

Before sticking your printed label on a CD, here are some quick tips:

- Wait! Make sure the label has completely dried.
- If you have a double label sheet, don't peel the printed label off until you print the second label. Run the label sheet back through your printer and then print the second label. If you take the first label off, the printer will most likely jam on your second print run.
- Are you making a bunch of copies? There are CD label applicators available, which are little

Figure 12. Click the Preview button to preview the background and text.

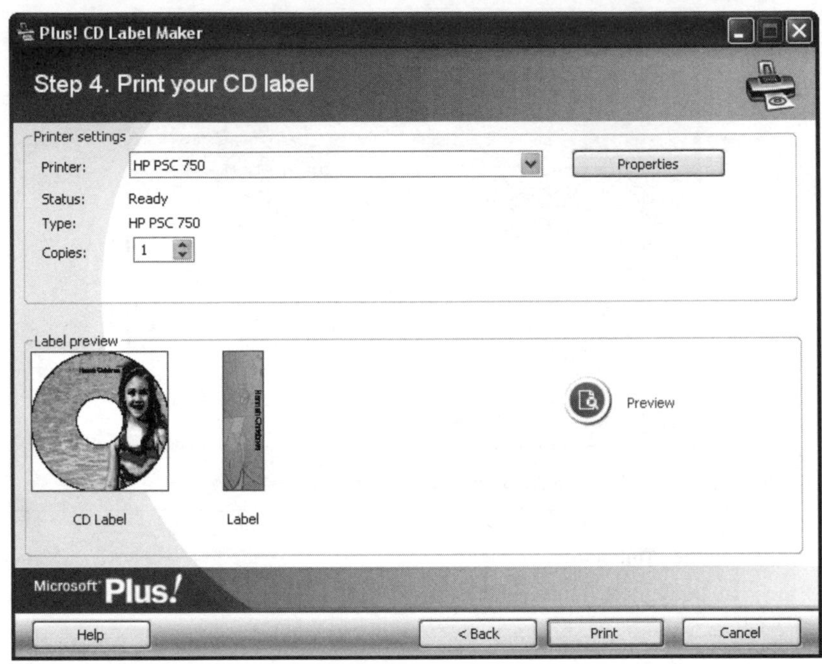

Figure 13. Choose the printer and number of copies.

devices that will hold your label and apply it exactly to your CD. They are inexpensive, available at most places where CD label paper is sold, and can be a real timesaver.

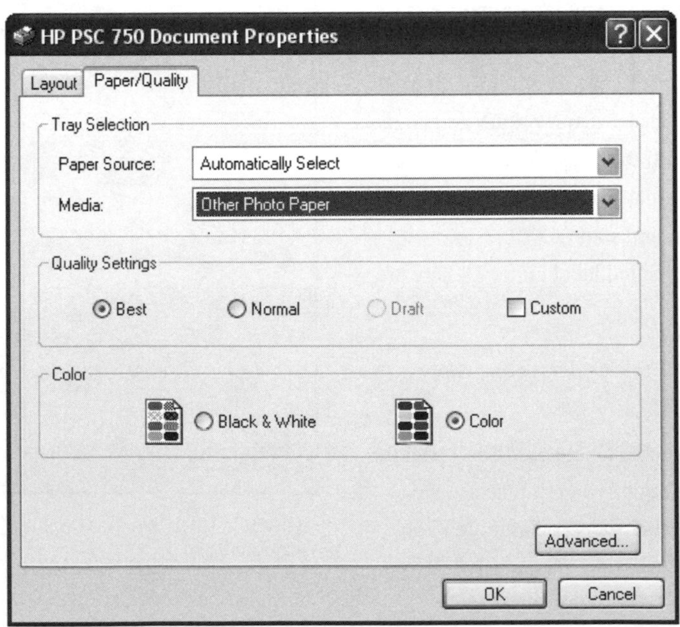

Figure 14. Tell your printer what you are printing.

Create Your Jewel Case Label with Plus! CD Label Maker

Just as you can use the Plus! CD Label Maker to create a CD label, you can also use it to create a custom jewel case insert. The process of creating the insert is almost exactly the same. You buy the jewel case insert label paper, select the correct template using the wizard, and then configure the text and background as you like. Generally, the jewel case label allows you to create a front and back insert card that you fold in half and put in the jewel case. You can add your own background image as usual, and manage the titles, fonts, and so forth. If you want to create an actual label with your song list, see the previous section.

By default, your song list will appear on the insert. The cool thing is you can edit the song list text directly without changing anything on the CD. For example, the first song on the CD might be "When I Fall In Love." You could leave the title and add your own text in parenthesis, such as

> "When I Fall In Love" (This was the first song we danced to.)

As you can see, this editing feature is really cool if you want to customize your song list and add your own text or comments for your personalized CD.

As shown in Figure 15, go to Step 3 in the wizard and click the Edit button next to the Track List field.

You can edit the track list directly in the Edit Track List dialog box, shown in Figure 16. Just make any changes you want (watch your spelling! There is no spellchecker built-in) and click OK.

That's it! You've made a custom CD!

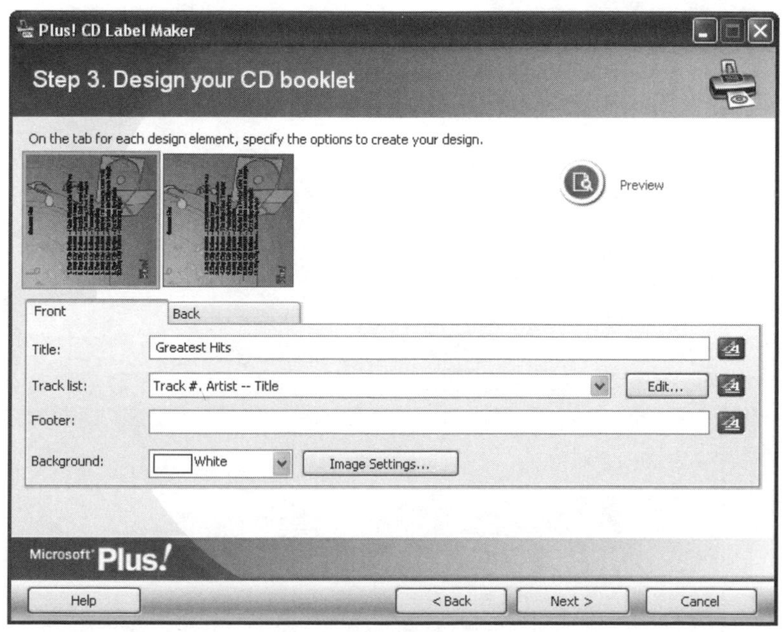

Figure 15. Go to Step 3 and click Edit to customize your song list.

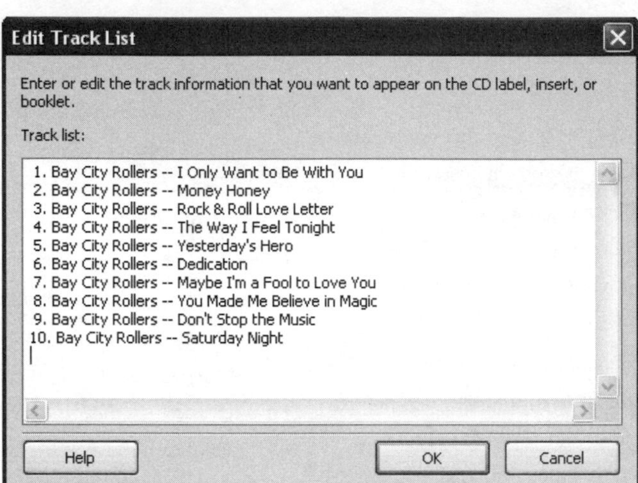

Figure 16. Make changes to the track list in the Edit Track List dialog box.

Did you know?

You Can Customize User Accounts with Pictures

By default, user accounts are represented with a picture that appears on the Welcome screen. At the Welcome screen, you click the user account picture to log on (and enter a password if necessary). You can change these picture icons using the Change Picture feature. You can select another picture from those provided or browse and select your own. Virtually any type of graphics file can be used for your account icon picture (such as a GIF, JPEG, or BMP file). You can choose pictures that are interesting to you; for a family computer, it is fun to use a picture of each family member who has an account on the screen. When you see the Welcome screen, you see your family members, and you simply click your own picture to log on. This idea is great for computer users such as younger children who are just beginning to read. The possibilities are all yours—explore and have fun!

4. If you want to change a password for the account, click the Change Password option and enter the password as instructed in the Password window. You can choose to enter a password hint if you like.
5. Use the Back button to return to the change list, and then make any additional changes that you want.

Select User Logon/Logoff Options

The final task you can perform in the User Accounts window is to select the logon and logoff options. If you click this task option, you see two check boxes, which are shown in Figure 12-4; by selecting these check boxes, you can enable the Welcome screen and Fast User Switching. Fast User Switching allows you to switch to another user account without closing any programs. I recommend that you keep these two options selected; however, do note that Fast User Switching doesn't work well with all programs, especially some antivirus programs and some PC management software.

Manage User Accounts with Computer Management

With the Computer Management console, you can manage local users and groups for your Windows XP computer, but this feature is available only on Windows XP Professional. Computer Management is available in the Administrative Tools folder in the Control Panel. (You must be logged on as an administrator to use this tool.) If you double-click the icon, you can expand Local Users and Groups and then select either the Users or Groups container. As you can see in Figure 12-5, all users are listed in the right console pane with a description.

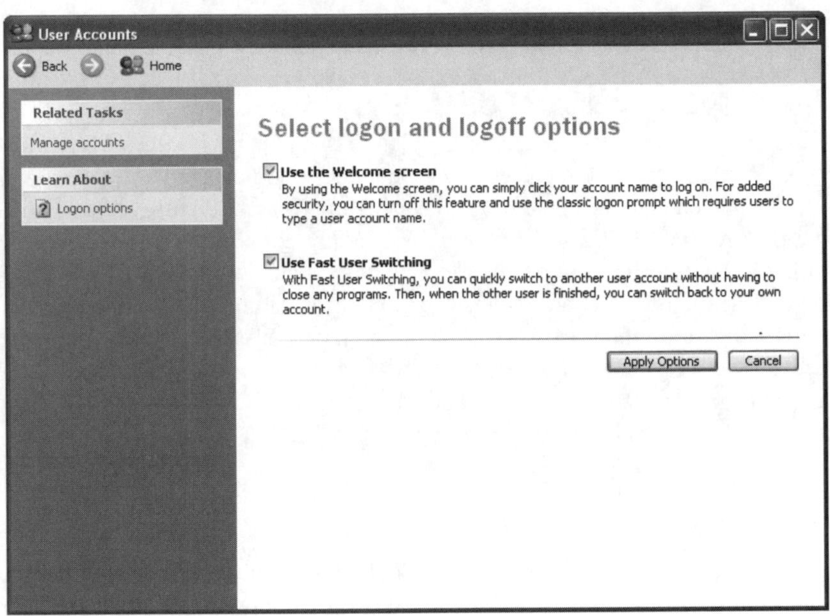

FIGURE 12-4 Logon/Logoff Options

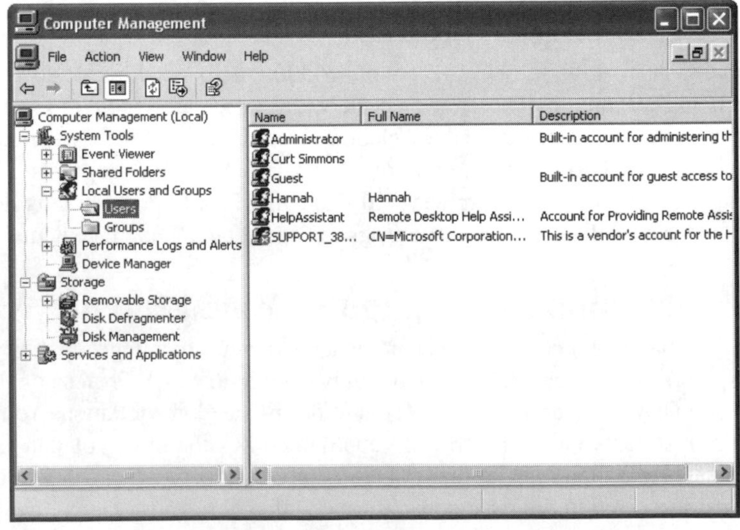

FIGURE 12-5 Local Users and Groups in Computer Management

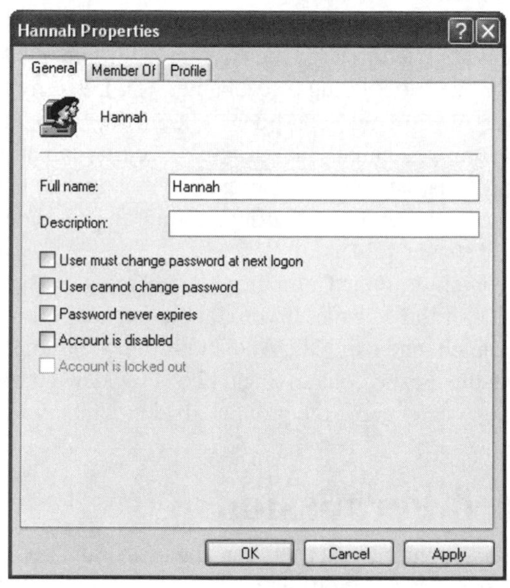

FIGURE 12-6 Security properties

You can double-click any user account in the right console pane to open the properties sheets for the account. As you can see in Figure 12-6, by selecting the desired check box, you can make a number of security-related changes, such as forcing a user to change his or her password at the next logon or restricting a user so that the password can never be changed. You can also disable the account from this location.

The Member Of tab lists the groups that the user is a member of. To add the user to a new group, click the Add button and select the group. You can click the Remove button to remove the user from any group. (See the next section to learn more about groups.) Finally, from the Profile tab, you can use a few fields to configure a path to the user's profile (if profiles are used). Profiles are more widely used in larger networking environments, and this feature isn't something you would typically enable for home or small office use.

If you want to create a new user by using the Computer Management console, just right-click the Users container in the left pane and choose New User.

Manage Groups

Groups are an effective way to organize users in terms of permissions. In fact, facilitating the permissions function is basically the only reason group accounts exist. Let's say that ten people use your Windows XP computer. Five of those users might be administrators, while the other five might have limited accounts. You can add those five limited users to the administrator group and then manage them as one entity rather than as five different accounts.

On a grander scale, groups are used in large networking environments for resource access in networks that aren't using Simple File Sharing (see Chapter 11). Let's say that your department has one printer. You want everyone in your department, but not users from another department, to be able to use the printer. Sure, you can use the printer's Security tab and add each user from your department to the permissions list, but an easier way to manage the users is to create a group account for them once, and then use the group account to give them access to network resources, such as printers and shared folders.

If you click the Groups container in the Computer Management console, you'll see a list of default groups on the right side of the console. If you double-click a group, you'll see a listing of the members, which you can change using the Add and Remove buttons. You can also create a new group by right-clicking the Group container and choosing New Group. Doing this opens a New Group window, where you can name the group and add members to the group.

Understand Advanced Permissions

Windows XP uses permissions to control what users can and cannot do, both on the local computer and on network shares. With permissions, you can grant certain users or groups specific rights while withholding those rights from others, if Simple File Sharing is not used and if you are using Windows XP Professional. If you are a Windows XP Home Edition user, you are limited to Simple File Sharing because it cannot be disabled—but this is really all you need anyway.

However, if you want to use advanced permissions, you can certainly do so on Windows XP Professional by turning off Simple File Sharing. When you do, you can use NTFS permissions to manage shared resources. This feature enhances Windows XP's versatility by allowing you to control both the entire computer and individual folders and files. So, in terms of security, permissions are used on the local machine to manage the actual user and define what he or she can do on that machine, and on the network folders to control what users can do with the contents of these folders. You can think of user permissions as "user access rights," while folder permissions are just that—permissions specific to a folder. You can learn more about NTFS in Chapter 19.

Through NTFS, Windows XP offers superior file and folder security. NTFS supports a number of permission features; but to use NTFS permissions, your shared folders must reside on an NTFS drive. FAT32 (see Chapter 19) also provides the simple folder permissions of Read, Change, and Full Control, but you do not get the fine level of control found in NTFS permissions. When you share a folder on an NTFS drive, you can right-click the folder and choose Properties to see the Security tab shown in Figure 12-7. You can select the desired group and then select the Allow or Deny check boxes to configure permissions for that group, or you can click the Add button and add other users and/or groups so that permissions can be set for them as well.

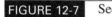

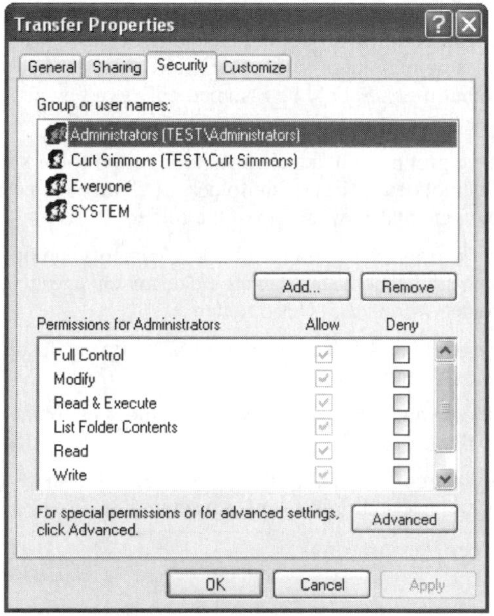

FIGURE 12-7 Security tab

NOTE *Remember that you will not see the Security tab if Simple File Sharing is enabled. Simple File Sharing cannot be disabled on Windows XP Home Edition.*

For any folder you share on an NTFS drive, you can configure the permissions for each group and user. So what exactly do the permissions mean? Table 12-1 explains the different NTFS folder permissions available.

TIP *It is important to note that Table 12-1 reflects these permissions from a grant perspective. However, you can also deny permission for each of these on the Security tab of any NTFS shared folder. In other words, for example, you can deny Write access so that a particular user or group cannot make editing changes or add new content to the shared folder.*

Now that you have taken a look at NTFS permissions, you may be wondering, "What if I need more control?" That's a good question—what should you do if you need to fine tune permissions for a particular user? For example, let's say that you want to give Bob Full Control permission to one of your folders, but you do not want Bob to be able to change permissions on the folder. How can you give Bob Full Control yet provide this one restriction?

Permission	Explanation
Full Control	User can perform any action, including deleting, with respect to a folder and all files or subfolders within that folder. Allows user to change permissions for other users. Should be assigned only to a few people who need complete control over a folder's contents.
Modify	User or group can make changes to files and folders within the shared folder, but cannot delete files or subfolders or change the permissions on the folder. User cannot take ownership of the folder.
Read & Execute	User or group can examine all folder contents and open files as well as launch applications, but cannot make any changes to or delete any files or folders within the shared folders.
List Folder Contents	Same as Read & Execute, but user or group can also view folder permissions for subfolders.
Read	User or group can read files within a folder but make no changes to the file or folder.
Write	User or group can make changes to files in the shared folder and create new files in the shared folder. Often used with the Read permission.

TABLE 12-1 File and Folder Permissions

For cases such as this, where a specialized permission needs to be made, you can access the Security tab of the desired folder and click the Advanced button. This action opens an Advanced Security Settings window, shown in Figure 12-8.

Permissions "Stay in the Family"

As you are assigning permissions to folders, it is important to remember that "inheritance" is in effect for all subfolders. This simply means that a folder within a shared folder inherits the permissions of the parent folder unless you specifically change those permissions. For example, let's say you have a shared folder called Cat. Inside Cat is a folder called Dog. Whatever permissions you have assigned for users and groups concerning the Cat folder will also apply to Dog, unless you specifically access the Security tab on the Dog folder and change them. The key is to remember that inheritance is in effect for folders and subfolders, so you should think carefully when sharing folders. After all, if you're working with many subfolders, you may not want other users wading around in them.

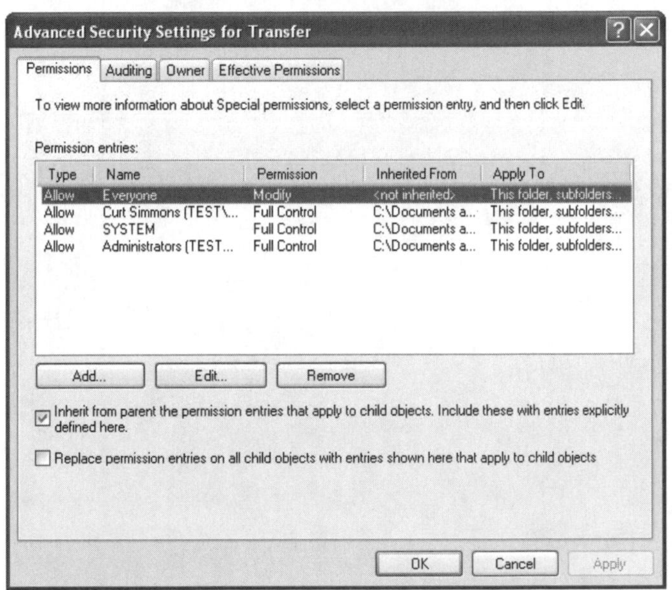

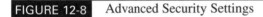

FIGURE 12-8 Advanced Security Settings

In the Permission Entries area, you can see the users and groups that you have configured for the folder so far. Select the user or group that you want, and then click the Edit button to see a Permission Entry window that more finely breaks down the possible actions of permissions.

It is important to remember, though, that these advanced permissions are options designed for incidental use and for professional networking situations. They are intended to give you flexibility in certain circumstances when the default permissions do not provide what you need. Under most circumstances, however, the default NTFS folder permissions are all you need for effective folder security.

Chapter 13

Windows XP Security and Remote Connections

How to...

- Use Windows Firewall and Security Center
- Configure Remote Desktop
- Use Remote Assistance

If the term *Internet firewall* sounds a little frightening, don't worry. A firewall is a good thing. In networks, a firewall is a piece of computer software or hardware that protects a network from intruders. For example, let's say that you own a small company with a network of 200 computers. Each user needs to access the Internet every day, so a primary Internet link travels from your company to an ISP. Although you need to use the Internet each day, you do not want people on the Internet getting inside your private network and stealing information from you. What do you do? The answer is a firewall.

Use Windows Firewall

Firewalls use various kinds of protocol tactics to check traffic as it flows in and out of the network. Based on rules that are configured by system administrators, certain kinds of traffic are allowed or not allowed, and some kinds of traffic can even be seen as threatening. In short, the firewall acts as a very paranoid traffic cop who makes certain that no one gets inside the private network. Firewalls are nothing new; they have been around for years, and most large, private networks today use some kind of firewall technology (and they spend thousands of dollars on it each year).

You may wonder, "That's great, but what does that have to do with me and my Windows XP computer?" Instead of firewalls that are limited to large networking environments, Windows XP includes its own firewall to help protect your computer from malicious people when you're on the Internet. You can think of the firewall found in Windows XP as a personal firewall; other companies also produce firewalls for the typical home or small office user (such as Norton Internet Security), and you can even find good free products, such as ZoneAlarm (www.zonelabs.com).

The next question that may come to mind concerns the need for a firewall. After all, as a home user, you may have been connecting to the Internet for years without a firewall on your computer. Why do you need one now? Any time you are using the Internet, your computer is open to potential attacks. With a dial-up connection, the attacks are limited because you are not connected to the Internet all the time. However, with the explosive growth of broadband connections (DSL, cable, and satellite), the need for a firewall becomes very important, because these computers are always connected to the Internet and therefore always exposed to danger. For this reason, Windows Firewall is included with Windows XP and is available for your use. When Windows XP was first released, the firewall was called Internet Connection Firewall, but this older version has been replaced with Windows Firewall, which is automatically installed on your computer when you install Service Pack 2. (For more information on installing Service Pack 2, visit www.microsoft.com/windowsxp.)

Understand How Windows Firewall Works

Windows Firewall is a *software solution* in Windows XP. This means that Windows Firewall uses code built into the Windows XP operating system to monitor and manage Internet traffic. As you might imagine, the process of managing traffic can become a rather complex topic, so I'm going to give you the important aspects of the process here and skip the boring technical details.

Windows Firewall is considered a *stateful* firewall. This means that Windows Firewall works with your Internet connection to examine traffic as it passes through the firewall both to and from your computer/network. Because Windows Firewall is stateful, it examines Internet traffic in terms of its live use. If something that is not allowed attempts to enter the firewall, Windows Firewall steps in and blocks the traffic from entering. Basically, no disallowed traffic ever passes the firewall. To use stateful inspection, Windows Firewall examines the destination of every piece of traffic coming from your computer or computers on your network. Whenever something is sent to the Internet (such as a URL request), Windows Firewall keeps a routing table to track your requests. When data comes to the firewall, Windows Firewall inspects it to see if it matches up with requests found in the routing table. If so, it is passed on to your computer or the requesting computer on your network. If not, it is blocked from entering the firewall. The end result is that any traffic you want from the Internet can enter the firewall, and anything you have not requested is blocked.

Issues with Windows Firewall

Before we get into more detail about Windows Firewall configuration, let me point out a few issues concerning the firewall's default behavior. You should keep these issues in mind as you set up Internet connections or home/small office networks:

- Windows Firewall should be enabled on any shared Internet connection in your home or small office network. You do not have to use a home or small office network to use Windows Firewall—if you want the protection, Windows Firewall works great on one computer, too.
- Windows Firewall works on a per-connection basis. For example, let's say your computer has a DSL connection and a modem connection (you use the modem connection in the event that the DSL connection goes down). You need to enable Windows Firewall on both the DSL and modem connections to have full protection. Windows Firewall is enabled per connection—not per computer.
- In a small network setting using Internet Connection Sharing (ICS), you should certainly enable Windows Firewall on the ICS connection. However, if other computers on the network have other ways to connect to the Internet (such as through modems), you need to enable Windows Firewall on each of those connections as well. Again, Windows Firewall works on a per-connection basis.
- Any configuration changes you make to Windows Firewall are for that particular connection only—they do not transfer from connection to connection. For example, if you have two connections and Windows Firewall is enabled on each of them, you must individually configure each connection as needed.

- Outlook Express will work fine with Windows Firewall and will continue to check for and download mail automatically.
- Windows Firewall should not be enabled on any computer's network adapter card that is used to connect to local computers. Doing so will prevent connectivity. Windows Firewall should be used only for connections to the Internet—not connections between computers on your private network.

NOTE *Windows Firewall, like ICS, is a home/small office solution. In environments where Windows XP is used with a Microsoft DNS/DHCP server and other large-scale networking services where other firewalls are in place, Windows Firewall should not be used. Chances are, if a DNS/DHCP server is in use, you're working in a large network and network administrators have taken care of setting up firewalls for you, so it's not something you need to worry about.*

Enable Windows Firewall

When you upgrade to Service Pack 2, Windows Firewall is activated by default. Naturally, you can deactivate it; you manage Windows Firewall through the new Security Center available in Service Pack 2. To activate (or deactivate) the firewall, open the Security Center window by clicking the Security Center icon in the Notification Area or the Control Panel. The Security Center window is shown in Figure 13-1.

If Windows Firewall is not activated, scroll to the bottom of the Security Center window and click the Windows Firewall icon under Manage Security Settings For. This action opens the General tab of the Windows Firewall dialog box, where you can click the On radio button to activate the Firewall, as shown in Figure 13-2.

Configure Windows Firewall Settings

If you open the Exceptions and Advanced tabs of the Windows Firewall dialog box, you'll see settings that govern how Windows Firewall works and what kinds of applications and services it allows. Again, you typically do not need to configure anything here if you are simply using the Internet and accessing Internet mail. However, if you are using certain applications or providing certain types of content to the Internet, you may need to configure some of these settings. The settings here can get a little complicated and tricky, however, so be forewarned!

Let's start with the Exceptions tab, shown in Figure 13-3. The Exceptions tab provides a list of programs and services running on your computer or network that you are allowing Internet users to access. For example, let's say that you want to use Remote Assistance on your Windows XP computer. (We'll explore Remote Assistance later in the section "Use Remote Assistance.") If Windows Firewall is in use, you need to check the Remote Assistance check box so that a Remote Assistance user can contact you. When you click this check box and then click OK, Windows Firewall basically reconfigures itself to allow certain kinds of content to pass through the firewall in order to meet these needs. Or, for example, let's say you want to use Remote Desktop (covered later in "Configure Remote Desktop") with someone on the Internet. By default, Windows Firewall will not allow this kind of communication, but if you enable it here, Windows Firewall understands that Remote Desktop should be allowed.

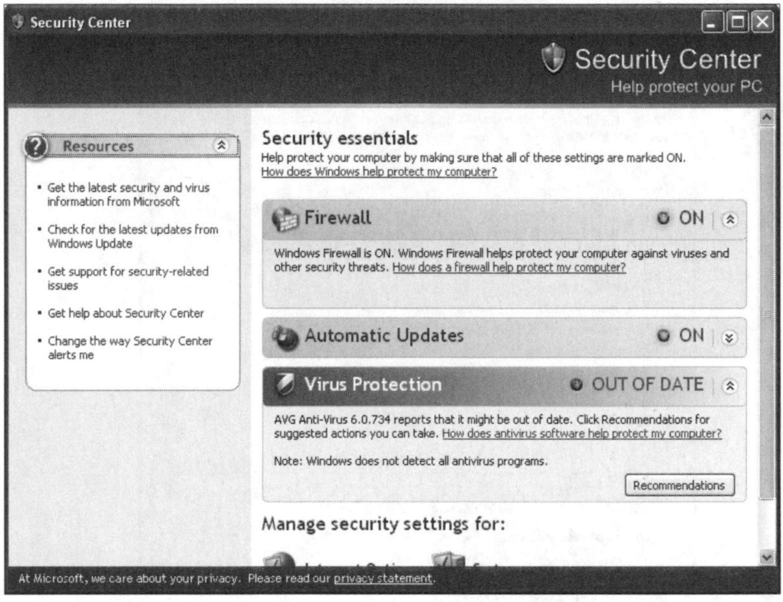

FIGURE 13-1 Security Center

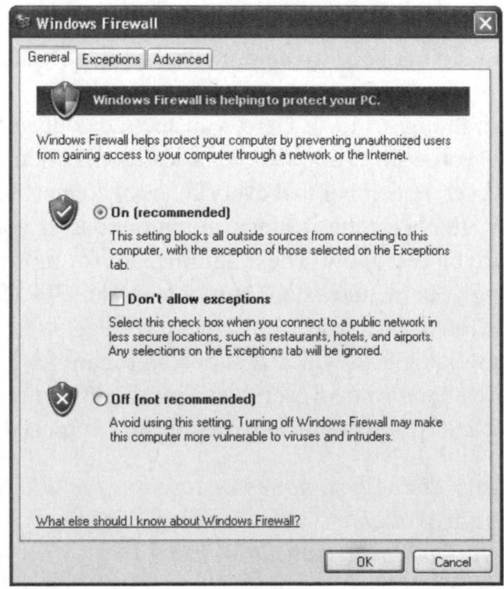

FIGURE 13-2 General tab of Windows Firewall dialog

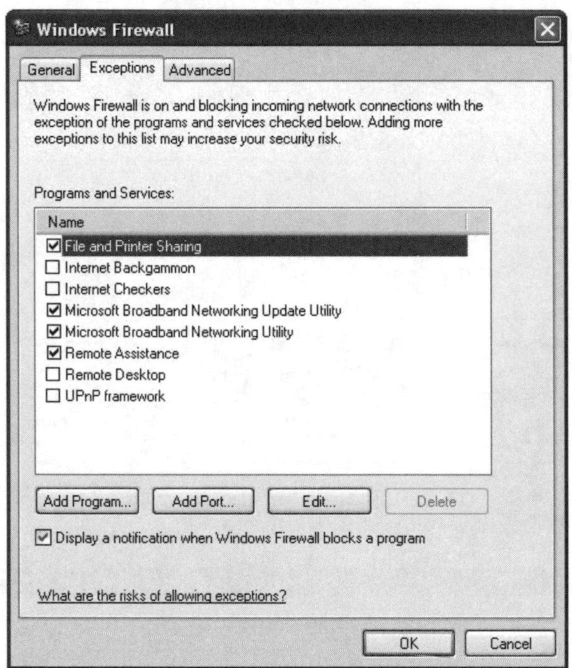

FIGURE 13-3 You can allow exceptions to the firewall.

If you are not offering any services to Internet clients, but you want to use the Internet only for Web surfing and e-mail, you do not need to do anything in this tab. Make sure none of the check boxes is selected.

The Advanced tab is shown in Figure 13-4. Here, you see the connections that Windows Firewall is enabled to protect. If you want to allow more or less connections, select or deselect the check boxes as necessary. However, remember that every Internet connection on your computer should be protected by the firewall. Notice the Settings button options. If you click Settings, you'll see another list of services that you can allow. These settings are for more advanced usage. For example, let's say you are using your Windows XP computer as an FTP (File Transfer Protocol) server for Internet clients. To allow FTP traffic, you'll need to select the FTP Server check box option on the Advanced Settings dialog box, which is shown in Figure 13-5. The same is true with any ICMP (Internet Control Message Protocol) services you might want to use. Again, these are advanced options, so don't enable any of them unless you are sure you need them.

In the Advanced Settings dialog box, notice the options for Web Server and Secure Web Server. These options are available if you are using Windows XP as a Web server. You do not need to enable these options to surf the Web.

FIGURE 13-4 Advanced tab

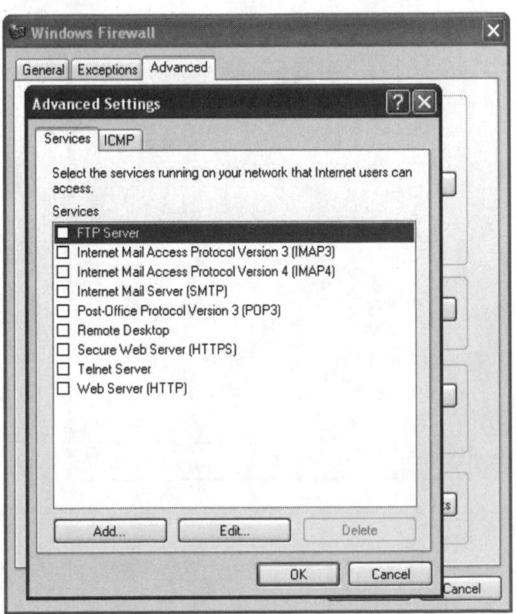

FIGURE 13-5 Advanced Settings

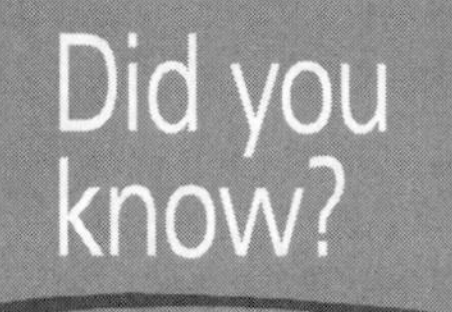

About Keeping Your Network Secure

Windows Firewall is designed to keep your computer or network secure, but it can do its job only if you keep it enabled and configured effectively. For this reason, you should never make any changes to the Services tab that you do not clearly understand. For example, let's say you enable the Web Server (HTTP) feature. This setting tells Windows Firewall that your computer is a Web server and that it should allow Web server requests and messages to pass through the firewall. However, if your computer is not really a Web server, then selecting this check box opens the door for intruders to get into your computer or network for no reason at all. Windows Firewall is one of those great features where less is more—do not enable anything extra unless it's absolutely necessary.

By default, the security log is stored in C:\Windows\pfirewall.log, but you can click the Settings button on the Security Logging section of the Windows Firewall dialog box to change the location. In the Log Settings dialog box, you'll notice that the log file has a maximum size of 4096KB (4MB) by default. You can increase or decrease this space if you like, but this default provides plenty of room. To enable logging for successful connections and dropped packets, select the desired check boxes, as shown in Figure 13-6.

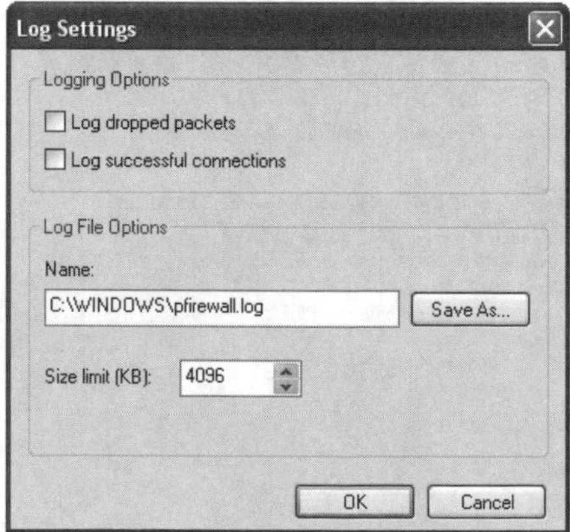

FIGURE 13-6 Log Settings dialog

You also see an ICMP section on the Advanced tab. ICMP handles a number of communication functions that test computer connectivity. A common one is the *ping* test (called *echo request* in the ICMP Settings dialog box), which tests another computer to see whether it is connected. Although ICMP messages are generally harmless, some attacks from the Internet act like ICMP messages, so by default, no ICMP messages are allowed on your network. Also, some ICMP messages can be used in a hostile manner, such as the infamous *ping of death*. Depending on your needs, however, you may want to enable some of these ICMP message types (or all of them). Just click the Settings button and enable the desired ICMP functions in the ICMP Settings dialog, shown in Figure 13-7; you can select a message type and read more about it in the Description portion of the dialog.

TIP *The best advice I can give you is not to enable ICMP messages unless you are sure that you need them. Doing so opens your computer or network to the possibility of attacks from the Internet. Of course, you don't want to be overly paranoid either, so feel free to enable these if necessary.*

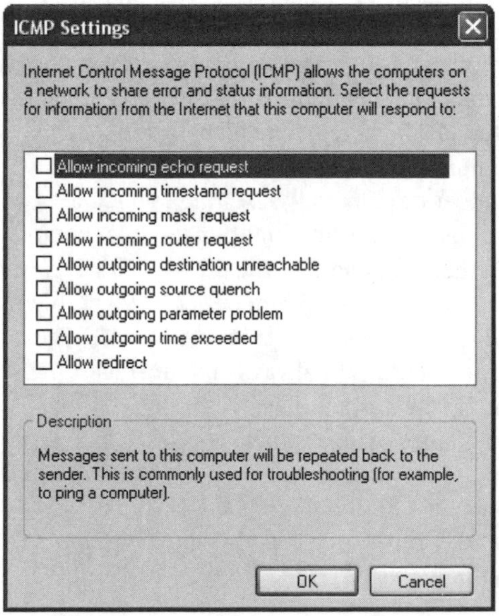

ICMP Settings

Internet Control Message Protocol (ICMP) allows the computers on a network to share error and status information. Select the requests for information from the Internet that this computer will respond to:

- Allow incoming echo request
- Allow incoming timestamp request
- Allow incoming mask request
- Allow incoming router request
- Allow outgoing destination unreachable
- Allow outgoing source quench
- Allow outgoing parameter problem
- Allow outgoing time exceeded
- Allow redirect

Description

Messages sent to this computer will be repeated back to the sender. This is commonly used for troubleshooting (for example, to ping a computer).

OK Cancel

FIGURE 13-7 ICMP Settings dialog

About the Security Center

The Security Center installed on your Windows XP computer is designed to be a simple interface that tells you whether your computer has certain security options enabled. All the Security Center really does is tell you whether Windows Firewall is enabled, as we've seen in the previous sections of this chapter. However, you can also check the Security Center to see if Automatic Updates are turned on and if virus protection is up-to-date. If not, the Security Center will tell you so (refer back to Figure 13-1). Other than providing that information, though, the Security Center doesn't do much.

Configure Remote Desktop

Windows XP supports a very cool feature called Remote Desktop. Consider this scenario: You use Windows XP Professional at the office, which is half an hour from your home. When you get home, you realize that you left some very important business unattended on your work computer. You also have a Windows computer at your home—now, what can you do? No problem—you can use your home computer to connect with the office computer, and then you can use the office computer with Remote Desktop just as if you were actually sitting there. Sound too good to be true? It's true, and this new feature works great.

Remote Desktop has a number of potentially exciting applications. You can access a remote computer and use the applications and information found on that computer seamlessly, just as if your hands were actually on the computer's keyboard. You can even use Remote Desktop to connect to another person's computer and help him or her solve problems through Windows XP's Remote Assistance feature, which is explored later in this chapter. The possibilities are endless. With Remote Desktop, a remote computer is always at your fingertips.

The Remote Desktop client updates an older technology called Terminal Services Client. Essentially, your computer can connect with a remote computer and, assuming proper permissions are in place, your computer can use the remote computer in a "dumb terminal" manner, as though you were actually sitting at the computer's location. Remote Desktop obviously works on Windows XP, but by using the XP installation CD-ROM, you can also add the Remote Desktop Connection tool to other Windows operating systems, such as Windows 9*x*, Me, NT 4.0, or 2000.

TIP

If you access a computer remotely, don't worry about onlookers. The remote computer is actually locked, so no one can walk by and see what you're doing on the computer in your physical absence. In other words, you are not logged on to the local computer and another person cannot use it locally.

Enable Remote Desktop

If you are currently logged on as the computer's administrator, you can enable the Remote Desktop feature on your Windows XP computer so that others can connect to it. Access System Properties in the Control Panel and click the Remote tab. As you can see in Figure 13-8, you can enable both Remote Assistance and Remote Desktop from this tab.

Once you enable Remote Desktop, you should consider two issues. The first is a user account. The remote computer must log on to your computer with a username and password, just as if you were actually sitting at the local computer. When you log on locally, you may be able to use a blank password, but the Remote Desktop connection requires a password. Think about the account you will log on with and make sure a password is configured for the account. If it is not, configure one using the User Accounts option in Control Panel (see Chapter 12 for specific instructions). You may consider creating a specific Remote Desktop account to use just for the Remote Desktop connection as well.

The second issue you need to consider is Windows Firewall. Remote Desktop will not work over Windows Firewall if Windows Firewall is enabled and not configured to pass Remote Desktop traffic. You can easily configure Windows Firewall to pass Remote Desktop traffic on the Exceptions tab of the Windows Firewall properties dialog. (See "Configure Windows Firewall Settings" earlier in this chapter for instructions.)

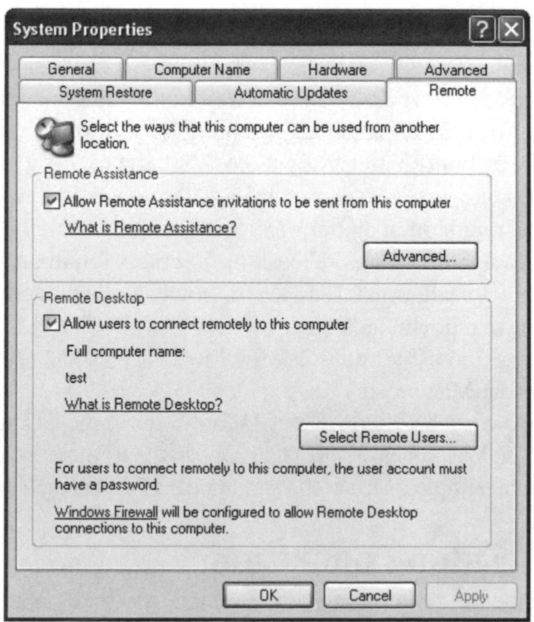

FIGURE 13-8 Remote tab

Once you have addressed these two issues, you need to determine which users are allowed to connect from a remote location. Let's say that you use Windows XP Professional at your office, and three other people use that computer with Limited accounts. You want to make certain that only your account can connect remotely. No problem. To configure the user(s) who can connect, click the Select Remote Users button on the Remote tab of the System Properties window, and then click the Add button on the Remote Desktop Users dialog box. A Select Users dialog box appears, as shown next. Enter the user account to which you want to give permission, or click the Advanced button and choose the user from the list. When you're done, click OK.

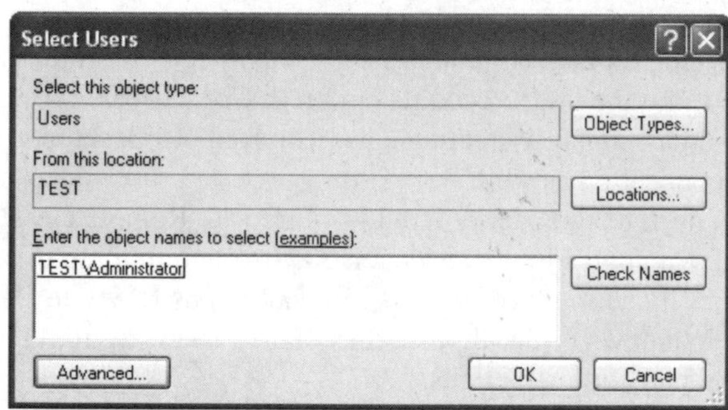

Configure the Remote Desktop Client Computer

Once you have enabled Remote Desktop on the host computer, you can then configure the remote computer to connect to the host. I have some great news—if the remote computer is running Windows XP Professional or Home Edition, there is nothing for you to do. The Remote Desktop Connection software is already built-in and ready to go. Move on to the next section, "Make a Remote Desktop Connection."

If you are using an earlier version of Windows, you'll need to install the Remote Desktop Connection software. This tool, called Remote Desktop Client, is found on your Windows XP Professional or Home Edition installation CD-ROM, or you can download it directly from www.microsoft.com/windowsxp/downloads/tools/rdclientdl.mspx. The Remote Desktop Client software will work on any version of Windows 95, 98, Me, NT, or 2000. (And a Remote Desktop version is also available for the Macintosh.)

To install the software from your Windows XP CD-ROM, insert the CD and click the Perform Additional Tasks option on the Welcome screen. Then choose the Remote Desktop Connection option that appears. Follow the simple instructions that appear in the next How To.

Make a Remote Desktop Connection

Once you have configured the host computer and the remote computer (if necessary), you are ready to make the Remote Desktop connection. On the remote computer, choose Start | All Programs | Accessories | Communications | Remote Desktop Connection. In the Remote Desktop

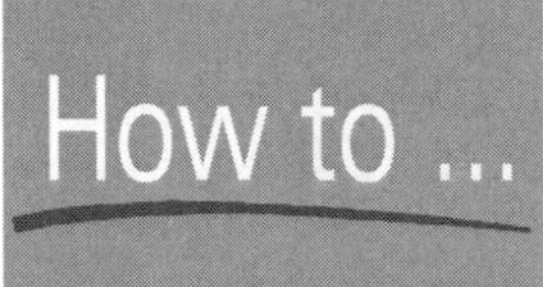

Install the Remote Desktop Web Connection

To install the Remote Desktop Web connection, follow these steps:

1. Open the Control Panel and double-click Add/Remove Programs.
2. Click the Add/Remove Windows Components button.
3. In the Setup window that appears, select Internet Information Services (IIS) and click the Details button.
4. Select World Wide Web service and click the Details button again.
5. In the Details window, select the Remote Desktop Web Connection check box and then click OK.
6. Click OK again, and then click Next. Windows XP will install and configure the component. You may need to insert your Windows XP CD-ROM to complete this action.
7. Once the installation is complete, click the Finish button.

Once you have installed the Web connection, you should be able to start a Remote Desktop session from a remote computer using Internet Explorer. Open Internet Explorer, and then type the address as **http://*ipaddress*/tsweb,** where *ipaddress* is the IP address of the Remote Desktop computer.

Connection dialog box that appears, shown in the following illustration, you can enter the name of the computer you want to connect to if the computer resides on your local area network (LAN), or, if you are connecting over the Internet, enter the TCP/IP address of the computer you want to connect to and click the Connect button.

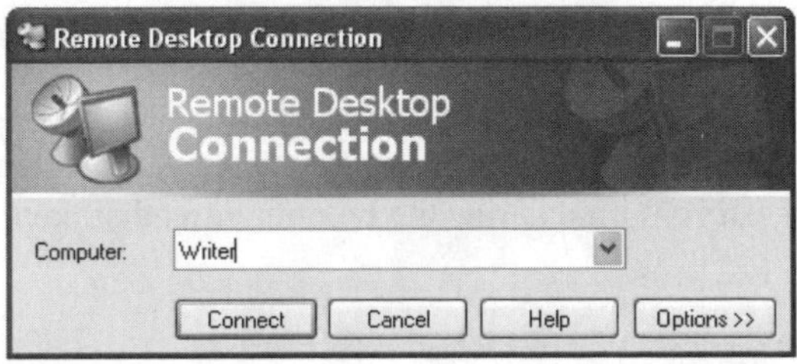

When the connection is made, you'll see a standard Windows dialog box where you enter a username and password and click OK. Once you log in, you can use the host computer just as if you were sitting at it.

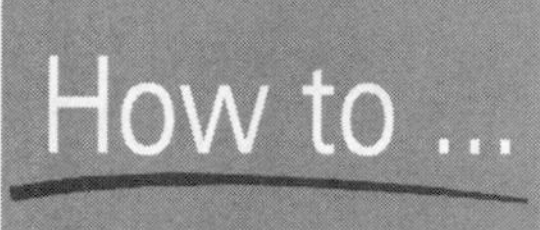

Connect Through a Corporate Firewall

This may be more information than you want to know, but if you are trying to connect to a work computer over a corporate firewall, you may encounter problems. Your corporate firewall may have blocked TCP/IP ports that Remote Desktop will need for the connection. In this case, a network administrator needs to open TCP port 3389. (That may not mean anything to you, but your network administrator will understand.) The point is that your corporate network will have to allow Remote Desktop connections if your work computer is protected by a network firewall. Typically, in this case, you'll connect remotely using the company's virtual private network (VPN) connection.

Manage Remote Desktop Performance

At first glance, it might not seem that Remote Desktop performance would be much of an issue. If you are using Remote Desktop over a LAN or DSL/cable connection, Remote Desktop performance isn't an issue. However, if you are using a dial-up connection from your home computer to your office, downloading all of your remote computer's graphics and other Desktop features can be time consuming, so Remote Desktop gives you some options to help you use less bandwidth. Using less bandwidth equals better performance, so if performance is an issue, you need to adjust the Experience settings of the Remote Desktop connection. Using the Experience tab, you can select your connection speed to optimize performance. Depending on your selection, the performance options will change. For example, if you are using a modem, the Desktop background is not displayed because it tends to use a lot of bandwidth.

Choose Start | All Programs | Accessories | Communications | Remote Desktop Connection. In the Remote Desktop Connection dialog box, click the Options button, and then click the Experience tab. As you can see in Figure 13-9, you can choose the speed of your connection. If you choose the Modem option, not all of the Remote Desktop features are used. The good news, however, is that the default settings provided here are just suggestions; you can change any of them by enabling or disabling the check boxes as desired. You may need to experiment with these settings to find those that work best for you. However, you should always leave Bitmap Caching enabled (checked) because it helps speed up your connection. This feature allows images to be saved in your local cache so that they can be reused during the session, instead of having to download them individually each time.

Manage the Display

The Display tab, shown in Figure 13-10, allows you to modify the options for the window containing the remote session. The supported resolutions range from Low to Full Screen.

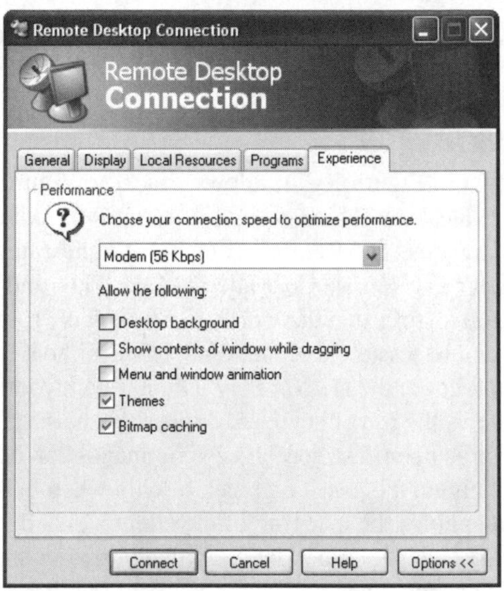

FIGURE 13-9 Experience tab

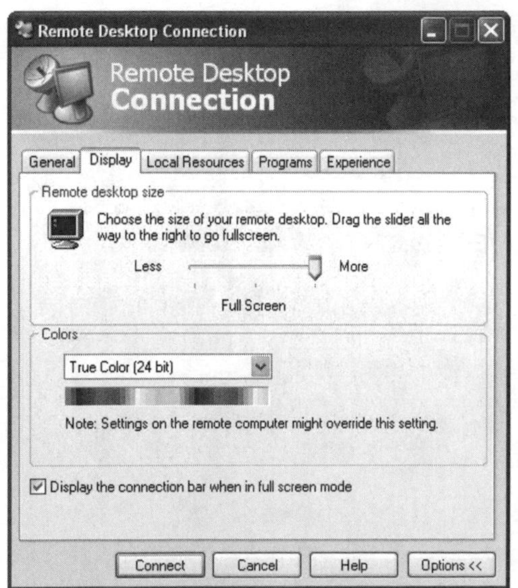

FIGURE 13-10 Display tab

13

You may also specify the color depth to use for the connections as well as decide whether or not to display the connection bar when in full-screen mode. The connection bar allows you to see the name or address of the computer hosting the session and to minimize or close the window.

Configure Local Resources

The Local Resources tab, shown in Figure 13-11, allows you to configure some of the newer features available with Remote Desktop. Three categories of options exist: Remote Computer Sound, Keyboard, and Local Devices. The Remote Computer Sound category allows you to specify one of three options: Leave at Remote Computer, Do Not Play, and Bring to This Computer (referring to the Remote Desktop client). In other words, depending on your choice, Windows event sounds can be heard on your remote session. Keep in mind, however, that sounds also increase bandwidth, so you may want to choose the Do Not Play option if bandwidth is an issue.

The Keyboard category allows the use of keyboard strokes (such as ALT-TAB) so that they will operate when the remote session is open. The special key commands can be configured to work only on the remote computer, only on the local computer, or only when in full-screen mode.

The Local Devices option enables the mapping of the client's disk drives, printers, and serial ports to the Remote Desktop host. For example, let's say that you are connected to your work computer from a home computer. You need to print a document that is on your work computer to your home computer's printer. This option allows you to do that. Or, let's say you want to be

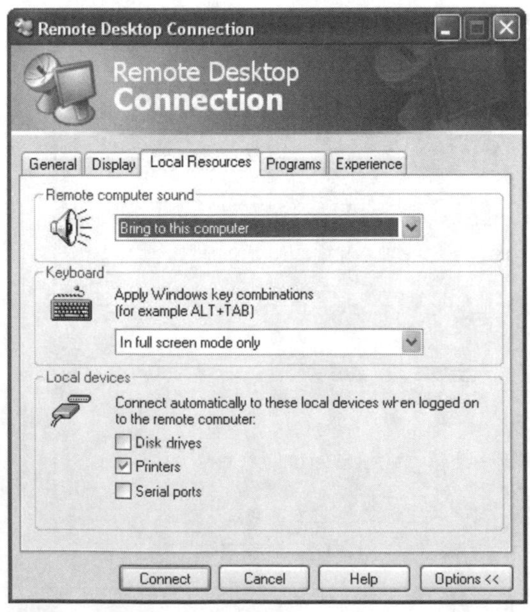

FIGURE 13-11 Local Resources tab

able to access information stored on drives on your local computer while in the Remote Desktop session. Selecting the Local Devices option Disk Drives makes your disk drives appear in the My Computer window of the remote computer so that you can access them.

Use Programs

The Programs tab can be used to launch a specific program when the user connects to the Remote Desktop host. In some cases, users will want to launch processes when they connect to the remote host, such as batch files or custom applications. This tab allows the user to specify the location of the files that should be started.

Use Remote Desktop Web Connection

Aside from a typical Remote Desktop connection using a LAN or VPN, Windows XP also supports connections over the Internet. This feature provides a Web utility that allows you to connect to the remote computer through a Web browser instead of having the Remote Desktop Client software installed on the remote computer. To use the Web connection feature, it must first be installed on the host computer. Follow the steps in the How To box "Install the Remote Desktop Web Connection" earlier in the chapter to install the Remote Desktop Web connection.

Use Remote Assistance

Remote Assistance is a new feature in Windows XP Professional and Windows XP Home Edition that enables users to help each other over the Internet. With this tool, one user who is deemed the "Expert" can view the Desktop of another user, deemed the "Novice." When properly authorized by the Novice, the Expert user can remotely use the Novice user's system to fix problems for the Novice user. For a Remote Assistance session to succeed, both users must be connected to the same network (the Internet, typically), must be using Windows XP, and the account requesting assistance (the Novice) must have administrative rights to the computer. Unfortunately, no other operating systems work with Remote Assistance—both computers must be running Windows XP. The good news is that Remote Assistance is easy to use and configure and can be helpful in many situations:

- It can be used on a company network where help desk personnel connect to remote computers and provide assistance.
- It can be used as a workaround for Remote Desktop. In actuality, Remote Assistance uses Terminal Services, just like Remote Desktop. The difference is that with Remote Assistance, a person has to be at each PC, and both Windows XP Professional and Home Edition can use the feature. This can be a quick and easy way to share data between two people over the Internet.

Remote Assistance works by sending Remote Assistance invitations. The Novice's computer uses either Windows Messenger (*not* MSN Messenger) or e-mail to send a Remote Assistance invitation to another, Expert, user. The Expert user accepts the invitation, which opens a terminal window showing the Desktop of the novice. The Expert can see the Novice's Desktop and exchange messages with the Novice. If the Novice wants the Expert to fix the computer, the Novice can give the Expert control of the computer. From this point, the Expert can manage the Novice's computer remotely.

As with Remote Desktop, firewalls can pose a problem for Remote Assistance. The good news is that Windows Messenger can typically get around the firewall, so use Windows Messenger instead of the e-mail option if you are having trouble.

Turn On Remote Assistance

Before your computer can use Remote Assistance, you must turn on the feature. Open the Control Panel and double-click System Properties. Click the Remote tab. You'll see an Allow Remote Assistance Invitations to Be Sent from This Computer check box. Select the check box to enable it.

Once you have enabled Remote Assistance, click the Advanced button. As you can see in the next illustration, you can use the Remote Assistance Settings dialog box to allow remote control of your computer. Keep in mind that if you do not enable Remote Control, the Expert user will be able to see your computer but not make any configuration changes. You can also specify a period of time that the invitation remains active. By default, an invitation is active for 30 days, but you can change this value if necessary.

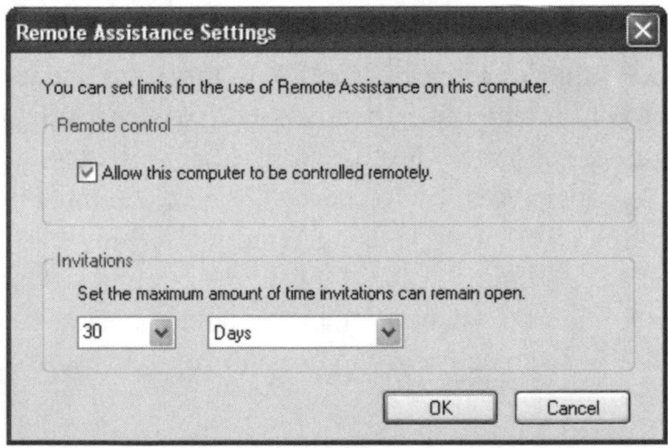

You need to enable Remote Assistance only if you plan on asking for assistance. You can accept Remote Assistance invitations from other people without enabling the feature on your computer.

Request Remote Assistance

If an end user (Novice) is ready to toss the computer through the nearest window, it is probably time to request some assistance. The Novice user will need to be able to send files to the Expert user who will be answering the call for help. This may mean using one of several methods, from using messaging software to saving a file to a floppy disk and hand-delivering it to the Expert. The logical place for the Novice to start is the Windows XP Help and Support Center. A component of this help feature provides easy access to the various methods of requesting a Remote Assistance session.

Follow these steps to create a Remote Assistance ticket:

1. Choose Start | Help and Support.
2. In the middle- to upper-right portion of the window that appears (the Help and Support Center), notice the section titled Ask for Assistance. Click the green square labeled Invite a Friend to Connect to Your Computer with Remote Assistance.
3. The Remote Assistance portion of the Help and Support Center will open. Click the link titled Invite Someone to Help You, shown in Figure 13-12.
4. In the next window that appears, choose the way you want to send the Remote Assistance invitation—either through Windows Messenger, e-mail, or by using a disk. Once you click the desired option, follow the rest of the instructions to complete the invitation.

Once the invitation is sent and received, the Expert user will be able to connect to your computer using the invitation and begin the help session.

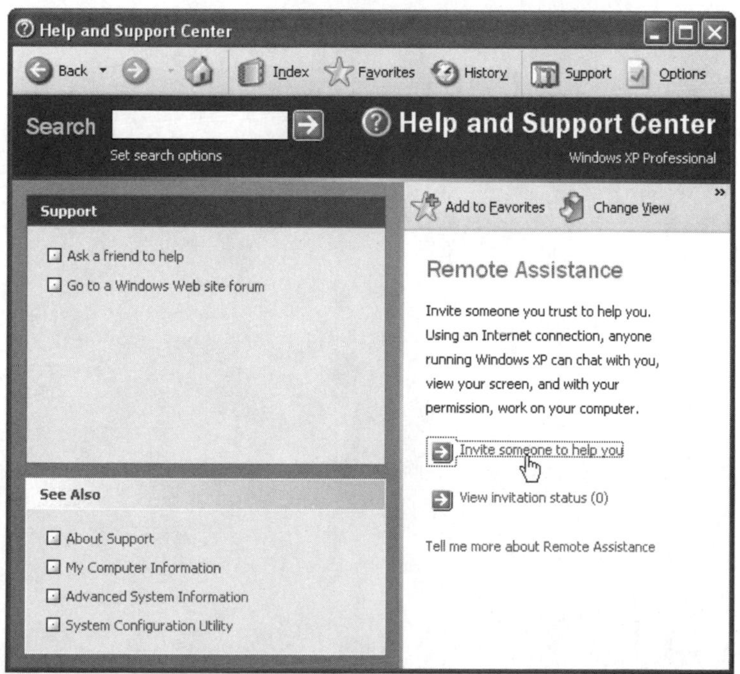

FIGURE 13-12 Invite Someone to Help You

Cool Things You Can Do with Windows XP

Chapter 14 Play Games

How to...

- Play games
- Manage game controllers
- Use Volume Control and Sound Recorder

Windows XP provides a stable system for game playing and multimedia. In fact, as game playing and multimedia have become so popular over the past few years, Windows XP is the best operating system Microsoft has produced to date for these purposes. In this chapter, you'll learn about two types of entertainment in Windows XP—game playing and sound recording. As you'll see, playing games and working with gaming hardware is a snap in Windows XP.

Manage Game Controllers

Game controllers are hardware devices that you attach to your computer. These devices enable you to play a certain type of game that requires the device. A typical example is a joystick. Joysticks have been around for some time now. If you're as old as I am, you remember owning your first joystick and trying to play the home version of PacMan on the Atari 2600 or some related game system (that dates me a little). In today's gaming market, all kinds of game controllers are in use—different kinds of yokes, gamepads, virtual reality devices, and many others.

No matter what type of device you want to use, you'll need to install it on Windows XP in order to work with the device. Installing a game controller is similar to installing any other piece of hardware in Windows XP. Typically, you attach the game controller to the correct port on your computer (following the controller's instructions). Windows XP will normally recognize the added device and automatically install it without any intervention from you. Some advanced game controllers may include an installation CD-ROM or floppy disk. If so, just follow the instructions for installation and you'll be all set.

NOTE *Make sure that any game controller you purchase is compatible with Windows XP. The device should tell you about compatibility right on the box.*

Once you have attached the game controller to your computer, you can manage and troubleshoot the device using Game Controllers in the Control Panel. Simply open the Control Panel and double-click the Game Controllers icon. The Game Controllers window, shown in Figure 14-1, shows you a list of game controllers currently installed on Windows XP.

NOTE *If you don't see a Game Controllers icon in the Control Panel, switch the Control Panel to Classic view.*

Using this window, you can add devices to and remove them from the computer, and you can access properties for the device—which may or may not have configurable options, depending on the game controller. If you choose to add a new device, click the Add button and the Add Game Controller window appears. From this window, you can select your device from the list and add it to your system, as shown in Figure 14-2.

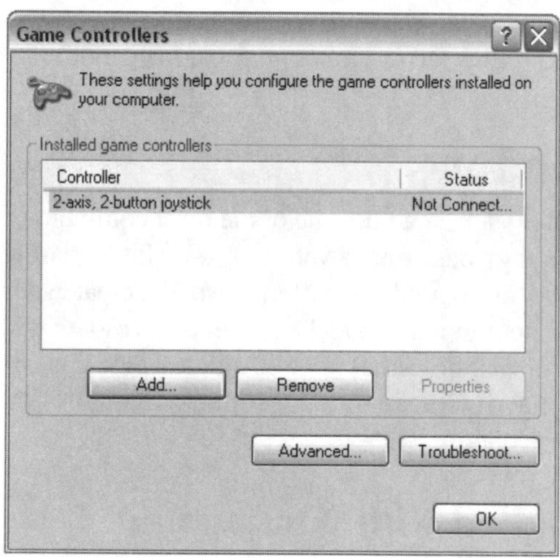

FIGURE 14-1 Game Controllers

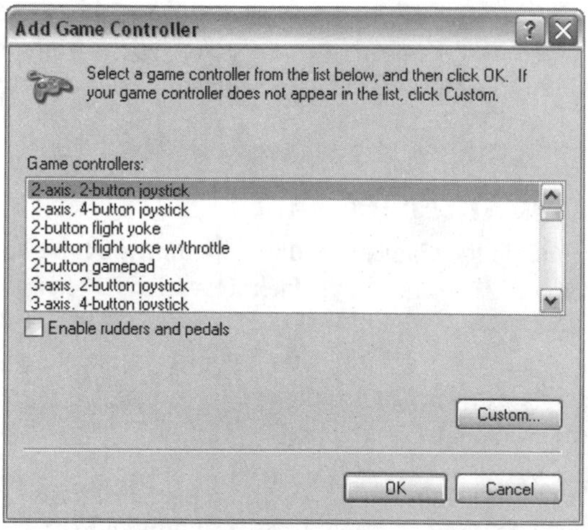

FIGURE 14-2 Add Game Controller

Windows XP should automatically detect and install game controllers. Under most circumstances, you should not have to add controllers manually to your system. You can, however, try manually adding an item if you are having installation problems.

Play Games with Windows XP

Let's face it, for all the great tasks a PC can do, one of the most common reasons we use the PC is to play games. Gaming technology has come a very long way in the past few years. With rich PC multimedia support, you can be transported into different worlds, create your own civilizations, race a car—you name it—you can do it in a game and experience awesome graphics and sound while playing. You can play games on Windows XP in three major ways: you can play the basic games included with Windows XP, play Internet games, or install other games that you purchase. The following sections explore these options.

Playing Games Installed with Windows XP

Unfortunately, operating systems do not offer a bunch of powerful games for free. You have to purchase those on your own and install them on your computer. However, Windows XP does include a few basic games you can play to pass the time: FreeCell, Hearts, Minesweeper, Pinball, Solitaire, and Spider Solitaire. Also included are several games that are designed for play with an Internet player: Internet Backgammon, Internet Checkers, Internet Hearts, Internet Reversi, and Internet Spades.

If you want to play one of these games, choose Start | All Programs | Games or choose Start | All Programs | Accessories | Games. A pop-out menu appears, where you can select the game of your choice. As with any Windows program, the game appears in a window with menu options, such as the Pinball game shown in Figure 14-3.

Playing Games on the Internet

The Internet game options found on the Games menu require that you have an Internet connection. Accessing these games takes you to Zone.com on the Internet, where you can play against an opponent on the Internet.

At www.zone.com ("the Zone"), information about your computer is gathered and an ID will be sent to you. No personal information is collected from you. Do you want to play? The following steps show you how it works:

1. Choose Start | All Programs | Games or choose Start | All Programs | Accessories | Games, and then select an Internet game. A window opens telling you about the game played on Zone.com, as shown with Internet Checkers in Figure 14-4.
2. Click the Play button. The game uses your Internet connection to explore Zone.com to find another player.
3. If a player is found, the game commences, as shown in Figure 14-5. Notice that you have the option of chatting with the other player as well (using a preselected list of comments, which prevents someone from calling you names you don't like).

FIGURE 14-3 Pinball game in Windows XP

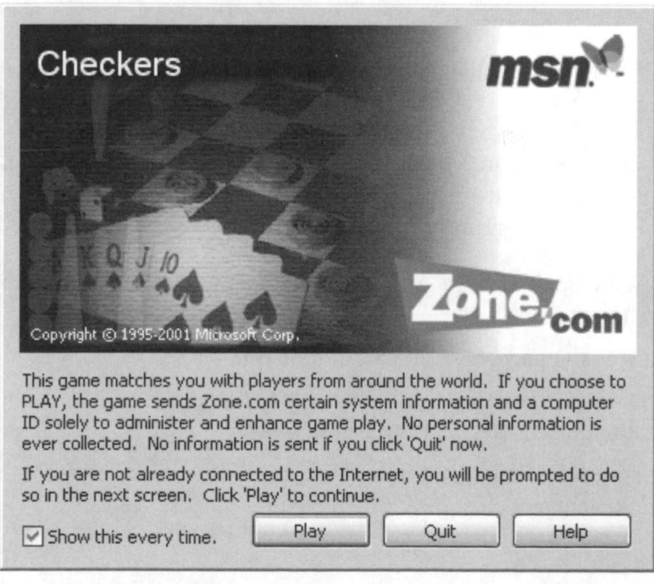

FIGURE 14-4 Game window on Zone.com

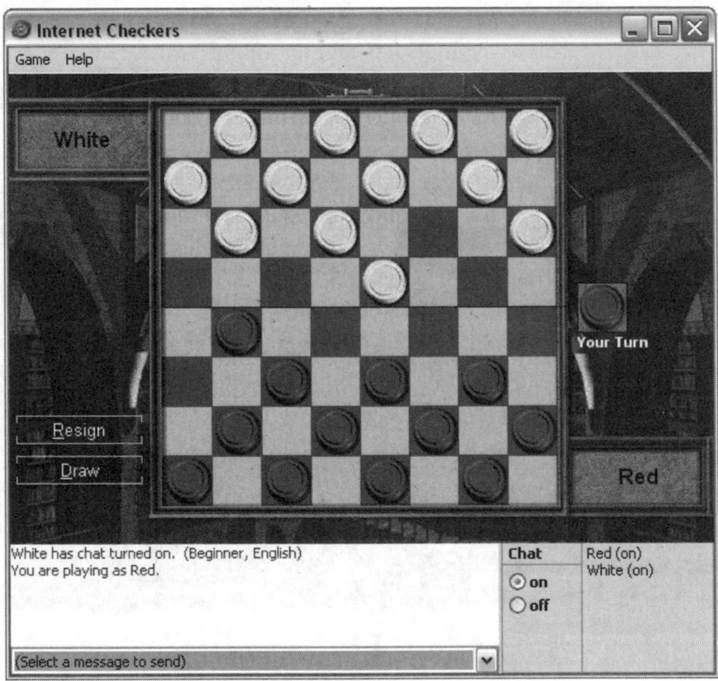

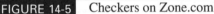

FIGURE 14-5 Checkers on Zone.com

So, what happens if you really like playing Internet games but don't want to play any of the games available with Windows XP? You can go to Zone.com, download some software, and start playing all kinds of free games on the Internet with other people. Obviously, there are Internet gaming sites other than Zone.com; but because the MSN Internet Gaming Zone is somewhat integrated with Windows XP, I do want to show you all you can do there. Follow these steps to start playing other games on Zone.com:

1. Open a Web browser, start an Internet connection, enter **www.zone.com** in the Address bar, and press ENTER.
2. Toward the top of the page, click the Sign In button.
3. The next window tells you that you'll need a .NET Passport to sign in, such as an MSN account, a Hotmail account, or a Passport account.
4. On the Zone.com page that opens after you sign in, you are asked to enter a nickname. Enter your nickname and click the Continue button.

5. You'll be asked to reenter your e-mail address. Do so and click Continue. On the confirmation page that appears, click the Yes button to make sure you get the MSN Gaming newsletter.
6. This takes you back to the main Zone.com page. At this point, you can click a game to find out more about it and begin playing. That's all there is to it!

NOTE *Although most of the game-playing sessions are free, you may have to purchase some games in order to play them on the Zone.*

Installing and Playing Your Own Games

You can purchase many different kinds of games at your local computer software store or on the Internet. As you might guess, virtually anything you would want is available. The trick when purchasing any game is not to get caught up in the excitement until you are sure the game is right for your system. As you consider purchasing a game, keep these points in mind:

- Check the minimum RAM requirements and make sure your computer meets them. A typical game will list the system requirements on the side of the box.
- The game may require certain graphics and sound capabilities. Make sure your current video and sound cards can support the requirements (such as True Color).
- The game may require that you purchase certain gaming peripherals, such as joysticks and other controllers. Make sure you know what you'll need before buying the game.
- Make sure the game is compatible with Windows XP.

With those considerations in mind, buy the game you want, and then read and follow the installation instructions. Most games include one or more CD-ROMs that guide you through the installation process. Once you've finished, refer to the owner's manual for information about playing the game, game options, and solving problems with the particular game.

Troubleshooting Game Problems

Naturally, it is impossible to offer every solution to every problem you might encounter with a game, particularly one you install. Always begin with the game's documentation. Sometimes the documentation can help you solve known issues or common problems. In addition, you can use the Windows XP Troubleshooter to help you solve a problem. I have listed some of the more common problems and their solutions in the following sections.

A Game Controller Doesn't Work

If you have a joystick or some other kind of game controller that doesn't work or is working erratically, first check the documentation for the hardware to see whether any immediate solutions are recommended. Check the Game Options icon in the Control Panel for the presence of the device. If you don't see it listed there, Windows XP doesn't think it is installed on the system. Check to make sure the device is plugged in correctly, and follow the manufacturer's instructions for installing the device. If the device works sporadically, you may need to access its properties in Game Options.

Click the Settings tab and click Calibrate to try to resolve the problem. If calibration does not solve the problem, the odds are good that the device driver is incorrect, corrupted, or needs to be updated. Try to reinstall the device driver or obtain an updated one from the manufacturer's Web site.

DirectX Problems

DirectX is a graphics software component used by many games. If you get DirectX error messages, the odds are good that you need to install the latest version of DirectX (found on the Windows Update Web site) or that you are using a newer version of DirectX that your game does not support. Check your game documentation for more information. If you are using an older video card, you may also experience incompatibility problems with DirectX.

Game Lockup

Lockups are generally caused when a game attempts to use hardware in some way that violates the integrity of the Windows XP operating system. This can cause a "hard lock." Press CTRL-ALT-DEL on your keyboard to get control of your system, or you may have to restart your PC. If this continues to happen with one particular game, it probably indicates software problems with the game. Consult the game documentation or manufacturer's Web site for more information.

Set Display Mode: DDERR_GENERIC

This error message can commonly occur if your video card resolution settings are too high for your video card to handle. You need to lower them to 256 colors on the Settings tab of the Display properties sheets.

Tired of playing a game, but you can't seem to make it stop? Just press the ESC key on your keyboard. This is a universal control that almost always halts a game and gives control of the operating system back to you.

Use Volume Controls and Sound Recorder

In the Entertainment menu in Accessories (Start | Entertainment | Accessories), you'll find two utilities—Volume Control and Sound Recorder. These are simple to use, and I just want to mention a few things about each of them.

Choosing Volume Control opens a window, shown in Figure 14-6, containing different slider controls so you can manage the volume of your speakers, microphone, and other Windows sound options.

NOTE

You can also access Volume Control by right-clicking the Volume icon in your System Tray and choosing Properties.

As you can see in Figure 14-6, the Volume Control window is a simple interface that is easy to use. One thing you might want to remember is that not all of your Volume Control options may be available by default. Choose Options | Properties, and you will see a list of volume controls you can add for different devices, as shown in Figure 14-7. Just select the check boxes of those you want to add, and then click OK. The rest is self-explanatory.

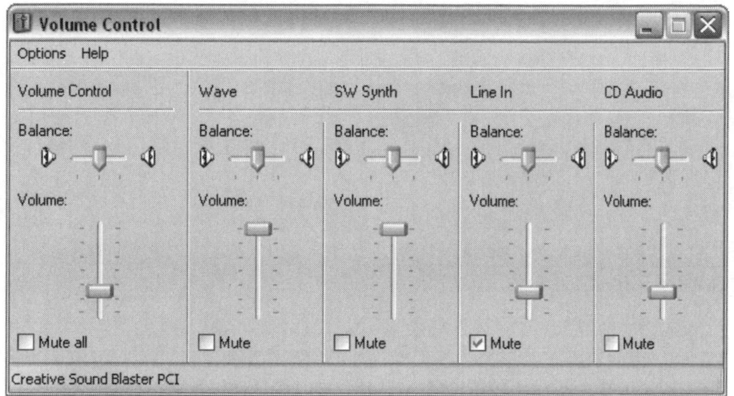

FIGURE 14-6 Volume Control

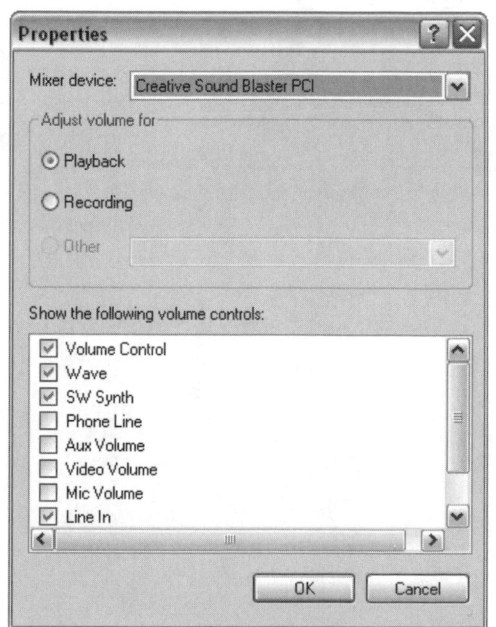

FIGURE 14-7 Properties options

FIGURE 14-8 Sound Recorder

Sound Recorder is a little utility that helps you record your voice (or whatever sound you want) using a microphone attached to your computer. The controls for Sound Recorder, shown in Figure 14-8, are similar to those on a tape recorder.

Click the record button to start recording. Once you have finished, you can save the recording as a file. The menu options offer standard choices, and you can play around with these settings to see which ones work best for you. Like Volume Control, Sound Recorder is easy to use—just spend some time with it and you'll be a recording pro in no time.

Chapter 15 Use Windows Media Player 10

How to…

- Play media with Windows Media Player
- Rip CD tracks and other media
- Create and manage playlists
- Manage a Library
- Configure Media Player

Windows Me introduced Windows Media Player 7, which was a gigantic improvement over previous versions of Media Player. Windows XP first appeared with Media Player 8, and later version 9, and now you can download the latest, Media Player 10, from www.microsoft.com/windows/windowsmedia/download. If you have used Media Player 9, using Media Player 10 will not need much of a learning curve, but Media Player 10 does include some new and very cool features. With Media Player 10, you can play and manage all kinds of multimedia, from CD/DVD music and movies to all kinds of downloadable multimedia files. Media Player 10 also gives you great media management features, and in this chapter, you will learn about them.

You can start Windows Media Player by choosing Start | All Programs | Windows Media Player. Depending on your system configuration, you may also see a shortcut to Media Player on your Desktop or on your Taskbar.

Once you open Media Player, you'll see a default interface. I say *default interface,* because you can completely change the interface using a variety of *skins* (which you will learn about later in this chapter in the section entitled "Skin Chooser"). The default interface provides you with a primary media area, a list of buttons on the top bar of Media Player (called features), and a standard toolbar. If you click a button, you can see the contents displayed in the window. Figure 15-1, for example, shows my Library.

You use Media Player by accessing the features on the top of the Media Player interface. By default, Media Player always opens to the Media Guide, which shows you the Internet page found at www.WindowsMedia.com. Each feature does something different, of course; the following sections explore the primary features and other aspects of working with Media Player.

Now Playing

Now Playing is your media play area and the primary area you will use—it lists or shows whatever type of media you are currently playing. When you insert most types of media into your PC, Windows Media Player will automatically launch. For example, let's say you want to listen to your favorite CD. All you need to do is put the CD into the CD-ROM drive; then Windows XP scans the CD, recognizes it as a music CD, and launches Windows Media Player. Media Player begins playing the CD, and information about the CD appears in the Now Playing area, as shown in Figure 15-2. If you decide to watch a home movie you have made with Movie Maker, the home movie will also be displayed in the Now Playing window.

FIGURE 15-1 Media Player Library

You can change and configure the Now Playing interface. Because the primary purpose of Now Playing is to provide a quick and easy interface to view and hear multimedia, specific configuration options for the media cannot be changed here; instead, you can adjust what is displayed in the Now Playing area and how the display looks.

First, if you look along the top of the display window (just under the button options), you see the following four buttons.

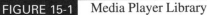

TIP *If you have trouble figuring out what buttons do what, hover your mouse over the button and a pop-out caption appears, telling you what the button is for.*

- **Select Now Playing Options** This option enables you to choose different visualizations, online stores, plug-ins, and enhancements, all of which are explored later in this chapter.
- **Toggle Visualizations** A visualization is a graphical display that moves with the music you are playing. You can use the forward and back arrows to switch to different visualizations.

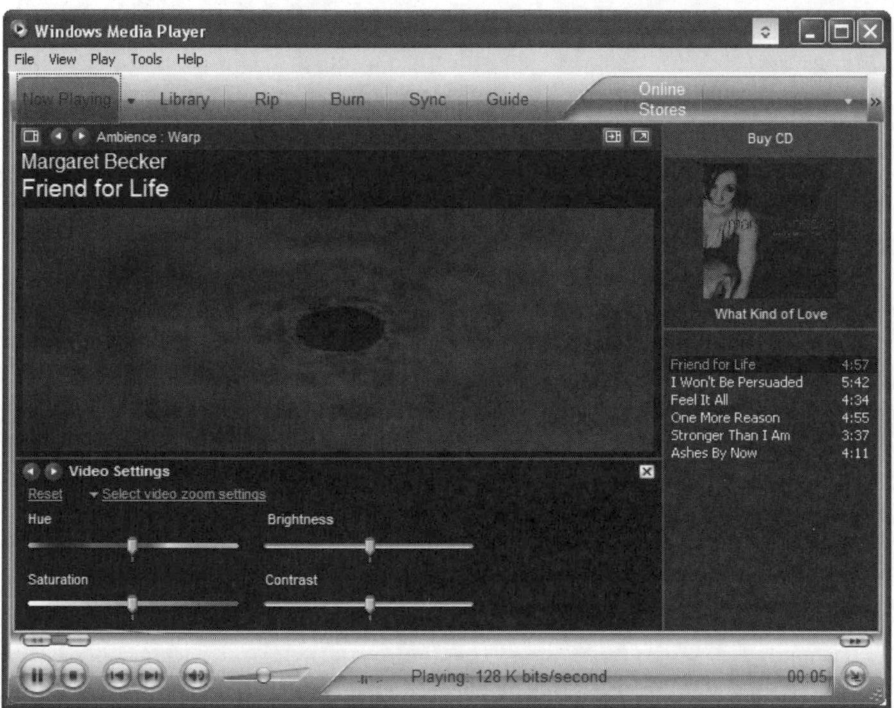

FIGURE 15-2 Now Playing area

- **Maximize the Video and Visualizations Pane** This option maximizes the area of the Now Playing window that displays video or visualizations (visualizations are explored in more detail later in this section). If you use this button, media is centered and the playlist is removed.
- **View Full Screen** This option allows you to view the Now Playing area full screen on your computer, which can be helpful if you are watching a movie clip.

You can also use the Online Stores drop-down menu in the upper-right corner of the window to find out more about and browse online stores.

Use the standard control buttons in the lower-left area of Media Player to play the media, stop playing the media, skip tracks forward and back, adjust the volume, and use related stereo or video controls. You can find these same controls in the Play menu at the top of the interface. At the bottom right of the interface, you also see button options to switch to skin mode. We'll explore skin mode later in the section "Skin Chooser."

TIP *If you don't see the menu bar across the top of the Media Player window, you can turn it on by clicking the little arrow button on the title bar interface to the right (it's near the minimize, maximize, and close buttons).*

Aside from the immediate button options available on the interface, you can use the View menu to change a number of items affecting the Now Playing area's interface:

- **Full Mode** The default display is shown to you in full mode. If you switch to compact mode, choose this option to return to full mode.
- **Skin Mode** This option allows you to choose a skin mode, which uses an overlay graphic to change the way Media Player looks.
- **Now Playing Options** This option provides a pop-out menu, where you can choose to do the following:
    - **Show Title** This option shows both the title and playlist option.
    - **Show Media Information** This displays title information about the media (such as the artist and songs, name of the video, and similar information).
    - **Show Playlist** For music media, this option shows the list of songs on the CD or the playlist you have created.
    - **Show Resize Bars** Resize bars appear between the different options you elect to show on the Now Playing area. The resize bars enable you to adjust the size of the components as you desire.
- **Visualizations** Visualizations give you a graphical view while you are playing audio-only media. For example, when you play a CD, the visualization options display interesting graphical patterns that move to the beat of the music. If you like this feature, the pop-out menu that appears here allows you to select the visualization you want to use. You can also change the visualization directly from the Now Playing area by clicking the visualization arrow buttons on the toolbar. You can see a sample visualization in Figure 15-3.

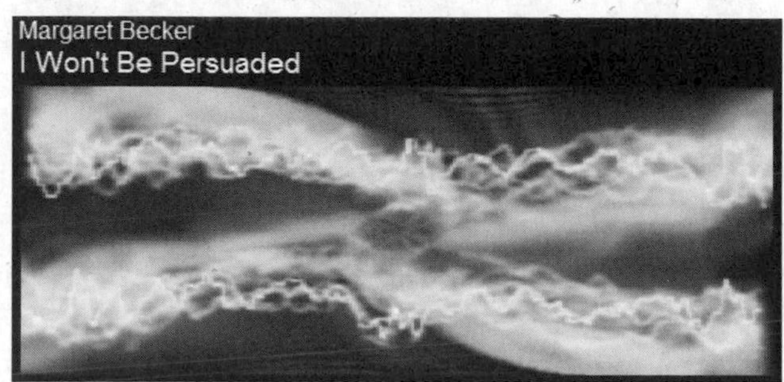

FIGURE 15-3 Visualization

NOTE

You can easily manage visualizations by choosing Tools | Options and then selecting the Plug-ins tab. You'll find a simple interface where you can add and remove visualization files.

- **Info Center View** This option displays the Info Center view, which downloads information about the media being played from the Internet.
- **Plug-Ins** Some media may require a *plug-in,* which is a small software program designed to work with Media Player. The Plug-Ins menu option allows you to see what plug-ins are installed and offers additional options for locating and managing plug-ins.
- **Enhancements** This option allows you to use some equalizer and volume-management features, as well as video settings when you are playing video. If you choose Enhancements | Show Enhancements, you can see a graphic equalizer in the Now Playing area, as shown in Figure 15-4, where you can adjust the EQ (equalization) and balance of sound.

TIP

Keep in mind that the Enhancements features can also be found by clicking the Select Now Playing Options button on the toolbar.

- **Statistics** When playing videos, choose this option to view statistics about the video transmission quality. The Statistics window may be particularly helpful when troubleshooting problems with streaming media.
- **Full Screen, Refresh, Video Size** The final options in the View menu provide basic viewing capabilities.

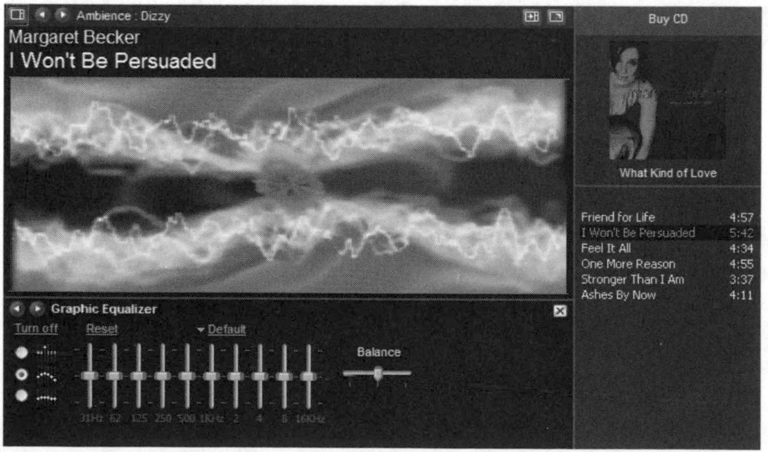

FIGURE 15-4 Graphic Equalizer

Get Visualizations from the Internet

Media Player offers quite a few visualization options when you choose View | Visualizations. However, if you are a visualizations junkie, you can also get more from the Web, and here's how:

1. In Media Player, choose Tools | Download | Visualizations. This action launches an Internet connection and takes you to the Windows Media Player site at www.windowsmedia.com/mg/visualizations.asp.
2. In the Web browser, inspect the visualizations available, and then click the one you want, which starts the download process.
3. When the File Download dialog box appears, choose to run the program from its current location, and then click OK.

Once the download is complete, installation is automatically started. The visualization is installed and now available in Media Player. That's all there is to it!

Library

All of your saved music and video files are stored in the Library under different categories so that you can easily access them, as shown in Figure 15-5.

On the left side of the interface, you see various categories with plus and minus-sign boxes next to them. Click a category, and you can see the songs or videos in your library for that category. For example, when I expand Album, I can select an album and see a list of songs I have copied to my computer from that album in the right pane. Just double-click a song or video clip to hear or see it.

So, how can you use the Library? Keep in mind that the Library's purpose is to help you keep track of files that you want. The Library is able to detect the type of multimedia you are using and add it to the appropriate category. You can search your Library by clicking the Search button at the top of the interface, and you can perform standard add, remove, and delete functions.

You can also use the Library to create a playlist of your favorite tunes or videos. The following sections show you how to use these options.

Adding an Item to the Library

To add a new item to the Library, click the Add button (plus sign) on the interface in the lower-left corner. A submenu pops out that enables you to add a track that is currently being played, a file, or media found on the Internet. If you want to add a file, a typical browse window appears for locating the file you want to add. If you want to add something from the Web, a window appears in which you can enter the URL of the media item.

FIGURE 15-5 Library interface

Creating a Playlist

At any given moment, I have about 10 favorite songs. The problem is that each song is by a different artist on a different CD. Media Player can solve that problem by allowing me to copy each of those songs and create a playlist so that each song is played in the order I want directly from my hard drive. Sound interesting? Here's how it works:

1. In Library, click the New button (found on the toolbar to the right) and choose Playlist from the menu that appears.
2. In the left pane, choose to access media in the Library by artist, album, or one of the other options on the drop-down menu. Then click the desired media to add it to your playlist.
3. You can browse through all of your media and generate a custom playlist this way, as you can see in the following illustration. When you're done, just enter a name for the playlist in the dialog box.

NOTE *You can quickly burn a playlist to a CD or synchronize with a device using the Start Burn and Start Sync buttons under the playlist.*

Rip

The Rip feature gives you information about the music CD you are currently listening to so that you can *rip,* or copy, the songs to your Library. If you are connected to the Internet, you'll see the names of the songs, artist name, and album name. If not, the tracks are simply listed as Track 1, Track 2, and so on, as you can see in Figure 15-6.

In the upper-right corner of the interface, you see Find Album Info and a View Album Info buttons. You can click these buttons to get additional information from the Internet about the album. Actually, this feature sometimes gives you additional information, and sometimes not, depending on how the album is listed. You may also be able to purchase the CD online from this interface.

You also see a Rip Music button, which may be what you really want to know about. You can copy any music track from a music CD so that the track is stored on your hard drive. This feature has two benefits. First, you can store songs you really like directly on your hard disk so that Media Player can play them without the music CD. Also, you can generate your own collection of favorites and create a playlist. The following sections tell you how to copy and configure copies of songs.

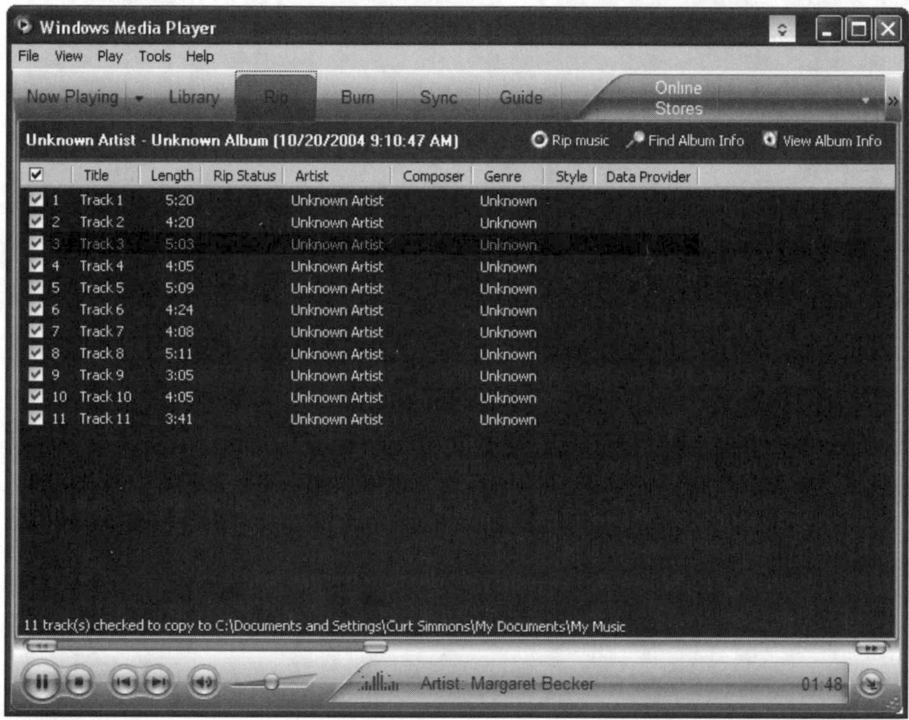

FIGURE 15-6 Rip track listing

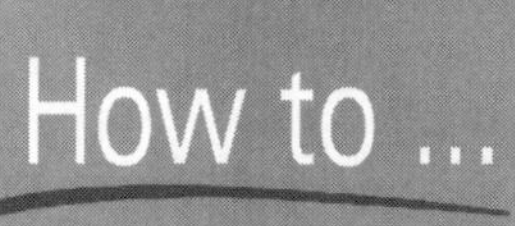

Make a Copy

To make a copy of a song from a CD, just follow these steps:

1. In Media Player, click the Rip button.
2. In the list of tracks, clear the check boxes next to the song(s) you do *not* want to copy. In other words, any songs with the check box enabled will be copied to your hard disk.
3. Click the Rip Music button. Depending on your configuration, you may be able to hear the song while it is being copied. The feature area shows you the progress of the copy as it occurs, although the ripping process proceeds much faster than actual playback of the song.
4. Once the rip is complete, the song is placed in your Library.

Configuring CD Audio Options

You can control how songs are recorded and managed in Media Player by choosing Tools | Options. Click the Rip Music tab, shown in Figure 15-7.

Under most circumstances, the default options configured on this tab are all you need, but at times you may want to change the default behavior. The following options are found on this tab:

- **Rip Music to This Location** By default, the location is My Documents\My Music. If you want to change this default location, click the Change button and select a different folder on your computer's hard drive.
- **Rip Settings** You can choose to copy music in either the Windows Media format or MP3. The Copy Protect Music check box simply means that Windows Media Player is keeping a license for you to copy the music and play it on your computer. It is illegal for you to e-mail copies of music to other people, however, or redistribute it by any other means. The other options are obvious. You can choose an Audio Quality setting by adjusting the slider bar. The higher the quality of the copy, the more hard drive space is consumed. Even at a lower quality, several megabytes of storage space will be needed for only a few songs.

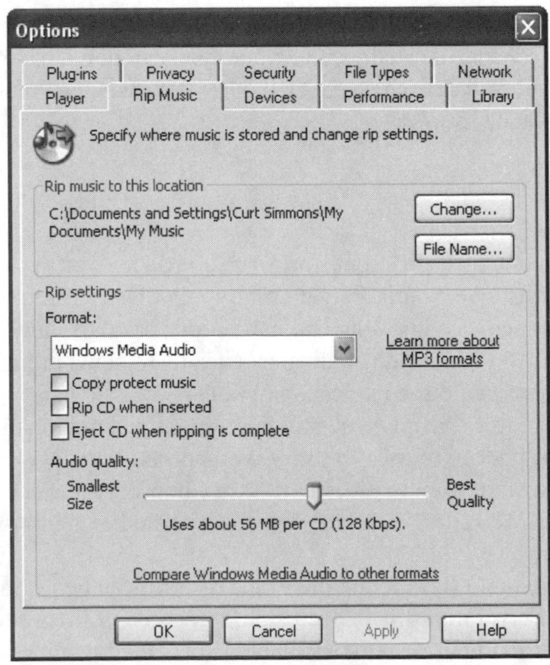

FIGURE 15-7 Rip Music tab

15

Music copies are automatically compressed to help save disk space. This is an internal feature that does not affect playback.

Burn

The Burn interface allows you to choose songs or playlists that you want to burn to a CD. First, though, your computer must have a CD-RW drive in order to burn CDs. Click the Burn button feature and use the drop-down menu on the toolbar to select the items you want to burn to your CD. Once you are done, place a CD-R disk in your CD-RW drive and click the Start Burn button.

Sync

The Sync interface looks almost exactly like the Burn interface, except you use this interface to synchronize songs with a portable device instead of burning them to a CD. Simply select the desired songs or playlists using the provided drop-down menu, make sure your device is connected and turned on, and then click Start Sync.

Guide

This button connects you to WindowsMedia.com, where you can download all kinds of music and movie files. This is a fun Web site, so do check it out. Obviously, you must be connected to the Internet for the Media Guide to work.

Skin Chooser

Media Player includes a number of different *skins*—or interface overlays—you can apply to Media Player. These skins give Media Player completely different looks, which you may find very appealing or very aggravating—depending on your point of view. For example, you can choose a skin that looks like the inside of an alien's head, as shown in Figure 15-8; one that looks like a heart; and a number of other interesting options.

As you can see, these are just for fun—you still have the same functionality in Media Player, regardless of what skin you choose to use. To use a skin, choose View | Go To | Skin Chooser. You can then choose the skin you want to use. In the Skin Chooser, you can click More Skins to connect to the Media Player Web site, where you can download other skins—you'll find several others available on this site.

Although most skins are fun, I have found that some of them can be aggravating. Sure, you maintain the same Media Player controls in each skin, but some of them seem to be more of a hindrance than a help. Experiment with the available skins and download some new ones so that you can find the one that is right for you—and remember, you don't have to use a skin at all.

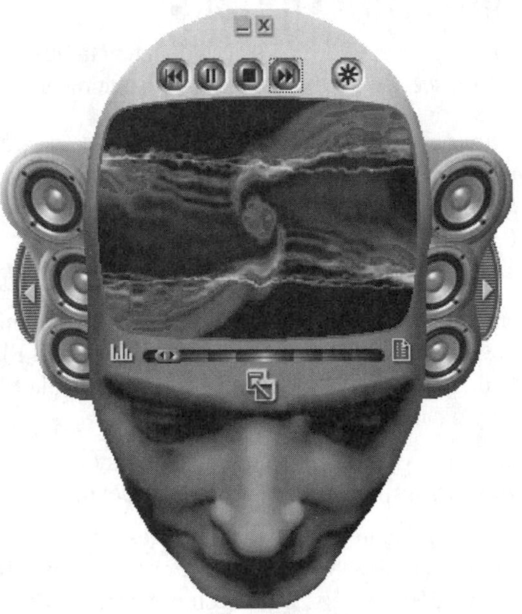

FIGURE 15-8 Personalize Media Player with a skin.

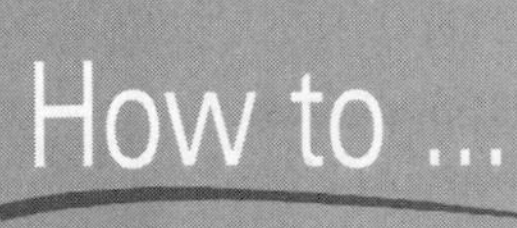

NOTE

If you're a skins fanatic, you can visit Web sites to download additional skins, such as www.skinz.org. Make sure the skin you select is compatible with Windows XP and Media Player 10, and note that some Web sites contain skins that are not appropriate for children—so parents beware. Also, if you install the Windows Plus! pack, some skins are added to Media Player as well. See Chapter 18 for details.

How to ... Download a Skin

To download a new skin, follow these easy steps:

1. In the Skin Chooser feature, click the More Skins button.
2. Windows XP launches an Internet connection and your Web browser, connecting you to www.windowsmedia.com.
3. Check out the skins available. When you find one you want to download, just click it. Download begins automatically, and the skin is installed in Windows Media Player.
4. When the installation is finished, click the Apply Skin button to start using the new skin.

Media Player Configuration Options

In addition to all the fun and frills of Media Player, you can do a few things that are more substantial. Choose Tools | Options, and you'll see several different tabs with a number of options on each tab.

NOTE *The default options are typically all you need, so this is not an interface where you need to wade around and make configuration changes. However, there may be instances when you need to use these options.*

The following list tells you what is available on each tab:

- **Player** This tab contains a number of basic check boxes. By default, your Media Player checks the Media Player Web site monthly for updates to Media Player. This setting is all you need. By default, Media Player opens and starts the Media Player Guide. You can change that behavior by clearing the check box on this tab.
- **Rip Music** This tab enables you to make setting adjustments concerning the copying of CD music. See the How To section "Make a Copy" for details.
- **Devices** This tab, shown in Figure 15-9, lists all devices found on your computer that can be used for media playback, such as your CD-ROM or DVD drive. If you select a drive and click Properties, a window appears, where you can choose whether to use analog or digital playback and copy. Typically, this tab is set to digital; but if you're having problems, you can try the analog setting. The Error Correction feature, available only with digital playback, allows Windows to attempt to resolve problems found in the digital media. This setting can be used, but you may notice a negative effect on the performance of your system—so I recommend you skip it unless you're having problems with digital media.
- **Performance** These settings affect how Media Player uses your Internet connection. You do not need to configure anything here, but I will note that, by default, Windows Media Player can detect your connection speed to the Internet. This allows Media Player to determine how best to handle media downloads. Make sure you leave this setting as is, because Media Player will perform better if it can detect your Internet connection speeds. See Chapter 8 to learn more about Internet connections.
- **Library** By default, Library gives other applications that tap into it read-only access, and no access is granted to anyone on the Internet. You should leave these settings alone.
- **Plug-Ins** This tab allows you to manage plug-ins by adding or removing them and accessing any available properties sheets.
- **Privacy** The Privacy settings are designed to keep you anonymous while you are connected to the Internet. You can peruse this list and make any changes concerning what Media Player can and cannot do, but in most cases, the default settings are all you need.

FIGURE 15-9 Devices tab

- **Security** The Security settings you have with Media Player simply determine whether or not Media Player can run scripts from the Internet and what Internet Explorer zone Media Player should use (you can configure IE security zones within Internet Explorer using Tools | Internet Options). Generally, you do not need to change these settings.
- **File Types** This tab lists every file type that Media Player can read. You don't need to do anything here unless you do not want Windows Media Player to be the default player for a particular file type. In that case, just clear the check box next to the file type's name. This feature can be helpful if you want to use another player, such as RealPlayer, instead of Windows Media Player to view or listen to certain kinds of content.
- **Network** This tab contains protocol usage settings and proxy server enabler settings. You don't need to change anything here unless your computer is on a network that uses a proxy server. Unless a network administrator instructs you to make changes, best leave this tab alone.

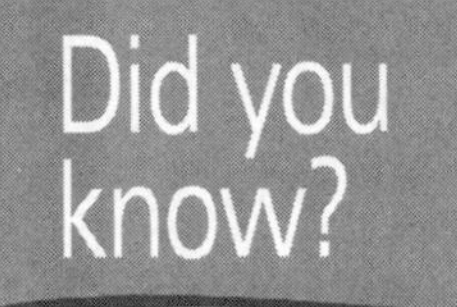

About Codecs

Notice the Download Codecs Automatically check box option on the Player tab, which is selected by default. A *codec* is a compressor/decompressor mathematical algorithm that is used for audio, video, and image files. The codec allows the file to be compressed and then uncompressed so that it can be read. Media Player must have codecs to be able to play files.

If a codec is used to compress a file, the same codec is used to decompress it. If Media Player does not have the correct codec, it will attempt to download it automatically for you. If you clear this check box option, Media Player will not be able to get the codecs it needs—so leave this check box selected!

Finally, from time to time, you can check the Media Player Web site for updates to Media Player. Media Player is an ever-growing animal, so you'll want to have the latest and greatest features as soon as they're available. You can easily check for updates by choosing Help | Check for Player Updates. This action connects you to the Internet, and it opens an Installation Options window so you can choose what new features you want to download and install.

Chapter 16

Create Movies with Windows Movie Maker 2.1

How to...

- Use Windows Movie Maker
- Import data into Windows Movie Maker
- Convert analog media to digital media
- Create and edit movies
- Add audio to movies

Over the past few years, computer users have demanded more from their computer systems. We want computer systems that will perform the important tasks that we need to accomplish, but we also want to use our computers as digital playgrounds. Windows XP helps meet the latter need by providing great digital media support, including support for digital video editing and analog-to-digital video conversion. That support is accomplished through a free application included in Windows XP called Windows Movie Maker.

First introduced with Windows Me, Windows Movie Maker is a basic video-editing tool that allows you to manage segments of video and even create your own video production. It has a number of useful features, and in this chapter, you'll explore Windows Movie Maker and see how it can help you manage and create video files. Before you get started, you should make sure that you have the current version of Movie Maker. To do so, just download Windows XP Service Pack 2, which includes Windows Movie Maker 2.1. Or, you can download it directly from http://www.microsoft.com/windowsxp/downloads/updates/moviemaker2.mspx.

Why Use Windows Movie Maker?

If you are like me, you tend to use a lot of videotape. You shoot everything from Aunt Ruth's birthday party to little Johnny's latest shenanigans. You may also have piles of still pictures—most of them not even in an album. Windows Movie Maker is designed to help you both manage and edit your home videos and pictures. You can use Windows Movie Maker to organize the data, edit it, save it, and even share it with others over the Internet. In short, Movie Maker gives you a way to manage those precious moments electronically and reduce the clutter around your house.

One of the greatest benefits of Movie Maker is that you can take analog video (such as your typical camcorder or VHS tape), import the analog video into your computer, and then manage it electronically. For example, you can store video data electronically and tuck the media disks away for safekeeping. Once thc video (and even pictures) are stored electronically, you can create multiple copies of them; store your movies on CDs, DVDs, Jaz disks, or Zip disks; and put them in a safety deposit box or other secure place for safekeeping.

Another great feature of Movie Maker is ease of editing. In any given videotaping session, you are likely to have some dull spots on tape. Consider this personal example: During the writing of this book, my wife gave birth to our daughter, Mattie. A few weeks after the commotion of the new birth, we sat down to watch the hospital video. We saw heartwarming moments and memories we never want to lose, but we were also faced with miles of boring videotape. Not wanting to miss anything on that special day, we filmed *everything*. Although *everything* seemed important at the time, in retrospect, I don't want to watch hours of videotape that shows "Here we are, waiting for the baby...."

With Windows Movie Maker, you can easily edit away the boring sections of video and keep the good stuff. By trimming clips and performing other editing tasks, your movies can become more interesting and entertaining, as well as shorter. The editing features can also help reduce the amount of storage space needed for the footage, and you can use it to join unrelated clips of video for a montage or another project.

Finally, you can have lots of fun with Movie Maker. Create your own home movies and edit in transitions, voice, background music, and much more. Get creative and stretch your brain—as you will see, there are tons of possibilities.

What Is Not So Great About Movie Maker

Believe me, I'm not completely enraptured with Windows Movie Maker; so for all of you skeptics and otherwise curious readers who want to know what is not so good about Windows Movie Maker, I'll give you my two cents in this section.

First, Windows Movie Maker is a free application included with your XP system—this should indicate to you that video-editing software is not Microsoft's main focus, and Movie Maker is, in fact, a *basic* video-editing package. This is not an advanced application. I've used video-editing software from other vendors that was much, much better, so I don't mind telling you up front that if you are really interested in getting into movie editing and production, you might want to look for a different software package that offers the power and tools that you need. However, Windows Movie Maker is free and readily available, and if you have basic video-editing needs, Movie Maker will work just fine. Overall, the software is intuitive and easy to use, as you will discover in this chapter.

Another specific caveat regarding Windows Movie Maker: When you create movies, you are forced to save those movies as Windows Media Video (WMV) files. You do not have the option of using other standard video formats, such as AVI or MPEG. Windows Movie Maker can read these types of files, but you can't save your work as one of them. The point here is that you, or anyone else who wants to view your movie, will need a Windows computer that has Windows Media Player installed to be able to play Movie Maker files. That may not seem like a big deal—but if you want to play the video on a system that does not have Windows Media Player, such as a Macintosh, you may have some compatibility problems. Again, this may not be a problem for you, but I think Windows Movie Maker should give us more file format options than it presently does.

Get Ready to Use Windows Movie Maker

If you read like I do, you may be tempted to skip over this section and get to the fun stuff, but I encourage you to read this section carefully to avoid a bunch of headaches and sorrow later on. Windows Movie Maker is a great tool, but to make it work, you have to spend a little time inspecting the hardware requirements. The trick, of course, is to get your analog or digital video and/or pictures inside your computer and into Windows Movie Maker.

First of all, let's consider the basic system requirements you need to run Movie Maker:

- **Pentium 600 MHz or equivalent** If you're using Windows Me on an older processor that is limping along, I'm afraid it won't have the power Movie Maker needs to process graphics and sound.
- **128MB of RAM** You need this minimum amount of RAM for Windows Movie Maker to function properly. If you want it to function well, you should have at least 256MB of RAM.
- **Up to 2GB of storage space** Movie files use a lot of storage space. Make sure your computer has plenty of room to store the movies you create.
- **A video card or video capture device** A standard video card will work just fine. If you want to capture analog video, you'll need a capture device that supports the feature.
- **A sound card or sound capture device** A standard sound card or device will work fine.

NOTE *Windows Movie Maker will look for and expect to find both a video and sound card or other capture device. If it doesn't find these, you'll receive a message telling you that your computer does not meet the Movie Maker requirements.*

Transferring Digital Images

Now that you know the basic requirements, let's spend a moment talking about getting video and pictures into your computer. First, if you are using a digital camera or camcorder, you're not likely to run into many problems. Because the media is already digital, you simply connect your camera or camcorder into your computer and follow the manufacturer's instructions for saving the digital content to your hard disk.

For the best performance, your computer needs an IEEE 1394 card, so you can import movies from a digital camcorder into your computer (especially important if you'll be using any streaming media devices). This type of card provides fast transfer from the camcorder to the computer and is highly recommended by Microsoft. You will need to do a little investigative work to determine whether your computer has this card, whether your digital camcorder supports it, and whether this transfer card is right for you. Consult your computer and camcorder documentation for more information.

Windows Movie Maker can recognize all kinds of graphics files, from AVI and MPEG to basic Web files such as JPEG and GIF. Once the files are loaded and saved onto your hard disk, you can use Windows Movie Maker to import and begin working with them.

Converting Analog to Digital

What about still pictures or analog video? What about a song you have written that you want to use as background music? Once you move out of the native digital arena, you then must use *capture devices* to move the analog information into your computer, where it is converted to digital information and saved. To do that, you need some kind of capture device that can import the data into your computer—these capture devices are video cards with video and audio input ports and sound cards with an audio input port. By connecting your analog camcorder or VCR to a composite video input or coax input port, you can receive the analog data from the camcorder or VCR and convert it to a digital format for use on your computer. In the same manner, your sound card can convert music and voice data from an analog device into a digital format that can be used on your computer.

TIP *Check out your capture device's instructions. Most devices tell you exactly how to connect the analog device to the card and capture video—and most even provide the cables you'll need to do so.*

You may already have a video capture device and sound card that support this process. If not, you can purchase new cards at your local computer store. They're not terribly expensive—generally anywhere from $100 to $200—but do make sure they are compatible with Windows XP; check the Windows XP Web site (www.microsoft.com/windowsxp) for continually updated information about compatible hardware. Also, if you owned one of these devices under Windows 98/Me/2000, you may need to download new drivers from the device's manufacturer so it will work correctly with Windows XP. Check out the manufacturer's Web site to see if an update is available.

NOTE *If you decide to buy a new capture device, make sure you know what kind of slot is available in your computer for the device—usually either PCI (Peripheral Component Interconnect) or AGP (Accelerated Graphics Port). Refer to your computer's documentation for more information about available ports.*

Once you connect your analog device to the capture devices, you can start the video on the analog device, and then use Windows Movie Maker to view and capture it—in a perfect world, anyway. Unfortunately, depending on your hardware, you can experience problems. Because of the variety of hardware available, it is impossible to offer solutions to all potential problems here, but I can give you a big tip that might save you some headaches. Usually, the capture device will ship with a CD-ROM containing the card's drivers and a program or two to help you capture video. Use the card's capture program and save the video in a common file format, such as AVI or MPG. You can then import the file into Movie Maker and begin your work from there. (See the upcoming section "Record and Import Video" for information about importing.)

TIP *Many capture devices save video files in their own default format, which may include compression not supported by Windows XP. When you start to save video using the device's program, make sure you are saving it in a format that is supported by Windows XP and Windows Movie Maker.*

Get to Know the Movie Maker Interface

Before you get started using Movie Maker, you'll need to take a few moments to familiarize yourself with the Movie Maker interface. Fortunately, the interface follows the typical Windows program interface, so it's not completely foreign to you. You can launch Windows Movie Maker by choosing Start | All Programs | Accessories | Windows Movie Maker. The basic interface, shown in Figure 16-1, appears.

FIGURE 16-1 Windows Movie Maker

The Windows Movie Maker interface comprises five major parts:

- **Toolbars** At the top of the interface, you see the Windows Movie Maker toolbars. You first see the menu options: File, Edit, View, Tools, Clip, Play, and Help. The menu options contain typical Windows menu features plus those specific to Windows Movie Maker. We'll be using these throughout the chapter. You also see a toolbar under the menus that presents typical toolbar options.
- **Tasks panes** The left side of the interface is called the Tasks pane. The Tasks pane lets you quickly access different features of Movie Maker.
- **Collections area** This area is at the middle of the interface. It is used to view and manage collections of data and view clips that you are working on at the moment. *Clips* are pieces of video or pictures, and you'll learn about those in a moment.

- **Monitor** The right side of the interface is called the Monitor. When you are working with video or still shots, the picture appears here. Standard start, stop, play, and other viewing buttons are located here.
- **Workspace** The bottom portion of the interface is called the Workspace. You use this area to edit video and/or combine still shots. The Workspace has two views: storyboard and timeline. You'll learn how to use the Workspace later in this chapter in the section "Getting Familiar with the Workspace."

Record and Import Video

Now that you have taken a look at the interface setup, you are ready to begin recording or importing video. You record video if you are streaming it live into your computer. For example, with your digital camcorder, analog camcorder, or other device (such as a DVD player or VCR), you can begin the streaming process, which appears in the Monitor area of Windows Movie Maker. To record the video as it appears, just follow these steps:

1. Begin playing the video from the desired device into your computer.
2. Choose Start | All Programs | Accessories | Windows Movie Maker to open the interface.
3. You will see the video appear on the Monitor. Choose File | Capture Video. A window appears where you can change the default recording options. Make sure the Create Clips check box is selected, and then click the Record button.
4. The video is recorded by Windows Movie Maker. Clips are being created and appear in the Collections area.
5. When you have finished recording, choose File | Stop Capture.
6. Click the Save button on the toolbar, or choose File | Save Project As.
7. The Save As window appears. By default, the project is saved in the My Videos folder found in My Documents. You can select an alternative location if you want. The file is saved as a Windows Movie Maker Project (with the extension .mswmm).

In addition to recording video, you can also import multimedia files—both video and audio (as well as still pictures). In many cases, you will choose to use the import feature simply because you can work with previously saved files. To import a file that has been previously saved, follow these steps:

1. In Windows Movie Maker, choose File | Import into Collections.
2. The Import File window opens, shown in Figure 16-2. By default, the import feature looks in the My Videos folder for a file to import, so you may have to navigate to another location on your computer if the file is stored elsewhere. Windows Movie Maker looks for all kinds of media files—select the one you want and click Open. Notice the Create Clips for Video Files check box. You should leave this check box enabled.
3. The file is imported into Windows Movie Maker. You can now work with it or save it as a project.

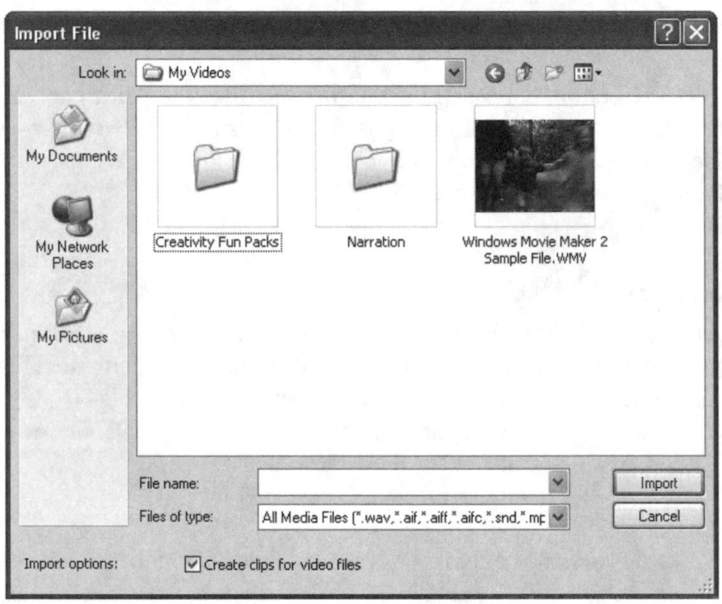

FIGURE 16-2 Import File window

When you import a file, the actual source file that you choose to import is not moved from its current location. Windows Movie Maker imports and uses the data but does not change the location of the existing source file. You are then free to use the source file for other purposes as needed.

Work with Collections and Clips

Collections are basically folders that contain clips of video or audio data. Collections provide a way for you to organize and save those clips as a project. Whenever you record or import media, Windows Movie Maker creates clips, by default. Windows XP creates clips to break apart video sequences into manageable chunks. Windows XP examines the video stream and attempts to segment it when the picture sequence changes. For example, I imported some video of a birthday party. One portion of the video contained the cake and presents, while the next showed the kids playing outside. Windows XP broke the two sequences into two different clips, which I can manage and use. This doesn't always work perfectly, but it does work well enough so that Windows Movie Maker can help you manage and edit your video more easily.

If you right-click any collection, you can delete the collection (which deletes all of the clips belonging to that collection), rename it, or import or record more clips into the collection. You can also create collections within collections. Because collections are just folder structures that enable you to organize clips, you can do what works best for you to keep your data organized in a suitable manner.

Make Movies

Now that you know how to record or import data and how to manage collections and clips, it's time to turn your attention to making movies. Using Windows Movie Maker, you record or import the clips you want to use, organize them into collections, edit them as desired, and then save the project. You are now ready to begin editing your video or still-shot clips. Keep in mind that you can combine video and still shots into one collection and blend them together as desired. You can also import background music and narrate a movie by recording your voice. The following sections show you how to perform all of these tasks.

Splitting Clips

Windows Movie Maker creates clips for you; however, you may need to split those clips into more manageable pieces. You can perform this function by using the *split* command. The following easy steps show you how:

1. Select the clip that you want to split in the Collections area.
2. In the Monitor area, click the Play button.
3. When the clip reaches the point at which you want to split it, click the Split Clip button in the Monitor area, as shown in Figure 16-3. You can also choose Clip | Split, or simply press CTRL-L on your keyboard. In the Collections area, the clip is split in two—the first part of the clip retains its original name, while the second clip contains the original name followed by *1*. You can change the name as desired.

FIGURE 16-3 Split Clip button

Combining Clips

Just as you can split a clip into two or more clips, you can also combine clips as needed. If you want to combine two or more clips, just follow these steps:

1. In the Collections area, select the clips that you want to combine: select the first clip, hold down the SHIFT key on your keyboard, and select the remaining clips that you want to combine.
2. Choose Clip | Combine. The clips are combined, using the first clip's name for the new file.

Getting Familiar with the Workspace

The Workspace at the bottom of the interface is where you edit and assemble movies. If you examine the interface, shown in Figure 16-4, you see a few buttons in the top left that correspond to areas in the Workspace. You can access volume controls, narration options, zoom controls, play and rewind buttons, and toggle between Timeline view and Storyboard views.

Creating a Storyboard

You can use the Workspace to create a storyboard or to sequence your clips together. You'll drag clips onto the Workspace area to create the storyboard. Begin by dragging the first clip in your movie to the video area of the Workspace. Once in position, you see the first frame of the video displayed in the Monitor. If you change to Timeline view, you can see how much time is consumed by the clip. By using the timeline, you can connect pieces of clips while monitoring the time frame of the whole movie. However, you will probably find that Storyboard view, shown in Figure 16-5, is initially easier to use when you are assembling your movie.

The zoom in and zoom out buttons at the top of the Workspace let you see more detail concerning the timeline (click the Show Timeline button to switch to Timeline view). While zoomed out, the storyboard is shown to you in increments of 10 seconds. You can zoom in and zoom out more to see the clips in whatever time measure you want.

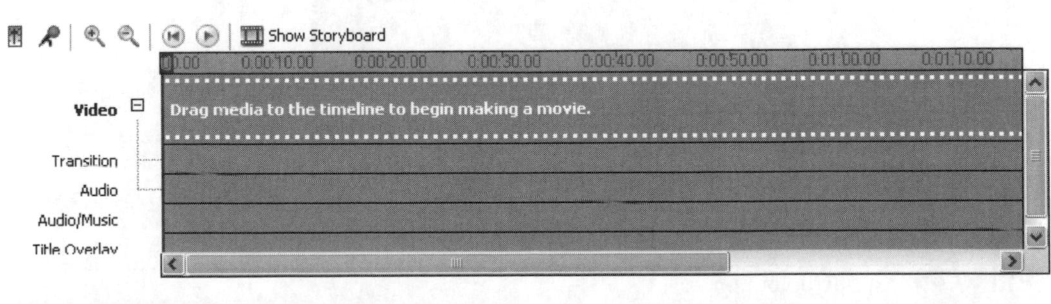

FIGURE 16-4 The Workspace

FIGURE 16-5 Storyboard view

NOTE *Feel free to mix video and still shots together on the storyboard. By default, imported still shots are given five seconds of time on a storyboard. You can change that value on the timeline by grabbing the edge of a photo and dragging to increase its duration.*

Trimming Clips

As you are working with clips in the storyboard, you will notice areas of your video that you want to cut out, or trim. These are often dull spots in the video where not much is happening. For example, let's say you have been videotaping your dog. Your dog does this great trick, but to capture the trick, you end up filming a boring minute or two waiting for the dog to perform. Now you want to lose the boring time when you create the movie—no problem; just trim off the excess.

In reality, the trim feature is very powerful because it gives you a fine level of control over your clips. You can use the timeline feature in the Workspace and trim away seconds of a clip that you do not want to use. You can trim clips in two ways; here's the first:

1. In the Workspace, select the clip you want to trim. The first frame of the clip appears in the Monitor.
2. The trimming process *keeps* the portion of videotape that you trim and discards the rest. That seems a little confusing, but it might help to think of it as trimming a piece of paper. You trim away the pieces you don't want in order to keep the primary piece. With the trim feature, you set a beginning and an end trim point, and everything outside of the area is trimmed away. To begin, click Play in the Monitor area.
3. Watch the clip until it reaches the place where you want to begin making the trim. Choose Clip | Set Start Trim Point. (Remember that anything *previous* to the beginning trim point will be discarded. The trimmed part is kept.)
4. When the clip reaches the point at which you want to stop trimming, choose Clip | Set End Trim Point. All video outside of the trim area is cut away.
5. If you don't want to keep the trim points you just set, choose Clip | Clear Trim Points.

As you can probably guess, the trim feature is useful—but a little confusing at first. Spend a few moments playing with the feature until you get the hang of how it works.

Creating Transitions

Windows Movie Maker provides several *transitions* that you can use between clips. You can also get more transitions by installing the Windows Plus! pack (see Chapter 18 for details). For example, let's say your movie contains clips of your vacation in Hawaii. You can use Movie Maker to assemble the clips and place transitions between them so the flow from clip to clip is more natural and less choppy.

You can easily create transitions in the Workspace. Follow these steps:

1. In the Workspace, make certain that Storyboard view is enabled.
2. Choose Tools | Video Transitions.
3. A transition box appears between each clip/photo on the storyboard. Drag a desired transition to a transition box on the storyboard. Each time you place a transition, an icon will appear in the transition box between each clip, as shown in Figure 16-6.
4. Click Play in the Monitor to see your movie play with the transitions.

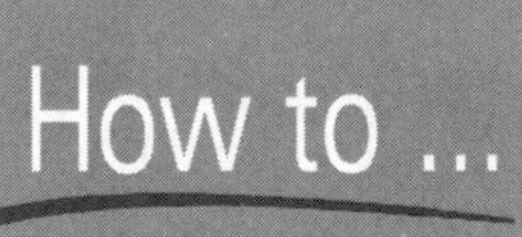

Add Effects

Movie Maker 2.1 also includes a number of effects you can add to any clip or photo. Like transitions, you can use the default effects, or you can install more effects on Movie Maker by purchasing the Windows Plus! pack (see Chapter 18). Effects cover all kinds of video/photo effects, such as blurring features, lighting features, and even an old-age film effect. These features are not necessary, of course, but they can add some cool features to your movies. To add an effect, just follow these steps:

1. Choose Tools | Video Effects.
2. Scroll through the effects and locate one that you want to use.
3. Drag the effect to the star icon on the desired clip in the storyboard (see Figure 16-6). Repeat this process for other clips to which you want to add effects.
4. Click Play in the Monitor to see your effect in action.

FIGURE 16-6 Transitions placed on the storyboard

Add Audio to Your Movies

Once you have placed clips on the storyboard, trimmed and transitioned as desired, you can add audio to your movie. For example, you can add narration, background music, or even additional background noise. If it's an audio file, you can add it to your movie.

You may wonder, "What if I want to keep the audio on my existing video?" For example, let's say you tape a family reunion. Everyone is talking and laughing, but you want to add soft background music to the movie. Can you add the music without ruining the original audio? Absolutely, and in this section I'll show you how.

Adding Audio

In the Workspace, an audio icon of the storyboard appears in the upper left, where you can manage audio levels and add narration. To record your voice or some background music or sounds, click the microphone icon. You should already have your computer microphone connected and tested, or make sure that any other sound input device that you want to use to record is ready.

If you have an existing audio file you want to use, use the import feature to import the audio file into your existing collection, and then just drag the audio file to the audio portion of the Workspace on the timeline.

To record an audio file, follow these steps:

1. In the Workspace, click the microphone icon. A window appears above the Workspace, listing the sound device that you will use to record the audio, as shown in Figure 16-7. If you have more than one sound device installed on your computer, use the drop-down menu to select a device as desired.
2. When you are ready to record, click the Start Narration button.
3. Name the file and save it. The file now appears in your Workspace timeline.

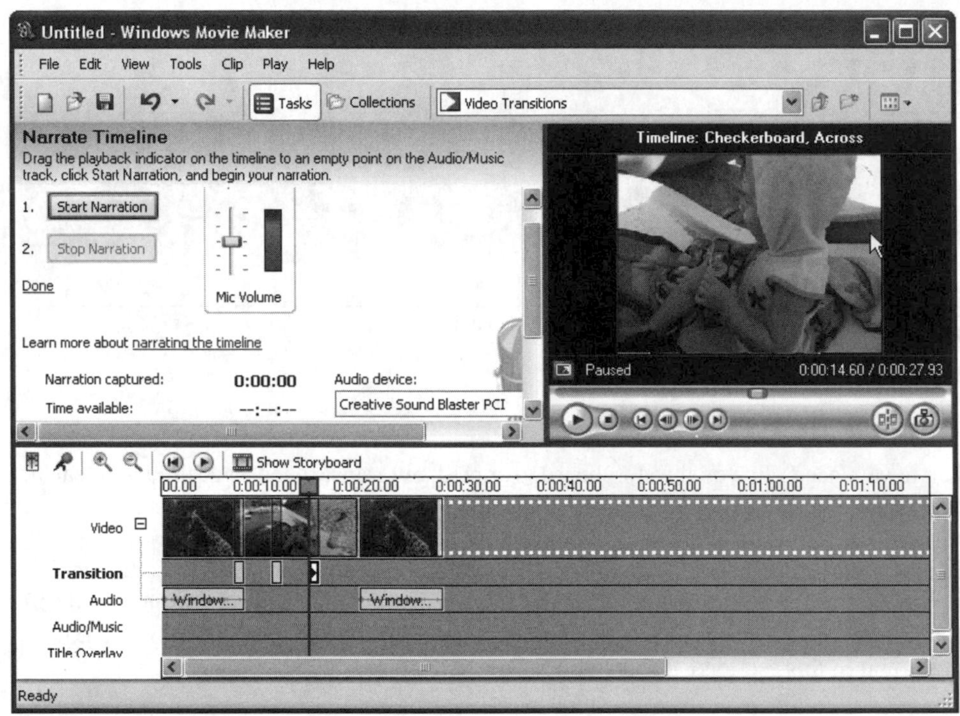

FIGURE 16-7 Record narration

NOTE *Recording narration or other background music or sounds does not erase the original video soundtrack—it simply adds another stream of sound to the existing movie.*

Adjusting Audio Levels

Once you add audio to your movie, you can adjust the audio level as needed. This is particularly helpful if you have two streams of audio—for example, a primary audio stream, such as voice, and a secondary audio stream, such as background music. By default, Movie Maker sets both streams to the same audio level, so you'll need to adjust them as appropriate. To adjust audio levels, follow these steps:

1. In Windows Movie Maker, click the Audio Levels button in Timeline view on the Workspace.
2. On the slider bar that appears, move the slider as needed (as shown in the following illustration). The video track contains your primary audio, and the audio track contains the secondary audio.

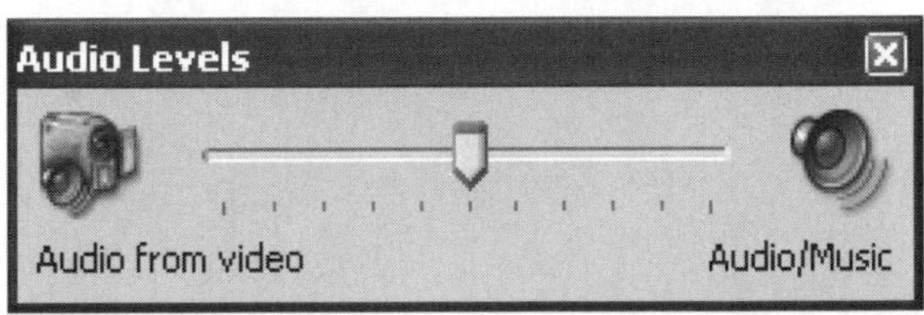

Save Movies

As you're working on your movie, you can save and close the entire project. When you're ready to begin working again, you can open the project and continue.

When your movie is finished, you can save it as a movie file so that Windows Media Player and other media software can read and play the movie. To save the movie, choose File | Save Movie File. Once you save the movie, you can view it with Windows Media Player.

Use Your Movies on the Web

As long as your friends and family have Windows Media Player on their PCs, you can e-mail your movies to them and they can watch them on their own computers.

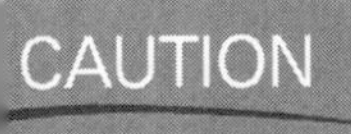

Multimedia files, such as movies, can be quite large, so be wary of sending a movie to someone who accesses the Internet with a regular dial-up modem. You really need high-bandwidth access, such as DSL or a cable modem, to send or receive multimedia files.

To send a movie via e-mail, choose File | Save Movie File. Choose either E-Mail or Web Server, and then follow the instructions that appear. You can also use this option to save your movie to My Computer, a recordable CD or other separate medium, or a digital video camera.

Chapter 17

Manage Digital Photos on Windows XP

How to...

- Work with digital photos
- Print digital photos
- Share and store digital photos

Digital photography has become an industry unto itself in the past few years. Digital cameras are better now than they have ever been, and millions of digital cameras are sold every year. Just take a walk into your favorite department or electronics store and glance at the available models. In many cases, you'll find that digital cameras are even pushing regular film cameras off the shelves! Although no one expects the film camera to die any time in the near future, the digital camera is here to stay. Windows XP gives you built-in tools and abilities that can help you manage digital photos and print them with greater ease and more flexibility than ever before. In the past, working with digital photos on a Windows computer, not to mention printing them in an effective manner, could be a difficult task. With Windows XP, however, you can spend time enjoying working with your photos, and this chapter will show you how.

Connect to Your PC

Before you can use digital photos on Windows XP, you'll need to connect your camera, card reader, or memory stick to Windows XP and download your photos. Most cameras, card readers, and memory sticks connect to your computer through a USB port. Since most of these products are plug-and-play, typically all you have to do is connect the device to a USB port and you are ready to go. However, you may have to install drivers or other software to connect your camera, so the best advice is to follow the manufacturer's instructions for downloading photos from your camera. Also, Windows XP has a wizard that you can use to install the camera on your system if you are having problems. See Chapter 7 for more information about installing a camera.

View and Manage Your Photos

Once your photos are downloaded to your Windows XP computer, you can begin using them in any way that you might want. Before doing so, it's a good idea to find out what is available to you and how you can view and manage your photos. The good news is that Windows XP is rather flexible and gives you several different options that you'll find helpful.

First of all, keep in mind that you can organize photos in any way that you want. This means that you can download all of your photos to a single folder, or you can create multiple folders and move them around as you like. Your photos may be downloaded to the My Pictures folder by default, and that's fine. However, let me point out that the My Pictures folder doesn't have any magical powers—it is simply a folder like any folder on Windows XP. I often organize my photos into various folders so I can identify them more easily. I typically organize them by event (vacations, birthdays, holidays, and so on), but you can create any kind of system that suits your needs. People who take a lot of digital photos often create a new folder for each month and put all of the photos for that month in one folder. There is no right or wrong answer, of course, but you'll want to decide on an organization method that works best for you. After all, there is nothing worse than taking a great digital photo and not being able to find it on your computer!

NOTE *If you happen to be using Adobe's Photoshop Album software to manage your digital photos, check out my book,* How to Do Everything with Photoshop Album *(McGraw-Hill/Osborne, 2003).*

Once you open a folder that has photos stored in it, you are ready to begin using your photos in a number of ways. As you can see in Figure 17-1, a folder containing photos has a Picture Tasks box that gives you several options, as well as a typical File and Folder Tasks box that can also be helpful. We'll explore the features you see here in upcoming sections, but I'll focus on a few direct features here. First of all, it is a good idea to open the View menu and find a View option that works well for you. Figure 17-1 shows Thumbnails view. This allows me to see the actual photo along with the file name.

On the View menu, you'll find the following options:

- **Filmstrip** This option presents your photos in a filmstrip fashion. You can select a photo and see a bigger image of it, and you can use the controls to click through all of your photos. You also have controls that allow you to rotate an image. Filmstrip view, shown in Figure 17-2, is really helpful if you want to get a good look at your photos.
- **Thumbnails** Shows you small photo views, as shown in Figure 17-1. This is a good way to see photos and file names at the same time.

FIGURE 17-1 Thumbnails view

17

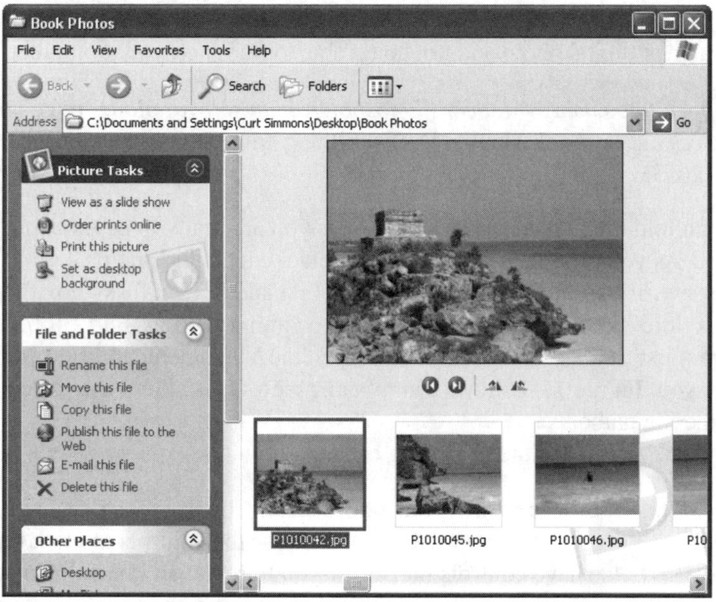

FIGURE 17-2 Filmstrip view

- **Tiles** Shows you icons (not photos), the file name, image size, and kind of image file (JPEG, TIFF, and so on).
- **Icons** Shows you smaller icons with only the file name.
- **List** Shows you even smaller icons and the file name. This view is useful to see a listing of photos so you can find the one you want by name.
- **Details** The same as List, but provides more information about each photo, such as size, type, date modified, and similar information.

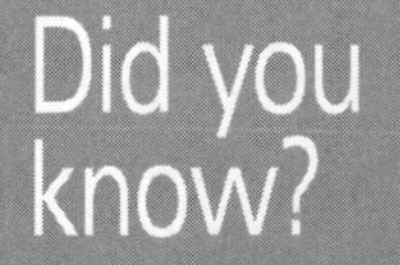

Make Sure You Back Up!

As with any file, photos can get corrupted or accidentally deleted from your system. You should have a backup plan in place so that you always have additional copies of your favorite photos stored elsewhere. This can be as simple as copying photos to a CD and putting that CD in a safe place, or it can be a full backup plan using the Windows Backup utility. You can find out more about using Windows Backup in Chapter 20.

View Your Photos as a Slide Show

Windows XP has a built-in slide show feature so that you can view the photos in a folder as a slide show. In the folder, just click the View As a Slide Show option that appears in the Picture Tasks box. Your photos will come to life in a full-screen, automatically advancing slide show. However, if you move your mouse, you'll see control options that let you manually advance or back up during the slide show, as you can see in the following illustration. You can also stop the slide show with the manual controls, or just press the ESC key on your keyboard.

In addition to these basic viewing options, you can also quickly access some features by right-clicking a photo. You'll see a context menu (the same one that appears when you right-click just about anything in Windows), but you also see some specific options that are useful in managing photos:

- **Preview** Opens the photo in Windows Picture and Fax Viewer, as shown in Figure 17-3. Windows Picture and Fax Viewer is not an image-editing program, but as you can see by the buttons at the bottom of the viewer, you can look through photo collections, view different sizes, see a slide show, zoom in or out, and rotate, delete, print, save, or open the image in whatever default image editor you have installed on your computer.
- **Edit** Opens the photo in the default image-editing program installed on your computer. This may be Microsoft Paint, Photoshop, Photoshop Elements, Paint Shop Pro, or another program you currently have installed.

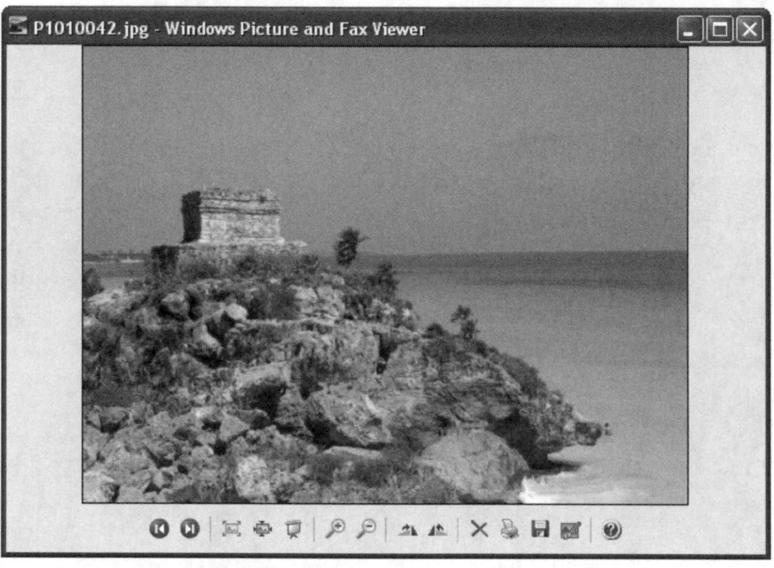

FIGURE 17-3 Preview your photo.

- **Print** Opens a photo-printing wizard, which you can learn more about in the "Print Your Photos" section later in this chapter.
- **Resize Pictures** Opens a quick and handy Resize Pictures dialog box, shown next. You can resize the photo, which creates a copy in a different size (your original photo is not tampered with, so don't worry). This helpful feature allows you to resize the photo to meet whatever need you have. Click the Advanced button to enter a custom size.

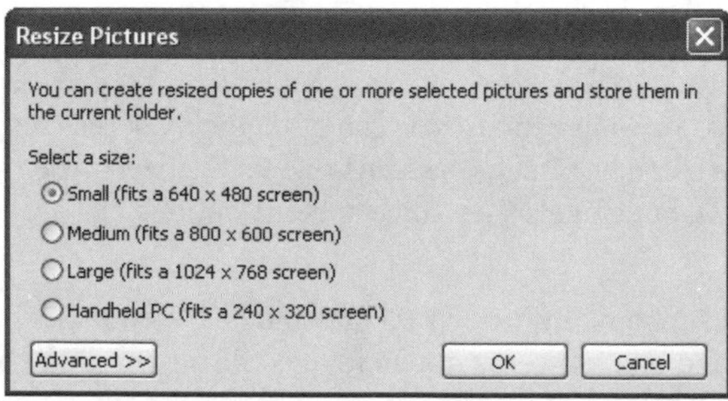

- **Rotate** Rotates your photo.
- **Set as Desktop Background** Immediately sets the photo as your Desktop background, which keeps you from having to wade through Display properties to make the change.

NOTE *You can also set a photo as the Desktop background by selecting it in a folder and clicking the Set as Desktop Background option found in the Picture Tasks box.*

Order Prints Online

One of the great things about digital photos is that you can print them on your home computer's printer with awesome quality, or you can upload them to an Internet store and have the store do it for you. The process is safe and easy, and you'll get your printed digital photos in the mail in a few days. Windows XP gives you a wizard to help you order prints online. Keep in mind that you do not have to use the wizard to order prints; you are free to access any Web site that provides prints and follow the site's instructions, but you may find the wizard helpful, especially if this is the first time you are ordering prints.

If you are wondering about which sites you should use to order prints, keep in mind that there are many to choose from (just search for "photo printers" on any search engine, such as www.msn.com), but I can recommend the following reputable printers. This list is not exclusive, but I have personally dealt with the following with quality results and service:

- www.snapfish.com
- www.ofoto.com
- www.photoworks.com
- www.clubphoto.com

If you want to order prints online using Windows XP's wizard help, just follow these steps:

1. Connect to the Internet.
2. Open the folder where your photos reside. In the Picture Tasks box, click Order Prints Online.
3. The Online Print Ordering Wizard appears. Click Next on the Welcome screen.
4. In the Change Your Picture Selection window, choose the photos you want to order. Simply clear the check box of any photo that you do not want to order. Click Next when you are done.

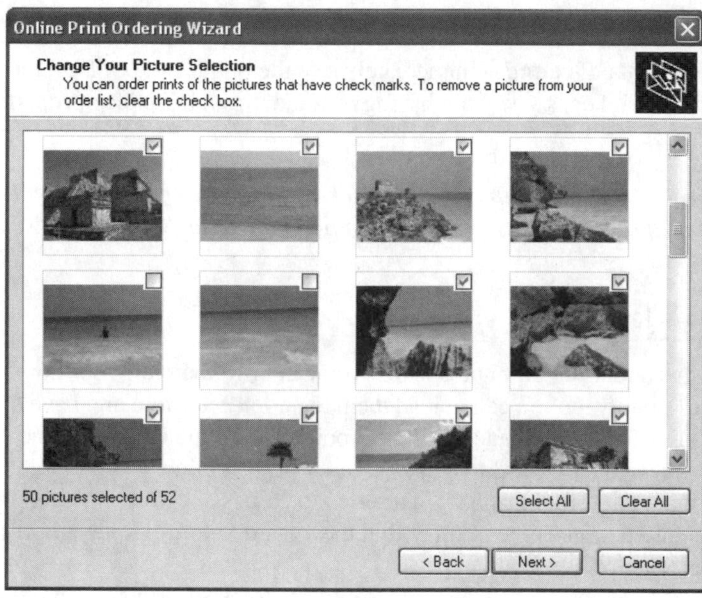
Online Print Ordering Wizard
Change Your Picture Selection
You can order prints of the pictures that have check marks. To remove a picture from your order list, clear the check box.
50 pictures selected of 52
Select All
Clear All
< Back
Next >
Cancel

5. The wizard connects to the Internet and downloads information. This may take a few moments, depending on the speed of your connection.
6. In the Select a Printing Company window that appears, select the photo company from which you want to order and click Next.

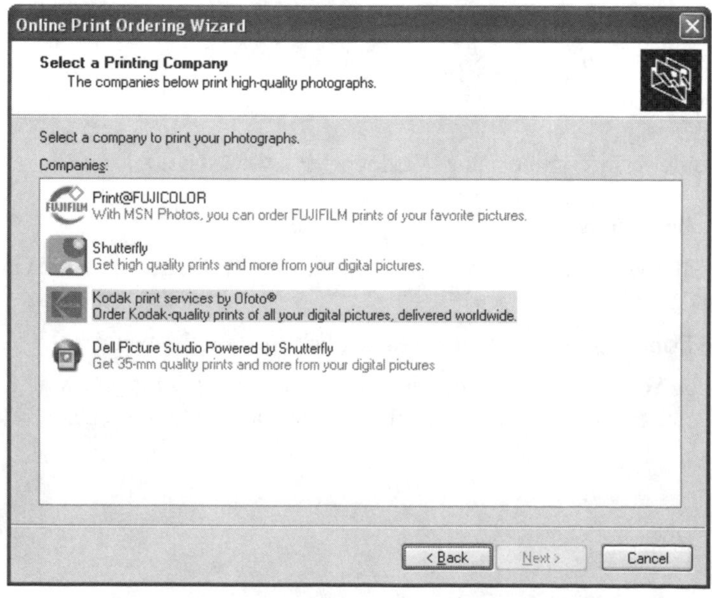
Online Print Ordering Wizard
Select a Printing Company
The companies below print high-quality photographs.
Select a company to print your photographs.
Companies:
Print@FUJICOLOR
With MSN Photos, you can order FUJIFILM prints of your favorite pictures.
Shutterfly
Get high quality prints and more from your digital pictures.
Kodak print services by Ofoto®
Order Kodak-quality prints of all your digital pictures, delivered worldwide.
Dell Picture Studio Powered by Shutterfly
Get 35-mm quality prints and more from your digital pictures
< Back
Next >
Cancel

7. The wizard downloads ordering information from the company you selected and displays it to you. Use the ordering window to select the number of prints you want, the size, and so forth, as shown in the following illustration. Scroll to the bottom of the window to see your subtotal when you are done, and then click Next.

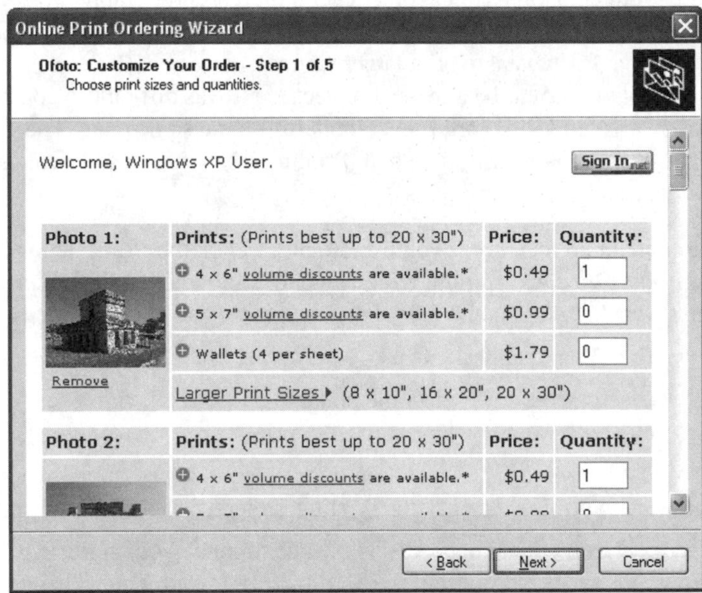

8. Depending on the company you selected, you then move through a series of windows where you establish an account and release your credit card and shipping information. This process is safe, so follow the remainder of the wizard screens to place your order.

Print Your Photos

In addition to ordering your photos online, you can also print them on your color printer. As a general rule, any inkjet printer can produce quality photos, even the inexpensive, $99, inkjet printers you see at discount department stores. Now, maybe you have tried to print your photos and ended up with terrible results. That is certainly not unusual, and there are two primary reasons why printed photos may not look great: paper and resolution.

First of all, you can't print quality photos on standard typing paper that you use to print text. The paper is not designed to hold the ink, so individual dots of ink run together, thus giving you a smeared and dull-looking photo. If you want to print effective photos, you must use photo paper. Photo paper, which is sold in packs at any department store, is designed to hold the ink and give you the results you want. Photo paper isn't cheap, of course, but you'll need to use it to print photos. Most brands you'll find at any department store work well, so before you go any further with printing, make sure you have some photo paper on hand.

The next issue is about resolution. *Resolution* refers to the number of pixels in a digital photo. Digital photos are made of tiny dots of color, pixels, that create images. The number of pixels you have in a photo determines the quality of the photo when it is printed. If not enough pixels are present, the pixels get stretched to make the size photo you want. For this reason, if you have a low-resolution photo, you can't print a quality 5×7 or 8×10 photo because there is not enough resolution. It is beyond the scope of this book to explore resolution and your camera settings, so I would suggest that you study your camera's manual or a general digital photography book so that you understand resolution more fully. Overall, though, the important thing to remember is that you need to shoot at a high resolution if you want to print larger photos, such as 8×10s.

In the past, printing photos could be a real chore because it was difficult to control the size of the printed photo and it was difficult to print several photos on the same page. The good news is that Windows XP fixes this problem with the Photo Printing Wizard. The following steps show you how to use the wizard to print your photos.

1. In the folder containing the photos you want to print, click the Print Pictures option in the Picture Tasks box. You can also right-click any photo and click Print, or select multiple photos by CTRL-clicking them, and then right-click them and click Print.
2. The Photo Printing Wizard appears. Click Next.
3. In the Picture Selection window, select the photos you want to print. Clear the check boxes next to any photos that you do not want to print.
4. In the Printing Options window, use the drop-down menu if necessary to select the printer to which you want to print. Then click the Printing Preferences button.
5. In the Properties dialog box that appears, shown next, make your selections. Make sure you choose a photo paper option from the Media drop-down menu. When you are done, click OK. This returns you to the Printing Options window. Click Next.

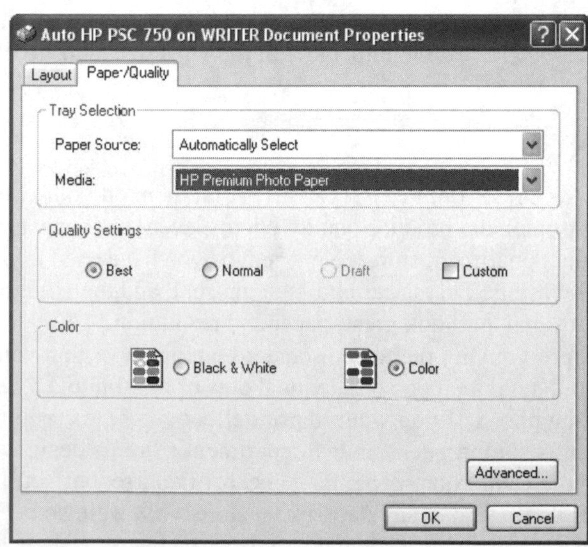

6. In the Layout Selection window that appears, choose what you want to print. You have options for full page, contact sheets, and a variety of sizes. As you can see in the following

illustration, I am printing three, 4×6 photos on a single page. Each photo is printed only once. Make your selections and click Next.

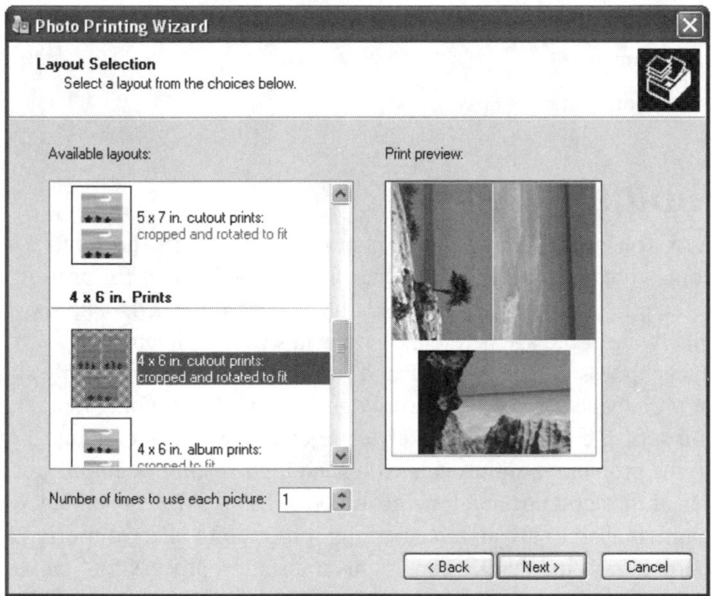

7. The photos are sent to the printer and printed. Click Finish.

Publish Photos on the Web

One of the great things about digital photos is that you can share them online either by posting them on a Web site or by e-mailing them to friends (see the next section to learn more about e-mail options). You can create your own Web sites using Web-authoring programs, or you can create accounts on sites that essentially allow you to create a home page by walking through an online wizard. You can also use Windows XP's Web Publishing Wizard to share your photos online. This option creates an account in MSN Groups, where you can post your photos and let other people see them.

Naturally, there are a lot of options for creating Web sites and showing pictures online. Some sites allow you to create online photo albums quickly and easily, so Windows XP's Web Publishing Wizard certainly isn't your only option. If you want to use the Web Publishing Wizard, just click the option to Publish This File to the Web in the File and Folder Tasks box, found in the folder's window with your photos. If you want to check out other options for sharing your photos online and creating a Web site, check out the following links:

- http://geocities.yahoo.com
- www.myfamily.com
- www.topcities.com
- http://picturecenter.kodak.com

- http://photos.msn.com
- http://photos.yahoo.com
- www.clubphoto.com
- www.snapfish.com
- www.webshots.com

E-Mail Your Photos

Consider this scenario: You take a high-resolution photo of your pet cat. The photo is a 2-megapixel TIFF file, which comes out to around 4MB in size. The photo is great for printing, but you also want to e-mail the photo to your friends. If you try to e-mail the 4MB photo over a dial-up connection, you'll likely die of old age before it ever reaches your recipients.

Let's face the facts: unless you have broadband service such as DSL or cable and all your recipients also have broadband service, you never want to e-mail something that large to anyone. If you can even get it sent, the photo would likely be rejected by your recipients' e-mail servers as being too big. So the problem is simply this: you need high-resolution photos for printing and you also need copies of those photos in a low-resolution JPEG format for sending over e-mail. In the past, that meant you had to use an image-editing program to alter your original file and skinny it down. No longer—Windows XP can do this translation process for you with just a few clicks. Here's what you do:

1. In the folder where your pictures are stored, select the photo you want to e-mail. You can select multiple photos by CTRL-clicking them. Then, either click the E-mail This File option found in the File and Folder Tasks box or just right-click the photo(s) and click Send To | Mail Recipient.
2. In the Send Pictures via E-mail window, choose the option to make your pictures smaller. If you click the Show More Options link, you see that you can determine the size that you want to make them, as shown in the following illustration. Make your selections and click OK.

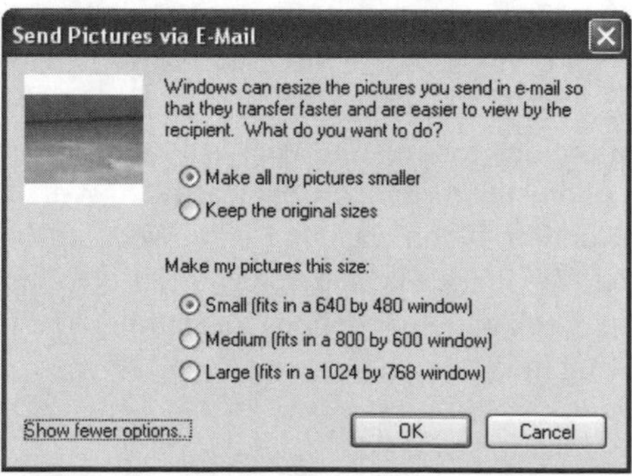

3. Windows XP prepares your images and puts them in an empty e-mail message using your default e-mail program. You can then enter the desired addresses, type a message, and click Send to send your photos.

Burn Your Photos to a CD

Like any file, you can burn photos to a CD to store them. You can use your CD-burning software as you would with any file, or you can click the Burn to CD link found in the Picture Tasks box in the folder with your photos (this option doesn't appear if you don't have a CD burner). Overall, burning photos to a CD works the same as burning any other file—Windows XP just tries to simplify the process by giving you a direct link in the Picture Tasks box.

If you have a CD burner, you can also right-click any file and click Send To, then choose your CD drive from the context menu that appears.

Chapter 18

Explore Windows XP Plus! Packs and PowerToys

How to...

- Use Microsoft Plus!
- Use Microsoft Plus! Digital Media Edition
- Run Windows XP PowerToys

Windows XP is, without a doubt, the coolest operating system Microsoft has produced to date. Although the operating system is great, you can add some fun and helpful features to Windows XP by downloading free PowerToys and by purchasing two inexpensive Plus! packs. PowerToys are small programs produced by Microsoft that are designed to enhance Windows XP or give you some additional management functionality. You can download them free from Microsoft, and you'll learn all about them in this chapter. Plus! packs are additional software CD-ROMs you can purchase at local and online computer stores. Under $30 each, the two available Plus! packs add more functionality and features to Windows XP that you may fall in love with. In this chapter, we'll explore all of these features so you can see what is available and how to use these additional software tools.

Use Microsoft Plus!

Microsoft Plus! is an additional CD-ROM of "goodies" you can purchase from any computer store. The Plus! pack contains some extra features for Windows XP, and if you are still deciding whether the Plus! pack is worth the $20 or so you'll spend for it, this section is just for you. If you already own the Plus! pack, this section will review its features and show you how to use it.

First things first. The Plus! pack is an add-on software enhancement for Windows XP. It is not an operating system, but rather a collection of tools and features that are installed on Windows XP as you would install any application. As such, you'll want to take a look at what you actually get with the Plus! pack before you part with your hard-earned money. The following list reveals its features:

- **Digital media** The Plus! pack gives you several pieces of software for digital media content, such as Voice Command for Windows Media Player, MP3 Audio Converter, CD Label Maker, Speaker Enhancement, Personal DJ, Windows Media Player skins, and additional 3-D Visualizations for Media Player.
- **Games** The Plus! pack gives you three additional games: Russian Square Plus! Edition, The Labyrinth Plus! Edition, and HyperBowl Plus! Edition.
- **Themes** The Plus! pack gives you additional Windows themes that you can apply to your Windows XP computer: Plus! Aquarium, Plus! Space, Plus! Nature, and Plus! da Vinci.
- **Screen savers** The Plus! pack gives you additional 3-D screen savers you can enjoy.

NOTE *The Plus! pack will work on either Windows XP Home or Professional edition.*

Plus! System Requirements

Before purchasing and installing the Plus! pack, you should be aware of the system requirements for running this software. More than likely, your system will easily meet the following requirements, but you should check them out just the same:

- Windows XP Home or Professional Edition
- A computer with at least a 500 MHz processor; 750 MHz or higher is recommended
- At least 64MB of RAM; 128MB is recommended
- 300MB of available disk space
- VGA video resolution; Super VGA (800×600) is recommended
- A 3-D graphics accelerator with 16MB of memory minimum; you'll need Direct3D version 8.0 API, which is supported with most modern video cards
- CD-ROM and/or DVD-ROM drive
- Keyboard and mouse (or other pointing device)

Exploring the Plus! Pack

Once you install the Plus! pack (which you can do by inserting the Plus! CD-ROM and following the instructions), you are ready to explore all that Plus! brings to you. Just choose Start | All Programs | Microsoft Plus!. This opens a standard Microsoft Plus! window, where you can access the different features of Plus!, as shown in Figure 18-1.

In the Plus! category, click the options—such as Digital Media, Games, Themes, or Screen Savers—to access the features. The following sections give you a review of what's available.

Voice Command for Windows Media Player

The Voice Command option for Windows Media Player allows you to use your computer's microphone to speak commands to Windows Media Player. For example, you can say, "Media Player, Play" so that it will start playing a song. You can also adjust the volume, skip between songs, show visualizations, and perform similar tasks. To use this feature, just click the Digital Media option in the Microsoft Plus! window and click the Start link under Voice Command for Windows Media Player. The utility will then walk you through a few training screens, where you can adjust your microphone and learn the available commands to which Media Player will respond. After that, you are ready to start using Voice Command.

MP3 Audio Converter

MP3 Audio Converter allows you to free up hard disk space by converting MP3 files to Windows Media files. This conversion will save about half the space a typical MP3 file uses. You get the same audio quality (using Windows Media Player), but the files are smaller. Of course, if you like to use media players other than Windows Media Player, don't perform this conversion,

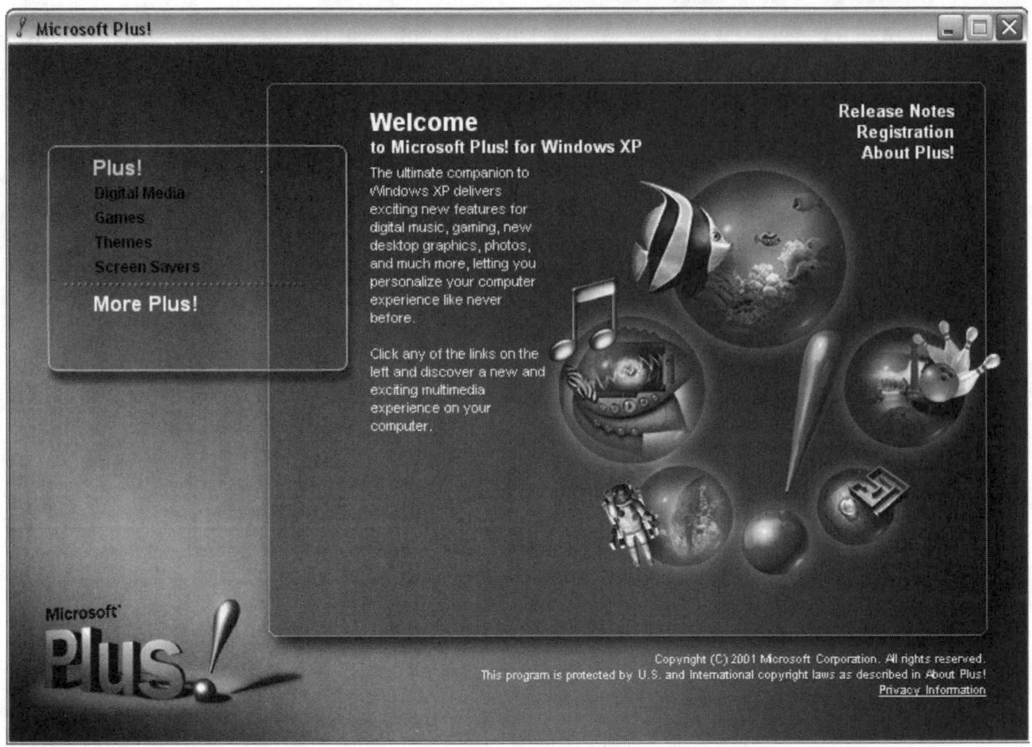

FIGURE 18-1 Microsoft Plus!

because the converted files will work only on Windows Media Player. In the Plus! window, click Digital Media, and then click Start under the MP3 Audio Converter option. A wizard appears that allows you to select the files you want to convert. After completing the wizard steps, the conversion takes place. That's all there is to it.

Remember that converted files will work only with Windows Media Player. There is no "undo convert" option, so make sure you don't need the MP3 version before running the wizard.

CD Label Maker

If you are into burning your own music CDs, Plus! can give you an added bonus by helping you print custom CD labels. You can buy CD label paper at any computer or department store, and then use CD Label Maker (found under Digital Media in the Plus! list) to make your labels and print them. Once again, a wizard appears that enables you to select the playlist, choose your type of CD paper, and give the label a title, background, and graphics. Finally, you print the new label(s) you have created. The process is fast and easy.

Speaker Enhancement

The Plus! pack provides Windows Media Player with a speaker enhancement that improves the quality of the music you hear from Windows Media Player. The process works by using a "speaker profile" for your type of speakers. Open Windows Media Player and choose Tools | Plus! Speaker Enhancement | Enable. A dialog box may appear, asking you to help choose your type of speakers.

Personal DJ

The Personal DJ option provides some enhancements to playlists for Windows Media Player. Using the Personal DJ, you can create a playlist from across your Media Library, and then determine how songs will be played. You can specify that some songs be played with more frequency than others and even control the overall duration of the playlist. This feature provides you with an easy way to create a playlist for a party, and then have Windows Media Player do the rest. Just choose the Personal DJ option in the Plus! window (under Digital Media), and then click the Start link. A simple wizard enables you to create the playlist, specify your settings, review and name the playlist, and then play it.

Media Player Skins and 3-D Visualizations

The Plus! pack adds to Windows Media Player more Media Player skins and visualizations that you can use. The new skins and visualizations are accessible within Windows Media Player, along with the basic skins and visualizations that come with Media Player. See Chapter 15 to learn more about using skins and visualizations.

Games

The games included with the Plus! pack are available in the Games category in the Plus! window, or you can access them directly by choosing Start | All Programs | Games (or Start | All Programs | Accessories | Games). Just follow the instructions given to you within the game to learn how to play the additional games.

Themes

Themes create the overall look and feel on your computer, including your Desktop settings, mouse pointers, icons, and other graphical features of Windows XP. In fact, the default Windows XP interface is a theme in and of itself. When you choose a different theme, your system is reconfigured and all aspects of the theme are applied. You can choose a theme directly from the Plus! window by selecting it, as shown in Figure 18-2, or you can choose a theme by accessing the Themes tab of the Display Properties window.

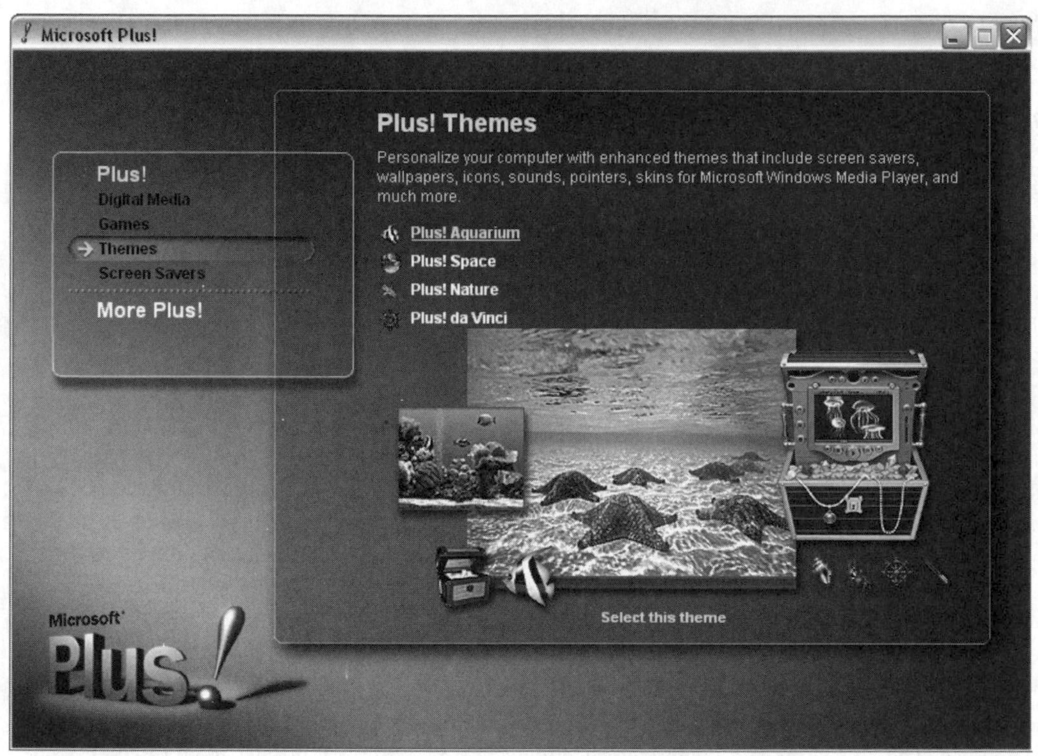

FIGURE 18-2 Theme options

Screen Savers

The Plus! pack adds some screen savers to Windows XP, such as Plus! Aquarium, Plus! Space, Plus! Nature, and Plus! Robot Circus. You can select these screen savers from the Microsoft Plus! window, or choose them directly from the Screen Saver tab of the Display Properties window.

Use Plus! Digital Media Edition

In addition to the Microsoft Plus! pack, you can also purchase an additional Plus! CD-ROM called Plus! Digital Media Edition ($15 to $20 at any computer store). Digital Media Edition (DME) gives you additional tools and enhancements for using digital media on Windows XP. The installation requirements are the same as for the Plus! pack (see the previous section), and you can easily install DME by inserting the CD-ROM and following the instructions that appear. Once the installation is complete, you can access the DME features by choosing Start | All Programs | Microsoft Plus! Digital Media Edition. The following sections review the features DME provides.

Alarm Clock

Plus! Alarm Clock is just that—an alarm clock you can use on your computer to wake you, alert you to upcoming meetings or events, and perform other time-related tasks. You can create alarms and even recurring alarms using Plus! Alarm Clock, as follows:

1. Choose Start | All Programs | Microsoft Plus! Digital Media Edition | Plus! Alarm Clock.
2. In the Plus! Alarm Clock window that appears, click the Create Alarm button.
3. In the Name and Schedule the Alarm window that appears, give the alarm a name, and determine when you want the alarm to sound (date and time). Then click Next.

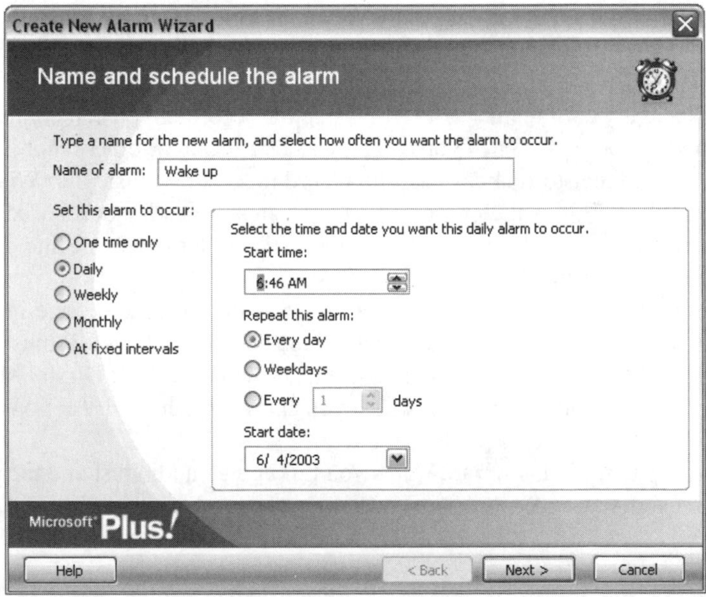

4. In the Alarm Music or Sound window, choose the alarm music or sound you want to play. Everything in Windows Media player is available to use. Remember to adjust the volume using the Volume button. Click Next.

5. Click Finish. The alarm appears in the Plus! Alarm Clock window. You can create additional alarms or change or delete an existing alarm at any time from this window.

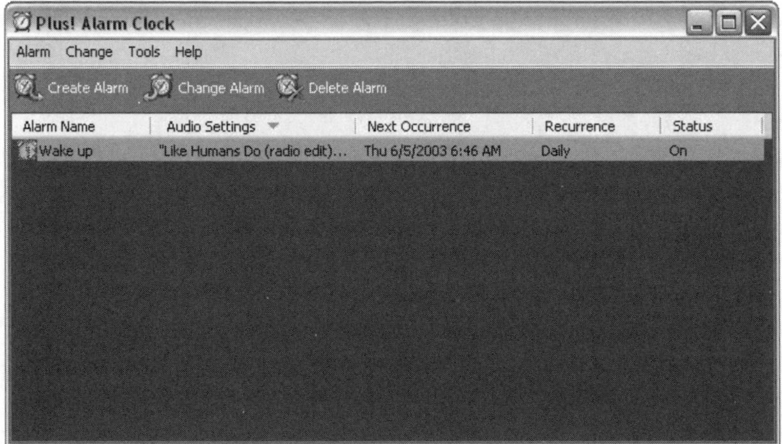

Analog Recorder

Analog Recorder is a really cool feature of DME. Using the recorder, you can connect a device, such as a stereo, to your computer. Then you can play analog music or other recordings, such as records, cassettes, or even reel-to-reel devices, and record the analog music into Windows XP. Analog Recorder can then digitize the music, which you can store in Windows Media Player or burn to a CD. Remember those old eight-track or cassette titles that you can't find on CD? Using this tool, you can record them and burn your own CDs.

To connect these devices to your computer, your sound card must have a line-in port (which most do), and your stereo or other device you want to connect to Windows XP must have a line-out port (most all do). If you choose Start | All Programs | Microsoft Plus! Digital Media Edition | Plus! Analog Recorder, a window appears in which you can get specific instructions and even diagrams for connecting your external audio device.

Once you are ready to record, a wizard walks you through an audio test and then the actual recording of your music. Analog Recorder can even help correct overall quality and sound from your analog source.

You can access the Analog Recorder Help files, which contain a wealth of information, from within the Analog Recorder Wizard, by clicking the Help button. It is a good idea to familiarize yourself with the Help files so you can make the most of Analog Recorder.

CD Label Maker and Plus! Dancer

The CD Label Maker included in DME is essentially the same as the CD Label Maker that appears in the Plus! pack. A wizard walks you through the steps to select your playlist, CD label printing paper, design, and so forth.

The Plus! Dancer feature shows you a small dancer in the lower-left portion of your computer screen. The dancer dances to music from Windows Media Player or even if no music is playing. Choose Start | All Programs | Microsoft Plus! Digital Media Edition | Plus! Dancer. A Dancer icon appears in your Notification Area, and if you right-click the icon and click Options, you can configure the dancer(s) you want to see and other basic options, as you can see in Figure 18-3. The dancers are obviously pure entertainment, but they are fun to watch.

Party Mode for Windows Media Player

Party Mode for Windows Media Player is a cool feature that is actually a Windows Media Player skin. When you use Party Mode, your computer can act as a jukebox. Users can select songs from Windows Media Player, but they cannot gain access to any other portions of your computer, so your personal files and data stay safe and sound while Media Player provides the pulse for your party.

To set up your party, just click the Party Mode Option found by choosing Start | All Programs | Microsoft Plus! Digital Media Edition. In the Specify Your Party Mode Settings window that appears, shown in Figure 18-4, choose the settings that you want and click the Start Party button.

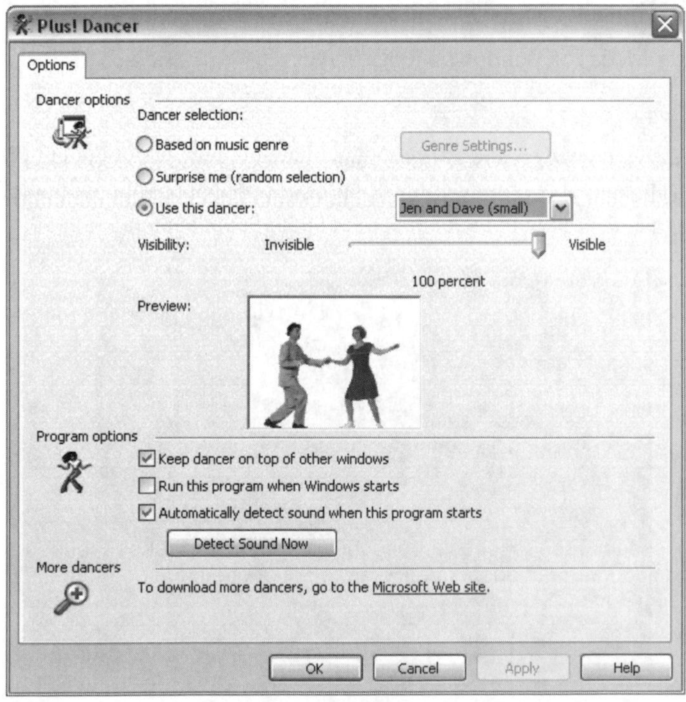

FIGURE 18-3 Plus! Dancer configuration options

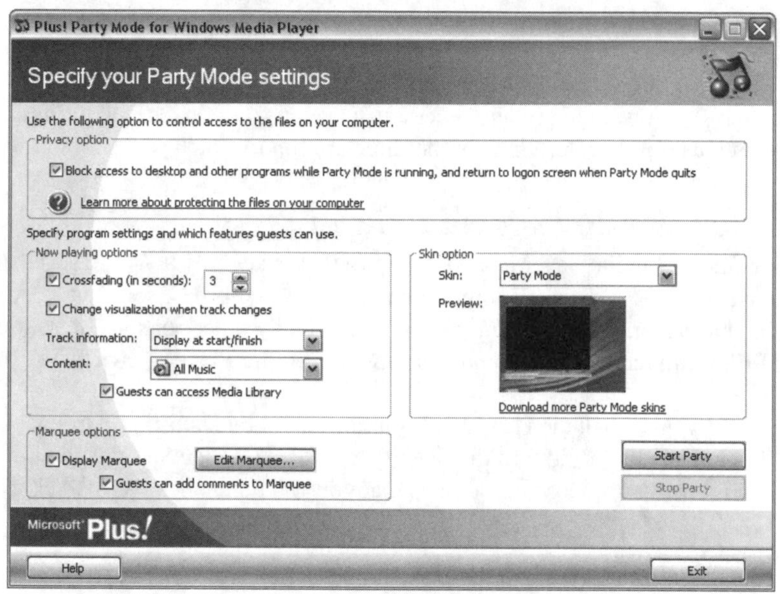

FIGURE 18-4 Party Mode for Windows Media Player

Once the party starts, the Windows XP interface changes to the jukebox skin, shown next. If you choose to exit the party, you are sent to the Windows logon screen so that you can log back in to Windows.

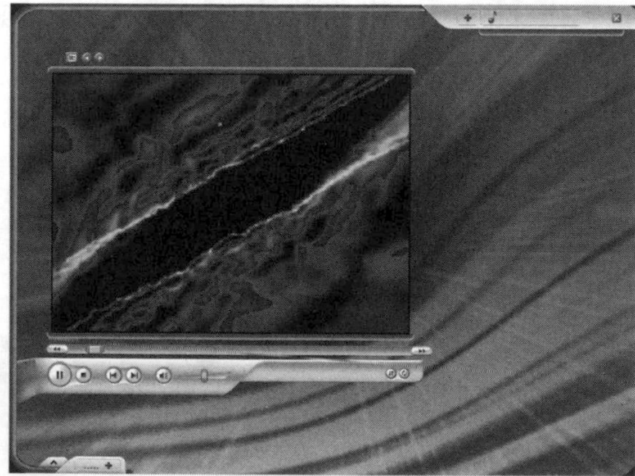

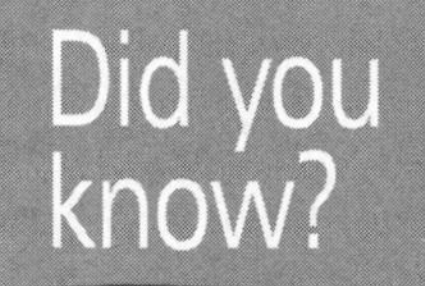

Party Mode Is Not Foolproof

Just because Party Mode provides a skin overlay to Windows XP does not mean that it is impossible for someone to access your personal files. You can avoid such access by configuring all user accounts so that passwords are required. If someone exits Party Mode, the Welcome screen appears. If you use blank passwords, all the user has to do is click a name to gain access. So use effective passwords on all user accounts. See Chapter 12 to learn more about configuring passwords for user accounts.

Photo Story

Photo Story allows you to assemble photos into a movie format using simulated movement. You can add narration to the story, and then save it in Windows Media Player or even burn it to CD. You'll want to make sure your microphone is configured and in good working order if you want to record narration. When you are ready, simply launch Photo Story by choosing Start | All Programs | Microsoft Plus! Digital Media Edition. A wizard walks you through the assembly of your photos, as shown in Figure 18-5. You can then record any narration, and even manage the

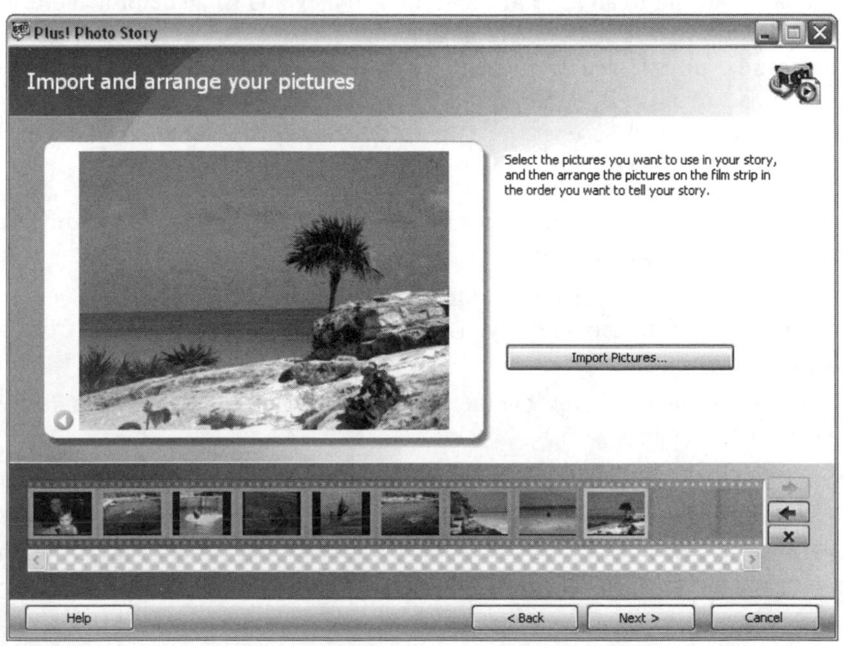

FIGURE 18-5 Photo Story assembly

panning motion that occurs during the story. You then follow the wizard and create a title page (with a background image if you want), add background music if you want, and finally save the photo story. The process is fairly simple; if you get stuck, be sure to check out the Help files by clicking the Help button.

NOTE *Your photo story is saved as a Windows Media file, and that is your only option. As such, only Windows Media Player can play your photo story.*

Effects and Transitions

DME adds 50 additional effects and transitions to Windows Movie Maker. You can use these transitions and effects in your Movie Maker movies. See Chapter 16 to learn more about using Windows Movie Maker 2.1.

Sync & Go

If you use a Pocket PC, you can easily transfer files from Windows Media Player to your pocket PC by using Sync & Go. This utility works with the Pocket PC synchronization software to make media file synchronization much easier and more flexible.

Use PowerToys

PowerToys are simple applications that perform a specific task or function. They are typically developed as an afterthought to an operating system, and they add some helpful and fun customization options to your Windows XP computer. We'll take a look at the PowerToys, see how to use them, and explore how they can help you customize your Windows XP experience.

You can download all of the PowerToys from Microsoft.com for free. You can choose to download the entire package, or you can select the specific toys you want to use and download only those. At the time of this writing, the following PowerToys are available:

- **Tweak UI** Enables you to configure some system settings that are not readily available in the Windows XP user interface.
- **Open Command Window Here** Adds an Open Command Window Here context menu option to file system folders so that you can easily get to the command line from within a folder.
- **Alt-Tab Replacement** Gives you the ease of switching between pages and seeing a preview of those pages.
- **Power Calculator** Provides graph and evaluate functions along with many different types of calculating conversions.
- **Image Resizer** Enables you to resize one or several image files at the same time by right-clicking them.

- **CD Slide Show Generator** Enables you to view images burned to a CD as a slide show. This tool also works on Windows 9*x* and Me computers.
- **Virtual Desktop Manager** Enables you to manage up to four Desktops on your Windows XP computer from the Windows Taskbar.
- **Taskbar Magnifier** Enables you to magnify part of your Windows XP screen from the Taskbar.
- **HTML Slide Show Wizard** Enables you to create an HTML slide show of your digital pictures that you can view locally or upload to a Web site.
- **Webcam Timershot** Enables you to take pictures at specified time intervals from a Webcam connected to your computer, and then save them to a desired location. It's your own mini-surveillance camera.

Downloading and Installing PowerToys

You can easily download and install PowerToys on your Windows XP computer. The good news is that most of the PowerToys are between 500 and 600KB in size, and you download them one at a time. Even with a slower modem connection, you'll be able to complete the downloads to your computer. To download PowerToys, point your Web browser to www.microsoft.com/windowsxp/downloads/powertoys/xppowertoys.mspx. This will take you to the PowerToys main page, shown in Figure 18-6.

Before you begin downloading PowerToys, you should note the following:

- PowerToys are created by Microsoft, but they are not supported by Microsoft. In other words, you can't get technical support from Microsoft for their use. Basically, you are on your own, but they are generally easy to use and problem free, so this really isn't a worry.
- If you have old PowerToys installed on your computer, you need to uninstall them before downloading and installing the new PowerToys.
- PowerToys work only with U.S.-English regional settings.
- PowerToys work on either Windows XP Home or Professional edition.
- Most PowerToys are user specific. This means you can use the PowerToys to customize your XP system, but the customization applies only to you—not to others who have an account on the local computer.

To download a PowerToy, click the desired PowerToy link on the right side of the PowerToys Web page (see Figure 18-6). A dialog box will appear, asking if and where you want to save the PowerToy. You can choose Open, which will start the download and installation, or just click Save to download the PowerToy without installing it. If you choose to download a PowerToy without installing it, double-click the download icon after the download is complete

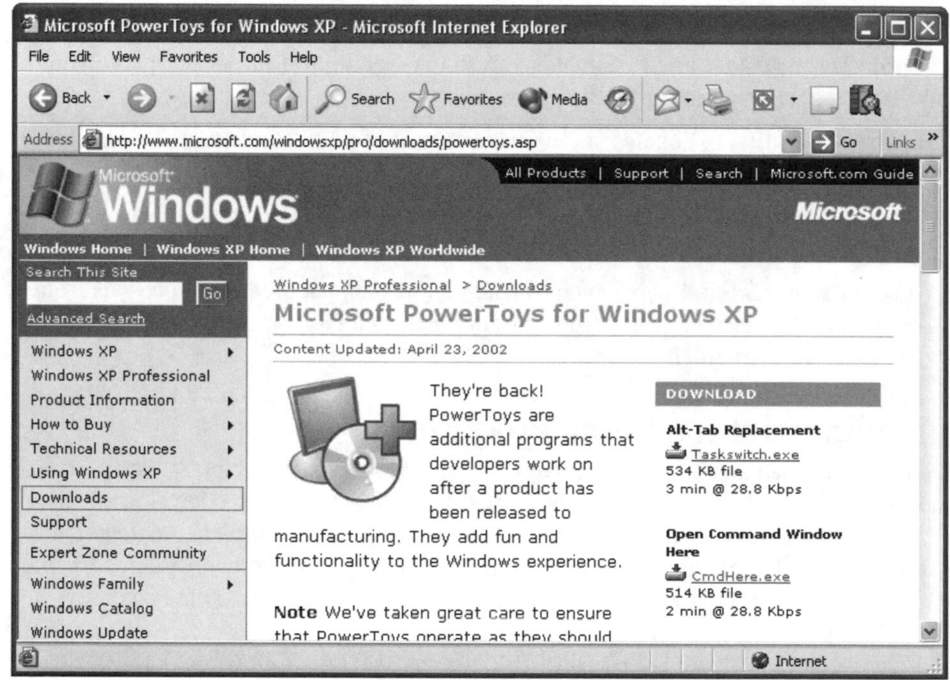

FIGURE 18-6 PowerToys Web page

to install the PowerToy. This will walk you through a very basic setup routine. After you install the PowerToys, you'll be able to access them by choosing Start | All Programs | PowerToys for Windows XP.

The following sections explore some of the common PowerToys.

Tweak UI

Tweak UI (User Interface) is a little tool that gives you access to some standard system settings that you can't configure through the default Windows XP tools and interface. You'll find some of these settings really useful, while a few do not readily seem as important. The tool is easy to use, and you can mix and match any of the settings that you want to use. Essentially, the tool gives you an interface to these settings that enables you to change them as you like, just as you would do with a standard Properties dialog box.

In the Tweak UI interface, shown next, the left column lists different settings categories. If you expand a category and choose a setting, you see the configurable options in the right pane. The following sections describe what is available in each category.

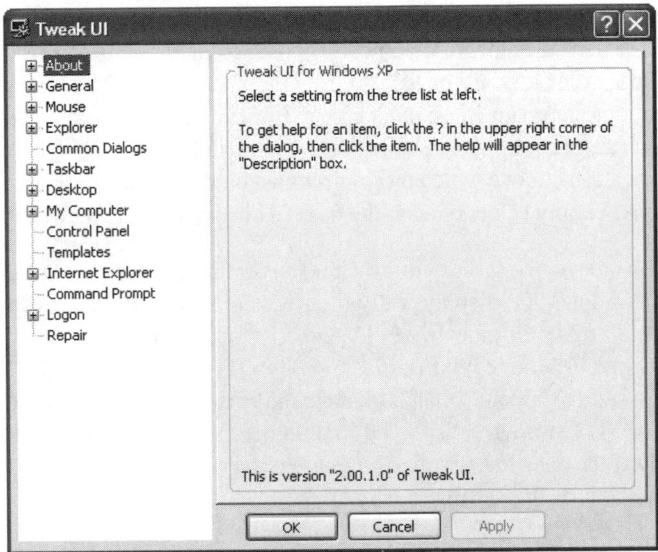

About The About category gives you a series of tips for using the Tweak UI interface. Also, the Policy option under About gives you direct access to the Group Policy Editor, which you can use to make a number of changes and enforce policies across all users on the Windows XP local computer (assuming you are the computer administrator).

General The General category has only one entry: Focus. Using this option, you can prevent applications from stealing focus from the current window you are working on. Rather than stealing focus, the Taskbar icon for the application will flash, letting you know the application needs your attention. Simply enable the setting and choose the Taskbar flashing option you want (continuous or flash a certain number of times).

Mouse The Mouse category gives you several settings to control mouse movements and behavior. You can manage the speed and mouse sensitivity to double-clicking and dragging. Under the Hover category, you can adjust the hover sensitivity and hover time. The Wheel category allows you to manage scrolling using the mouse wheel. The X-Mouse option allows you to configure activation for windows that follow the mouse movements. This keeps you from having to click the mouse to bring a window into focus.

Explorer The Explorer category gives you a number of settings that control some basic Windows interface functionality. If you select the Explorer category, you see several check box options that enable you to manage different features of Windows—everything from displaying Help on the Start menu to enabling Windows hot keys. Select a setting to read more about its features in the description section of the page.

If you expand Explorer and select Common Dialogs, you can create a custom Places bar where you show either default places or custom places you choose, such as My Documents, My Music, and History. Overall, this option gives you more flexibility to get to the items you most frequently use.

Taskbar and XP Start Menu The Taskbar category gives you several options to manage your Taskbar. If you select the Taskbar category, you can choose to enable balloon tips and receive a warning when disk space runs low. If you select Grouping under the Taskbar category, you can configure how applications are grouped on the Taskbar. For example, you can group least-used applications first or you can group applications with the most windows first. If you select XP Start Menu Under Taskbar, you can choose which programs to list on the frequently used programs section of the Start menu. Simply select or clear the desired check boxes next to each application.

Desktop The Desktop category enables you to choose what icons you want to display on the Desktop. By default, Windows XP displays only the Recycle Bin on the Desktop, but you can easily add Internet Explorer, My Computer, My Documents, or My Network Places to the Desktop icons by selecting the available check boxes.

Under the Desktop category, you can also manage the First Icon option. You can choose to have My Documents or My Computer displayed first on the Desktop. Note that this is a per-user setting that works only if the user has permission to alter My Computer settings. Also, you may need to log off and back on for the setting to take effect.

My Computer The My Computer category allows you to manage which drives and folders you see in My Computer. Simply expand this category and choose Drives, Special Folders, or AutoPlay. You can determine what you see in My Computer from these options and determine what is done with AutoPlay for each icon or folder.

Under the Control Panel section of My Computer, you can choose to enable or hide certain Control Panel icons. For example, you could hide Accessibility Options, Add Hardware, and so forth. Some people choose to use this option to make the Control Panel neater by removing icons that are not typically used. Note that removing the options here only removes the icon from the Control Panel—it does not uninstall the Control Panel option. You can add the icons back at any time by returning to this window option and enabling the desired check boxes.

Under the Templates option, you can control what kind of document Windows offers to make when you right-click and choose New from the context menu. Just enable or clear the desired check boxes here as desired.

Internet Explorer Under the Internet Explorer category, you can choose to use a custom toolbar background for Internet Explorer by selecting the option and clicking the Change button to select a new bitmap image that you have on your computer. Also under the Internet Explorer category, you can edit the Search function so that searches within IE are directed to certain search engines. Under View Source, you can manage what program is used to view Web page code source (it is Notepad by default).

Under the Command Prompt option, you can choose a couple of completion options that determine the character used for command prompt file name completion. You can also specify word separators.

Logon The Logon category allows you to determine the users that appear on the Welcome screen and whether the Autoexec.bat file is parsed at logon (this option is selected by default). You can select the Autologon option and have the system log you on automatically at system startup, and you can also configure whether or not to maintain RAS (Remote Access Server) connections after logoff.

Finally, you also see a Repair option that you can use so that Tweak UI can rebuild icons and remove unused icons from Internet Explorer. From the drop-down menu, you can choose different folders you want to repair, such as the Fonts, My Music, and My Pictures.

Open Command Window Here

This PowerToy gives you a context menu option to open a command window from any file system window in which you happen to be working. This feature enables you to open a command prompt without first going to Accessories or choosing Start | Run and entering **cmd.** You can right-click any icon in any file system window and choose Open a Command Window from the context menu that appears.

Alt-Tab Replacement

You can use the ALT-TAB keys to toggle between multiple windows on your screen. The Alt-Tab Replacement PowerToy gives you an enhancement to ALT-TAB. Once you install the Alt-Tab Replacement PowerToy, you see a small window showing the actual content of the windows to which you want to switch. Basically, this little option can make using multiple windows in the same application easier because you can see exactly what you are switching to before doing so. Just press ALT-TAB and then continue holding the ALT key to use your mouse or keyboard arrow keys to select the window to which you want to toggle.

Power Calculator

The Power Calculator PowerToy is just that—a power calculator that performs graphing functions and other conversions that are not available on the standard Windows XP calculator. As you can see here, the Power Calculator contains standard charting and graphing features. Use the Functions menu to access basic operations, trig functions, log functions, and user functions. From the Conversions menu, you can easily convert length, mass, time, velocity, and temperature to different values. Use the View menu to access Numeric, History, and Advanced views. Choose File | Help to learn more about using different functions and features.

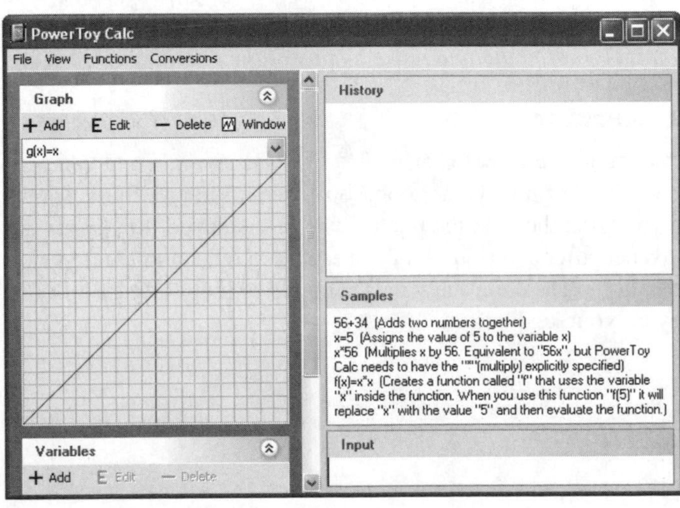

18

Image Resizer

Image Resizer is a great little tool if you work with digital images on a frequent basis. As its name suggests, you can use Image Resizer to resize images or groups of images quickly and easily. With this feature, you don't have to open the images in an image editor and resize them through that program. You can do so more easily with Image Resizer. Once installed, just follow these steps to resize your images:

1. Right-click an image or collection of images and choose the Resize Pictures option.
2. In the Resize Pictures dialog box that appears, choose the size to which you want to resize the photos. This action creates a copy of the photos and stores them in the current folder. It does not alter your original photos.
3. Click the Advanced button to extend the options, as shown here. You can create a custom size, choose to make photos smaller but not larger, and choose to resize the original photo. Click OK when you're done.

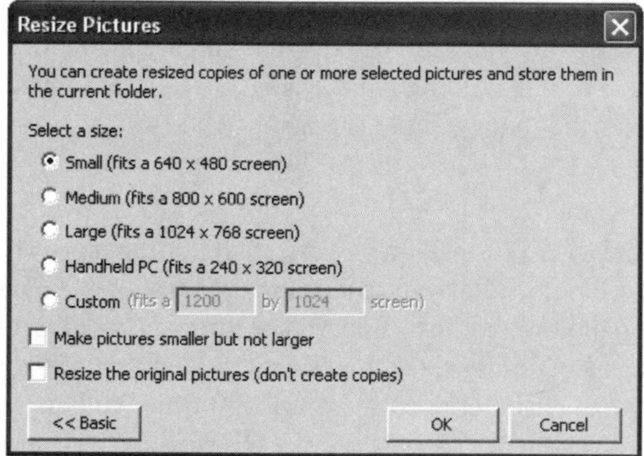

Exercise caution when resizing original photos. Resizing an original photo will reduce its quality and may make it unusable for your printing needs. As a general rule, always maintain your original photo and make a copy of the photo when resizing.

CD Slide Show Generator

This PowerToy allows you to view photos on a CD as a slide show. When you open the CD that you create using the CD Slide Show Generator, you'll see a View as Slide Show link under Picture Tasks. When you click the link, the photos will be displayed full screen one at a time and will automatically advance after a period of a few seconds (you can manually advance them by clicking your mouse button). The slide show will continue to loop through all of the photos until you press the ESC key on your keyboard.

Virtual Desktop Manager

Virtual Desktop Manager allows you to use up to four different Desktops on your Windows XP computer at the same time, just by toggling between them using the Taskbar. For example, one Desktop can have one background and applications open while another Desktop uses a different background and applications. You'll see a Taskbar icon that you can click to switch between the different Desktops. It's like having up to four computers in one.

To use Virtual Desktop Manager, first install it and then follow these steps:

1. Right-click an empty area of the Taskbar, and choose Toolbars | Desktop Manager. Virtual Desktop Manager appears on the toolbar.

2. To switch between Desktops, simply click each one, and then change each Desktop as desired. To adjust the background and applications open on each Desktop, switch between the Desktops by clicking the number icons on the Taskbar and configure each as you want.
3. To see a preview of your Desktops, click the green Preview button next to the Desktop buttons on Desktop Manager. You'll see each Desktop on the screen, and you can click between them.

Taskbar Magnifier

If you have problems seeing some of the items that appear on your screen or you have to work with a bunch of small icons or small text, Taskbar Magnifier may be able to help you a bit. This magnifier is a lot like the magnifier you can use from Accessibility Options in Control Panel, but this one stays on your Taskbar as an icon until you turn it off.

Simply install Taskbar Magnifier, right-click an empty area of your Taskbar, and choose Toolbars | Taskbar Magnifier. Taskbar Magnifier appears on your Taskbar. Anything you move your mouse over appears in the magnifier area on the Taskbar.

HTML Slide Show Generator

HTML Slide Show Generator is a wizard that you can use to assemble a collection of digital photos into a slide show. After you make the slide show, you can view it in any browser, which means you can easily e-mail it to someone, burn it onto a CD, or upload it to your Web site. This PowerToy is a quick and easy way to create photo slide shows. After you install HTML Slide Show Generator, just follow these steps:

1. Choose Start | All Programs | PowerToys for Windows XP | Slide Show Wizard.
2. Click Next on the Welcome screen.
3. In the Image window, click the Add Image or Add Folder button to add images or folders to your collections. All of the photos you add here will be used in the slide show.

4. In the Select Options for Your Slide Show window, enter a name for the slide show and your name for the author (if you like). By default, the slide show is saved in My Documents\My Slide Shows, but you can change the location by clicking the Browse button and selecting a different location. Under the Picture Size category, choose a desired picture size. Keep in mind that if you are posting the photo to the Web, smaller sizes such as 640×480 work best. If you are going to be using the slide show on your computer only or on a CD, choose a larger size or keep the current size. Under Slide Show Type, you can choose between Simple and Advanced, and you can also choose to display the slide show full screen. Make your selections and click Next.

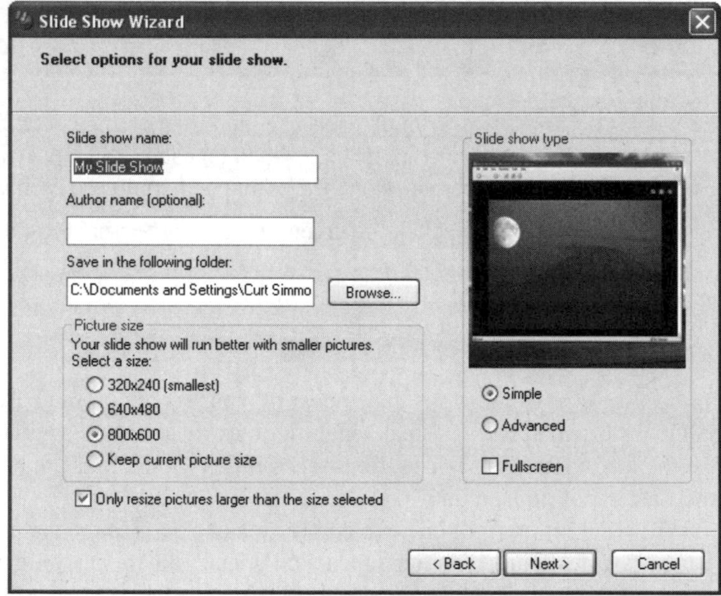

5. After the slide show is created, the Finish screen displays. If you want to view the slide show from this window, click the View the Slide Show Now button.

Webcam Timershot

The Webcam Timershot PowerToy uses a Webcam attached to your PC to take photos at specified intervals. Basically, it is a way to create a collection of photos of a room or office, primarily for security purposes. Once you install Webcam Timershot, choose Start | All Programs | PowerToys for Windows XP | Timershot to launch the program. The window that appears allows you to see the photos taken and adjust the properties for the timershot. For example, you can determine how often to take a photo, where to save the photo, and whether to save all photos or just the last photo taken. You can even save your photos to a network location so that you can take photos of a remote location and see them from a network share.

If you love PowerToys, you'll find a PowerToys Fun Pack at www.microsoft.com/windowsxp/downloads. Enjoy!

Part IV

Optimize, Troubleshoot, and Fix Windows XP

Chapter 19

Take Care of Windows XP

How to...

- Access disk properties
- Run disk tools
- Configure and manage scheduled tasks
- Automatically install Windows update

Windows XP is an advanced operating system that, for the most part, is able to take care of itself. Hardware management, and even error correction, can be done automatically; unlike with computer systems of the past, you don't have to spend much of your time thinking about care and maintenance. However, Windows XP provides you with tools that will help keep the XP system running at its peak. In this chapter, we'll explore those tools, how you can use them, and how they help your system run better. Most of the tools you will see in this chapter have to do with hard disk maintenance. You should check out the information in this chapter, and be sure you also read Chapter 20, which covers more advanced disk management features in Windows XP.

Hard Disk Basics

Before we explore hard disk maintenance, we should first take a quick look at hard disk basics. After all, it is much easier to maintain and care for a part of your computer if you have some basic understanding of it. Every Windows XP computer has at least one hard disk. A hard disk is made up of a platter (or multiple platters) that holds magnetic material. This platter is hard, not flexible like other types of storage media, such as magnetic tape. When the operating system needs either to read from or write information to the disk, the platter spins—often faster than 100 mph—and data is read from or written to the disk in small chunks called *bytes*. This is why you hear a churning noise from within your computer when you open or save files, open programs, or perform other memory-related actions on your computer.

You can think of the hard disk as the computer's storage area. All applications, files, folders—practically everything that is installed or exists on your computer—resides on the hard disk, including the Windows XP operating system itself. Because the hard disk is one giant storage area, it is important to keep the disk in tip-top running shape, and the tools found in Windows XP can easily help you optimize the hard disk.

File System Basics

As mentioned, a hard disk is a storage area where all files, applications, and other types of system information are stored. When you want to view a file or even open a program, Windows XP accesses the hard disk to retrieve the information. However, hard disks are basically blank slates, and Windows XP cannot store information on a hard disk until it has been partitioned and formatted. *Partitioning* is a process that logically divides the disk into different segments that can be managed independently. *Formatting* is a process that logically divides the disk into sections so

To Tweak or Not to Tweak

As an operator of a Web site geared toward helping beginners maintain a pleasurable Windows XP experience, it's obvious to me that most visitors are obsessed with tweaking their system, when in fact Windows XP is, for the most part, ready to go for the average user.

About half of the e-mails I receive are from users trying to recover from a malfunctioning system due to a registry tweak that was totally unnecessary for their environment, and in many cases these tweaks would have provided a minimal performance increase.

One of my favorite and safest ways to apply various tweaks is through one of the PowerToys called Tweak UI (available from Microsoft—see Chapter 18). You can toggle tweaks on or off though an easy-to-understand interface with minimal risk. Tweak everything from your mouse to your Desktop, including the adjustment of the quality and size of thumbnail images in Windows Explorer.

A plethora of useful functions is already included with Windows XP, most of which are rarely utilized. The tools are there. It's up to you to find them, learn about them, and use them in a way that fits your needs.

I enjoy using Windows XP for its ability to function, look, and feel the way I want it to, and the ease with which it took me to get it that way. Happy tweaking!

—Michael
www.tweak.us

that information can be stored on the disk in an organized way. Think of the hard disk as a filing cabinet, and the file system as the folders that are placed in the filing cabinet. Windows XP uses a file system to organize data so that it can be easily recorded and retrieved. Without a file system, Windows XP would have no way to keep track of the information stored on the hard drive.

Windows XP supports two different kinds of file systems: FAT32 and NTFS. FAT32 was used by Windows 95 SE and Windows 98, as well as Windows Me (and also supported by Windows 2000), and NTFS was used by Windows NT and Windows 2000. In truth, Windows XP works just like Windows 2000, because it can read either FAT32 or NTFS. Without getting into too many gory details, the following two sections tell you about each type of file system.

FAT32

FAT32—the acronym stands for *file allocation table*—is a basic file system that has been around for quite some time. FAT12 was the original FAT file system, and it was used to organize and manage small disks. FAT32 came onto the scene when large (more than 1GB) hard drives became popular a few years back. FAT32 is a simple file system that Windows XP can use to manage your computer's hard disks. FAT32 supports very basic folder security.

NTFS

NTFS is a file system that was first introduced with Windows NT. NTFS is a much more complex file system than FAT32, and it supports both folder and file security. This means that you can place security restrictions on folders, and you can finely control access to resources with users and groups. NTFS is also supported in Windows XP and is considered a much more powerful file system than FAT32.

You can format your computer's hard drive with either FAT32 or NTFS—Chapter 20 explores this issue in more detail.

Set Hard Disk Properties

As you have learned throughout this book, almost everything in Windows XP has properties pages—a place where you can get more information about a feature or component. Your hard disks, removable disks, and CD/DVD-ROM drives are no exception. If you open My Computer from your Start menu, you'll see an icon for each drive available on your computer. You will see your C drive; a floppy drive; a CD/DVD-ROM drive; possibly other drives, such as a Zip or Jaz drive; and even portable devices if they are attached to your computer, as shown in Figure 19-1.

As you can see in Figure 19-1, my own computer has two hard disks (C and F), a floppy drive, a CD-ROM drive, and a Zip drive. You can also inspect your computer's disk drives using the Computer Management console found in Administrative Tools in the Control Panel, as shown in Figure 19-2. The Computer Management console is a powerful tool that we will explore in more detail in Chapter 20.

If you right-click any of the hard disks and choose Properties, you see a standard properties sheet with four basic tabs. Each tap contains some maintenance and management features, and the following sections examine each of them individually. Also note that you can right-click any removable storage media, such as floppy drives and CD-ROM drives, and choose Properties to view their properties sheets as well.

The tools and options presented in the following sections apply only to writable disks—not read-only CD-ROM or DVD-ROM disks.

General Tab

One of the best things about the General tab is the pie graph, shown in Figure 19-3. You can access your drive's General tab at any time and see exactly how much disk space is used and how much disk space is free (available for use). You get this usage information for any writable disk, including your floppy drive.

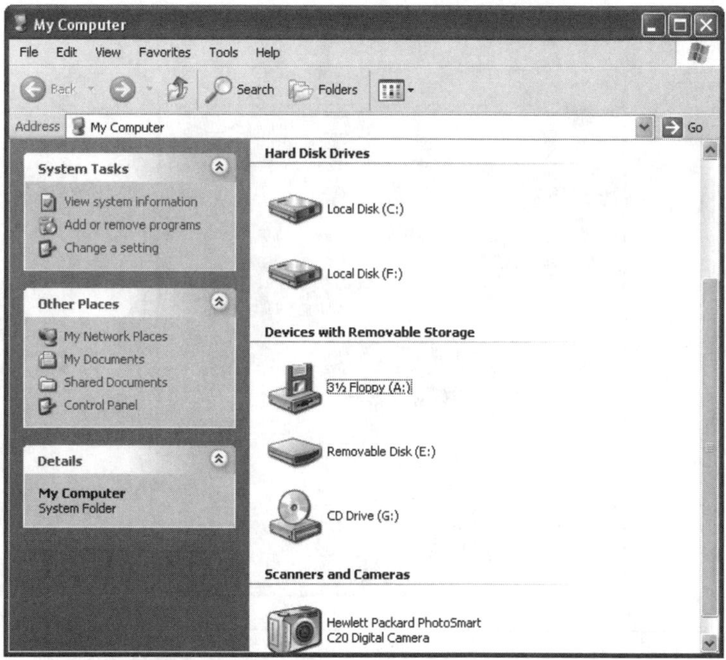

FIGURE 19-1 My Computer contents

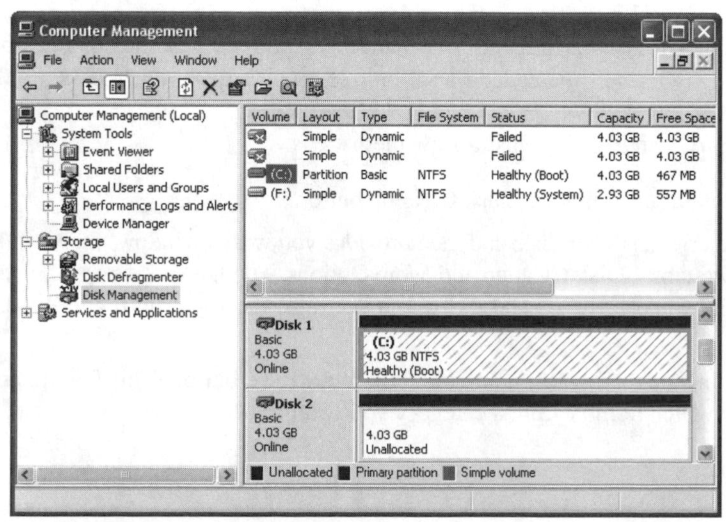

FIGURE 19-2 Computer Management console

19

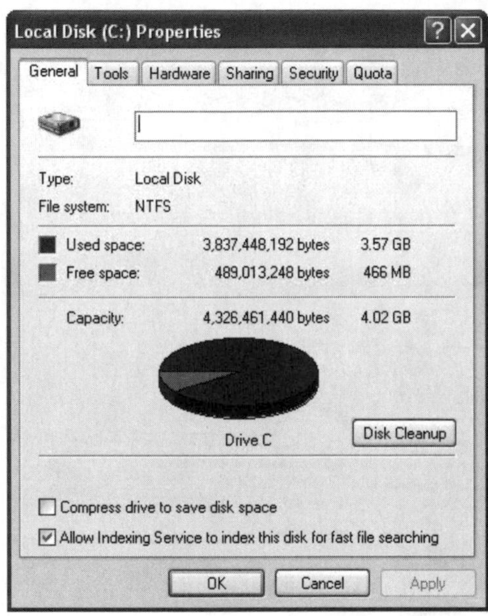

FIGURE 19-3 General tab

In addition to getting information quickly, you can do only two other things on the General tab. First, you can enter a label for the disk. The label isn't anything usable to you, so most people don't put anything here. The other option on the General tab is the Disk Cleanup option, which you will find useful from time to time.

Disk Cleanup is a utility that inspects your hard disk and looks for files that can be safety deleted. By deleting unused or unneeded files, you free up disk space that can be used for other purposes.

To run the Disk Cleanup utility, just follow these steps:

1. On the General tab, click the Disk Cleanup button.
2. Disk Cleanup scans your disk, and then provides you with a window, shown in Figure 19-4, that has two tabs—Disk Cleanup and More Options. The Disk Cleanup tab lists categories of potential "delete" items and the amount of disk space you will gain by emptying each one.
3. To inspect a category, select it and click the View Files button. This feature enables you to specify which items within a category you want to delete.

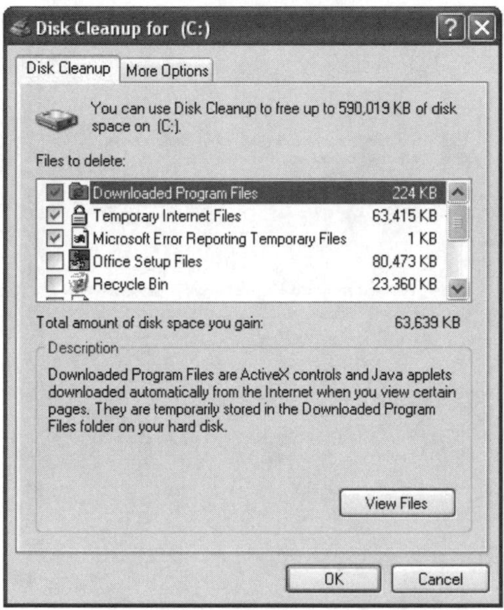

FIGURE 19-4 Disk Cleanup utility

4. When you are sure of what items/categories you want to delete, select the check boxes next to those categories, and then click OK.
5. Also notice the More Options tab, shown in Figure 19-5. Disk Cleanup inspects basic temporary storage areas on your computer, but you can use the More Options tab to specify different cleanup options. The Clean Up buttons take you to other areas on your computer, such as Windows Setup and Add/Remove Programs, where you can remove unwanted items.

It is important that you remember that Disk Cleanup examines only certain areas of your computer, such as temporary files and downloaded Internet items. Disk Cleanup does not inspect every possible category of items that can be deleted—much of that work is left to you. So, how often should you use Disk Cleanup? A typical user should run this utility once every three months to see if any unused files can be deleted to free up disk space.

Tools

The Tools tab gives you three important tools you can use to keep your computer disks happy and working efficiently, shown in Figure 19-6. The following sections tell you all about these tools.

FIGURE 19-5 More Options tab

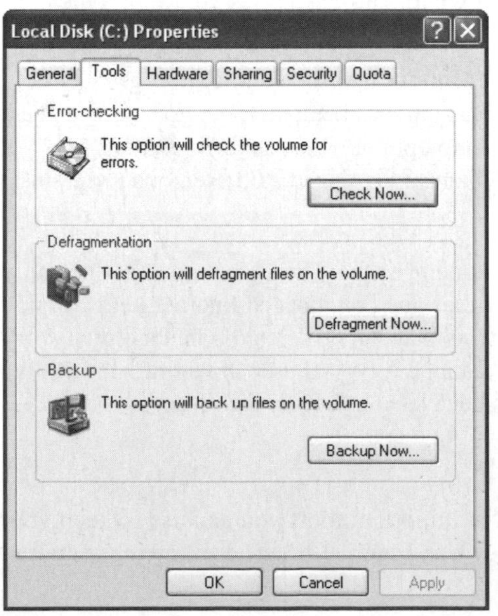

FIGURE 19-6 Tools tab

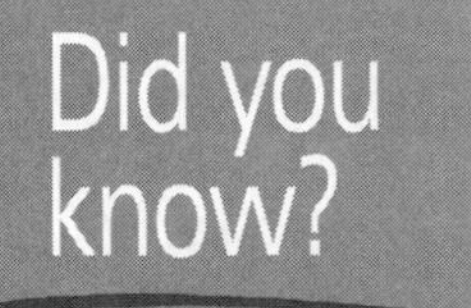

About Conserving Disk Space

If you have a newer computer, conserving disk space probably isn't a big concern to you—after all, it is not uncommon for a typical computer to ship with a 20GB or larger hard drive. That's a lot of storage space; but if you use Windows Movie Maker and Windows Media Player a lot and hang onto all of your video and multimedia files, you will need a lot of disk space. Here are some quick and helpful tips to conserve disk space on your computer:

- Uninstall games and programs you do not use. Programs take up a lot of space; if you aren't playing all 10 of those games you installed, get rid of them. You can always reinstall one if you need it later—but in the meantime, free up that disk space!
- Old personal files can easily be saved to floppies, CDs, or Zip disks for storage.
- Check Add/Remove Programs from time to time. If you download a lot of utilities from the Internet, you may need to remove those that are unneeded or unwanted.
- Use folder compression (see Chapter 4). Compression helps save disk space and doesn't interfere with your work.

Error Checking

The first tool option you see is Error Checking. If you click the Check Now button, the Error Checking tool is opened, as shown in Figure 19-7, so you can check your disk for errors. The small dialog box gives you the options to fix errors that are found automatically, and to scan for and attempt recovery of bad sectors.

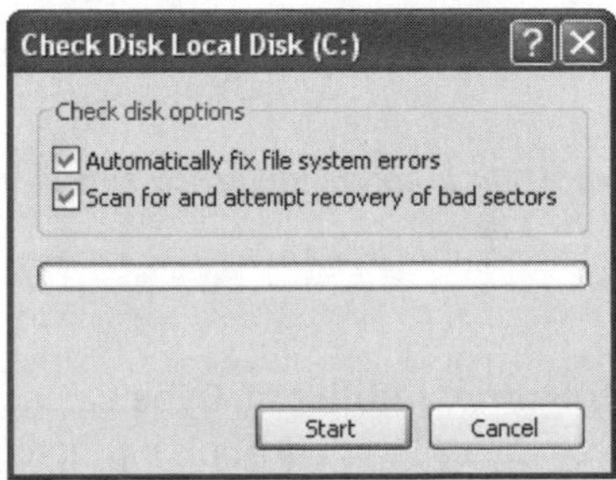

FIGURE 19-7 Error Checking tool

Avoid Disk Errors

Disk errors are part of life and nothing to be too concerned about, as long as you allow Error Checking to fix them from time to time. Although a number of different actions and problems can cause disk errors, here are some operation tips to help you avoid them:

- Always turn off your computer from the Start menu. This enables Windows to shut down in a proper manner. Avoid shutting down your computer by just turning off the power button.
- Uninstall programs by using the program's uninstall feature or Add/Remove Programs in the Control Panel. Do not delete a program's folder to uninstall it unless no other way works.
- If you experience a lockup or some other problem that forces a hard reboot, allow Error Checking to run at reboot to catch any new errors.

If you don't have the Automatically Fix File System Errors check box enabled, Error Checking will prompt you to OK its fix for every error it finds (which can get really annoying).

The Scan For and Attempt Recovery of Bad Sectors option allows Error Checking to check the file system of the disk and attempt to resolve any problems that exist with sectors on the physical disk. As a general rule, you should also enable this option when using Error Checking so that you can get a more thorough disk examination.

So, now that you know what the options are, what should you do? First, let me note that Error Checking is automatically run during reboot after an improper system shutdown. Let's say your computer locks up, and you have to turn the power off, and then turn it back on. During reboot, Error Checking will check your file and folder structure. If you use your computer a lot, it doesn't hurt to run the Error Checking test every few weeks, just to make sure your files and folders are up to par.

TIP

Error Checking may take half an hour or longer to run, depending on the size of the disk being scanned.

Disk Defragmenter

Windows XP includes a Disk Defragmenter utility that you can access from the Tools tab (or through Start | All Programs | Accessories | System Tools). Before you use Disk Defragmenter, I'll need to tell you a little bit about fragmentation so you'll understand the process.

Fragmentation is a normal part of disk usage, and it occurs at the file system level. Windows XP is not able to use a disk of any kind unless the disk is formatted. Formatting logically divides the disk into sectors and regions—basically making a grid out of the disk so that blocks of data can be stored on the disk. The grid allows Windows XP to keep up with which block of data is stored where; otherwise, the disk would become a big confusing mess. To create this grid, Windows XP uses a file system (FAT32 or NTFS), as discussed earlier in this chapter. Once the file system is in place, Windows XP can write and read data to and from the hard disk.

In Windows XP, data generally is stored on the disk in a *contiguous* manner. This just means that data is stored in order. For example, let's say you're working again on that Great American Novel. When you save the document, it is divided into pieces—or blocks of data—and stored in a "row" on the disk. Later, when you make changes to the document, those changes are stored at the end of the row. Over time, as you save, edit, and delete different files, changes to those files are moved to available, but noncontiguous, storage blocks on the disk, so that files become *fragmented*—in other words, they are not stored in a contiguous manner. When you want to open a file, Windows XP must gather the fragmented pieces together from your hard disk. Because the pieces are in different places, this can take longer than it should. The short of it is simply that heavily fragmented drives can cause Windows XP to run slower than it should.

The Disk Defragmenter utility takes all of the data on your hard disk and reorganizes it so that it is stored in a contiguous format—or at least close to it. The Disk Defragmenter utility found in Windows XP is the same one found in Windows 2000. If you have used Disk Defragmenter in Windows Me or 9*x,* you'll notice that the Disk Defragmenter utility in Windows XP looks different.

You will see a section listing all disks on the computer, as well as an analysis display and defragmentation display. Click the Analyze button to have XP analyze the disk to see whether it needs to be defragmented, as shown in Figure 19-8. Once the analysis (which is rather quick) is complete, a message appears telling you whether or not you need to defragment the drive.

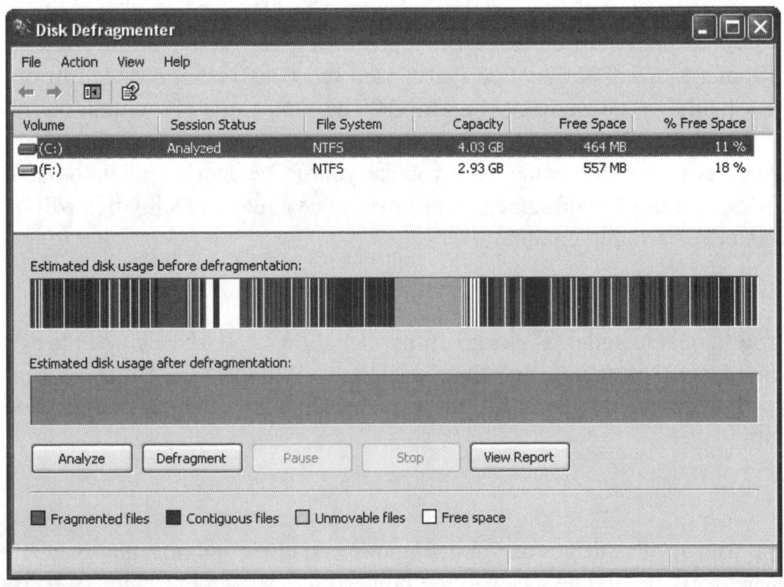

FIGURE 19-8 Disk Defragmenter

Share Drives

Let's say you have a home network. One of your PC's floppy or CD-ROM drives stops working. What can you do until it's fixed? Easy solution—have the PC access a shared drive of the same type from another computer in the network. You can also share Zip or Jaz drives so that any computer on your network can access them as well. As you can see, sharing these drives can save you time and money, and it's very easy to implement. To share a drive, follow these steps:

1. In My Computer, right-click the drive you want to share, and then choose Properties.
2. Click the Sharing tab. If no Sharing tab appears, networking is not set up on your computer. See Chapter 11 for details.
3. Click the Shared As radio button and give the share a recognizable name.
4. Configure permissions as desired.

If you want to defragment the drive, just click the Defragment button. You can watch the display change as the Disk Defragmenter utility reorganizes information. Note that the utility will not get 100 percent of your files reorganized—this is normal and nothing to be concerned about. Defragmentation may take some time to complete, especially for large hard drives, so do be patient.

Once defragmentation is complete, you can click the View Report button to find out more information about the condition of the disk. The report will give you overall information about the number of fragments, the disk size, free space, used space, and other related information.

So, how often should you defragment your drives? The simple rule of thumb is based on how often you use your computer. If you are a typical home user, you should run the Disk Defragmenter utility about once every two or three months. If you use your PC every day (all day) like me, and you use a lot of files, you should defragment your drives once a month. Doing this will help keep your file system in peak operating condition.

Backup

Windows XP Professional includes a Backup utility that allows you to back up entire disks or individual folders to a backup storage location. If you are a Windows XP Home Edition user, don't despair, you can get the Backup utility as well. See Chapter 20 to learn more about Windows Backup.

Hardware

The Hardware tab lists the disk drives on your computer and gives you information about each one (including whether or not the disk is working properly), as shown in Figure 19-9. You can also

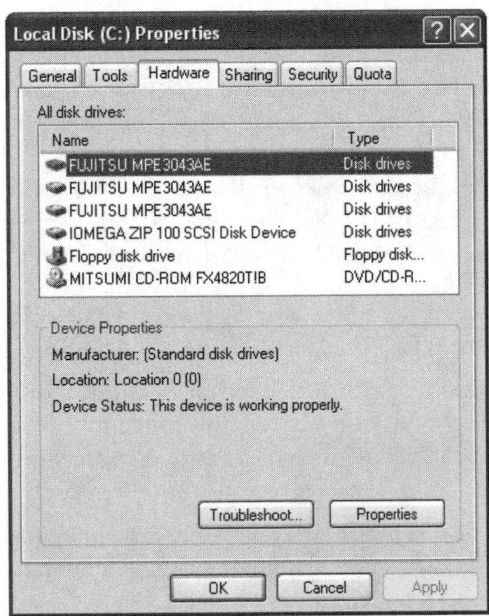

FIGURE 19-9 Hardware tab

click the Troubleshoot button to get help if you are having drive problems; and you can click the Properties button, which opens the standard Device Manager properties sheets for the hard disk.

Sharing

Just as with folders, you can share any drive on your computer so that others on a network can access it. The Sharing tab you see is just like all other Sharing tabs in Windows XP (you can learn more about network shares in Chapter 11). Under most circumstances, you would not want to give someone else full access to your entire hard drive, but you may want to give someone access to a CD-ROM or Zip drive.

If You're Using NTFS Drives

If your drives are formatted with NTFS, you will see one or two additional tabs on the disk's properties sheets. If you are using Windows XP Professional in a domain environment, you may see a Security tab where you can set permissions for various users and groups in your domain. Follow the instructions provided by your network administrator to use this tab.

Finally, you see a Quota tab. Windows XP supports a Disk Quotas feature, which first appeared in the Windows 2000 operating system. Disk quotas are designed for network computers where a computer's hard drive is shared with other network users. For example, let's say that your

Windows XP computer is shared on a network. Your computer has two hard drives, one of which is shared. Network users can store documents in various folders on this drive, and, essentially, your computer acts like a file server. You can configure how much disk space users may consume on the drive by using disk quotas. This feature prevents a user from storing information on the drive that may be inappropriate or unnecessary. If you are not sharing drives on a network, you have no need to configure anything on this tab. However, if you are using your Windows XP computer as a storage/file server on a network, read on to learn about disk quota configuration.

The Quota tab, shown in Figure 19-10, allows you to set quota configurations for the particular hard disk you are using. As you can see, you have some standard configuration options, allowing you to do the following:

- Enable quota management (which is already done by default).
- Deny disk space to users once they have exceeded their quota limits. By default, quota management warns users only when they are over the limit; but if you need to impose strict quota limits, you can choose to deny them disk space until they remove files to free up usable disk space.
- Set a limit based on size (such as 1MB), as well as a warning level. For example, if you set a limit of 1MB of storage space, you might want to configure the warning level to appear when a user reaches 800KB.
- Log an event when a user exceeds the quota limit or meets the warning level.

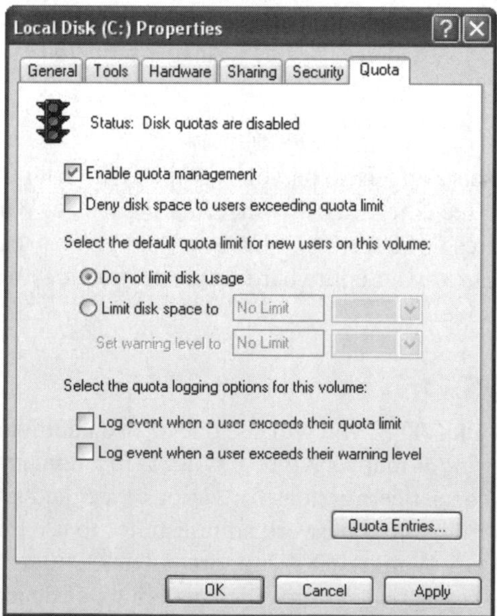

FIGURE 19-10 Quota tab

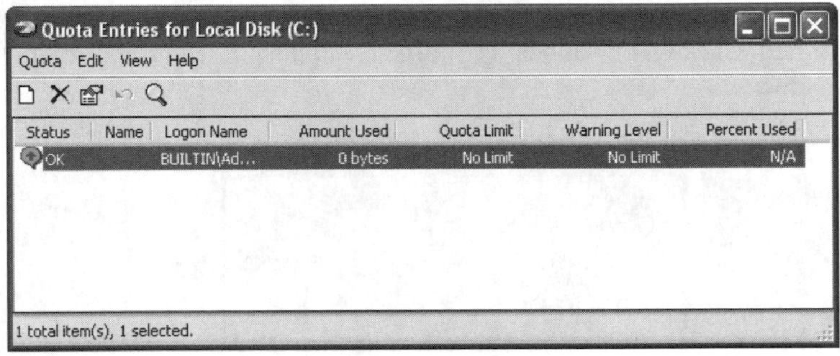

FIGURE 19-11 Quota Entries

Simply select these check box and radio button options as needed to configure quota behavior. Next, you need to click the Quota Entries button found at the bottom of the Quota tab. Doing this opens the Quota Entries window for the drive, as shown in Figure 19-11.

You use this window to create, edit, and manage quota entries. You can also make editorial changes to any quota entries you configure, and you can delete entries by selecting the entry and then using the window menus.

To create a quota entry, follow these steps:

1. On the Quota tab, click the Quota Entries button.
2. In the Quota Entries window, choose Quota | New Quota Entry.
3. The Select Users window appears. Use the Object Types button and Locations button to select the desired user or group on your network. You can also use the Advanced button to perform a more detailed search of the Windows 2000 network directory (Active Directory). Once you have selected the desired user/group, the entry appears in the Select Users window, as shown here. Click OK.

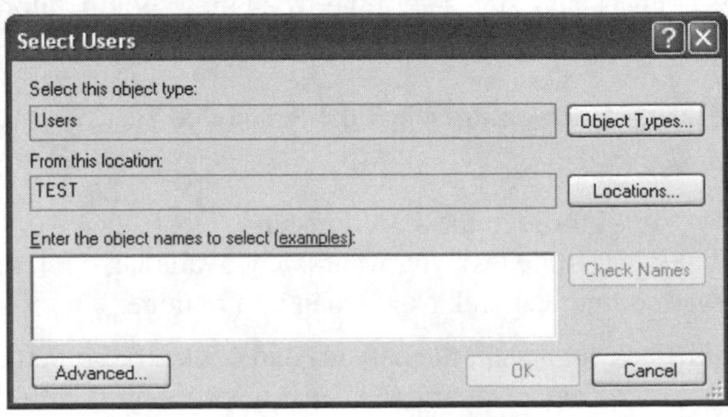

4. The Add New Quota Entry window appears. You can choose not to limit disk space usage for that particular user, or you can limit disk space by placing a limit level and warning level as desired. Click OK when you've finished, and the new entry appears in the Quota Entries window.

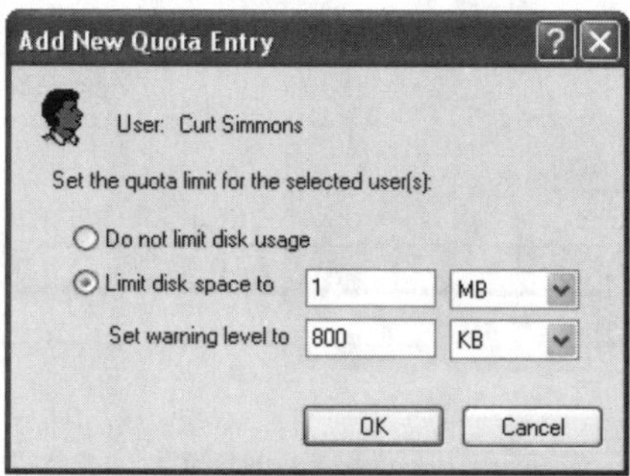

Schedule Tasks

Remember how I said that you should run Disk Defragmenter, Error Checking, and Disk Cleanup at regular intervals? What if you don't want to remember and keep up with these housekeeping tasks? The good news is you don't have to. You can use a Windows XP feature called Scheduled Tasks so you can schedule these utilities to run automatically on your computer at certain times and on certain days.

You'll find Scheduled Tasks as an icon in the Control Panel or in Accessories | System Tools. Scheduled Tasks is actually a folder, and when you open it, you see a Scheduled Task Wizard and two preconfigured scheduled tasks that automatically run on your computer. Windows XP needs these preconfigured tasks, so leave them in the folder. However, you can also create your own.

Scheduled Task Wizard

You can use the Scheduled Task Wizard to create additional scheduled tasks for your PC. The wizard enables you to select tasks, and then determine when they should automatically run on your computer. Fortunately, configuring the scheduled task is easy. Just follow these steps:

1. In the Scheduled Tasks folder, double-click the Scheduled Task Wizard icon.
2. Click Next on the Welcome screen.
3. In the next window, scroll through the selections and select a task you want to schedule, as shown in Figure 19-12. If the task you want is not available, click the Browse button and locate it on your computer. Click Next when you're done.
4. Enter a name for the task (or accept the default) and click a radio button to indicate how often you want the task to run, such as daily, weekly, or monthly. Make your selection and click Next.

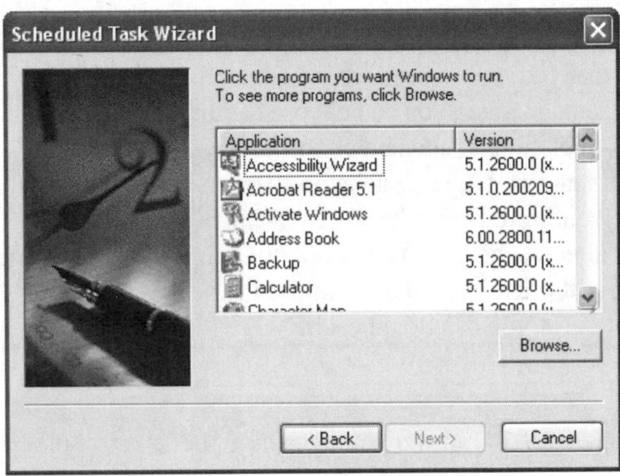

FIGURE 19-12 Choose the task.

5. In the next window, select the days/times you want the task to run, as shown in Figure 19-13. This window may vary, according to your selection in Step 4. Click Next.
6. In the Credentials window, enter your username and password. Click Next.
7. In the Completion window, click the Finish button. The scheduled task now appears in your Scheduled Tasks folder.

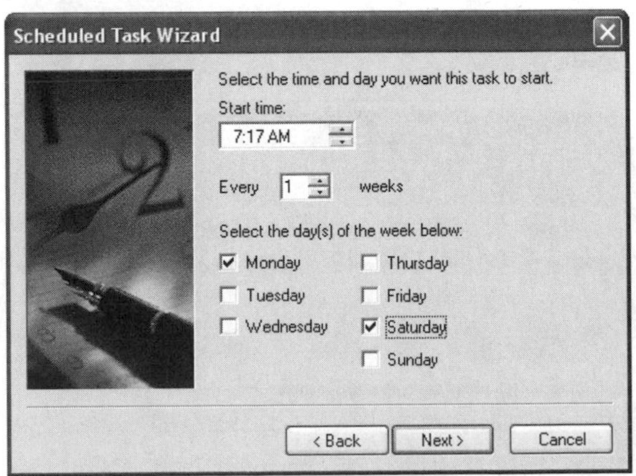

FIGURE 19-13 Schedule the task.

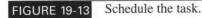

Managing Scheduled Tasks

Once you have created scheduled tasks, the icons for those tasks reside in the Scheduled Tasks folder. If you later decide that you do not need the scheduled task, right-click its icon in the folder and choose Delete. In the same manner, you can choose to run the scheduled task manually at an unscheduled time by right-clicking the icon and choosing Run.

Another piece of good news is that you can access the task's properties sheet and change basically anything you've configured with the wizard. This is a great feature, because your needs may change, and you can alter a scheduled task without having to delete it and create a new one. To edit a scheduled task, right-click its icon and choose Properties. Three tabs appear, and the following sections tell you what you can do on each.

Task

The Task tab, shown in Figure 19-14, allows you to change the location of a particular task and the settings for the task.

When a task is scheduled, the Scheduled Task Wizard notes the location of the program on your computer. When it is time to run the task, the scheduled task starts the program. However, what happens if that program is later moved to a different folder? The Scheduled Task Wizard will not be able to find the program, so it will not run. You can use this tab to change the location

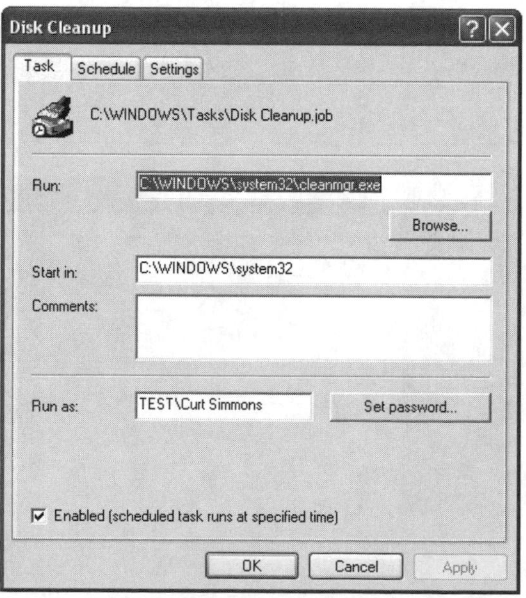

FIGURE 19-14 Task tab

for the task so that it points to the new location of the program on your computer. In most cases, you won't need to do this, but if you are running custom programs, you may need to change the information here if the program is moved.

Schedule

The Schedule tab, shown in Figure 19-15, gives you an easy interface where you can change the schedule of the task. Let's say you originally scheduled Error Checking to run at 8:00 P.M. once every two weeks. However, you have been using your computer a lot in the evenings, and Error Checking has been interrupting you. No problem—just change the start time to a more convenient one on this tab. As you can see, you can change anything about the task's schedule here.

Settings

The Settings tab gives you several good options—ones that are not presented to you when you run the wizard, so you will want to check out this tab, shown in Figure 19-16.

As you can see, the options on this tab are rather self-explanatory, but I do want to mention a couple of things you might want to consider. Notice that you have the option of stopping a task if it has run for a certain period of time. For longer tasks, such as disk defragmenting, this can be a good safety check, in case another program is interfering with the task and causing it to start over…and over…and over—you get the point. You should, however, not configure this setting too low; 24 hours is your best minimum.

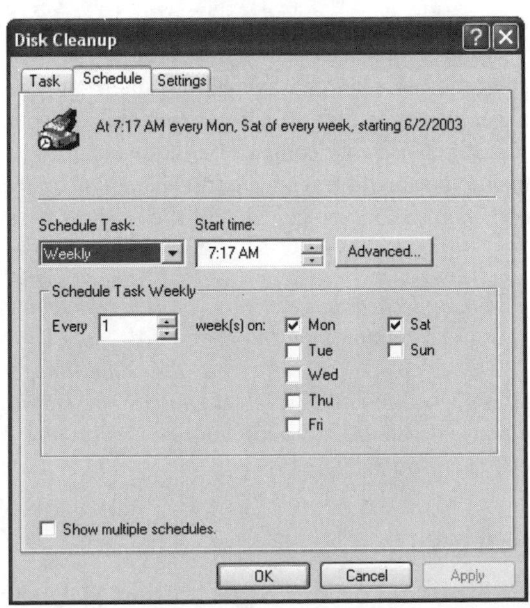

FIGURE 19-15 Schedule tab

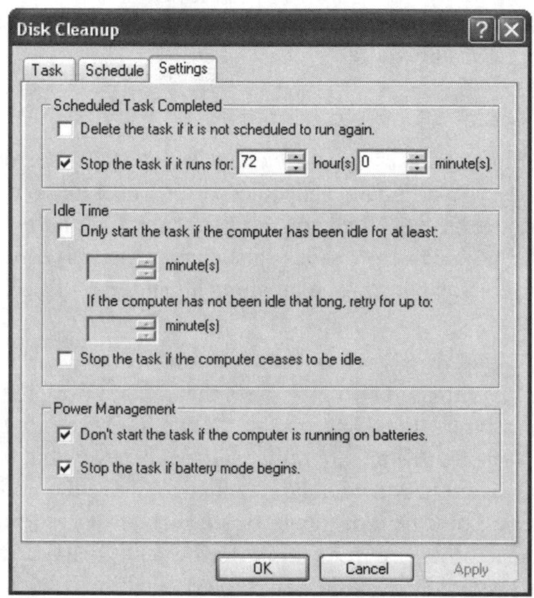

FIGURE 19-16 Settings tab

Also, the Idle Time option can be very useful. You can schedule a task to run at a certain time, but what if you are using the computer when the task is supposed to run? Without the Idle Time feature enabled on this window, the task runs anyway and may interrupt your work or play. You can use the Idle Time feature so that the task waits until the computer has been idle for a certain number of minutes, which you specify. If you use your computer a lot, this feature can be very handy.

Under Power Management, you should leave the options enabled concerning batteries if you are using a laptop computer. If you're not, you can clear these settings because they do not apply to a desktop PC anyway.

NOTE *You can configure as many scheduled tasks as you like; however, each task should be configured to run at a different time. In other words, some programs, like Error Checking and Disk Defragmenter, cannot run at the same time. Also, use as many scheduled tasks as you need, but don't overschedule them. Having too many tasks running at close intervals sometimes causes more confusion than necessary and may degrade Windows XP performance.*

Use Automatic Updates

Automatic Updates is a great feature of Windows XP that enables you to update Windows XP automatically as fixes and software updates are released from Microsoft. In fact, if you haven't installed Service Pack 2 (SP2), you can do so quickly and easily through Automatic Updates.

NOTE *SP2, along with many other updates from Microsoft, are often several megabytes in size. If you are using a dial-up Internet connection, you can expect the update process to take quite a bit of time to download.*

To make certain that your computer is automatically updated as fixes are released from Microsoft, you can turn on Automatic Updates. If you have already downloaded SP2, Automatic Updates is turned on by default and an icon for it appears in the Control Panel. If you haven't downloaded SP2, choose Start | All Programs | Automatic Updates to start the process.

If you open Automatic Updates in the Control Panel, you see a single configuration window, shown in Figure 19-17, that enables you to choose a setting. The following options are available:

- **Automatic** This is the default setting. Automatic Updates checks for updates automatically, downloads them, and installs them without any intervention from you. Note that you can choose the download time you wish. If your computer has an always-connected broadband connection, every day during the middle of the night works great, but your computer must be turned on for the process to work.

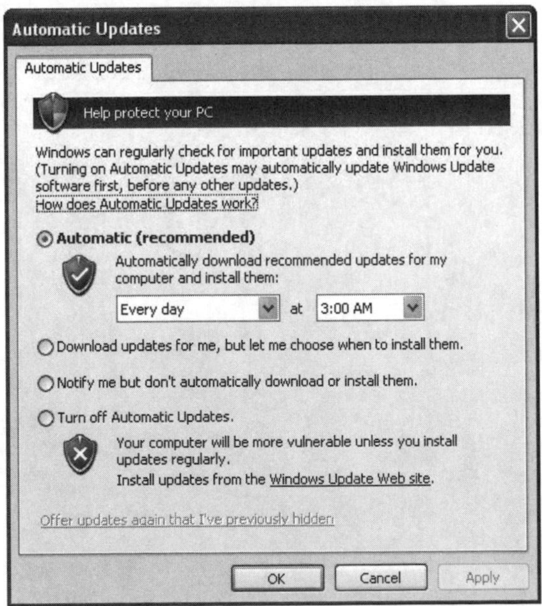

FIGURE 19-17 Automatic Updates

- **Download Updates for Me, But Let Me Choose When to Install Them** This option downloads the updates but doesn't install them until you are ready.
- **Notify Me But Don't Automatically Download or Install Them** You'll receive a notice telling you that Automatic Updates are available, but you choose when to download and install them.
- **Turn Off Automatic Updates** This option turns off the feature, which isn't recommended.

Chapter 20 Manage Disks

How to...

- Configure Windows XP disk volumes
- Use XP backup and restore features
- Explore Removable Storage

Windows XP includes a number of features that make disk management easy. As you work with Windows, the importance of effective disk management cannot be overstated—after all, it is the hard disk(s) on your computer that must store all of your information, including the Windows XP operating system. The more you know about effective disk management and how to administer and maintain hard disks on your system, the more likely you are to have a computer that runs in peak condition and never to lose data from your hard disk. In this chapter, we'll explore several disk management features in Windows XP.

Manage Disks

The Computer Management console, which is found in the Administrative Tools folder in the Control Panel, provides a section called Storage. If you click the plus sign next to Storage you see three categories available, one of which is Disk Management, as shown in Figure 20-1. I'll address Removable Storage later in this chapter, and you can learn about Disk Defragmenter in Chapter 19. Click Disk Management, and the Disk Management console, by default, provides you with an interface to manage the drives on your computer.

If you spend a few moments clicking around in the Disk Management console, you'll see that both the list and graphical portions tell the same things about your disks—the layout, type, file system, status, capacity, and so on. Disk Management in Windows XP and the options that are available will probably be new to you, and they will certainly be new if you have been using only Windows 9*x* or Me in the past. The following sections explore these management concepts and tasks so you can see how to manage the hard disks on your computer.

Understanding Dynamic Disks

Dynamic disks, which first came onto the scene with Windows 2000, give you more management and configuration options than basic disks. First, I need to define these two terms. A *basic disk* in Windows XP refers to standard disk configurations in earlier versions of Windows, such as 9*x* and NT. With a basic disk, you can configure different drives by segmenting the disk into different partitions, and you can perform basic disk-management tasks. *Dynamic disks,* on the other hand, give you more flexibility, allow you to make changes without rebooting, and use volumes instead of partitions. Essentially, from your perspective, a partition and a volume are really the same thing—both logically segment the disk—but dynamic disks do not have volume number limits, and you can change drive letters and paths on the fly. In short, dynamic disks give you the full range of disk features available in Windows XP, while basic disks are supported for backward compatibility.

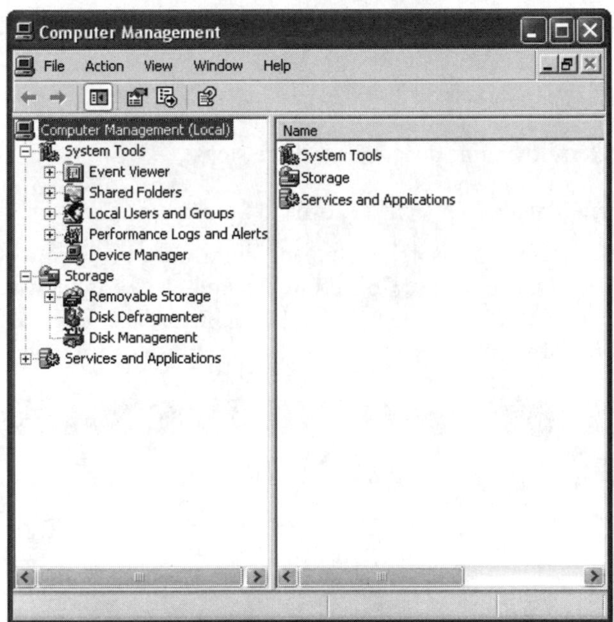

FIGURE 20-1 Disk Management console

Now, if all of this seems like alien gibberish to you, don't worry. If you are a home user or even an office user, you probably do not need to worry about the differences between basic disks and dynamic disks, and you probably will not need to make any disk changes at all. However, dynamic disks will be an important feature if your computer has several hard disks or if you are an intermediate-level user who wants to take full advantage of all that Windows XP disk management has to offer.

NOTE *If you are using a dual-boot system where multiple operating systems are available on your computer, do not convert any disks that house a "down-level" operating system, such as Windows 9x or Me.*

If you want to convert a disk to a dynamic disk, at least 1MB of free disk space must be available on the disk for the conversion to take place. Once the upgrade is complete, you cannot reverse it unless you delete all of the volumes (and hence, all of the information) from the disk. You must also be logged on as the computer's administrator to complete any disk conversion actions.

To begin, you must first convert any basic disks on your computer to dynamic disks. This process is easy and safe, and the following How To box gives you the steps.

NOTE *You cannot upgrade removable media, such as CD-ROMs or Zip disks, to dynamic disks. Dynamic disks are supported only for fixed disks. You cannot use dynamic disks on portable computers.*

Convert to Dynamic Disks

To convert a basic disk to a dynamic disk, follow these steps:

1. In the Computer Management console, expand Storage and select Disk Management.
2. In the Disk Management console's right pane, right-click the disk number (such as Disk 0 or Disk 1), and choose Convert to Dynamic Disk, as shown next. If you do not see the graphical view, choose View | Graphical View for either the top or bottom portion of the window.

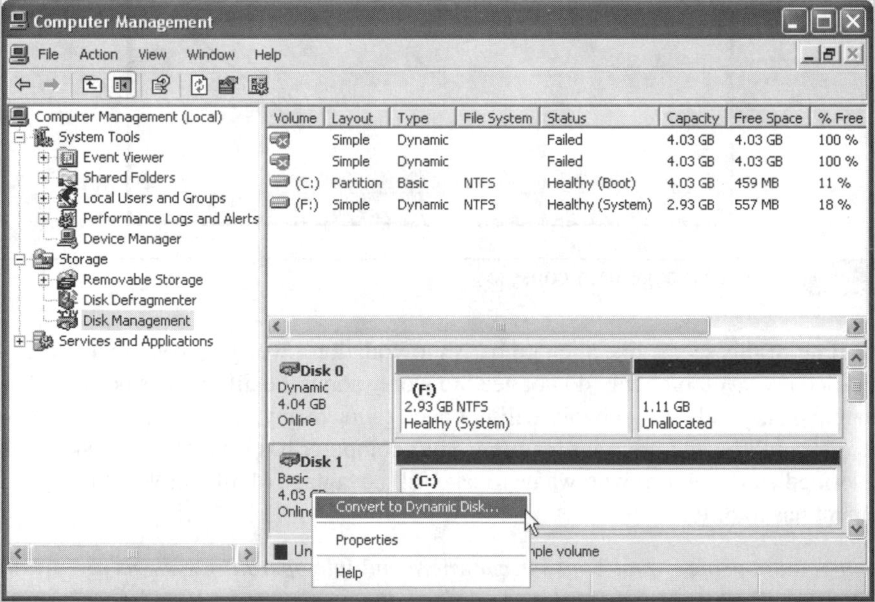

3. In the Convert to Dynamic Disk window, select all the drives that you want to convert. If only one drive needs converting, that is all you will see here. If more than one needs converting, you have the option of selecting them and converting them all at the same time. This process is safe, so feel free to convert more than one disk at a time if needed. Make your selections and click OK.
4. A window appears listing the disk(s) that will be converted. Click the Convert button to continue.
5. A message appears telling you that you will not be able to start another operating system from any volume on these disks. Click Yes to continue.

The disk is converted and now appears as a dynamic disk in the console.

Understanding Disk Status

Dynamic disks provide status information to you in the Disk Management console (see the "Convert to Dynamic Disks" How To). A number of possible status indications can be displayed, and these enable you to determine what might be wrong with a disk.

The actual disk state is shown in the graphical portion of the window under the disk number (Disk 0, Disk 1, and so on). Disks may display the following states:

- **Online** The disk is functioning properly.
- **Online (Errors)** The disk is functioning, but input/output errors have been detected. Run the Error Checking tool by right-clicking the desired disk and then choosing Properties | Tools to try to correct the problems.
- **Offline/Missing** The disk is not functioning or is not accessible. Possible hardware problems may be causing this state. Right-click the disk number in the console and choose the Reactivate Disk option.
- **Foreign** A new disk from another Windows XP computer has been installed on your computer, but it has not been set up for use on your computer. Right-click the disk and choose Import Foreign Disk to set it up for use on your computer.
- **Unreadable** The disk is not accessible because of failure or corruption. You can try to reactivate the disk by right-clicking the disk number in the console and choosing Reactivate Disk.
- **Unrecognized** The disk is formatted with a file system that is not recognized. This error occurs when you install a new disk into the computer that came from another operating system. You can reformat the disk so that Windows can use it, but any existing data on the disk will be lost.

In addition to these disk states, each volume found on each disk also displays a status, which is shown in the Disk Management console. The following status readings may be seen:

- **Healthy** The volume is functioning properly.
- **Healthy (At Risk)** The volume is functioning, but errors have been detected. Run the Error Checking tool to attempt to fix the problems.
- **Initializing** You have created a new volume, and Windows XP is preparing it for use. This status will change to Healthy once the initialization is complete.
- **Failed** The volume cannot be automatically started and has failed.

Formatting a Disk

In some circumstances, you may need to reformat a hard disk. When you format a disk, all information on that disk is erased and a new file system is created. Obviously, you will lose any data stored on the disk, so a format operation should not be taken lightly and should be performed only if absolutely necessary. The Windows XP system does not allow you to reformat a disk that holds the operating system software, because this action would delete the software from your computer. However, if your computer has other hard drives, you are free to reformat those.

To reformat a disk, right-click the drive (such as D, E, and so on) and choose Format. The Format window appears, as shown in Figure 20-2. Use the File System drop-down menu to select the desired file system, and give the volume a label. You may wish to use the Quick Format option, which essentially erases the information from the disk and creates a new file system for you. Click Start to continue.

NTFS is the file system of choice for Windows XP. So what do you do if you upgraded to Windows XP and your disks are still formatted with FAT? How can you get NTFS without losing data on the drives? The answer is simple—you can use a `convert` command at the command prompt. The process converts the disk volume to NTFS and retains all of your information. The process is quick and painless, and the How To box shows you how.

Creating a New Volume

A *volume* is simply a portion of a hard disk that acts like a separate disk. Volumes give you a way of organizing hard drives for storage purposes. Depending on your storage needs, you may want to divide one or more of your computer's hard drives into logical volumes.

Windows XP makes volume creation easy. At any time, you can create a new volume on any hard disk on your computer, provided enough free disk space is currently available to create the volume. Note that creating a new volume does not damage any existing information on your drive, so there is no danger to current data.

To create a new volume, follow these steps:

1. On the disk where you want to create the new volume, right-click the Disk number (Disk 0, Disk 1, and so on) and choose New Volume.
2. The New Volume Wizard appears. Click Next on the Welcome screen.

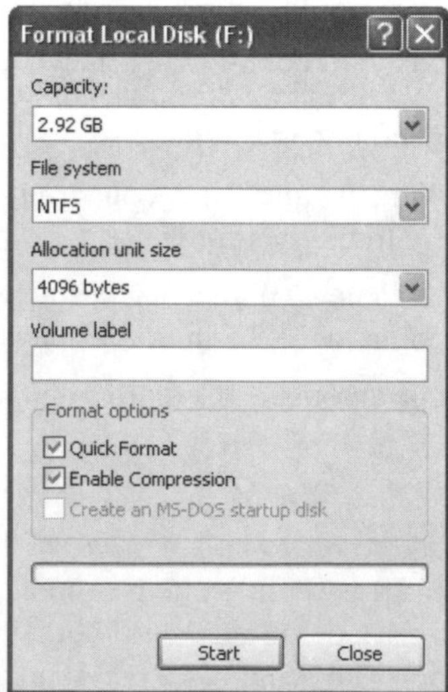

FIGURE 20-2 Format window

Convert a Drive to NTFS

To convert a drive to NTFS, follow these steps:

1. Choose Start | Run, type **CMD,** and then click OK.
2. At the command prompt, type **Convert** ***driveletter*****: /FS:NTFS** where *driveletter* represents the volume you want to format. For example, if I wanted to convert a volume labeled E, I would type **Convert E: /FS:NTFS.** Press ENTER.
3. The conversion takes place. When you reopen the Disk Management console, you will see that the desired drive is now formatted with NTFS.

3. In the Select Volume Type window, select Simple Volume and click Next.
4. In the Select Disks window, the maximum amount of free disk space that can be used is displayed in the right window. You can choose to use this amount of free disk space by clicking Next, or you can adjust it in the Select the Amount of Space in MB field. Make your selection and click Next.
5. In the Assign Drive Letter or Path window, use the drop-down menu to assign a drive letter. You can also mount the volume to an empty NTFS folder. This feature allows the drive to act like a folder on your hard disk and have a friendly name. You can also choose not to assign a drive or path, but this option is not typically recommended. Make your selection and click Next.
6. The Format Volume window appears. Choose the file system you want to use on the volume (preferably NTFS) and click Next.
7. Click Finish. The new volume is created and now appears in the Disk Management console.

Assigning a Different Drive Letter and Path to a Volume

You may need to reorganize volume labels or paths at different times, and the Disk Management console makes these changes easy. For example, let's say I have a volume labeled Drive H, and I want to assign that volume to an empty NTFS folder and give it the friendly name Company Documents. I am then going to store all kinds of company documents on that volume and share the volume on the network. I can easily make this change by right-clicking the volume and choosing Change Drive Letter and Path. I then select the volume that I want to change and click the Change button, which opens a dialog box in which I can make the desired changes.

Extending a Volume

What happens if you are storing information on a particular volume and the volume begins to run short of disk space? If additional free disk space is available on the actual disk to which the volume belongs, you can easily make the volume larger by extending it. This action does not damage any of the current data stored on the volume and is perfectly safe. To extend a volume, right-click it and choose Extend Volume. This action opens a simple wizard that guides you through the steps of making the volume size larger.

Other Volume Solutions

Windows XP Professional provides some additional management features that are not found in Windows XP Home Edition, and we will take a look at those in the rest of this chapter. In addition to simple volumes, Windows XP also supports other volume solutions, namely the *spanned volume* and the *striped volume.* You use the same New Volume Wizard to create these types of volumes, and the process is rather self-explanatory. To determine whether a spanned or striped volume is right for you, consider the following features of each.

Spanned Volume

A spanned volume combines various pieces of unformatted free space on several different hard disks to create one logical volume. For example, let's say your computer has four hard drives. On each of three drives, you have 2MB of free space, and on the last drive, you have 5MB of free space. Alone, none of these pieces of free space amounts to much storage room, but the spanned volume allows you to combine all of these free spaces into one logical volume, which would be 11MB in size—something actually useful. To you, it appears as another volume to which you can save data. Windows XP handles all of the management tasks of writing and reading data to and from various disks for you. The result is that you get more storage space by combining bits and pieces of storage on various drives that might not otherwise be useful.

To create a spanned volume, you must have unformatted free space on at least 2 physical disks (up to 32 physical disks). The space you combine can vary—there are really no rules except the 2-disk minimum. However, once you create the spanned volume, you cannot reclaim a portion of it without deleting the entire spanned volume. This means you would have to move any data to other volumes before deleting the spanned volume. Also, this solution offers no *fault tolerance*. That means if one of the hard disks fails, the entire volume is lost, even though the other disks may still be functioning with no problems.

Striped Volume

The striped volume is a lot like the spanned volume. You combine free pieces of disk space on from 2 to 32 physical disks for storage purposes, but the striped volume writes data across the disk evenly and in blocks. This feature makes the read/write time faster, but it requires that the pieces of free space be of equal size when creating the striped volume. The only reason for using a striped volume over a spanned volume is performance. The striped volume also provides no fault tolerance—if one disk fails, all data on the volume is lost.

To create a spanned volume or striped volume, use the Disk Management console to select an area of free space on one of the disks, right-click it, and choose Create Volume. Follow the New Volume Wizard steps to create the desired volume type and combine the desired areas of free space.

Use Windows XP Backup and Restore

I cannot overstate the importance of backing up your data. When you save a file to a computer's hard drive, it is safely held there until the next time you need it—unless something happens and the computer crashes. If you have used computers for any length of time, you know that sinking feeling in the pit of your stomach when you fear you have just lost an important file.

Backing up your data makes certain that the prospect of losing information never becomes reality. Should something happen to your computer, the data is safely backed up somewhere safe, and you can retrieve it once the computer is up and running again. Fortunately, Windows XP Professional provides built-in backup and restore features that are easier to use and more flexible than ever before. In the following sections, you'll learn all about backing up and restoring data on your computer.

Backing Up Data

You can back up data in a number of ways: You can save data to a floppy disk, on a CD-R or CD-RW disc, or even to a Zip or Jaz disk. You can manually save the files you want; should a problem ever occur, you would still have your data. However, backing up important information this way is time consuming and heavily dependent on you. Why not let Windows XP automatically handle this task for you?

Windows XP includes advanced backup features that enable you to store backup data to any kind of removable media (such as tape drives, Zip drives, CD-RW drives, and so on), or you can even save backup files to a network share. The idea is to get data copied off your computer so that it is in another location should your computer fail.

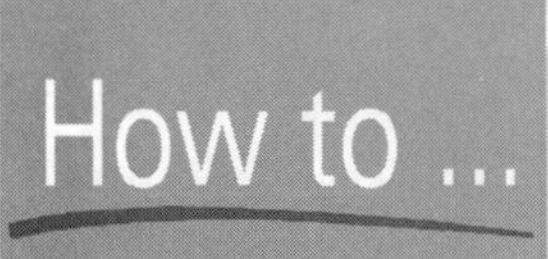

Install the Backup Utility on Windows XP Home Edition

If you are using Windows XP Home Edition, Windows Backup is not included as part of your operating system. However, you can find it lurking about on your Windows XP Home Edition installation CD-ROM, from which you can install it to your system.

1. Insert the CD-ROM and look in\valueadd\msft\ntbackup.
2. The file that you install is called NTBACKUP.MSI. Just double-click this file to start the installation.

Once you install the Backup utility, it will work according to the instructions in the upcoming sections.

To help you accomplish your backup goals, Windows XP gives you a helpful wizard, which provides a number of different options. The following steps walk you through this wizard and explain the available options to you:

1. Choose Start | All Programs | Accessories | System Tools | Backup.
2. The Backup Utility Wizard appears. Notice that on the Welcome screen, you have the option of using Advanced Mode. I'll explore that option for you later in the chapter (in the "Using Backup Advanced Mode" section); click Next.
3. On the Backup or Restore window, you have the options of performing a backup or restoring files. Click the Backup Files and Settings radio button, and then click Next.
4. In the next window, you can choose to back up everything on your computer, only certain drives and files, or only System State data. System State data refers to a collection of network and security settings, and you will not typically back up these unless specifically directed to do so by a network administrator. Make a selection and click Next.
5. If you chose to back up selected files, an Explorer-type window appears, where you can select the drives, folders, or even specific files that you want to back up. Select the check boxes for the items you want to back up and click Next.

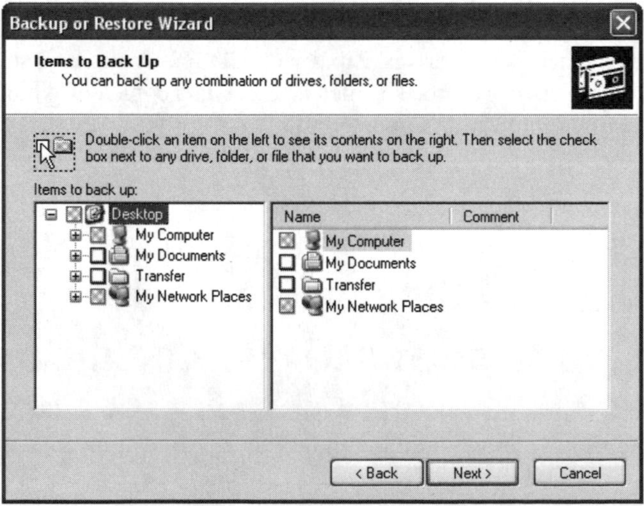

6. Choose the location where you want to store backup files. Use the Browse button to select a removable media drive or even a network location. If your computer has multiple hard drives, you can even save the backup file to a different hard drive. Also note that the backup file will be named backup.bkf by default. You can change this name if you like, but you should not change the .bkf extension. For example, I rename my backup files to represent the date of the backup (such as 0612.bkf for June 12). Make your selections and click Next.
7. You now reach the completion window. You can click Finish to start the backup job. However, before doing so, notice the Advanced button. This option will give you some

additional backup features you may want to consider before completing the backup. Click the Advanced button.

8. In the Type of Backup window, you see a drop-down menu that allows you to choose a type of backup. By default, a typical backup is *normal,* which means a backup file is created. However, you can also choose other types of backup options—such as *incremental,* which backs up files only if they have not been previously backed up, or *differential,* which backs up files only if they have changed since the last backup. These backup options are important and do require some additional planning and study on your part. See the Windows XP Help files for more detailed information about these options. Also, you see a check box option to back up data that is in Remote Storage. Windows XP provides a Removable Storage feature, explored later in this chapter, which tracks data stored on removable storage, such as CD-ROMs, Zip drives, and other types of removable storage media. Make any desired selections and click Next.
9. The next window asks whether you want Windows XP to verify data once it has been backed up, which is a good idea. You can also use compression if it is available on the storage device. Also, you can choose to disable volume snapshot, which allows Windows XP to save files even if they are in use at the time of the backup. Make any desired selections and click Next.
10. In the Backup Options window, you have the option of replacing an existing backup file that might exist in the same location or appending the new backup file to the old one. By default, the append option is selected. Click Next.
11. You can choose a backup label, which is the date and time by default. You can change this if you want. Click Next.
12. You can choose to run the backup now or later. If you choose later, you'll need to click the Set Schedule button to create a schedule when the backup should run.
13. Click Finish. The Backup process occurs, and a window presents the status.

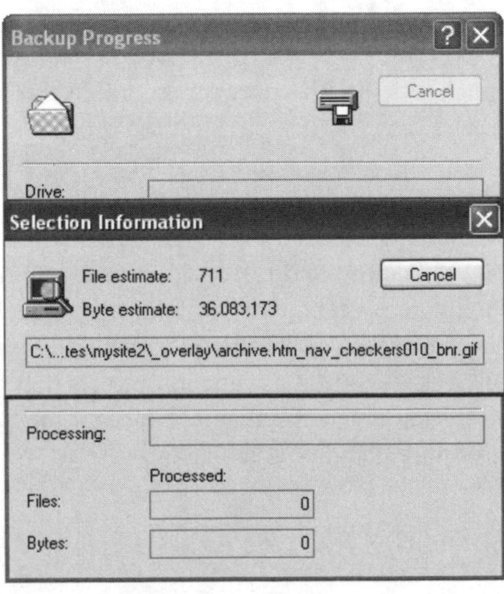

How to ... Use the Restore Wizard

To use the Restore Wizard, just follow these steps:

1. Choose Start | All Programs | Accessories | System Tools | Backup.
2. Click Next on the Welcome screen.
3. In the Select an Operation window, click the Restore Files from a Previous Backup radio button, and then click Next.
4. In the What to Restore window, select the files that you want to restore in the left pane and the backup media to be used in the restore in the right pane. Click Next.
5. Click Finish. You see a progress window that tells you when the backup is complete.

Using Backup Recovery

Okay, the moment you have been dreading actually happens, and, because of a system failure, you lose some files, or even a complete drive, on your computer. If you have followed an effective backup plan and you are regularly backing up data, you can recover that data quite easily by using the Backup utility. To recover backup data, you'll use the Restore Wizard. Follow the steps in the How To box.

Keep in mind that the larger the backup or restore data, the more time will be required to complete the job.

Using Backup Advanced Mode

Once you've used the Backup Wizard a few times, you'll become a pro in configuring backup jobs, and using the wizard will get a little tedious. Recognizing that this will happen, Windows XP provides an Advanced Mode feature that you can click on the Welcome screen of the Backup Wizard. This option opens the Backup Utility window, which contains Welcome, Backup, Restore And Manage Media, and Schedule Jobs tabs, as you can see in Figure 20-3.

If you spend a few moments looking around here, you'll discover that the tabs provided simply give you a way to configure backup and restore processes without the wizard. You can access the exact same options using these tabs without wading through the wizard screens. For example, open the Backup tab. On this tab, you can configure what you want to back up, and you can even choose Tools | Options to get the advanced options that you have when using the wizard. There is absolutely no difference in using this interface or the wizard—you just may like this one more as you learn to configure backup jobs.

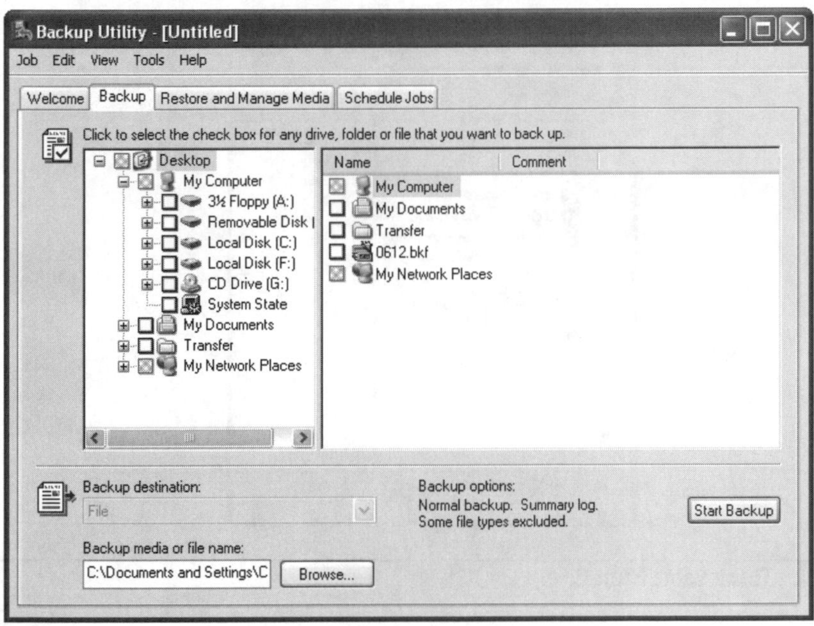

FIGURE 20-3 Backup Utility options

Use Removable Storage

Removable Storage is a feature that Windows XP continues to provide. Removable Storage gives you and Windows XP a way to keep track of data that is stored on removable storage media, such as CD-ROMs, Zip disks, tape libraries, and related media. Windows XP can keep track of what data is stored on what media by organizing that data into libraries. Removable Storage is also available in the Computer Management console, as shown in Figure 20-4.

Removable Storage is designed to control devices that handle multiple items, such as CD changers or jukeboxes, which are used to store large amounts of data on removable disks. With these devices and Removable Storage, a bunch of disks or CDs can be managed and loaded. Windows XP keeps track of data that is written on each disk; it can access the appropriate disk (using the changer) to retrieve the data. As you can see, for environments that use such devices, the Removable Storage feature can be very important, but it is not a feature intended for the typical home or office user.

I'll be brief and honest concerning Removable Storage—it can be helpful in certain circumstances where a large amount of data is being stored in many removable storage media disks; but for the most part, Removable Storage is confusing and not particularly helpful to the

FIGURE 20-4 Removable Storage

home or office user. In fact, Removable Storage is designed for a system that is primarily used as a file server or storage computer that connects with certain types of media devices. Because most all of you reading this book will not use the Removable Storage feature, I'll not delve any deeper into the subject. However, if you want to learn more, you'll find detailed information in the Windows XP Help files.

NOTE *You don't have to do anything with Removable Storage to store data on Zip, CD-ROM, or floppy drives found on your computer. Removable Storage is used to manage the storage of a lot of data on multiple disks, but is not a feature required to store data on removable media.*

Chapter 21

Solve Problems with Windows XP

How to...

- Use System Information
- Use the Performance Monitor
- Use problem-solving tools
- Troubleshoot your computer
- Use System Restore

Windows XP is a complicated operating system, full of features and functions, many of which go on behind the scenes. As with any complex operating system, you may experience both performance and functionality problems from time to time. I'll be the first to say, however, that Windows XP is as solid as a rock. In most cases, you can say goodbye to all those aggravating lockups and weird behavior problems you saw in Windows Me and 9*x*. If you've used Windows 2000, you'll see the same stability and performance in XP—with a friendlier attitude. In this chapter, we'll explore some tools and optimization features that can help you keep XP in tiptop shape and even get out of jams from time to time.

Use System Information

First introduced in Windows 98, System Information is a powerful tool that provides all kinds of information about your computer system, and it includes some additional tools that can fix problems on your system, as you can see in Figure 21-1. You can access System Information by choosing Start | All Programs | Accessories | System Tools | System Information. System Information can be slow to start because it has to collect a lot of information, so be patient.

TIP *You can quickly reach System Information by choosing Start | Run, then typing* ***msinfo32,*** *and then clicking OK.*

If you take a look at the left pane, you see a list of information categories. If you click the plus (+) sign next to each category, you can select specific topics for which you want to gather information. It is important to note here that you cannot configure or actually do anything with System Information, with the exception of the troubleshooting tools, but System Information is designed to give you...well, *information.* Why? you might ask. The answer is simple. The more information you can gather about your computer, the more likely you are to solve problems with your computer. On a more practical note, System Information is very useful to telephone support personnel, who you may need to call in the event of a problem you can't solve. Although having outside support is very helpful, it is always best if you can solve your own PC problems; the next several sections tell you all about the information you can gain in each major category, and I'll point out some tips for you along the way.

Voices from the Community

Fixing a Slow System

You should never have to reboot Windows XP due to system slowdown or general instability. If you feel your system is running sluggishly, follow these steps:

1. Press CTRL+ALT+DEL to open the Windows Task Manager.
2. Open the Performance tab. Under the Totals category, if the number of handles is greater than 15,000, you know something is eating up too many of your resources. To find out where this is happening, open the Processes tab and choose View | Select Columns. Select the Handle Count check box and click OK.
3. Look for processes that use more than 2000 handles. If you find a process that fits the bill, you may want to consider terminating that process (unless it's svchost.exe because it typically uses more resources, which is OK). This will help make Windows run faster and more reliable and keep you from having to reboot.

—Brad Wardell
President & CEO
Stardock Corporation
www.stardock.com

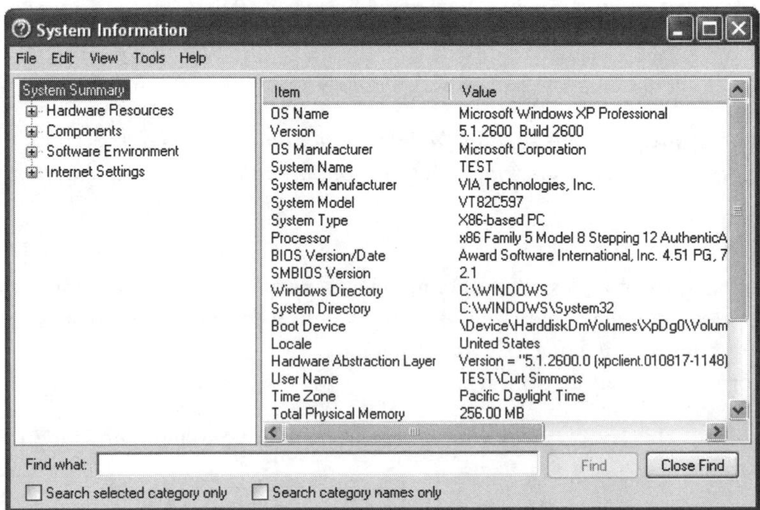

FIGURE 21-1 System Information

System Summary

When you first open System Information, the default view is the System Summary. This view provides an overview of your computer. You see everything from the operating system to the total amount of RAM installed on your computer. This page is excellent to access if you want a quick report about the basics of your computer. You can print this page from the File menu.

Hardware Resources

The Hardware Resources category of System Information gives you a complete look at the hardware on your computer. This section is an excellent place to see exactly what's installed, what's working and what's not, and whether any conflicts exist.

Should conflicts be encountered, you'll see warning messages in yellow and conflict or error messages in red. This helps you quickly identify problems. By expanding Hardware Resources in the left pane, you see the following categories from which you can select and view:

- **Conflicts/Sharing** This option tells whether any hardware conflicts are occurring between devices. In some cases, hardware devices share certain computer resources, and this section tells you about those as well.
- **DMA (direct memory access)** This option tells you what devices have direct access to memory resources.
- **Forced Hardware** If you have problems installing a device and it has been "forced" onto your system using manual settings, the device will be listed here.
- **I/O (input/output system)** This information gives a report about input/output operation. Technical support personnel may find this information useful.
- **IRQs (interrupt request lines)** Each device uses an IRQ to access your computer's processor. This option tells you which device is using which IRQ.
- **Memory** This option provides a list of memory resource assignments per device.

NOTE *If you are having problems finding the information that you need, try typing information into the Find What field that appears at the bottom of the System Information window.*

Components

The Components category provides a list of components installed and used on your system. Some of these include additional submenus as well. System Information will display problems in yellow and red lettering so you can easily identify them.

You gain information about the following:

- **Multimedia** This option gives you information about your audio and video configuration.
- **CD-ROM** Information is listed here about your CD-ROM drive.

- **Sound Device** Information about your sound card is listed here.
- **Display** Information about your display appears here.
- **Infrared** If you are using any infrared ports, they are listed here.
- **Input** Get information about your keyboard and mouse or other pointing device here.
- **Modem** Modem information is listed here.
- **Network** Network adapters, protocols, and WinSock information is provided here.
- **Ports** Get information about ports on your computer (such as serial and parallel ports).
- **Storage** Get information about the drives on your computer here.
- **Printing** Find out about printers and print drivers here.
- **Problem Devices** If any devices are not working correctly, they are listed here. This is a very useful option to find troublesome devices.
- **USB (universal serial bus)** USB configuration and devices are listed here.

Software Environment

The Software Environment category provides information about the software configuration of Windows XP. If any errors occur, you'll see them appear in red or yellow. This category can be very helpful to technical support personnel who are helping you solve a problem with Windows XP.

You see the following information in this category:

- **System Drivers** This section lists the drivers that manage your computer's software environment.
- **Signed Drivers** This section provides a list of installed drivers that are certified by Microsoft, as well as any other drivers that are not signed or whose status is not available.
- **Environment Variables** This section lists items such as your TEMP file, which is used for temporary files and other variables in the software environment.
- **Print Jobs** This option gives you the information found in your print queue.
- **Network Connections** All network connections currently held by your computer are listed here.
- **Running Tasks** This option lists all of the tasks on your computer that are currently running.
- **Loaded Modules** This option lists all software modules currently loaded.
- **Services** This section lists the services, such as automatic updates, fax, and much more, that are currently installed on your computer.
- **Program Groups** This option lists all program groups currently configured on your computer.

- **Startup Programs** This option lists all programs that are configured to run automatically when your computer starts up.
- **OLE Registration (object linking and embedding)** Windows XP uses OLE to allow the various system components and programs to communicate with each other. OLE information is listed here.
- **Windows Error Reporting** This section provides a listing of software errors reported by the system.

The Windows Error Reporting section, which is new in Windows XP, is a great feature, because it lists all of the application lockups and related service problems. If you are having trouble, this can be a great place to find the culprit!

Internet Settings

You'll find the following information in this category:

- **Summary** Access this option for a quick summary of IE's configuration.
- **File Versions** This lists all files and file versions used by IE.
- **Connectivity** Access this page to see a review of IE's connectivity configuration. These are the settings you configure in Internet Options in IE.
- **Cache** IE uses a cache to store temporary Internet files. Access this option to learn more about the cache size and see a list of objects in the cache.
- **Content** Examine security and content settings here.
- **Security** View zone security configuration here.

You may see additional categories for some of your software, such as Microsoft Office.

System Information Tools

System Information also has a Tools menu that gives you easy access to some features and tools in Windows XP. If you check out this menu, you see right away that you can access the Backup tool, the Network Connections folder, the Add Hardware Wizard, and Disk Cleanup. You can also access Net Diagnostics and System Restore here. In addition, you can access three tools that we have not discussed in this book, and the next three sections explore these tools and show you how they can help you.

File Signature Verification Utility

To protect Windows XP, files that are in use by the operating system are *signed* by Microsoft to ensure compatibility and security. You can use the Signature Verification Utility to make certain that files that are not signed are not in use on your system. By default, Windows XP gives you a warning message before you install unsigned files. You can use this tool to gather that information. When you open Signature Verification, click the Start button to run the verification scan. Once the scan is complete, you see a report showing all of the unsigned files on your system. Generally, you don't need to use this tool, but if you have installed some programs on your computer that are giving you problems, you can run this utility to check for signatures.

DirectX Diagnostic Tool

DirectX is a graphics technology that enables you to play really cool games. However, you can have problems with various versions of DirectX and its operation with your system components. The DirectX Diagnostic Tool gives you an easy interface with a bunch of tabs, as shown in Figure 21-2.

The DirectX Files tab reports a variety of information to you. The Display, Sound, Music, Input, and Network tabs provide information about how DirectX is interacting with these system resources. Each of these tabs also contains a Test button so you can directly test how DirectX is interacting with the hardware. This is a great tool that can help you identify exactly which incompatibilities are occurring with DirectX and your hardware.

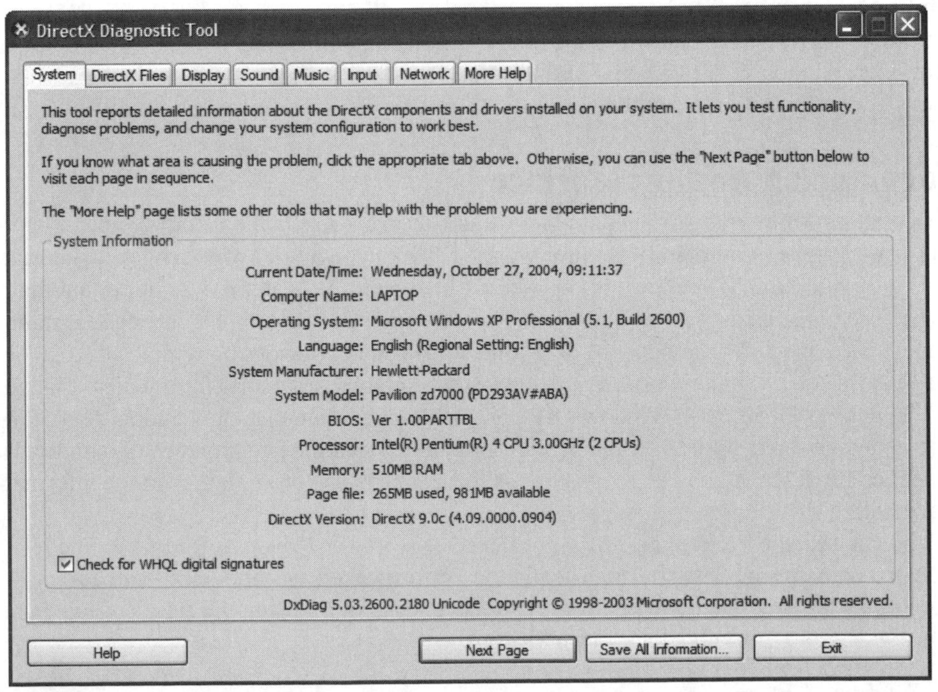

FIGURE 21-2 DirectX Diagnostic Tool

Dr. Watson

Dr. Watson is a Windows tool that can inspect your system and generate a detailed report after a system fault has occurred. Dr. Watson can tell you what went wrong and sometimes suggest what can be done to fix the problem. Should you ever need to contact technical support, the support technician may have you run Dr. Watson to take a "snapshot" of your system; once the snapshot is taken, the report can potentially be used to solve the problem.

You can run this tool yourself, of course. The results are usually easy to understand. If you see a particular application or device listed, you may need to try reinstalling the application or device in question—or just remove it from Windows XP altogether.

Use the Performance Monitor

If you've spent any time with a Windows 2000 computer, you probably know a thing or two about the Performance Monitor. The Performance Monitor, which is included in Windows XP, enables you to gather real-time server data about the performance of various system components and processes. You can examine this data and locate potential performance problems. Once you identify the source of performance problems, you can then take an appropriate course of action to solve those problems.

The Performance Monitor may seem a little intimidating at first, and it can be a complex tool. Don't worry, though—if you study this section and spend a little time with the Performance Monitor, you can learn a lot about the performance of your computer system quickly and easily.

Performance Monitor Interface

The Performance Monitor tool is available in Administrative Tools in the Control Panel. Before showing you how the Performance Monitor works, I'll give you a brief overview of its interface, as shown in Figure 21-3. If you have never used the Performance Monitor, it is important that you spend some time using it so you can learn how it works. Fortunately, the interface is rather easy and intuitive, and you can be a pro in no time after you begin working with it.

The Performance Monitor works by creating charts, graphs, or reports for counters that you select. A *counter* is a particular Windows XP component or service that can be monitored. By adding counters to the console, you can view information about the performance of a particular component or service. You can use as many or as few counters as you wish to gain the information that you need.

As you can see, the Performance Monitor interface is a basic Windows interface. The left console pane contains the System Monitor and the Performance Logs and Alerts categories. However, you primarily interact with the Performance Monitor by using the right console pane, which is divided into three divisions (from the top):

- **Toolbar** The toolbar contains icons you will use regularly to generate the types of charts and information that you want. The toolbar contains the following button options, shown from left to right in the following illustration: New Counter Set, Clear Display,

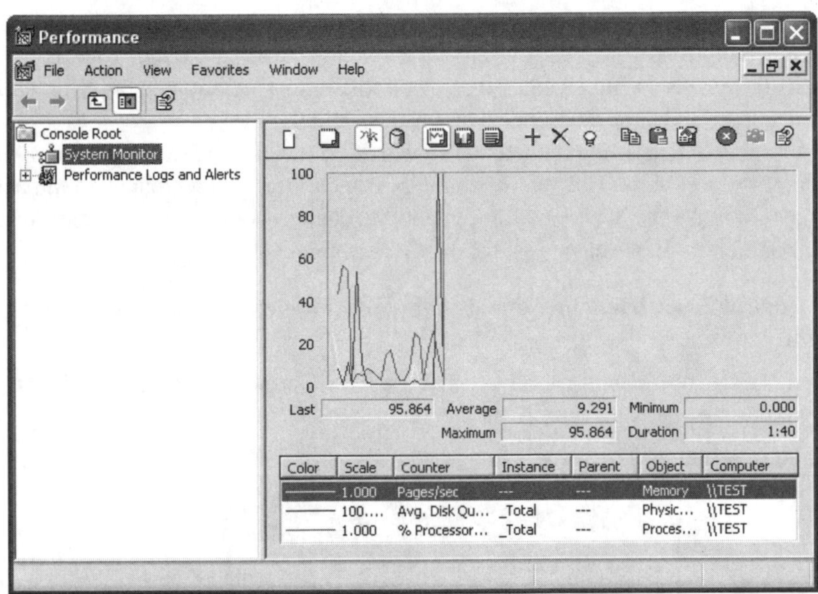

FIGURE 21-3 Performance Monitor

View Current Activity, View Log File Data, View Chart, View Histogram, View Report, Add Counter, Delete, Highlight, Copy Properties, Paste Counter List, Properties, Freeze Display, Update Data, and Help. You use the toolbar to manage the Performance monitor as needed.

- **Information area** The information area contains the chart, histogram, or report that you want to view. Click the desired button on the toolbar to view counter information in the desired format.
- **Counter list** The bottom portion of the window contains the counter list. All of the counters displayed in this list are currently being reported in the information area. You can easily remove or add counters to the list using the toolbar. Each counter in the list is given a different color for charting and histogram purposes.

Using the Performance Monitor

The primary functionality of the Performance Monitor is through the use of counters. Without counters, there is no way to break down performance information and view various components and services. As you might guess, a number of different counters can give you information on all kinds of system processes and services.

With an understanding of the counters available to you, you can use the Performance Monitor to gain valuable data for making decisions about performance and optimization in your environment. You can monitor activity for a period of time and then save the data to a log file. You can even set up logs and alerts so that data will be gathered on a periodic basis automatically and you will be alerted if certain values fall below a baseline that you determine.

Your first action is to determine the manner in which you want to view information—in chart, histogram, or report view. The type of counters you choose to view may also impact your choice; but once you make the decision, you can add the desired counters to the chart, histogram, or log. Adding counters is rather easy; just follow these steps:

1. In the Control Panel, open the Administrative Tools folder and double-click the Performance icon.
2. On the Performance Monitor toolbar, click the New Counter Set button, and then select the type of view you want (graph, histogram, or report).
3. Click the Add button. The Add Counters window appears.

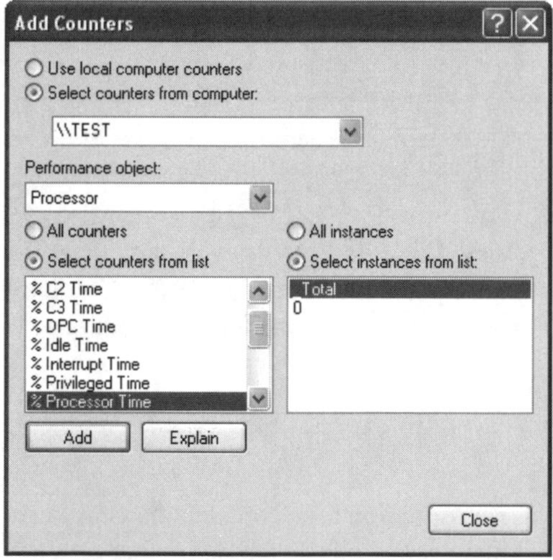

4. Click the Performance Object drop-down menu and select the object that you want to monitor. For example, if your computer seems to be having memory problems or is running very slowly, you might want to choose the Memory or Processor object.
5. Click the Select Counters from List radio button, and then select desired counters in the list and click the Add button. If you want an explanation of the counter, select it and click the Explain button. Also, notice that you can click the All Counters radio button to select all counters. For some counters, you can select an instance from the list that appears in the right box. Continue to select objects/counters as desired until you have finished, and then click the Close button.

6. The counters you selected are now added to the window and are charted (or reported, depending on your selection). You can change charting or reporting views at any time, and you can remove counters from the console by selecting the counter and clicking the Delete button.
7. If you want to save the data you are currently charting, you can right-click the chart and save it as an HTML file. You can also save the data as a Performance Monitor Alert.

Using Counter Logs

In addition to the live collection of data, you can also set up a counter log so that desired counters are recorded and logged at the intervals you specify. This feature is very handy if you need to collect data over a period of time, but do not wish to do so manually. To configure counter logs, you simply create a new counter log, add the counters that you want to the log, and then configure the additional log elements.

To create a counter log, follow these steps:

1. In the left console pane of the Performance Monitor, expand Performance Logs and Alerts. Right-click Counter Logs and choose New Log Settings. Enter a name in the dialog box that appears and click OK.
2. The Log File Settings window appears with three tabs. On the General tab, shown next, you see the log name and the location where it will be stored (C:\PerfLogs, by default). Click the Add Counters button to add the desired counters that the log will record. At the bottom of the window, use the scroll boxes to determine how often data is collected (15 seconds is the default).

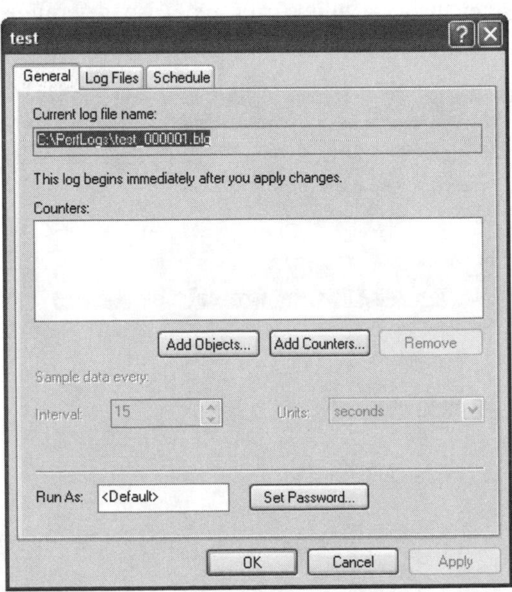

3. Click the Log Files tab. You can make changes on this tab to the manner in which the log file is saved and its maximum size.
4. Click the Schedule tab. Use this tab to determine when logging should start and stop. Click OK to save your changes.

Creating a Performance Alert

The Performance Monitor also provides a performance alert feature with which you can configure a counter to be monitored against a baseline of performance. Then, if the performance measured by that counter falls below that configured baseline, a certain action or actions can be carried out. The Performance Monitor supports the actions of logging an event to the Application Event Log, sending a network message, starting a performance data log, or running a program for performance alerts.

However, it is important that you configure alerts only for items that are very important. If you configure too many alerts, you may end up with too much information that is difficult to sort through. So determine what action you absolutely want performed when baseline levels are not met, and then configure those alerts accordingly.

To create a performance alert, follow these steps:

1. Open the Performance Monitor.
2. In the left console pane, expand Performance Logs and Alerts. Right-click Alerts and choose New Alert Settings. Enter a name in the dialog box that appears and click OK.
3. On the General tab, shown next, use the Add button to add desired counter(s), and then create a baseline with the Alert When the Value Is and Limit fields. When performance falls below the baseline, the alert will be triggered. Also, determine how often you want to sample data that pertains to this alert by making selections at the bottom of the window.

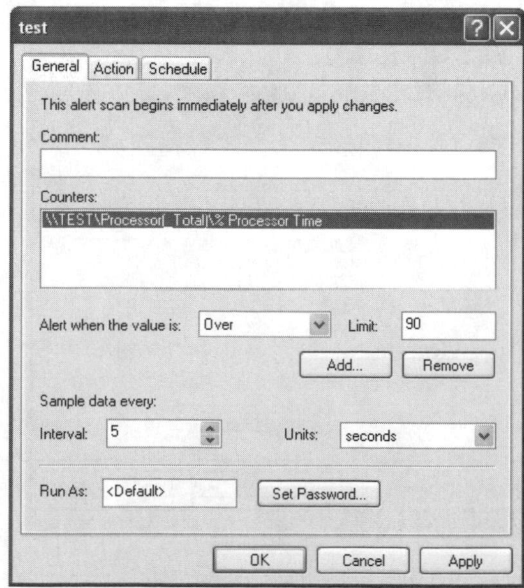

4. Click the Action tab. Select the desired action(s) and configure the necessary options.
5. Click the Schedule tab. Configure the options to start and stop the scan at the desired times. Click OK to save the alert.

Use System Properties to Optimize Windows XP

You access System Properties in the Control Panel (or by right-clicking My Computer and choosing Properties if you're using a My Computer icon). When you access System Properties, you will see an Advanced tab, among others, as shown in Figure 21-4.

A Performance section on the tab lets you deal with performance issues, and we'll take a look at your options in the following sections.

Performance Options

If you click the Settings button under Performance, you see a Performance Options window with a Visual Effects tab and an Advanced tab. The Visual Effects tab, shown in Figure 21-5, gives you another place to manage the way Windows handles the user interface in terms of icons, animation, and other factors. The more visual effects that are in use, the more system resources

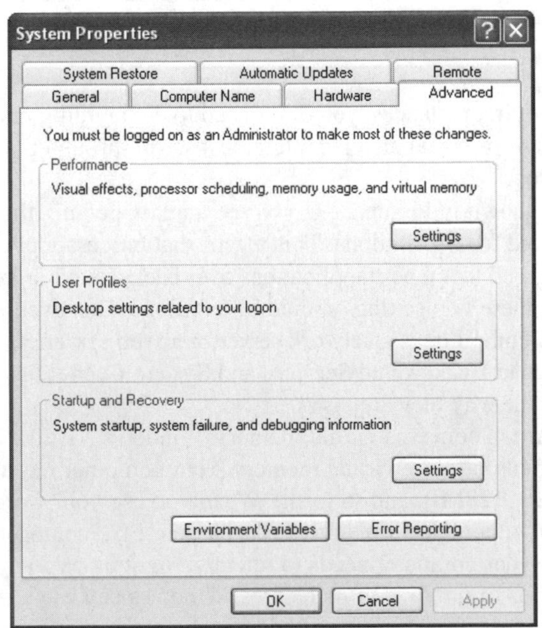

FIGURE 21-4 System Properties

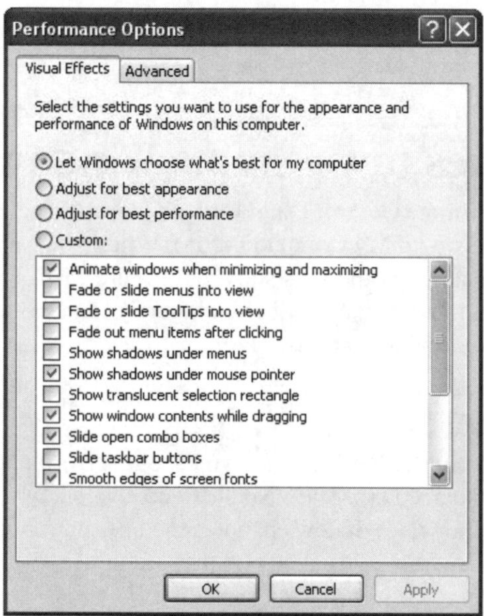

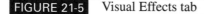

FIGURE 21-5 Visual Effects tab

are consumed. Under most circumstances, you don't need to do anything on the Visual Effects tab; but if you want to disable a visual effects feature, just scroll through the list and clear the check box next to the option.

On the Advanced tab, shown in Figure 21-6, you see that, by default, the processor and memory usage are optimized for applications. This means that processor cycles and memory usage are primarily configured to support applications over background or system process functions. For most users, these two settings should be left alone. However, if you are using your Windows XP Professional computer as a network server or a Web server, you might consider changing these two settings to Background Services and System Cache. For most of us, though, these settings are just fine the way they are.

The final portion of the tab concerns virtual memory. Windows XP, like other Windows operating systems, is configured to use virtual memory. Your computer has a certain amount of memory installed (96MB, 128MB, and so forth). When you use your word processor, open applications, surf the Internet, and perform other tasks on your PC, memory is used to hold programming information your computer needs to run the programs. When you have too many open programs, RAM begins to run low. In such cases, Windows can use a portion of your hard disk to store information temporarily. This is called *virtual* memory because it is not *real* RAM, but rather storage room borrowed from the hard drive. Windows XP is programmed to set its own virtual memory settings, as you can see in Figure 21-6.

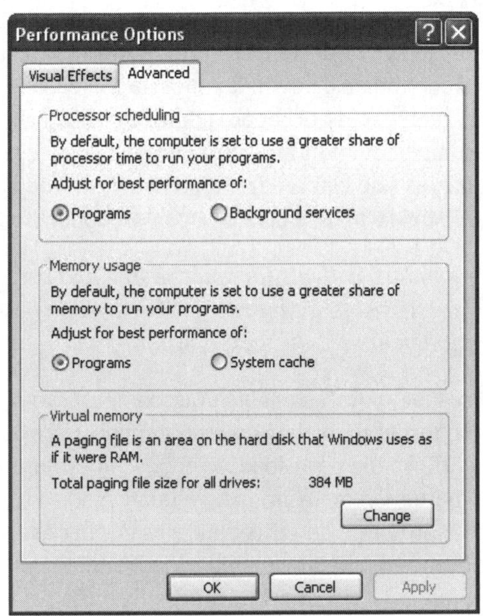

FIGURE 21-6 Advanced tab

Did you know?

Virtual Memory Is Not a Replacement for More RAM

Many people who learn a few things about virtual memory think they can configure their own settings to make Windows use more hard disk space—a replacement for physical RAM. This simply is not the case. Windows XP can handle these settings, and overriding Windows XP's settings is normally a bad idea. Virtual memory is used for overflow information—it is not designed to be a replacement for physical RAM chips. If you need a RAM upgrade, tinkering with virtual memory will not solve the problem—and, in fact, doing so may create more problems. My advice: leave this setting alone! If your system needs more RAM, your best bet is to part with a few hard-earned dollars and install more RAM on your computer.

You can click Change and configure the Virtual Memory settings yourself, but this action is *not at all recommended.* Your best performance option is to allow Windows to continue using its own Virtual Memory settings—believe me, they are the best!

Use Automatic Updates

Automatic updates, first introduced in Windows Me, allow Windows to check Microsoft.com automatically for operating system updates, download those updates, and tell you when they are ready to be installed. It is a relatively hands-off approach to keeping your computer current and updated. You can access the management window for automatic updates in System Properties under the Automatic Updates tab, as you can see in Figure 21-7, or you can click the Automatic Updates icon found in Control Panel (which is added once you update to Service Pack 2).

The downloads your computer collects for you are free and are generally safe because they come directly from Microsoft. If you're a little worried about your computer downloading information behind your back, don't be—you're in good hands.

Using the Automatic Updates tab, you can enable your computer to download needed updates automatically and prompt you to install them, have your computer tell you that a download needs to occur so you can manually perform the download, or choose not to use automatic updates at all. Just click the appropriate radio button on the Automatic Updates tab.

Automatic updates have one problem, and this concerns connectivity to the Internet. Automatic updates will work best with any always-on broadband connection, such as cable, DSL, or satellite. With these kinds of connections, downloads can occur at any time without your having to dial a connection to an ISP. Without always-on access, your computer will

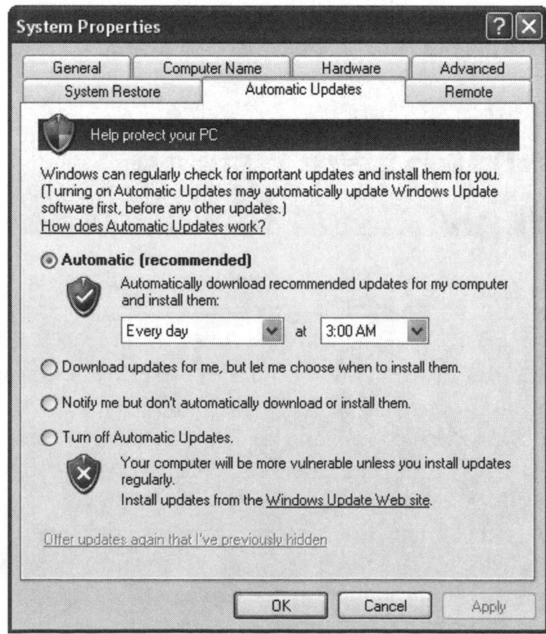

FIGURE 21-7 Automatic Updates tab

attempt to dial up a connection for you and download the files. This may not be a bad thing, but if you do not want your computer dialing up an ISP connection without you, you may want to consider turning off automatic updates. You can always try this feature and turn it off if later it is not working for you.

Troubleshooting Tips

When you experience a problem in Windows, you can take some positive actions, or you can take some panic-driven actions that are usually not very wise. So, without getting into the murky details of troubleshooting, here's my list of troubleshooting tips you should always follow:

- *Relax.* If Windows XP experiences a problem, don't get in a hurry. Your systems will not self-destruct to leak poisonous gas into the room and kill you. In other words, a problem with your system does not mean that it needs to go to the computer ER—don't be in a hurry.
- *Think.* What were you doing when the problem occurred? Consider grabbing a piece of scratch paper and writing down exactly what you were doing—what applications were open when the problem occurred. If serious problems exist with Windows XP, you may need this information later. If you see an error message, write it down. You may need it later when you're talking with a help technician or consulting other help resources.
- *Act.* Try one thing at a time to resolve the problem. With each action you take, write down what you did. Do not randomly press keys—do one thing at a time in an organized manner.

Now, you may think, "But that's just it—what action should I try?" The rest of this chapter answers that very question.

Using CTRL-ALT-DEL

Although you will not experience the system lockup problems that you did in previous versions of Windows, you may encounter an application that stops responding from time to time. In Windows 9*x,* this would often bring your entire system to a standstill, but that is typically not the case in Windows XP. A system lockup occurs when an application is naughty and doesn't behave the way it should. The application can interfere with Windows XP functionality, causing the application itself to lock. This means that you can't do anything with the application by clicking buttons or doing anything else. In some cases, two applications that are open can interfere with each other, causing them both to lock.

In the case of a system lock, you should use your keyboard and press CTRL-ALT-DEL one time. This action will open the Windows Task Manager dialog box, shown in Figure 21-8, where you can select the name of the program and click End Task on the Applications tab. This action forces the task to end so you can get control of your computer. If you have any unsaved data in your application at the time it locked up, I'm afraid you will probably lose that data (save data frequently when working to avoid loss). While you're looking at the Task Manager, you can also explore the Processes, Performance, Networking, and Users tabs to find out current system information.

FIGURE 21-8 Task Manager

NOTE *If you press CTRL-ALT-DEL twice, your computer will restart.*

In some cases, pressing CTRL-ALT-DEL will not give you control of the computer. This problem happens when errors occur within Windows XP, possibly associated with an application, that cause the operating system to "hard lock." In this situation, pressing CTRL-ALT-DEL doesn't do anything. You can't do anything by pressing keys on your keyboard, and your mouse pointer is useless. In such cases, the only way to get control of Windows XP is to turn off the computer using your computer's power switch. Just crawl under your desk, turn off the switch, wait at least 10 seconds, and then turn the switch back on so your computer can begin rebooting. Error Checking will automatically run during the reboot, and you should let it finish its check for file system errors. Again, a complete hard lock is not common in Windows XP, but you may experience the problem just the same.

Use Windows Help

Windows XP has the best Help files that have ever been produced by Microsoft. They are easier to use, more attractive, and contain a wealth of information both locally on your machine and on the Internet. You can easily access Windows Help by choosing Start | Help and Support. The Windows Help interface appears.

The Windows Help program has several major parts. The Help screen shows a number of topics and tasks from which you can select, as well as a Search option and a place for getting outside assistance. The following sections address the Help features.

Why You Should Wait 10 Seconds

As a general rule, you should never reboot your computer using the power switch—always use the Shut Down or Restart option in Windows XP. However, if your system locks up, you have no choice but to use the power switch. When this happens, turn the switch off, wait at least 10 seconds, and then turn it back on. Why 10 seconds? The power switch simply cuts the power to the computer, and 10 seconds gives your computer enough time to dump all of the data in RAM and stop the hard disk from spinning. If you turn the switch off and on too quickly, you could damage your computer's components.

Help Center

When you first open the Help files, you find yourself in the initial Help and Support Center, shown in Figure 21-9. This is the starting point of accessing Help; and as you can probably guess, this page is used to mimic a Web page because the Windows Help files are HTML based, just like a Web page. As you use Help, you'll notice hyperlinks that enable you to jump from the Help files to additional help resources on the Internet.

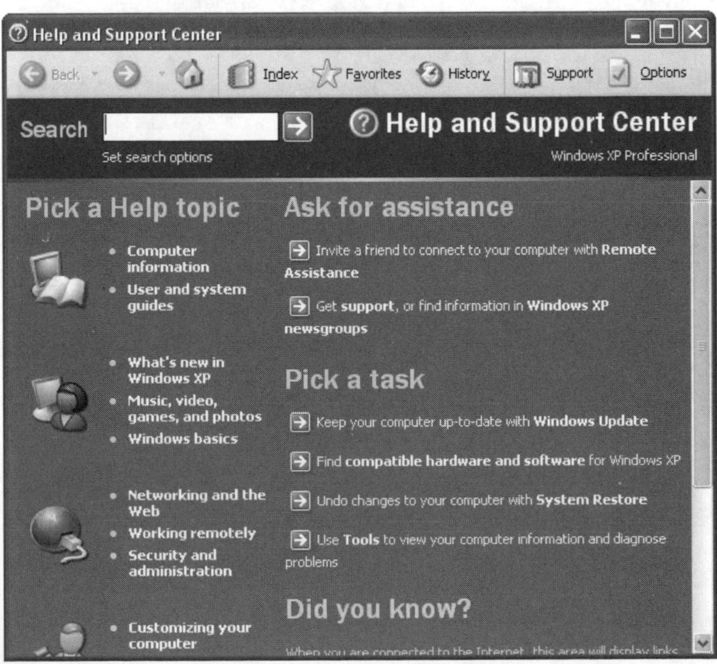

FIGURE 21-9 Help and Support Center

In the window, you'll see some generic categories that can help you get moving in the right direction, such as Networking, Games, Sound, Video, and so on. You also see sections where you can fix a problem or find more resources.

Index

The Index option in Help is just like any other index—the only difference is that this one grabs the information for you instead of you having to look it up (see Figure 21-10). To use the index, click the Index icon on the Help bar (at the top of the Help and Support Center window).

In the left side of the window, you see the entire index displayed in alphabetical order. Just use the scroll bar to locate a topic you want, select it, and then click the Display button. The information about that topic appears in the right pane. You can read the information, click the Print button to print a copy (which is really nice), and even reorganize the window by clicking the Change View button.

TIP *If you don't want to scroll down the list of index topics, you can just type in a keyword for an item in the Search box above the index. The closest matches to your search request will appear.*

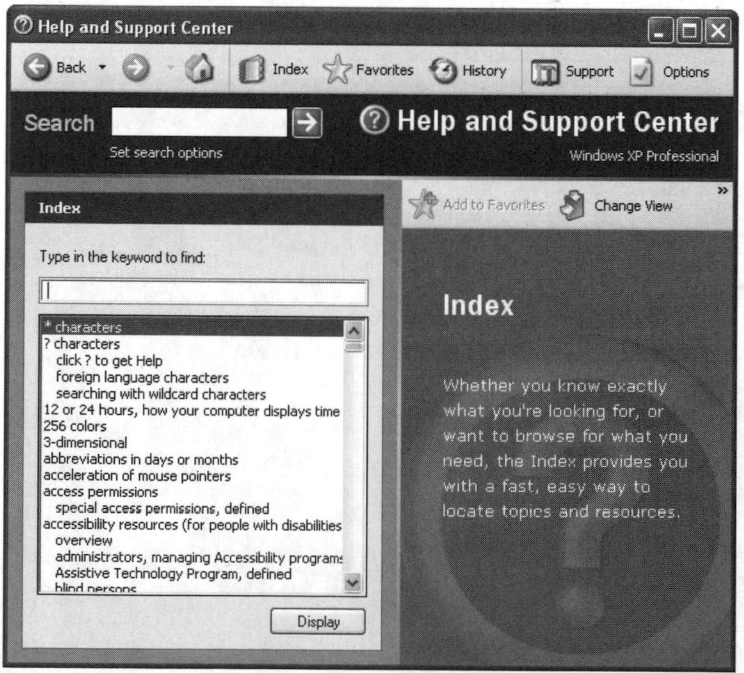

FIGURE 21-10 Help Index

Favorites

The Favorites option works a lot like Favorites in Internet Explorer. Whenever you find a Help page that you want to visit again, click the Add to Favorites button and the page will be added to a Favorites list. Whenever you want to see that list, click the Favorites menu option at the top of the window to see a list of your favorite Help topics.

History

Just as with Internet Explorer, History keeps track of all of the pages you have visited on the Internet from the Help and Support interface. You can check out the History and revisit any of these pages by double-clicking the link that appears in the History list.

Support

If you are having serious problems with Windows XP that you can't seem to resolve, you can access the Support option of Windows Help (shown in Figure 21-11) so you can get help in one of two different ways: by asking a friend or by going to a Windows Web site forum.

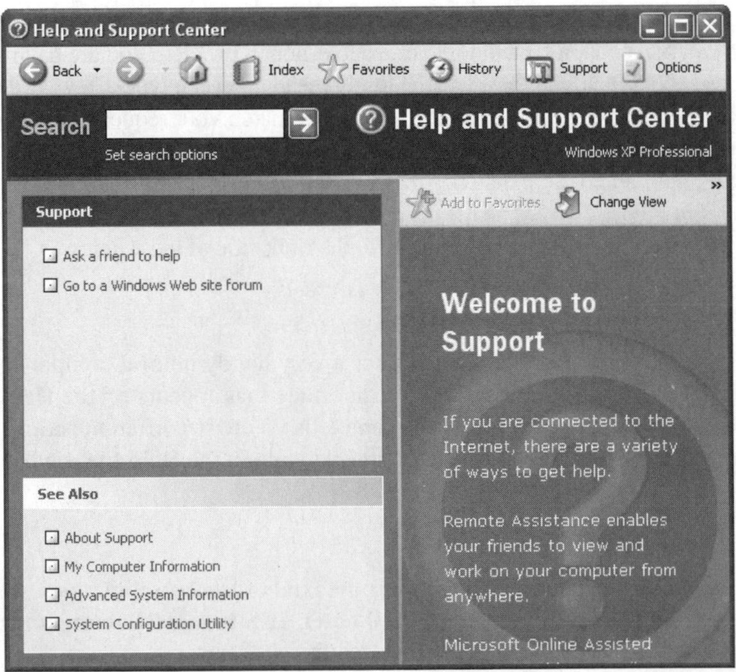

FIGURE 21-11 Support option

If you click the Ask a Friend to Help option, you can create a remote assistance file that you can send to a friend so he or she can help you with your problem. This feature is called Remote Assistance and it is a new and cool feature of Support. Let's say you have a cousin who is a computer genius. You're having problems with your computer and you want your cousin to take a look. Unfortunately, she lives 1000 miles away. What to do? No problem—as long as your cousin is using Windows XP or a later operating system, you can invite her to take a look at your computer and see what you are doing over the Internet. The Support window gives you easy, step-by-step instructions to generate this remote Help connection. You can find out more about this feature in Chapter 13.

The second option is Go to a Windows Web Site Forum. This feature allows you to access online newsgroups and resources so you can try to find the answer to your problem. The content, though, comes from other users, so you'll sometimes find mistakes. Still, this feature can be helpful. You'll need an active Internet connection to use the feature.

Options

This section allows you to change the interface of Help and Support and even share Help with others. The options presented here are very simple and self-explanatory.

Searching Windows Help

One of the primary ways you will use Windows Help is to search for topics. You use the Search feature to find information about a certain topic or troubleshoot a problem you are having. The Windows Help files support text searches, which simply means you can type a keyword or keywords into the Search box. Windows XP will try to find topics that match your request. The Search box appears in the upper-right corner of the Help window. Just type the subject you want and click Go. Windows Help will return all possible matches for your subject. For example, I have searched for the words *Media Player* in Figure 21-12. The results are displayed in the left side of the window. I can double-click any of the items to see the information in the right side of the window.

Using Windows Troubleshooters

Within the Windows Help interface, you can access a very handy helpful component called a "troubleshooter." A troubleshooter is an HTML interface that appears on the Help window. The troubleshooter asks you a series of questions and tells you to try different actions to resolve a problem you are having. Many troubleshooters are available in the Help files, and they are very easy to use. Just follow these steps:

1. Choose Start | Help.
2. In the Help window, type in the Search box the kind of troubleshooter you want. For example, you might type **modem troubleshooter, ICS troubleshooter,** or **sound card troubleshooter.** To see a full list, just type **troubleshooter.**

NOTE *Obviously, a troubleshooter does not exist for every possible problem you might experience with Windows, but troubleshooters can be found for most hardware devices.*

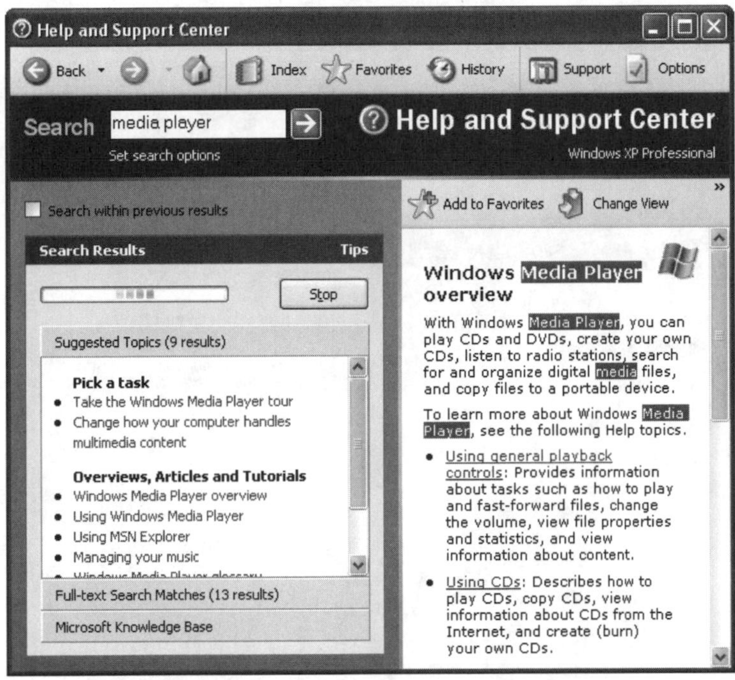

FIGURE 21-12 Search Results

3. Begin the troubleshooter by clicking an appropriate link that is returned from your search, and then click the Next button to continue, as shown in Figure 21-13.
4. Continue following the troubleshooter instructions to attempt to solve the problem.

Use Safe Mode

Safe Mode is a Windows XP feature that enables you to start Windows with a minimal number of drivers. Safe Mode is used in instances when you cannot start Windows normally. Safe Mode is used to fix problems with your system—it essentially gets Windows up and running, but that's about it. Most major XP features do not work in Safe Mode.

So, why would you use Safe Mode? Let's consider an example. Let's say you have installed Fly-By-Night's Most Excellent Video Card (okay, it's just an example). You install the card and driver for the card. When you restart Windows XP, it boots, but then you get a "fatal exception" blue screen just before your Desktop appears. You try this over and over with the same result. More than likely, the video card's driver is not working correctly with Windows XP. You can boot the computer into Safe Mode, and Windows will load a basic VGA driver to use with the card. Once booted, you can use Device Manager to remove or update the bad driver.

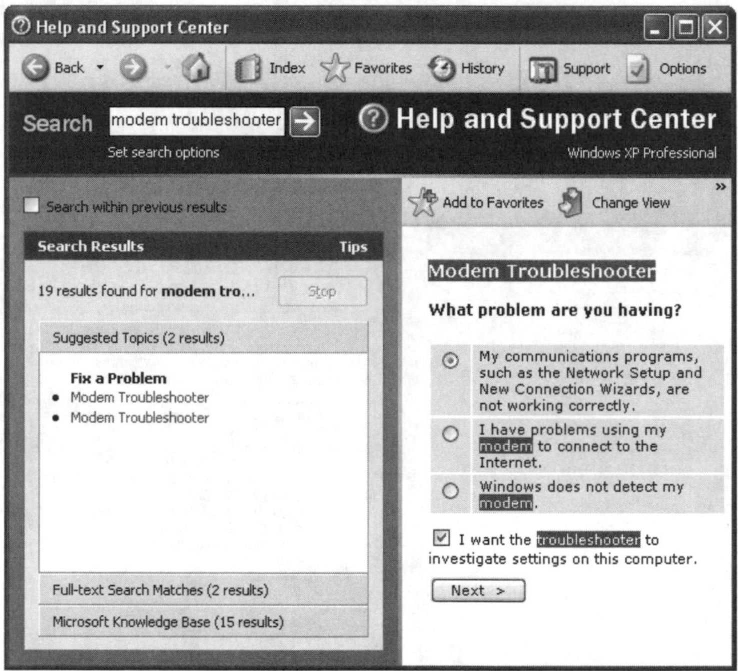

FIGURE 21-13 Begin the troubleshooter

A number of other repair tools (which we'll explore later in this chapter) require you to boot your computer into Safe Mode in order to work. Before showing you how to boot into Safe Mode, let me mention that you can choose some other boot options along with Safe Mode. You can access all of these options by using the Windows Startup menu, which you'll see if you hold down the CTRL key on your keyboard when you turn on your computer. (If CTRL doesn't seem to work, press the F8 key on the keyboard when you start the computer.) You'll see a Startup menu that allows you to choose Safe Mode, Safe Mode with Networking, and some other options. When your computer boots in Safe Mode, you can access the tools and Help you need to try to solve the problem. When you've finished, just reboot the computer and it will boot into normal mode.

Use System Restore

As you have learned to use Windows XP, you no doubt have found several of its new features very helpful and fun, and maybe others less so. However, I can emphatically say that System Restore is a great feature of Windows XP and one that can get you out of all sorts of trouble. What if your computer won't start? What if you install a bad application that wrecks your computer? What if little Johnny decides to delete C:\Windows? No problem—just use System

Voices from the Community

When Things Go Wrong

The most common request I receive from my service is for help in regaining data lost (documents, pictures, and other data) due to various problems with computers or operating systems. Although numerous third-party applications are out there that can help users with file recovery, by far the best way to prevent this problem is to be vigilant with your computer and back up regularly. The best way to do this is to use Windows XP itself. You can copy your My Documents folder to a floppy disk or CD/DVD or backup your whole computer.

You can do this in two ways. The first way is to use a little known application called Backup. If you Use Windows XP Professional, you will find Backup by choosing Start | All Programs | Accessories | System Tools | Backup.

Windows XP Home Edition does not have this facility, but you can still add it by inserting your Windows XP Home/Media Edition Disk and browsing to *X*:\Valueadd\MSFT\NTBackup (where *X* is your CD-ROM drive). Double-click the file called Ntbackup.msi to start a wizard that installs Backup. Follow the instructions in the wizard, and when you have completed the wizard, click Finish.

If, like me, you forget to back up important data, you can rely on Backup to remember for you, because it has a schedule facility to run backups automatically.

The second way to backup is to use the Files and Settings Transfer wizard. You will find the Files and Settings Transfer Wizard in Windows XP Professional/Home/Media Editions by choosing Start | All Programs | Accessories | System Tools | Files and Settings Transfer Wizard. The Files and Settings Transfer Wizard is a brilliant application you can use to transfer (by cable or CD/DVD) all your personal settings and files to a new computer quickly and seamlessly, so your new computer is as familiar as your old one. I prefer to use it to back up my computer once a month. To do this, I choose to export my files and settings to my Desktop, and then I copy them to a rewritable DVD.

—David Potter
Widescreen XP
www.wide-screen.co.uk

Restore and put your computer back just like it was before the problem, tragedy, or accident happened…with only a few mouse clicks from you. I've used System Restore numerous times after fouling up Windows XP with my experiments, and I must say that it has worked flawlessly for me without fail.

Are you intrigued? I know you are if you have ever worked with Windows, because bad configuration problems can be a serious troubleshooting problem. System Restore leaves that legacy behind, because you can easily restore your computer to a previous state. The following sections show you how to use System Restore.

System Restore Requirements

System Restore is automatically installed and configured on Windows XP if your computer has at least 200MB of free disk space after Windows XP is installed. If your computer does not have 200MB of free disk space, System Restore is installed, but it is not set up to run. System Restore functions by saving information about your system so that it can be restored in the event of a problem. In order for System Restore to function correctly, 200MB of free disk space is required, and, in reality, System Restore may need much more. Fortunately, if you are using a newer computer, you most likely have plenty of free disk space, and System Restore is already operational on your computer.

Enabling System Restore

If your computer did not have 200MB of free disk space upon initial installation, but you have made 200MB or more of free disk space available, you can enable System Restore so that it begins functioning on your Windows XP computer. To enable System Restore, just follow these steps:

1. In the Control Panel, double-click System, or right-click My Computer and choose Properties.
2. Click the System Restore tab.
3. Make sure the Turn Off System Restore on All Drives check box is clear. This will enable System Restore.
4. Click OK and click OK again on the System Properties window.

Creating Restore Points

System Restore functions by creating restore points. A *restore point* is a "snapshot" of your computer's configuration that is stored on your hard disk. If System Restore needs to be used, it accesses a restore point to reconfigure your computer. This process brings your computer back to a stable state—a place where it was when the system was stable. Restore points enable your computer to "travel back in time" and be configured as it was when it was stable.

It is very important to note here that System Restore restores your operating system and applications only. It does not save and restore any files. For example, let's say you accidentally delete the Great American Novel you are working on. System Restore cannot be used to get your novel back. Incidentally, System Restore does not affect other files, such as e-mail and Web pages. Performing a System Restore does not make you lose new e-mail or files—it only configures your system settings and application settings.

System Restore automatically creates restore points for you, so, in general, there is no need to create a restore point manually. However, what if you are about to try some configuration option or configure some software that you know may be risky or that has caused you problems

How to ... Adjust System Restore Disk Usage

By default, System Restore is given 12 percent of your hard disk space when you install Windows XP, assuming that 12 percent is at least 200MB. If you access System Properties and click the System Restore tab, and then click the Settings button, you'll see a slider bar on the Hard Disk tab that indicates the total amount of disk space System Restore is allowed to use. You can raise or lower this amount by moving the slider bar. However, keep in mind that System Restore must have at least 200MB, and if you want System Restore to function really well, you should leave this setting at its 12 percent default level.

in the past? Before trying the configuration or software, you can manually create a restore point so you can later restore your system to its present state. To create a restore point, just follow these easy steps:

1. Choose Start | All Programs | Accessories | System Tools | System Restore.
2. In the System Restore window, click the Create a Restore Point button, and then click Next.
3. In the window that appears, enter a description. You may want to include information that will help you distinguish the restore point from others. The date and time of the restore point are added automatically, so you don't need to include those. Click Next.
4. The restore point is created. Click OK and you're done.

Running System Restore

The eventful day finally arrives and you (or someone else) has done something bad to your computer. Now it doesn't boot or it acts erratically. Whatever the problem, you can use System Restore to restore your computer settings as they were at an earlier time when it was functioning appropriately. The following two sections show you how to use System Restore.

If You Can Boot Windows…

If you can boot into Windows, follow these steps:

1. Choose Start | All Programs | Accessories | System Tools | System Restore.
2. Click the Restore My Computer to an Earlier Time radio button, and then click Next.
3. A calendar and selection list is presented, as shown in Figure 21-14. You can select different days to find a desired restore point. If you did not create a restore point, you should choose to use the latest one available. The latest one will be listed first in the current or previous day window. Select a restore point and click Next.

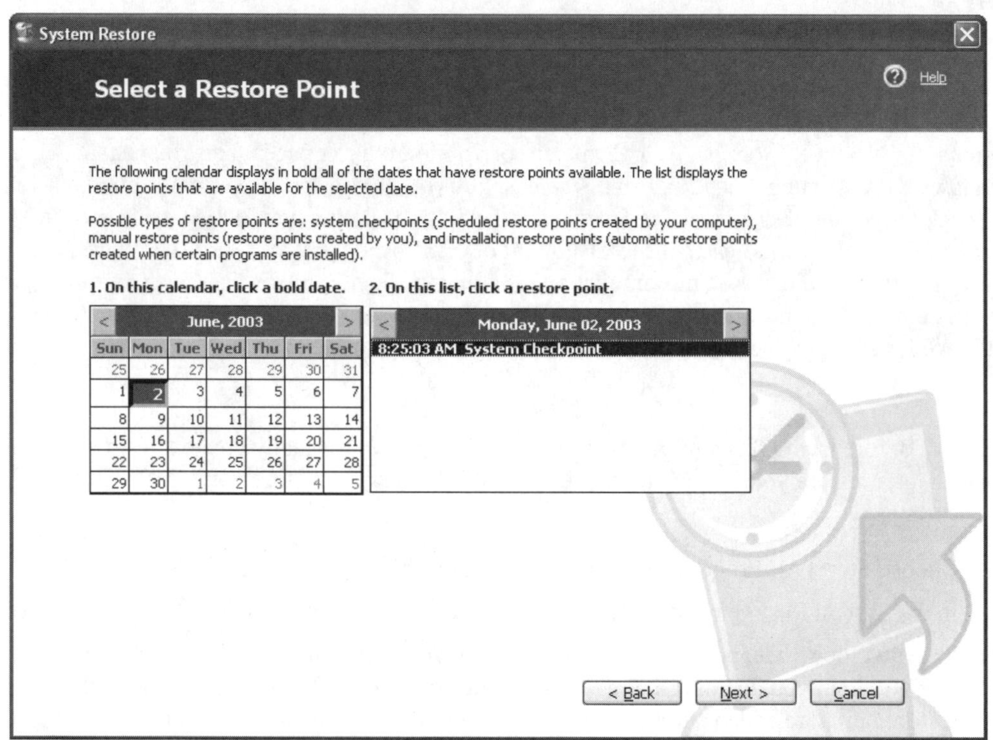

FIGURE 21-14 Select a restore point.

4. A message appears, telling you to save all files and close all open applications. Do so at this time, and then click the Next button.
5. Restoration takes place on your computer, and your computer automatically reboots once the restoration is complete. Click OK on the restoration message that appears once you reboot.

If You Cannot Boot Windows…

If you cannot boot Windows, follow these steps to run System Restore:

1. Turn on your computer and hold down the CTRL or the F8 key until you see the Startup menu options.
2. Choose Safe Mode, and then press the ENTER button.
3. Once Windows boots, the Help screen that appears gives you the option to restore your computer. Click the System Restore link.

What to Do If You Selected the Wrong Restoration Point

Let's say you run a restoration to solve a problem, but the point from which you chose to restore the data was not early enough. In other words, Windows XP created a restore point while the current problem existed. What then? No problem. Simply undo the last restoration and then run the restoration again, but select an earlier restore point to fix the problem.

4. Click the Restore My Computer to an Earlier Time radio button and then click Next.
5. A calendar and selection list is presented to you. You can select different days to find a desired restore point. If you did not create a restore point, you should choose to use the latest one available. The latest one will be listed first in the current or previous day window. Select a restore point and click Next.
6. A message appears telling you to save all files and close all open applications. Do so at this time, and then click the Next button.
7. Your computer automatically reboots once the restoration is complete. Click OK on the restoration message that appears after booting has taken place.

NOTE *Current documents, files, e-mail, and similar items are not affected during a restoration. However, if you installed an application after the last restore point was made, you will need to reinstall that application.*

Undoing a Restoration

As I have mentioned, I think System Restore is the best new feature of Windows XP. It can save you a world of pain and agony. But what happens if restoration doesn't go so well? What if a problem with the restoration leaves Windows XP in worse shape, or even unbootable? Good news—restoration is completely reversible, and the following two sections show you how to reverse a restoration.

Reversing Restoration If You Can Boot Your Computer

To reverse a restoration if you can boot your computer, follow these steps:

1. Choose Start | All Programs | Accessories | System Tools | System Restore.
2. In the System Restore window, click the Undo My Last Restoration radio button, and then click Next.

NOTE *The Undo My Last Restoration option does not appear unless you have previously run a restoration.*

3. Close any open files or applications, click OK, and then click Next.
4. The previous restoration is removed and your computer reboots. Click OK to the restoration message that appears after reboot.

Undoing a Restoration If You Cannot Boot into Windows

If you cannot boot into Windows and you need to undo a restoration, just follow these steps:

1. Turn on your computer and hold down the CTRL or the F8 key until you see the Startup menu options.
2. Choose Safe Mode and then press the ENTER button.
3. Once Windows boots, the Help screen that appears gives you the option of restoring your computer. Click the System Restore link.
4. Click the Undo My Last Restoration radio button, and then click Next.
5. A message appears, telling you to save all files and close all open applications. Do so at this time, and then click the Next button.
6. Your computer is rebooted once the restoration has been removed.

Appendix

Install Windows XP

How to...

- Prepare for a Windows XP upgrade
- Upgrade to Windows XP
- Get a computer with no operating system ready for installation
- Clean install Windows XP
- Activate Windows XP

If you're like me, you would almost rather have a root canal than install a new operating system. Why? The answer is simple. Any time you install an operating system, whether it be an upgrade or a clean install on a computer with no operating system, you stand the risk of experiencing problems. But you can relax—Windows XP is rather easy to install, and as long as you are sure that your computer's hardware is ready for Windows XP, you are likely to experience no problems at all. This appendix is designed to help you plan and actually perform the installation. If you purchased your computer with Windows XP preinstalled and for some reason you need to reinstall it, you should also check the manufacturer's instructions for installations, as they may be different than the information presented in this appendix.

Upgrade to Windows XP

Most home or office users who purchase Windows XP do so to upgrade their existing PC. This means that you are likely to have a computer that runs Windows 98, Me, NT, 2000, or XP Home Edition (if you're upgrading to Professional), and you want to upgrade that system so that it runs Windows XP. Unless you are buying a new PC with Windows XP already preinstalled from the factory, you have purchased a Windows XP upgrade CD-ROM so you can have the latest and greatest from Microsoft.

In a perfect world, upgrading your home or office PC would be a piece of cake. You pop the installation CD into your CD-ROM drive, answer a few questions from the setup program, and setup installs Windows XP without any problem whatsoever. When you find that perfect world, let me know, so I can move there, too. The reality is that any number of problems can happen when upgrading to Windows XP. However, if you upgrade smartly, the likelihood of encountering installation failure or problems is low. The trick is to do a bit of homework before installing Windows XP to make sure your existing PC and operating system are ready. It is all too tempting to start the installation and hope for the best; but to upgrade smartly, you need to play detective for a few minutes and make certain all is well in your computer's environment before starting the upgrade. Upgrading smartly will help prevent a number of potential problems and help you find issues affecting the installation before you ever begin.

So, how do you upgrade smartly? The following sections explore the tasks you should perform before attempting an upgrade to Windows XP.

Check the System Requirements

One big mistake computer users often make when attempting an upgrade or install is not to check the system requirements. Every piece of software, whether it is an operating system or an application, has certain requirements that must be met before the software will function properly or before it can even be installed. Your computer must have hardware that can handle the Windows XP software; so before ever attempting the installation, you should check out your computer to see whether any potential problems exists. Windows XP is very demanding, and one of the main causes of upgrade problems is the lack of proper system resources—so be careful! Check out the information in the following sections to make sure your computer is ready for Windows XP.

Processor

A computer's processor can be thought of as the computer's brain. The processor "processes" information that the operating system or an application needs. For example, if you want your computer to multiply 467×345, that request is sent to the processor for completion. Once the processor performs the computation, it is returned to the requesting application (such as your system's calculator). In the past, processors were not very fast, because operating systems and applications were not terribly complicated. However, with today's operating systems and applications, your computer's processor will have to be fast enough to handle Windows XP and all of the many tasks it can perform.

For a Windows XP installation, you need a processor that is at least a Pentium (or equivalent) 233 megahertz (MHz)—the megahertz number is the speed at which the processor can run. By today's standards, 233 MHz is pretty slow. Most new PCs today contain 2 to 3 gigahertz (GHz) processors, which puts you in great shape for Windows XP. It is important to note here that 233 MHz is the bare-bones minimum. Windows XP will run on this processor, but it will not work fast. In reality, you always want the fastest processor you can afford, because you will see the best performance with a fast processor.

NOTE *If your computer currently runs Windows 2000 and your system works well with Windows 2000 (in other words, if the computer does not slowly limp along), your computer will be able to handle Windows XP just fine.*

If you check your computer's processor and find that it is not at least a 233 MHz processor, what should you do? You have two options. First, you can buy a new processor for your computer and install it as an upgrade. This involves buying the processor and paying someone to install it (unless you know a thing or two about hardware). In some cases, this is a great solution, but be careful. You may be able to purchase a new computer for not much more money, so think carefully and shop smartly before deciding to upgrade your computer's processor.

TIP *If your processor is too slow for Windows XP, the odds are good that other components are too old as well. In most cases, upgrading your processor usually means you'll have to upgrade other components, such as RAM. This is why buying a new computer is often the best option.*

Random Access Memory

You have probably heard the term *random access memory* (*RAM*) plenty of times, even if you do not have your head stuck in the computer world. RAM is the amount of memory your computer contains to run current applications and processes. RAM enables you to work with a Microsoft Word document while also surfing the Internet; it enables you to draw pictures and run programs—anything that you do on your computer requires RAM. Simply put, the more RAM you have, the faster and better your computer will run, and the happier you will be. For a Windows XP installation, you need at least 64 megabytes (MB) of RAM. As with your processor speed requirement, 64MB is a bare minimum, and Microsoft recommends that you have 128MB. Most computer systems today are sold with at least 256MB of RAM, and many with more than that. As with the processor, think carefully before upgrading your RAM. Check your other system components and make certain they do not need to be upgraded as well. The odds are good that they do, and you may be able to buy a new computer with the same money you would spend on upgrades.

Hard Disk Space

Windows XP will need some of your hard disk space for storage during and after the installation. Your computer's hard disk stores any data that you choose to save, as well as your operating system itself. To upgrade to Windows XP, you must have 650MB of free hard disk space. This means that you must have that much spare room on your hard disk so Windows XP can store its files. To check your computer's hard disk space, double-click the My Computer icon on your Desktop. You see your C drive in the window. Right-click the C drive icon, and then choose Properties. The General tab of the properties sheet shows you the amount of used and free space your disk contains.

What if you do not have enough free disk space? Then you need to free up some disk space by removing data from your hard disk. Removed items can include files, Internet pages, and even applications that you no longer use. You'll need to make some decisions about what you want to remove, but you must free up enough disk space for the installation to be successful.

Other Requirements

Your processor, RAM, and disk space requirements are of utmost importance, but some other system requirements should be met to make the most of Windows XP. These requirements are virtually a given (unless your computer was built in the '70s), so just take a minute to make sure you have these:

- VGA or higher-resolution monitor
- CD-ROM or DVD-ROM drive (Windows XP isn't fussy about the drive speed)
- A mouse or other similar pointing device
- A keyboard

I told you those were easy. Now, you may also want to check a few other items. These are not required for a Windows XP installation, but they may impact how well your system works with Windows XP and how happy you will be with its functionality.

- If you plan to access the Internet (which I hope you do), you need at least a 56 Kbps modem. The standard dial-up speed is 56 Kbps, and you now have a number of broadband options available, including DSL, cable, wireless, and satellite. None of these are required, of course, but while you are upgrading your system, this is an excellent time to look at your Internet connectivity speed and consider upgrading to a faster service if necessary. If you plan on using DSL, cable, wireless, or satellite, be sure to contact your Internet Service Provider to find out if your computer will have to meet any specific hardware needs.
- To make use of all Windows XP has to offer, you should have a good sound card, speakers (or headphones), and a good video card. A plethora of video and sound card products are compatible with Windows, so check your local computer store for information and pricing.
- You may consider adding other components to your system, such as a DVD-ROM drive so you can run DVD games and movies on your computer. You can also use Windows XP to watch TV on your computer through a TV tuner card. You can always add these options to your system after installation, but now is a good time to consider them.
- If you want to connect to a local area network (LAN), you need some kind of network adapter card. See Chapter 11 for more information.

Back Up Your Data

From painful past experience, I have learned always to back up any data that I do not want to lose before ever tinkering with my operating system—and that includes an upgrade. If everything goes well during your upgrade, the computer will preserve all of your data and settings, and you will not need any data you have backed up because it will still reside on your computer. However, if things do not go so well, you will desperately need a backup of your critical data—the data you cannot afford to lose. This includes documents, spreadsheets, Internet information—you name it. Spend some time on your computer finding everything you can't live without, and then back up that data.

You can back up your data in a number of ways. First, Windows 98, Me, and 2000 all include a Backup utility found in Accessories. You can use the Backup utility to create a backup file. You must then save this backup file to another location, such as a tape drive or even the hard drive of another computer. You may also have other backup programs and backup media you have purchased. If not, backing up your data doesn't have to be difficult. Simply copy any files you don't want to lose to a CD/DVD, floppy disk, a Zip or Jaz drive, or USB removable storage. If you have only a floppy drive, you may need several disks to make sure you save all of your data, but your time and effort will be well spent if something should happen during the installation.

Check Out Your Device Drivers

Every device attached to your computer, such as your printer, scanner, or modem, has a *driver.* A driver is a piece of software code that enables your computer to interact with the hardware device. Think of a driver as a car steering wheel. To interact with your car and make it do what you want, you use a steering wheel to communicate with it, along with other controls like the brake and gas pedal. For your computer to communicate and control a device, a driver must be installed. When you install a device, you usually use a floppy disk or CD-ROM that comes from the factory with your device. This installation media installs a driver that Windows can use. Windows has its own driver database as well, and in many cases, Windows can install and use one of its drivers to manage a device.

Drivers are always changing. When a new device is released—for example, a printer—the driver ships with it. However, as operating systems change, new drivers are developed so your printer can work with the new operating systems. Before upgrading to Windows XP, you should visit manufacturers' Web sites for your computer's devices. Look for new drivers for your particular models and see if you can download any. Download the drivers to a floppy disk and keep them. You may need these new drivers when you install Windows XP, to ensure that your hardware works well with your new operating system. Check your device manufacturer's documentation for more information about downloading updated drivers. Even if you do not need to update drivers, you do need to round up your floppies and CD-ROMs so you have access to your existing drivers in case you need them during installation.

Check for Viruses and Disable Antivirus Software

Before upgrading to Windows XP, you should run a full virus check on your computer system using an antivirus program, such as one from McAfee or Symantec. You may currently have one of these programs, or you may need to buy one. If you use the Internet, you should certainly have virus-detection software to make sure you can both detect and disinfect your computer in the case of a virus. Antivirus software is normally under $50 and well worth your investment. If you do not have antivirus software, you can purchase it both on the Internet and at any computer store, and in many department stores as well.

Refer to your owner's instructions and run a complete virus scan of your system. Make sure your software has current virus definitions so it can detect the presence of a newer virus. Current definitions can be downloaded from the manufacturer's Web site. Once the virus scan is complete and you have removed any viruses, you need to disable your antivirus software before running setup. Antivirus software will interfere with Windows XP installation, so make certain you check the antivirus documentation and disable the software accordingly.

Shut Down All Programs

Before running Windows XP setup, make certain that you shut down all programs that are running and that you disconnect from the Internet. Also, if you have any programs that protect your Master Boot Record (MBR) by encrypting it, you need to uninstall that application. Some applications on the market today help protect your computer against sabotage or data theft by encrypting certain portions of your operating system so they cannot be read by unauthorized persons. This software is not normally installed as a part of a purchase package, but do check your original documentation and make certain you do not have any applications like this installed. If you do, uninstall them before attempting to run setup. These applications will cause the Windows XP upgrade to fail if they are running.

Upgrade to Windows XP

Finally, after doing your detective work, you are ready to begin the upgrade to Windows XP. Before you get started, make sure you have everything gathered that you will need. First, you'll need the Windows XP CD-ROM and the product key. You can find the product key on a sticker on the back of your CD-ROM jewel case. You should also have any disks or CD-ROMs containing drivers for your hardware in case Windows XP cannot install one of the devices.

Now that you have your materials and you have taken some time to check out your computer and make certain it is ready for the upgrade, you are ready to begin. The following steps walk you through the upgrade and describe each piece of the upgrade process to you:

1. Insert your Windows XP CD-ROM into your computer's CD-ROM drive. A message appears, asking, "What do you want to do?" Click the option to install Windows XP. If the message does not appear, your computer is having problems reading the auto launcher, which is no big deal. Just open My Computer and double-click your CD-ROM drive icon. Your computer opens the CD-ROM and you see a folder called i386 and an icon called Setup inside the folder. Double-click this icon to start the installation.
2. Setup begins by checking your system and preparing the Setup Wizard. This will probably take less than one minute.
3. The Windows XP installation Welcome screen appears. The Welcome screen prompts you to select a type of installation, either upgrade or clean install. Use the clean install option if your operating system is not supported as an upgrade path (such as Windows 95). If your current operating system *is* supported, choose the upgrade option, unless you simply want to get rid of all of your previous settings and applications from Windows. Click the Next button to continue.
4. The Licensing Agreement window appears. This window gives you all the laws and rules about using your new software. It's very interesting to read (yawn), but you should read it and you must click the I Accept This Agreement radio button for installation to continue. Click this button, and then click the Next button.
5. The Product Key window appears. Locate your product key found on your CD-ROM jewel case and type the key into the provided fields just as it appears on the CD-ROM case. Click the Next button when you've finished.

NOTE *As you type your Product Key, you don't have to worry about typing capital letters. The product key is not case-sensitive.*

6. A Windows Setup window appears in which you can choose language options, advanced options, and accessibility options for your install. If you are interested in any of these features, just click the appropriate button to select the options that are available. Click Next.
7. Windows XP asks whether you want to upgrade your file system to NTFS. You can learn more about NTFS in Chapter 19; as a general rule, you should choose to use the NTFS file system for best performance. Make your selection and click Next.

8. The Dynamic Update window appears. This feature enables XP to check Microsoft.com for updates that can be installed during your installation. Your computer must be currently configured with an Internet connection for this to work. If it is, choose the Yes button and click Next.
9. At this point, the interactive part of setup is over. This means that Windows XP will not need your assistance any longer to complete setup. The only exception is if Windows XP needs a hardware driver from you. Under most circumstances, however, you don't have to do anything else and you can leave your computer unattended for the next half hour or so.

If installation does not go so well and you have problems starting Windows XP, see Chapter 21 for helpful troubleshooting tips.

Install Windows XP on a Computer with No Operating System

You may need to install Windows XP on a computer that does not have an operating system. For example, let's say you purchase a computer from a direct supplier or even over the Internet. These machines are often sold "unformatted" and without an operating system. Or, perhaps your Windows 98 computer has too many goofy system problems you don't want to contend with and you want to clean install Windows XP so that it does not use and keep all of those older operating system files. No matter what your reason, you can clean install Windows XP on a computer that has an operating system, as well as on systems that do not.

This discussion brings up an important question. Should you format an existing hard drive and blow away your old operating system so you can clean install Windows XP? Not usually. It is best if you upgrade your existing operating system to Windows XP to preserve your system and hardware settings. However, in some cases, you may wish to clean install to get away from problems in your older operating system. This is, of course, fine; but as a rule of thumb, always choose an upgrade over a clean install for Windows XP.

Prepare for a Clean Installation

Just like an upgrade, you need to spend a little time preparing for the clean installation. This means that you need to examine your computer's hardware and make certain the computer meets at least the minimum hardware requirements. You also need to locate floppy disks and CD-ROMs that contain drivers for your computer's hardware. The Windows XP CD-ROM is a bootable CD-ROM. This means that if you place the CD-ROM in the CD-ROM drive and turn on the computer, the installation CD-ROM can start the computer for you and begin installation automatically. If your computer does not boot from CD-ROM (most all of them do these days), you can use a Windows 98/Me/2000 startup disk to start the computer so that you can begin installation. Refer to the appropriate Help files on those operating systems for more specific instructions. Beyond booting from a CD-ROM, a clean install of Windows XP functions in the same manner as an upgrade to Windows XP, so refer to the section "Upgrade to Windows XP" earlier in this appendix for the steps to follow.

Activate Windows XP

Windows XP includes a new feature not found in previous versions of Windows, called *activation.* In a nutshell, Windows activation is a new feature Microsoft uses to protect the licensing of software. The activation feature prevents someone from installing Windows on a bunch of computers using the same software CD-ROM. Essentially, activation is just a new step in the key and licensing agreement portion of setup.

Once you install Windows XP, you have 30 days to activate the operating system with Microsoft. The activation doesn't need any information from you—so don't worry, this isn't like Big Brother or anything. The activation process records a serial number from your computer's hardware and couples it with your CD-ROM installation code. This way, if someone tries to install Windows XP on a bunch of computers with a single CD-ROM, activation will recognize that the key has already been used and will not allow the activation to continue. Once the 30-day period expires, Windows XP will cease to function.

You can activate your Windows XP computer in two ways: You can do it over the Internet or by manually calling the Microsoft product activation call center. Depending on your version of Windows XP, you may have seen the Activation prompt during setup. If not, you can access the Activation tool found in Start | All Programs | Activate Windows. Either way, the process is rather easy and straightforward. To activate your computer using a modem, just follow the onscreen prompts. If you need to call Microsoft to activate Windows, refer to the Windows XP documentation that came with your installation CD-ROM. That's all there is to it.

Index

B

C

D

E

F

G

H

I

K

L

M

N

Q

R

S

U

V

W

X

Z

INTERNATIONAL CONTACT INFORMATION

AUSTRALIA
McGraw-Hill Book Company
Australia Pty. Ltd.
TEL +61-2-9900-1800
FAX +61-2-9878-8881
http://www.mcgraw-hill.com.au
books-it_sydney@mcgraw-hill.com

CANADA
McGraw-Hill Ryerson Ltd.
TEL +905-430-5000
FAX +905-430-5020
http://www.mcgraw-hill.ca

GREECE, MIDDLE EAST, & AFRICA (Excluding South Africa)
McGraw-Hill Hellas
TEL +30-210-6560-990
TEL +30-210-6560-993
TEL +30-210-6560-994
FAX +30-210-6545-525

MEXICO (Also serving Latin America)
McGraw-Hill Interamericana Editores
S.A. de C.V.
TEL +525-1500-5108
FAX +525-117-1589
http://www.mcgraw-hill.com.mx
carlos_ruiz@mcgraw-hill.com

SINGAPORE (Serving Asia)
McGraw-Hill Book Company
TEL +65-6863-1580
FAX +65-6862-3354
http://www.mcgraw-hill.com.sg
mghasia@mcgraw-hill.com

SOUTH AFRICA
McGraw-Hill South Africa
TEL +27-11-622-7512
FAX +27-11-622-9045
robyn_swanepoel@mcgraw-hill.com

SPAIN
McGraw-Hill/
Interamericana de España, S.A.U.
TEL +34-91-180-3000
FAX +34-91-372-8513
http://www.mcgraw-hill.es
professional@mcgraw-hill.es

UNITED KINGDOM, NORTHERN, EASTERN, & CENTRAL EUROPE
McGraw-Hill Education Europe
TEL +44-1-628-502500
FAX +44-1-628-770224
http://www.mcgraw-hill.co.uk
emea_queries@mcgraw-hill.com

ALL OTHER INQUIRIES Contact:
McGraw-Hill/Osborne
TEL +1-510-420-7700
FAX +1-510-420-7703
http://www.osborne.com
omg_international@mcgraw-hill.com

Mc
Graw
Hill
OSBORNE
www.osborne.com